The
Goddess
and
The
Shaman

Photo © David Brazil

J. A. KENT HAS taught university courses in the fields of educational and developmental psychology. She has also practiced and taught High Magic and Wicca. She has degrees in teaching, a post-graduate degree in counseling/psychotherapy, and a doctorate in social ecology from the University of Western Sydney. She is a natural psychic and has been trained in herbal medicine, homeopathic medicine, and hypnotherapy.

J. A. KENT, PhD

The
Goddess
and
The
Shaman

The Art and Science
of Magical Healing

Llewellyn Publications
Woodbury, Minnesota

FIRST EDITION
Second Printing, 2018

Book design by Rebecca Zins
Cover design by Lisa Novak
Cover image: "Epona, Goddess of Horse" © Helena Nelson-Reed

Llewellyn Publications is a registered trademark of Llewellyn Worldwide Ltd.

Library of Congress Cataloging-in-Publication Data
Names: Kent, J. A., 1952– author.
Title: The goddess and the shaman : the art and science of magical healing /
  J. A. Kent, PhD.
Description: First Edition. | Woodbury : Llewellyn Worldwide, Ltd, 2016. |
  Includes bibliographical references.
Identifiers: LCCN 2015041372 (print) | LCCN 2015043430 (ebook) | ISBN
  9780738740423 | ISBN 9780738748726 ()
Subjects: LCSH: Goddesses. | Goddess religion. | Shamanism. | Magic. |
  Occultism. | Healing—Miscellanea.
Classification: LCC BL473.5 .K46 2016 (print) | LCC BL473.5 (ebook) | DDC
  203/.1—dc23
LC record available at http://lccn.loc.gov/2015041372

Llewellyn Publications
A Division of Llewellyn Worldwide Ltd.
2143 Wooddale Drive
Woodbury, MN 55125-2989

www.llewellyn.com
Printed in the United States of America

This work is dedicated to the Great Mother,
ruler of the worlds.

May it be of some aid to all the seekers
who are struggling to understand the
mysteries of life on earth.

Contents

Foreword

I WAS PRIVILEGED TO have accompanied Jane on the journey of search
and discovery that has led to this book. That journey changed me, as it
changed her, and as it has the power to change many others who will
come to read this book. So I am delighted to have been given the opportunity to write some preliminary words here.

The task of writing a foreword for this particular book seems so easy
that it makes it actually difficult. Jane writes so eloquently and well that
she has already said everything that needs to be said, without any need
for a preamble or foreword. Anything I say will surely just get in the way
and delay that miraculous and productive encounter between writer and
reader that completes the meaning of every good book, especially one
like this that is not packed with abstract concepts in turgid prose. Jane
does her very capable best to communicate her strong and important
message.

But as the long Goddess tradition Jane belongs to knows so well,
understanding does not come through clear words alone. Without structured experience, words communicate nothing that matters. In that tradition ritual plays an important role, including being a site and set of
practices that stand on the threshold of a deeper grasp of the meanings
that matter. Delays and indirections are a normal and functional part of
the journey.

I am more scholar than mystic, yet I have to try to bridge those different, often incompatible worlds as I write a foreword to this book that brings together extensive empirical research and a lifetime of spiritual experience. But perhaps my particular combination of strengths and weaknesses equips me to mediate the unique qualities of this book for at least one kind of reader it may find, to their surprise and maybe to the publisher's too.

The readers I have in mind are rational skeptics who were educated to take pride in being militantly uninterested in a book with a theme like this, a book whose basic premise is that the Goddess and her world have always existed, now just as much as in earlier times, recognized more and more as the source of healing and sanity the world needs as never before.

Jane sees signs that the time of the Goddess is re-emerging again. This would not be plausible or welcome news to this kind of reader. Yet maybe there is something in their heart or their life that intuits that something like this may just possibly be a truth they need. In the normal run of things these readers would not even think to open this book, yet they need to, even more than those more likely to buy and enjoy it. Jane's approach is especially attuned to such readers, with their skepticism and the seeds of a deeper understanding alike. Most writers on the Goddess have already written these readers off as targets for their books, with good reason. Why dilute their work for the sake of people who won't buy it or listen anyway?

This is not a polemical book, trying to convince such skeptics to rethink their skepticism, but that may be a reason why it may finish up doing that better than if it had tried to do so. Every book constructs the community of its readers. The community this one envisages is unusually broad and inclusive, and that is its strength, not a weakness.

The book does not have a single voice, Jane's, speaking from her position of spiritual knowledge, though she does that. She also weaves together a choir of voices who believe and don't believe across a broad spectrum. It describes not so much the content of enlightenment but different kinds of encounters with it. These are the voices the skeptics will hear if they give the book a chance. They hear or overhear voices who are not preaching or proselytizing but trying to understand, sharing their experiences with Jane in all their compelling complexity. All readers, skeptics and non-skeptics alike, are drawn into the intimate conversations of this fascinating, welcoming community of witnesses. In human terms it is the best kind of introduction to ideas that otherwise might be rejected as too challenging.

Her book begins by summarizing what Goddess scholars have shown about the Goddess tradition. For those who already know this work, the book is a reaffirmation. But for my imagined skeptical readers, it may just seem what they think they have heard before, though of course they did not get it the first time either. This part of the book is not new and is not meant to be. This is a foundational premise, a chain that links the deep past with experience today, spiritual intuitions with grounded research. Jane contributes a well-wrought link to this chain.

I find it helpful to see this Goddess premise as being like the cosmic pole, the axis mundi that was a core belief in the age of the Goddess. This axis was the hinge around which the universe turned. Likewise, the world of this book turns around the Goddess Principle, its principle of coherence. If only my skeptical readers could hold on to it, all the contradictions and problems they feel about the Goddess would seem as natural as the progression from day to night and back to day again.

I find the idea of the axis mundi a rich image for many qualities of this book, as well as the world of the Goddess. Here is how it was described by Plato long ago in his *Timaeus*, the text in which he announced the story of Atlantis. His enigmatic words are worth repeating here:

> And the earth our foster mother, winding as she does about the axis
> of the universe, he devised to be guardian and maker of day and
> night, and first and oldest of the gods born within the heavens.

My skeptical readers might be surprised here, on this threshold before they have even got inside Jane's actual text, that the revered philosopher Plato, writing in 350 BC, reports that the earth is a goddess, the oldest of the gods. His later patriarchal commentators could be relied on to ignore the phrase, but there it is, like a fossil preserved in the amber of his ancient text.

Plato's text hints at something important to later devotees of the Goddess, which Jane brings out strongly in her book. This version of the Goddess is not simply a benign force, a foster mother and guardian. The word Plato uses for her, which is translated here by the bland word "maker," is *demiourgos*, which translators of Plato elsewhere usually transliterate as *demiurge*. This is a powerful, ambivalent creative figure, creator of day and night, darkness and light.

This image of the Goddess describes a spinner, as the Goddess is represented in many ancient traditions. Weaving is arguably the first form of technology invented by humans, by women more likely than by men. Weaving is a complex and miraculous act. In it the many become one, the humble and the weak becoming part of something that is stronger than any of them could be on their own.

That is the miracle Jane performs with her many voices. By the alchemy of weaving, that first gift of the Goddess to humanity, the sum of Jane's witnesses is far greater than the individual parts. That is why this book can take readers by surprise by the time they reach the end. It is impossible to say or feel when suddenly the case has become irresistible. No particular example stands out. Jane's guiding hand arranges them intuitively, knowing what follows what, how point and counter-point work together. It is a subtle and skillful technique of persuasion, as painless as it is powerful.

Yet there is one distinctive quality of this book that does not fit so well this image of weaving difference harmoniously into a single web or the axis mundi where day turns to night and back again in a gentle rhythm. For many witnesses in this book, light keeps turning to darkness as rapidly, disturbingly, and inexplicably as in a total eclipse, an event which ancient people dreaded.

This sense is captured in the powerful, beautiful idea of ontological shock, one of the most original and challenging ideas in this whole book. I will not explain it here because Jane introduces it so much better than I ever could. Here it is sufficient to say that this idea concerns problematic transitions felt as disturbance or shock between the two worlds, the Goddess's world of the Elphame and the everyday secular world that is the only one rational, skeptical readers think they know.

This is the emotional range that makes this an unusual and great book. In its honesty it encompasses many different degrees of belief and unbelief in a creative, productive tension. That is why I believe that sooner or later it will expand its sphere of influence. It will assist and be part of the slow return of the Goddess, which Jane has seen, or hopes for—as do I.

Professor Bob Hodge
Institute for Culture and Society
University of Western Sydney

Preface

ALTHOUGH I HAD BEEN raised and educated within a reality dominated by the ideas of positivism and scientific materialism, from early childhood I had experienced events that contradicted these particular paradigms. Intellectually I saw myself as a rational, scientific skeptic. I lived within the scientific materialist reality, but I was dimly aware that I also possessed a different, mysterious form of consciousness. Although I couldn't really categorize it, it involved seeing and hearing things that "weren't there" and other strange phenomena. My mother had told me that as a tiny tot I was strongly telepathic. My ontological position was therefore confusing. Ontology is the philosophical study of being and existence, and it relates to who we think we are and how we experience the world. It defines reality and it colors questions of identity and self-acceptance.

Epistemology is the study of how we know things. The epistemological position of scientific materialism only supports knowledge that is gained through the intellect and the brain; it confines research to physical reality and tries to invalidate any knowledge said to be gained through intuition, inspiration, or contact with intelligences or entities from another level of reality. Anything construed as metaphysical is considered to be irrational and anathema to this way of knowing.

Positivism is a philosophy of science that promotes the belief that the only authoritative information comes from an examination and observation of data by the physical senses (on the assumption that the senses are reliable) and from logical and mathematical exploration. Scientific materialism is a kind of fundamentalism that believes all phenomena—including mental phenomena and consciousness itself—can be reduced to material functions. In this view the brain materializes the mind, or the mind is a product of the brain. Both positivism and scientific materialism assume no other level of reality exists beyond the physical.

My otherworldly experiences challenged the ontological and epistemological parameters of the Western intellectual discourse model. Within this model experiences claimed to be from another reality could be understood only as delusions, fantasies, or the products of a diseased brain. It is also the foundation of a dogma. That is, it is a discourse model that makes dogmatic foundational assumptions about the boundaries of reality and excludes alternative ideas without testing them. A discourse model enables a theorist/writer to tell a story with certain clear parameters that keep it discreet, consistent, and manageable. Strangely, relative to the Western theoretical discourse model I seemed rational, capable, and functional, and I definitely did not have a diseased brain.

At about age seven I made and consecrated a talisman, a small wooden black cat, that I wore on a chain around my neck concealed under my clothes. I'm not sure how I came by it. Whenever I wanted something I would touch or tap it to activate it. It was infallible, and looking back it seemed to have real power but I never told anyone about it. I intuited that it was something that should be kept secret. How did I know to do this?

When I was nine I saw my grandfather in spirit form shortly after his death. He was walking about the house and stopped to pat me on the head. "I'm okay, sweetheart. Don't worry," he said. It felt halfway normal. As a child and young teenager I experienced other random and strange phenomena but at that stage I didn't try to integrate them, to codify them, or to really make a serious attempt to understand them. I didn't have a frame of reference for them, so I did what many people do:

I tucked them away in the background of my psyche with a fleeting thought that one day I might make rational sense of them.

I had no expectation that as a young adult the spiritual world would become a lasting and important part of my personal reality and something that I would struggle to understand and to integrate into my subsequent and uncomfortably shifting and expanding worldview.

For a time I described myself as an agnostic. I was unsure about the existence of a Divinity. I was amazed when friends spoke about their Christian beliefs with a high degree of emotional fervor. I found it impossible to believe almost anything and had valued and sought knowledge rather than belief. I tried very hard to believe the Christian stories, but I just couldn't make myself do it. It all seemed rather childish and silly to me. At first I thought that there must have been something deeply wrong with me, but finally I had to accept myself for the person that I am. I am naturally a critical and analytical thinker but an open minded and imaginative one. I've always had a sneaking suspicion that just about anything is possible but believe that it is important to be skeptical and scrutinizing at the same time.

As a young adult I continued to experience events that indicated the possibility of contact with another subtle level of reality that existed apart from yet permeated the physical world. Those mysterious and confusing contacts gathered intensity and culminated in a psychological crisis of confidence I called "ontological shock." This is the mind's struggle to reconcile and to integrate two diametrically opposed models of reality. I see it now as a conflict between the intellect and the intuition, but ultimately it is a conflict that can be resolved. There is a third way. We can be rational and logical and at the same time understand that there are other levels of reality that we can explore with the inner senses. It really is a question of widening our horizons. The intellect and the intuition can be reunited to create a more complete reality and a more complete individual.

The intellect or concrete mind is grounded in physical existence. It must go through the processes of logical inquiry in order to come to conclusions. But the intuition or the higher mind, being more flexible, imaginative, and adventurous, can range more widely and into the subtle levels of reality. It can know something directly without going through the processes of step-by-step analysis. I now see the intuition as our human contact with the universal mind. But when your culture says one thing and your experience says another, it can feel like the ground beneath your feet is shifting. It's not just uncomfortable. It can induce powerful self-doubt, and it can be downright scary.

Over time and through personal experience and experimental practice I found that both my worldview and my epistemological position had changed radically. I knew that other levels of reality existed and that it was possible to know and understand those realities through direct experience of them, through past-life memory both of ideas and skills that have been developed to the point of mastery, through intuitive processes, through prophetic dreams, through telepathic contact, and through discarnate spiritual guidance and communication. I began to understand that the gaining of "knowledge" is not just an intellectual process. There are other ways of knowing, and I believe we can understand their presence, their efficacy, their nature, and their potential in a rational way. Some of the claims I make in this book have been not only mined through mundane research but through educated guesses, past-life memories, information provided by my discarnate spiritual master teacher, strong dreams, and direct experience of the subtle worlds themselves.

A lot more detail about these matters is discussed in chapter 1, so I will not elaborate further here. What I will say is that the material gathered for this book has come from many different sources, some rational and some extra-rational but none of them "irrational." Altogether I think all the different sources combine to give a rounded, integrated, and coherent view of the subtle world and how it works, how it can be utilized, and how it interfaces with physical reality.

My partner and I had also spent many years reading our way through vast numbers of magical texts and discussing what we were reading. All of these activities gave me a way of connecting the dots and understanding ideas and experiences from many different perspectives. I had previously formally studied in the fields of history, comparative religion, linguistics, political science, and philosophy; this prior work had helped me think more broadly as well as be able see how many things that seemed to be superficially separated actually had many important links and commonalities. All this educational discipline helped me to stay reasonably grounded when confronted by events that precipitated fearful responses to ontological shock.

Because the dominant cultural narrative dismisses any type of "psychic" experiences, I searched for a model of reality that could embrace them. I discovered the presence of a mystical and magical tradition that was largely concealed within our culture that had its roots in ancient pre-Christian Paganism, alchemy, Hermetic philosophy, the holy Qabalah, and elements of Greek, Egyptian, and Gnostic mysticism. It is generally referred to as the Western magical tradition. I tend to see it as the lost shaman tradition of the West. Over time the tradition has evolved and broadened to embrace the many modern varieties of Witchcraft groups, High Magical groups, and the many practicing groups that have taken inspiration from indigenous shamanic traditions of various kinds. The common thread that links them all is an understanding that beyond the physical world there exist rich and diverse levels of subtle spiritual worlds that are communicative, contactable, and can be utilized for learning and healing.

I was to eventually find there was meaning and order in my apparently chaotic experiences of the subtle world and that, to my shock and surprise, I had been "chosen by spirit" in the initiatory tradition of the universal shaman. This book, therefore, gives some insight into how a shaman is "made" in the contemporary era. It was interesting for me to see that nearly all Westerners I researched who had a similar initiatory experience had reacted in a similar way. They all went through the experience of ontological shock before getting to the stage where they could accept the experiences for what they were—real contact with the worlds of spirit. In traditional societies this experience would be accepted and honored; in Western society it was generally accepted reluctantly and with a lot of accompanying soul searching and self-doubt.

The Western magical tradition provided me with a workable theoretical map of the subtle world and how it interfaces the physical, as well an archetypal symbol: the Great Goddess. The Goddess discourse model of reality is animistic. She is the subtle yet conscious and intelligent spiritual reality that underpins the physical universe and the interconnected web of energy that links everything in both the visible and the invisible worlds. The Hopi give her the title "Grandmother Spider," indicating that she is both the Weaver and the Web: that she is both within and without the worlds. She is both immanent and transcendent.

The old Goddess was patiently standing at the end of every avenue that I explored. Everything came back to her, and everything made sense because of her. All in all, this discourse model made everything much clearer and simpler than the scientific materialist or positivist model of how the world works.

I wanted to construct an integrated and coherent theoretical model that satisfied my need for what I thought and believed to be a rational process, although it was traditionally described and debunked as irrational by dominant forces in our culture. It was clear to me that reality was far more complex, interesting, and scary than the way in which traditional science had allowed it to be. The other purpose was to think through the idea of ontological shock that I had experienced so intensely and that many of my patients had also encountered in different ways. I was starting to see ontological shock as a kind of war between the intellect and the intuition (or the concrete mind and the higher mind) that created instability, but to qualify this, it was an instability that created an opportunity for rapid mental, emotional, and spiritual growth if one could cope with the pressure and intensity. Ontological shock was painful but ultimately, when one took a deep breath and worked through the pain, it was not so bad.

This book drew its first breath as a doctoral dissertation. The research subject area of the dissertation was basically in applied psychology, but because of its somewhat controversial nature I had put together a qualitative research proposal and applied to the faculty of Social Ecology at the University of Western Sydney. This school had a reputation for innovation and for daring to go where more conventional and conservative universities feared to go. Qualitative research is designed to explore issues, understand phenomena, and make sense of unstructured data. It seeks an in-depth understanding to decipher personal perceptions and uses one-on-one interviews or small focus groups to question a sample of research subjects about their personal thoughts and reactions to certain experiences. It is often used as a research methodology in the social sciences. My research made extensive use of one-on-one in-depth interviews.

Social ecology is a "big picture" kind of discipline. One of its attractions for me was that it is able to put back together ideas and disciplines that have been severed from each other even though it is clear that they are really very closely related. In this era of very narrow academic specialization, social ecology suited me very well because I would describe myself as a "big picture" kind of person. In light of this, my doctoral thesis, although it had a strongly psychological focus, was a fusion work that linked and in a sense reunited the subjects of psychology, psychotherapy, anthropology, and consciousness studies. My approach to all of these interlinking disciplines, however, was tinted with a certain expertise that I had accrued through my years of study, practice, and certain hairraising experience in magic and the Craft. So I could compare, for example, what orthodox psychology has to say about certain matters with what magical psychology has to say about them. There are very considerable differences!

Generally, orthodox psychology has a scientific materialist and positivist perspective and so believes that everything can be explained by reference to the physical world, but magical psychology understands that in order to come to grips with "strange" phenomena it is necessary to go to the subtle levels of reality to find true meaning. Magical psychology has a more spiritual focus. Magical psychology views the brain, the mind, and consciousness itself to be interactive but separate: that is, the mind is separate from the brain. My personal experience with altered states of consciousness and out-of-body experiences confirms this to be true.

In the orthodox psychological view the brain for some (unknown) reason decides to originate and generate "strange" effects like visions, for example, but in the magical view the brain is a sophisticated kind of computer/receiver. It organizes data, receives information from the senses and the "world," and stores it. The storage process is imperfect, and stored memory can become corrupted. The brain doesn't generate anything at all. Magical psychology would say that strange effects like visions that present themselves to the screen of consciousness come from another level of reality and can therefore be considered as real events, just not events that have their origins in the physical world.

Both conventional psychology and conventional psychiatry, however, dismiss these kinds of psychic events as delusions that are generated by a chemically unbalanced and malfunctioning brain. In this view a person who is having visions or hearing voices would be regarded as psychotic. Orthodox practitioners generally would not agree that there exist other levels of reality that have an influence upon the physical world. They subscribe to the generally accepted doctrine of scientific materialism that still has a stranglehold upon conventional thinking. Despite this cultural hegemony recent research indicates there are many people in the Western world who think that other levels of reality do exist and that these levels communicate with us in various ways to our benefit. For example, many people report having had an experience of seeing and communicating with a loved one after physical death. They consider these reassuring events as real experiences, not delusions. They do not exhibit any symptoms of psychosis and are perfectly functioning and contributing members of society. Orthodoxy has what I think is a very unconvincing and tortured explanation for this quite common experience where the brain suddenly becomes compassionate and creates a hallucination of the departed loved one in order to offer consolation to the grieving widow/ family member/friend, etc. Occam's razor suggests that the simplest explanation is most probably right—the observer is actually seeing the person in their subtle body after they have shed their physical body like a serpent cyclically sheds its skin. I think it is safe to say that every traditional and ancient culture believes that spirits do exist and that they can cause problems after death if the right rituals are not performed or if the departed have not received correct instruction in what to expect and what to do.

They are not immediately transported to sit with God or Jesus, for example, or have eternal peace or eternal sleep in a cozy grave that looks like a bed. Neither do they lounge about on clouds playing harps or other musical instruments badly. Our "enlightened" culture has turned the normal, natural, and beautiful process of dying into a childish fantasy. Death is a time of transition of consciousness into the subtle world. Therefore consciousness is not annihilated at physical death; individual consciousness survives death. Consciousness is a movable point like a torch beam that casts a shaft of light into the vast darkness of the "unknowable" void. My research and personal experience also confirms this is so.

I think that the doctrine of scientific materialism is a limiting and old-fashioned reductionist view of reality, but it is a view that dominates at the level of our entrenched social institutions: the centers of learning, the law, conventional medicine, Christian institutions, and politics and science in general. It also gives tacit permission for the rampant and ravaging exploitation of the natural physical world because it does not admit of any spiritual basis or value that underpins it all. The universe is viewed as basically inanimate. It is time for this limiting dogma to go!

By comparison, the magical worldview of both traditional shamanism and modern shamanism is animistic—that is, the universe is filled with life and intelligence on all levels. It is a living, conscious, and communicative system. We can learn from it as opposed to learning about it. The physical universe is the body of the divine entity—the Great Goddess. The subtle reality is the consciousness of this divine creative force. We live and move and have our being within this vast consciousness, as does everything that exists. Recent research also indicates that many people in the Western world, despite the scientific materialist view that nature is to be dominated and subjugated, believe that nature is sacred and that humanity has a sacred duty to protect it and all its life streams. There is a universal and growing wave of revulsion toward the ruinous exploitation of the natural world for greed and profit. This revulsion extends toward cruelty to animals that are used as resources and to the careless and profit-driven destruction of both farmland and wilderness areas by disgusting practices like fracking.

With the arrival of Christianity in the Western world, the psychic and spiritual world of Paganism progressively became depopulated, and the ecological web of the old religions and traditions, with their ideas of interconnection and interrelationship with the natural world, faded into obscurity. The devitalizing process that Christianity began was finished off by rational science, which delivered the coup de grace and turned the Western cultural landscape from an organic, communicative, conscious, and magical world into a stark and mechanical reality. This is the dark world we have inherited. In it humanity dominates and exploits other life streams to their detriment, increasing irrelevance and finally their extinction. In the meta-narrative or discourse model of the Great Goddess there is room in the world for all life streams to have their place and flourish in an interactive and enlightened balance that is based on knowledge and respect.

Thou or It, Organism or Mechanism?

It seems obvious that there are two paradigms operating in the world today. The first, of course, is the scientific materialist paradigm that is still current but passing. The second is what I call the Goddess paradigm. It is a modern restoration of ancient Pagan and traditional ideas about the sacred and an awareness of human reality. It is gradually emerging as people are coming to understand and accept some of its important concepts. A paradigm in this sense means a framework of ideas, thought patterns, and theories that define reality. In an important sense it is thinking that changes paradigms and therefore changes reality. Hermetic science tells us that mind is a first principle and that matter comes out of mind and not the other way around.

The science of ecology and its different branches underscores the concept of interconnectedness and relationship. The Gaia hypothesis that the planet Earth is a self-regulating single living being made up of complex systems suggests to me that some organizing consciousness and foundational intelligence must be present. At a magical level we can understand this complexity because we have an understanding of how the elementals work in the subtle world to sustain the physical. In terms of open-minded scientific investigation, I believe the cosmic Goddess could be called the "unified field" that is the Holy Grail of theoretical physics. The concept of dark matter suggests that the universe is not mostly empty space but that something of finer material density underlies the visible physical universe. Its gravitational effects can be observed. The idea that mind, thought, or expectations can influence the outcomes of experimental work was a shocking and radical concept in its day but one that is observably accurate if not universally accepted. Some people don't want to see what they don't want to see. The fact that water can hold a charge of thoughts and emotions was also a very radical concept but now is generally well accepted and established. The list goes on. Ideas about the nature of reality are rapidly changing and becoming more magical and spiritual. I believe that what is called a paradigm shift is taking place slowly but surely.

At the leading edge even science itself is becoming more magical, especially in physics at the theoretical and speculative level. At the entrenched dogmatic level it is digging in and becoming more defensive, closed-minded, militant, angry, and strident as its power is gradually ebbing away. There is nothing wrong with the scientific method if it is used properly, but it is not universally applicable in every situation and it cannot give answers or solutions to problems that are out of its jurisdiction. We need a different kind of science for that purpose.

I had previously completed a post-graduate degree in counseling and psychotherapy, so the doctoral thesis had a good foundation on which to build a strong case for the theoretical discourse model I was proposing, especially in the area of healing. I will describe this in greater detail in chapter 3, but for the moment I will simply say that the archetype of the Great Goddess provided the theoretical or discourse model for the experimental work I had done in education, psychotherapy, and healing in general and in an investigation into what constitutes modern shamanism. These three are my areas of special expertise. The discourse model enabled me to pull the threads together so that the project did not disintegrate into three separate fields.

I had come to see that the discourse model I needed in order to tell the story I wanted to tell involved not just the archetype or template / original pattern of the Great Goddess but also the archetype of the Shaman. In my view these two archetypes are inextricably linked. The Shaman is the bridge or the link between the physical world and the subtle world because the Shaman has the ability to change consciousness and to travel by many different means and routes into the subtle world in order to gain knowledge and insight at a causal level.

The second part of the Shaman's journey is to return to normal waking consciousness and the material world in order to bring back that special knowledge that will heal the pain of their suffering clients. Shamans are traditionally the teachers and healers of their communities. They have some expert knowledge of both the physical and the subtle worlds—and the interactions between the two. The dual archetype of the Goddess and the Shaman is fundamentally about healing from the subtle worlds.

The word *shaman* has migrated into European and other languages from its Siberian Tungus origins. Of course there are many other terms from different cultural origins that describe the same thing, but the word shaman has become almost a universal term. Most reasonably educated people have some idea of what a shaman does, and the term in the public mind is now pretty much free from the pejorative connotations of terms like "witch doctor" or "sorcerer." I use the word shaman to describe high-level magical workers from whatever culture because I believe that there are strong commonalities in the ways they work apart from the cultural dressing and cultural differences. Some writers, mostly academics, focus on the differences and uniqueness of each shamanic tradition, but I believe that every culture has always had shamans or magical workers who have practiced in similar ways with the aim of changing consciousness and of travelling into the Elphame to gain knowledge and insight.

The idea that there are fundamental differences in ways that human share experiences is not one I subscribe to—the shamanic experience is one of the many fundamental attributes of being human. I focus on the similarities rather than on differences because I believe there is a single foundation to our spiritual and magical nature and purpose despite notional superficial differences. To me the crucial thing is that shamanism is not a religion peculiar to a special group but a set of spiritual technologies that facilitate the changing of consciousness in various ways.

An archetype is the original model, template, or design upon which other and later ideas are compounded. The Great Goddess, for example, is the original Divinity upon which all other ideas of goddesses are modeled, and the archetype of the Shaman is the original mythological template for magic workers (but magic workers who work in life-enhancing ways and who are constrained by the ethical principles of a goddess reality). These principles are clearly laid down in Hermetic philosophy and in other similar magical codes. The Shaman archetype also represents the notional "ideal" of the human condition through evolution of spiritual technology that leads to rational contact with the divine world.

The first prong of my doctoral research project was an investigation into some experimental work that I had conducted into what I had described as education with the Goddess in the classroom. This work showed that when Goddess principles were adopted in education, all bullying and disengagement ceased, and even the most reluctant and hopeless students began achieving at an unexpectedly high level. This research is not part of the current work but is the subject of a future book I am in the process of writing. I have included a mention of it to show the extent of the research project in toto.

The second prong of the investigation involved researching a group of my former patients who had presented for treatment with a range of mental, emotional, and physical problems that had not responded to conventional medical and psychiatric treatment or to ordinary alternative medical treatments like herbal medicine or homeopathy. (I am also trained as a medical herbalist, homeopathic physician, naturopath, and nutritionist.) With these difficult and unresponsive cases, and in order to find cures for their presenting conditions, I had experimented with ideas and methodologies gleaned from my studies and experiences in the Western magical/mystical tradition.

What these former patients had to say about their treatment and the subsequent transformations of their lives and their conscious awareness was interesting and generally very positive. It seemed that publication of this work could be helpful to many people who were suffering from similar intractable conditions that had their origins not in the physical world but in the second, more subtle foundational reality that I now call the "Elphame." It was also surprising to me to find that many health problems, both physical and nonphysical, do not have their origins in the current life but can originate from past-life situations and follow a person from lifetime to lifetime until a resolution is established. I interviewed ten former patients who had experienced treatments that had their origins in various techniques and practices of the Western magical tradition. I also interviewed my former partner James because he had been a collaborator and co-therapist in one of the important case studies in chapter 13.

The Elphame is a generic term that I use to describe the Goddess: the foundational subtle reality that forms the intelligent basis of the physical world of forms. The Aztecs called the physical world of forms "the painted world," suggesting that it is something like a stage set where we come to act out our roles and relationships for a time. The physical world is in a process of continual cyclic change and flux. It is an ephemeral world. As humans we don't like it. We try to fix it to prevent it from moving and changing too much, but of course we have no power over it.

It seems from my research that we return to the ephemeral physical world from time to time, usually for a period of intense learning, then retire to the subtle spiritual world that is our natural home, as we are naturally spirit in transitory human form. It is this spiritual fact that according to American Egyptologist and linguist Dr. Alvin Boyd Kuhn formed the basis of the initiated teachings of the Egyptian and Greek mystery schools. What we learn in the physical world, frequently through traumatic experiences, is that these experiences are symbolic of a deeper spiritual truth and reality.

The Elphame is also a term used by some Craft groups with which I am familiar. I realize that it is not universally used in Wiccan circles, but I like it as a shorthand way of describing the intelligent levels of cosmic mind. I find many of the other terms that are used to name this Goddess world to be imprecise and clunky. The term "astral" is misleading, and the phrase "non-ordinary reality" as used by Michael Harner and the Foundation for Shamanic Studies seems awkward and prosaic to me. "Elphame" seems a bit more shiny, mysterious, feminine, even glamorous. Queen of Elphame seems like an appropriate title for the cosmic Queen of Heaven—"Aparantos," the shining one, the hidden light of the physical word.

The title "Queen of Elphame" is, of course, a reference to the Great Goddess, but it is sometimes used as a title for the Wiccan high priestess because she consciously carries the energy of the Goddess herself. The verbatim interviews with this group of eleven people who had encounters with the cosmic Goddess and the subtle worlds in various ways are included in the book. I think they make for engrossing and almost hypnotic reading.

The subtle reality has many levels or grades, but to differentiate amongst them is not part of this current work. The term Elphame includes all these levels for convenience's sake, and for the purposes of this book I am contrasting and comparing the physical world with the subtle world and observing how they have a mutual influence. Reality looks very different when the Elphame is included and factored into the equation, and many things that are invisible when the dim and scratched lens of scientific materialism is used suddenly become visible and understandable. With the right microscope or a clearer lens a new world is suddenly revealed. The Goddess model of reality suddenly supplies the right microscope through which a vastly expanded vision of reality becomes possible, and as many of the interview subjects have said, "It made sense! Something finally made sense!"

Although materialist science would describe this process as "irrational," I contend that it is a rational process that can be embraced by the human mind and brain. It only takes a slight mental shift that gives permission to imagine what the world would look like if it were repopulated by spiritual entities. If normal waking consciousness is rational, then perhaps a better description of altered states of consciousness might be "extra-rational" or "suprarational" rather than "irrational." That is, consciousness can move beyond the limited logical and concrete ways of habitual thinking into areas we could describe as intuitive, emotional, psychic, aesthetic, and magical, as I contend that knowledge that is gained through these processes is as legitimate as knowledge gained through so-called logical and empirical processes. It is also probably important to note that what is now called "irrational" was once normal and rational. In fact, until the purposeful eradication of the inner ecology, disbelief in spirits would have been thought of as madness.

It is possible that what we describe in our culture as "mental illness" has an emotional basis that has a great deal to do with a separation or severing, either partial or complete, of the personality self from its spiritual foundation, the higher self or soul from its nurturing spiritual environment—the matrix of the natural world. From a shaman perspective the denial of the reality of the spiritual in our scientific/technological culture generally creates a schizoid and traumatized environment in which we live and move and have our fragmented being. Most of us are incomplete people living within a suffocating world desperately seeking oxygen through reunification. Understanding the rational intelligence of the Goddess model helps you to breathe deeply again.

The third group of people I interviewed were what I describe as modern shaman-healers. They worked confidently and knowledgeably from the second subtle reality to bring about healing in the physical world. Their work included telepathic communication, dowsing as a diagnostic tool, hands-on diagnosis and healing, and the use of many different kinds of "energy medicines," including the changing of consciousness to work with both humans and animals in spirit or from the Elphame.

They had a common ontology or worldview that was holistic and animistic. That is, they saw a world that is very different to the mechanistic model. Their world is integrated and interrelated, communicative and intelligent, and has a spiritual purpose. Everything to them is alive, interconnected, and conscious. Like the traditional shaman-healers from traditional and ancient cultures, these people work from the second reality, the Elphame, by an act of changing consciousness.

Shamanism is not a religion as we usually understand it; rather, it is a spiritual technology employed for the act of changing consciousness. Some cultures use drugs in a controlled and ritualistic manner, others use dance or drumming, some use types of meditative processes, but basically all these techniques are a means to shut down the intellectualizing part of the mind and brain to allow them to access to the unconscious and the intuitive. The unconscious is the part of the mind that is connected to the universal spiritual reality and what we would call the higher self—our conscience, higher mind, or soul that is an intermediary between humanity and Divinity. The group of modern shamans I call the Grail Family (after Caitlín Matthews) simply use a process they call "clicking over" to describe how they move from ordinary waking consciousness to altered states that allow them to enter the Elphame.

I believe that the term "Holy Grail" in literature is a veiled reference to the Great Goddess. The Grail Family of chapter 16 includes all magical workers both traditional and modern who are able to enter the Elphame and gain knowledge and power there. They are the sons and daughters of the Great Goddess in consciousness. They keep the sacred tradition alive and pass on the flame of initiation from generation to generation and sometimes, through necessity, in deepest secrecy. The members of the Grail Family are the conscious transmitters of the hidden light and are able to employ a magical/spiritual technology acquired from their contact with the Elphame to heal and teach.

The ten verbatim interviews I conducted with people I describe as modern shamans are included in the book, interwoven throughout chapters 16 through 18, "The Grail Family," "The Modern Shamans," and "Animals and the Elphame," respectively.

Superficially it might seem that these three research fields lacked a unifying structure that was capable of relating them to each other to create a seamless and unified piece of work. It was the discourse model of the Goddess, however, that provided the glue that held the fields together to create what has been described as a "seamless work."

This book goes outside the materialist medical discourse in an attempt to shed some light on these important issues. It contends that for many of those who find their experiences of the Elphame to be detrimental, cures can be affected by using shamanic methods of healing. My experience of developing and using magical treatments indicates that they have been safe, effective, and lasting. These procedures can be fitted within a coherent and validating ontological frame, and the verbatim interviews of the later chapters are testament to those claims. This is essentially a book about true healing and not about just the amelioration of symptoms.

I believe the ideas in this book can be influential in helping people understand how our current worldview has created a dark reality that does not help us understand how to refine ourselves spiritually or understand that there are consequences for our actions. Living only in the physical world, it is virtually impossible to see the long-term effects of our actions and take responsibility for them because everything is separate and distinct from everything else. There are no psychic links or connections and certainly no spiritual reality to suggest we need to be more cautious and thoughtful.

For those involved in the Western mysteries this book will weave together many threads to create a synthetic and discernible pattern of insights that previously perhaps will have appeared to be diffuse and confusingly disconnected.

For the intelligent and curious seeker it will open up a way of thinking about the mystical and the magical in a rational and ordered way that can provide safe entry into the subtle world that I call the Elphame.

For the inquiring and inquisitive general reader I think it is an interesting and intriguing journey that gives some understanding of how the magical and the political are intertwined and mutually influential, although they might seem superficially to be strange bedfellows.

For the more open-minded and thoughtful rational skeptics who may pick up this book it is my hope that they might have the courage to suspend disbelief and follow the train of argument to see whether it has some validity and that there are other ways of knowing and being that encompass the intuitive, the emotional, and the suprarational. I have nothing against intellect and order but believe that these powers need to be balanced by the more feminine powers of emotion and intuition in order to have a more complete understanding of reality.

This book works on several levels. Firstly it is about my personal struggle to work through and integrate the intellectual, emotional, and spiritual challenges that were precipitated by the confronting and disturbing intrusion of energies from another dimension. Secondly it is about how the Goddess and the Shaman ontology and epistemology was developed as a tool for interpreting and responding to the physical and psychological needs of my patients, often when no other more conventional treatment had worked. On a global or universal level the archetype shows that the "world," or physical reality in general, is underpinned and permeated by a foundational consciousness and intention rather than by mechanism and randomness. We can use this old/new knowledge for the benefit of all life streams.

I present this work to the Great One in gratitude and reverence. In a sense, it is a libation—a distillation of learning and experience poured out freely and lovingly onto our beautiful world. My hope is that it might bring an aha moment to those who read it. It carries my love and possibly some small wisdom to all the brave seekers of the world.

Blessed be.

A Dream of the Great Goddess

I am sleeping and I suddenly become conscious that I am in another reality inside a strong dream. I am standing on a ladder polishing and filing into shape what appears to be a large translucent tile. It is a wonderful vibrant green color and has a strangely shaped curved edge that strikes me as curious. I apply some adhesive with a brush and begin to place the tile on a surface, thinking it is a wall. As I do this I realize it is not a wall surface or anything inanimate. It is a living form! I suddenly and shockingly become aware that the surface I am restoring is part of the midsection of a vast serpent's body. Its length is so great that it stretches out of sight in both directions. Neither head nor tail is visible, but I sense intelligence, consciousness, and communication are present. I feel an emotional connection and response.

I am doing the final shaping and polishing of what I now see are large serpent scales, repairing a section of the body that has been badly damaged. I am doing it lovingly and carefully, restoring it to perfection. The repair is seamless and undetectable. I feel satisfaction in my work.

One part of my consciousness is afraid. It shouts to the part that is concentrating on the restoration work: "Yikes! It's a huge snake! Why aren't you afraid? Why aren't you running away? Are you mad? Let's get out of here!"

The part of my psyche doing the restoration work is serene: "There's nothing to fear," she says calmly. "To do this work is to our honor and our greatest good." The fearful part is startled, surprised, yet grudgingly admiring that "we" are so brave. The images begin to fade.

I am awake and reflective but aware that I am still conscious in another reality. I begin to analyze the dream as I am experiencing it. The experience has the power and clarity of a vision with none of the sometimes confusing, ephemeral, and transitory ambience of a normal dream. It is a strong dream, sometimes called a "big dream" by Australian indigenous people—a communication from what they would describe as the Dreamtime. My consciousness shifts and gradually returns to awareness in the ordinary physical world, and the dream world fades.

• • • •

THE DREAM OCCURRED A few years before I became deeply involved with Wicca and hence with the archetype of the Old Goddess herself in a way that was more closely acquainted. It was, therefore, powerfully prophetic about what was to come, and it was the guiding inspiration for much of my subsequent thinking both magical and mundane.

As the dream symbolism describes it, the seemingly inanimate becomes a vast and powerful living being. What I originally misperceived as inorganic, lifeless, and something more like a good idea than a living reality suddenly and unexpectedly morphs into the life force itself.

The dream is prophetic, speaking of something of which, at the time, I am only dimly aware. The great serpent is the Great Goddess, I realize, and I am a Wiccan high priestess. I serve and honor the Goddess, but the dream seems to be saying that my life and my work at some future time will somehow change to become involved with the restoration of the archetype of the Goddess in the world.

As my life unfolds, the restoration of the serpent gradually becomes more important to me. As I write, reflect, and pursue my research into the meaning and potential of the archetype, she also seems to shift and lose objectivity and distance. I develop a certain personal emotional closeness with the Goddess. I consciously become part of her as the process of magical initiation opens before me and gains momentum. I see clearly that the Great Goddess is a reality in which we live and move and have our being and that everything exists within a vast ocean of consciousness energy that is a living spiritual reality. I had kind of known this intellectually, but to know it emotionally and in a grounded and experiential way is quite a different proposition. It feels more real and emotionally believable. It changes everything.

The dream prophesies my transformation of consciousness and the gaining of a deeper realization of the serpent symbol's meaning. I begin to look at the natural world in a different, more integrated way as I understand that there is intelligence and consciousness in everything. Animals, plants, stones—all have their own particular consciousness and deserve and require respect and honoring. We can communicate with these other life streams telepathically using the universal web of connectedness. The natural world communicates with me, and I begin to see and sense the world in very much the same way that traditional shaman cultures see it and feel connected to it.

There is a point where the past becomes the future—that is, a moment in time when I find myself engaged in the work that the dream prophesies. The serpent is the life force, and I work to serve it and restore an understanding of its significance, purpose, and functionality. My consciousness expands, and I begin to see through the misleading simplicity of the dream images to grasp something of their multilayered complexities of meaning. I remember the dream and realize I am living it. I begin to understand that my life and work are intimately connected to the repair and restoration of an understanding of the feminine power of Divinity.

The dream reveals that one part of me senses the danger in doing this work and wants to flee from it. It seems safer to remain numb and obedient, cocooned within the dominant group delusion. The Western world has moved in another direction and roughly abandoned the Old Goddess as an anachronism, but the option of willful ignorance is not really possible. The other self, balanced on the ladder, has climbed higher and gained a more exalted view. She can see further. She is in touch with a higher spiritual world. She is visionary, and she is in charge. Taking the long view, she sees there is a rightness and fitness in doing the restoration work, and not only in a personal sense. She sees that humanity may also benefit psychologically and emotionally from re-establishing a connection with the life source and from applying insights gained by that experience to "real" living in the physical world.

The dream elegantly expresses the psychic conflict I frequently experience as I move between mundane reality and the spiritual world and that I later investigate and describe as ontological shock. The mind simultaneously knows and does not know something, and a state of paralyzing conflict is induced. The dream is an encapsulation of the book, and the book is an exposition of that dream. The two forms are intimately connected, two sides of the one psyche that dramatically indicate the difference between the intuition and the intellect, and two sides of a larger binary reality. The dream, however, clearly shows the limitations of the intellect fearful and fixed in physical reality vis-à-vis the loftier magical and spiritual vision of the intuition that is capable of imagining and embracing other possibilities.

The dream also describes the ancient symbol of the serpent as having the capacity to slot seamlessly into our modern psyches. ("The repair is seamless and undetectable.") The restored section fits perfectly into the whole. Restoration of the serpent means a renewal of the Goddess archetype and everything that powerful and benign symbol represents. It indicates the possibility of life lived courageously, without fear of what lies beyond the boundaries of the physical world: holism, interrelationship, connectivity, health, regeneration, and transformation.

The serpent is a powerful symbol of the Goddess. It gives an understanding of the law of cycles, death, rebirth, immortality, and spiritual growth. It promises rejuvenation for humanity on every level: physical, emotional, mental, and spiritual. We are in desperate need of it. We are slowly realizing as a culture that the intellect is not supreme. It is fallible and does not give good guidance for action in the long term, which is why most political and technological solutions to the world's problems usually ultimately fail. They are usually short term and reactive and driven by intellectual hubris. We need our poets, our strong dreamers, and our visionaries, who can help to tune us into a spiritual reality that can nourish and guide our actions in the long term.

This dream is also, paradoxically, at once deceptively simple and enticingly complex. The enacted meaning works on two levels of reality simultaneously and moves with a kind of naturalness between one state and another; it describes an interaction between two realms. One level describes the legitimate knowledge of consensual reality and the other, the forbidden knowledge of a subtle world long since dismissed as delusional by Western science and demonized by Western religion. But the dream reconnects the two worlds and honors and legitimizes both.

1

The Seeker, the Dreamer, the Pagan, and the Rebel

Horatio: O day and night, but this is wondrous strange!
Hamlet: And therefore as a stranger give it welcome.
There are more things in heaven and earth, Horatio,
than are dreamt of in your philosophy. (Shakespeare, *Hamlet*)

MY INTEREST IN ACTIVELY investigating the Elphame was triggered by my need to find a way of understanding powerful and destabilizing personal "psychic" experiences that could not be explained rationally or psychologically. My direct and unfolding experience of contact with the Elphame represents an ongoing awakening to a different and shifting way of understanding reality. I was in the uncomfortable position of continually "remaking the world" and so it seems necessary to give some further detailed examples of the kinds of events that have led me to make such a radical departure from the consensus Western view of reality. What follows is a small but representative series of strange and dramatic life experiences that I originally found to be doubtful and disturbing but that with the benefit of time, hindsight, and familiarity I now accept as valid.

I began to see repeating patterns in these personal experiences and in those of the people I interviewed. The theme of initiation and ordeal, the theme of ontological shock, and the theme of the spiritual journey, for example, reached directly into their lives. The whole subject of shamanism and how a shaman is made is also particularly relevant to any discussion of the Goddess model of reality because the shaman is the one who has direct and controlled experience of that reality. The biographical vignettes that follow provide an insider description of the concept and process of being "chosen by spirit" and "made" into a shaman.

I know that my personal story is exotic and may set challenges for some readers. Can this record be trusted? The question hangs in the air, and although the rationalist tradition would deny my experiences as valid, I maintain that they are as real and as clear as any written description can make them. This spiritual journey I am on has taken me wholesale into the "irrational," extra-rational, or suprarational world of the Elphame, but this does not mean the "rational" should be discarded because both the rational and the intuitive or super-rational give valuable and necessary different perspectives. Unlike the polarized black-and-white world of mainstream Western thought, they offer not mutually exclusive positions for evaluation but a combined third way that is both magical and rational. This is the territory between the worlds that I inhabit and the book as a whole inhabits. It seems reasonable, then, and not presumptuous to ask the unprejudiced reader to join us there.

As I scan my life looking for seminal events I allow my consciousness to drift back in reverie through the mists of memory. The first intuitive image that arises spontaneously on the screen of consciousness is of a vast landscape. I have an overview from above it. Through the swirling clouds of fog I see many piercing mountain peaks. Some are dark and barren, cold and repelling; others are sunlit and snow-clad; some have craggy overhangs that suggest they are difficult to climb but that the effort is well worthwhile—they will give a clear vision of the pattern and meaning that is inherent in everything that has happened. These images are the symbolic peak experiences of my life and indicators that the learning they represent is important, even transformational. I am looking for markers in childhood and young adulthood that may give some indication of the future person I was to become. I float closer to one of the illuminated peaks of memory. I feel an inner jolt as a detailed image appears.

I see myself aged about three, standing alone somewhere outdoors and in a moment of quiet reflection thinking my first clearly remembered rational thought: *Who am I?* It was followed closely by *What am I doing here?* The recovery of the image brings a chain of associated thoughts and feelings that connect with a psychic network. I sense a powerful energy beneath the network that drives it and that seems to be at the level of life purpose or direction. I had considered those were normal questions that humans asked themselves and have been surprised that the many people I have subsequently asked about this have told me that the questions have never occurred to them and certainly not in early childhood. Some of my patients told me that those kinds of questions sometimes arose in adult life, usually at a time of personal crisis or painful loss. This precocious questioning was to become a repeating motif woven throughout the pattern of my life's journey.

Eventually, as my ego became capable of comprehending that there were other people in the world who also had needs and wants, I began to identify with humanity and to ask *Who are we? What are we doing here?* And as I gained some further maturity and a greater capacity for abstract thought, the more sophisticated version of these questions became *What is the essential nature of human identity? What is our relationship to the cosmos?*

I was also fascinated as a small child by the concepts of life and death, and have another memory-vision of myself, probably around the same age, examining a dead bird and puzzling over how it was the same and yet so very different to the other birds that were flying around nearby. I tried to force my child's mind to cope with this paradox and to find an answer to penetrate the veil of what I sensed to be an important mystery. I asked myself something like *What was the thing that caused the flying birds to be animated, the lack of which caused the dead bird to lie so still?* I knew it was not asleep, and I also knew that some important factor was missing. I had an unformed intuition that some of the answers to these important questions were to be found shrouded by the mystery of death.

Childhood was a frustrating time for me as I tried to force my mind to penetrate the veils that concealed the secrets of existence but continually came up against a barrier through which the mind could not pass. It was as though I had a deep spiritual and philosophical intuitive understanding but lacked the precise language to give it a sophisticated form. I thought that either the mind was the wrong instrument for this purpose or that it was not sufficiently sharpened and I would have to wait out childhood to see if greater age and experience would create the mental focus that could pierce through to the heart of the mystery. I was ultimately to discover that the intellect was not the right instrument for the purpose, but it did provide some imperfect language that could extend meaning through the process of metaphor and analogy to describe and communicate something of the essence of the mystical experience.

At age five I was expelled from Sunday school for persistently engaging in religious and philosophical arguments with my teacher. I wanted knowledge, not belief or allegory, and thought that I could tell the difference. Somehow I knew intuitively there was a difference between what Laurence Gardner, a researcher into the Paganism of the "Ring Lord" tradition, calls "churchianity" and true spirituality, and like many small children I had an infallible nose for cant and hypocrisy.

At about age nine a hawk appeared in my life and took up residence in a tree outside the window of the bedroom I shared with my sister. We understood the hawk was special in some way, so we spent a lot of time talking to him, feeding him, and telling him about our secret lives and asking him about his travels. I was later to find that in many shamanic cultures birds are regarded as messengers of the gods, and throughout my life I have had many remarkable and magical encounters with birds.

It was an exciting event when the hawk returned each year, and we would hold a celebration in his honor. We regarded him as a kind of protective deity who came each year to check on our progress and show us that there was another world to which he could travel that was magical, mystical, and enchanted. I wished I could travel to that mystical otherworld that seemed unknown to our parents; they seemed so preoccupied with mundane matters that they could give no guidance on how to access that ethereal place. In retrospect I realize that what transpired between myself and the hawk was telepathic communication; my grandmother and mother later confirmed that as a young child I had a strong telepathic ability.

My maternal grandfather was an important figure of my childhood and one adult who had not lost his sense of the magical. He had designed and built an extensive and beautiful enchanted garden where we would spend hours looking at plants and insects, picking fruit and vegetables, feeding the chooks, and making bouquets of flowers. There were little grottoes and cool rockeries filled with delicate and gracefully levitating ferns whose fronds seemed to float and breathe, mysterious and strangely striped tiger lilies, and delicately perfumed rock lilies glowing rich and creamy in the cool dampness and shade.

Here a child could safely hide and dream and talk to the nature spirits who cared for the garden's inhabitants. There I felt nurtured and connected to a vast and benign presence. Inwardly I see myself at the bottom of the garden standing in a huge field of blue, pink, and white violets, and fruit trees in blossom: plums, peaches, and citrus. The scent of orange blossom and violets overwhelmed the senses. It was delightful to lie among the violets, allowing the opiate perfume to carry my mind away to a mysterious place where everything was still and deeply quiet as I watched through my eyelashes the shifting patterns of clouds across the blue wash of sky. Time was frozen and I entered another world. The garden was a microcosm, a secret place of beauty, peacefulness, and excitement. Grandfather was an enchanter, a spellbinding storyteller, a funmaker with a whimsical sense of humor and one adult who understood the heart of a child.

My maternal grandmother was Welsh. In the manner of the Celtic people, she had powerful visions and prophetic dreams. She had trained as a spirit medium and her religious orientation was strongly Pagan. On New Year's Eve, for example, she would gather up the children, and with everybody armed with drums, bells, whistles, trumpets, and other improvised percussion instruments, she would lead us on a fierce expedition around the house and garden, everybody shouting, jumping, thumping, clanging, and banging in order to drive out any evil spirits that might have been lounging about the place, looking for an opportunity to create mischief. She was strongly humanitarian and was always rescuing people. She once said to me, "I'm a better Christian than all those mealy-mouthed hypocrites who rush off to church every Sunday and never lift a finger to really help anyone!" I wondered why she said she was a better Christian when she seemed like a perfectly good Pagan to me.

Another flashing peak image arises and I see myself again at nine years old when my grandfather died and a light went out in my life. The person who had given me unconditional love was gone, although his physical departure did not make that much difference to Grandmother, as she carried on their earthly dialogue after death as though he were still powerfully present and as if it were the most normal thing in the world. In passing conversation she would often confide that she had been "talking to your grandfather last night, and he thinks…"

She was demonstrably sane, so I suppose I must have unconsciously accepted at quite an early age that talking to spirits was what one did and that the barrier between the living and the dead was not the gaping abyss that most people believed it to be. I realize with a flash of insight how close I had been to both my maternal grandparents and how they had given me the dual gifts of unconditional acceptance and a sanctuary where I could safely and authentically be myself.

Consciousness floats on and another vision emerges. I see myself at the scene of my grandfather's death. At the moment of his passing my grandmother, my mother, and other members of the family behaved strangely. They began screaming, sobbing, moaning, tearing their hair, and collapsing. I remember standing in shock and wonderment, watching the adults behaving as though they were psychotic. Somehow I had expected that death, when it came, would be quiet and dignified. I did not cry although I had been very close to this grandfather. I had a different understanding of what death meant, but this was more like an intuition and once more I struggled to give it shape in words. It was many years later when I was thirty and having an acupuncture treatment that I suddenly began spontaneously weeping, and I understood that I had not done the necessary grieving for his loss. I heard my child's voice saying through the tears, "Don't leave me. Don't leave me with these people who don't understand me."

My father, who had noticed my shock at my mother's strange behavior at the moment of my grandfather's death, said something interesting and important to me. He had been born in Sri Lanka of a Sinhalese mother and an English father and had lived there until his late teens. "You know," he said, "in India and Ceylon people don't behave like this. They believe that when a person dies it is a time to celebrate because the person's worldly duties are over and they have become free of the limitations of being in the physical world. They also believe that you don't just get one life, but you come back many times to learn all the things you need to learn. They call it reincarnation."

It was as though a big piece of the puzzle I had set for myself at the age of three fell into place. A light came on in my brain, and I believe I actually physically felt the neural pathways rearrange themselves. My world picture shifted and expanded. I intuitively knew it was right. If we come here to learn through our life experiences during many lifetimes, then it made the mystery of death a rational process because I had intuited it was important that the mystical should not be predicated on faith alone but also on knowledge and reason.

After my grandfather's death I began to ponder questions of health, asking myself *What is perfect health?* Health and disease became the lower analogues of life and death in my mind, and they were important mysteries I would investigate as my life unfolded. As an adult I eventually trained as a nutritionist, naturopath, medical herbalist, and homeopath and used diet, herbal medicines, and homeopathic remedies, as well as several modalities that could be best described as shamanic techniques of healing. I also trained as a psychotherapist because I had begun to realize through my healing work that thoughts and emotions powerfully influence physical health and, as many indigenous shamans believe, have upset the balance and relationship with the natural world.

My mother recently reminded me that when I was a young child one of my favorite games was mixing up "medicines" from the ingredients of the kitchen pantry and asking her what illnesses they could cure. The Jungian psychotherapist James Hillman maintains that there are clues in the play of childhood to what will be our life path as an adult. It seems in retrospect there were strong signs that I was destined to become a healer who worked in altered states of consciousness.

Memories of school begin emerging. Having a quick and intuitive mind, I was easily bored by drill and repetition and escaped into the fantasy world of books. I became a voracious reader. My imagination soared, and I became adept at working in the world I later came to know by its magical name, the Elphame—the plane of dreams and imagination.

At some point during my early teen years I heard a radio documentary discussion during which one of the participants said that the physical world had been almost completely explored and there was virtually nothing left to discover. I was dismayed to hear this because I had read all the travel books I could find about journeys to exotic places, even to the point of poring over the atlas for hours at a time imagining what all the places with strange, evocative, foreign-sounding names might be like. When the interviewee said, however, that the inner world—the world of the psyche—was virtually unknown territory, I think I determined at that moment that this would be the world I would explore. I would search for the secret door I knew existed somewhere that would open onto the pathway of deeper knowledge.

Between the ages of seventeen and twenty-two I went through an intense period of exploration. My restless curiosity and drive to know started me on a quest to explore the world's classical literature, philosophy, psychology, and religion. At the age of eighteen I was fortunate enough to spend two years at college studying philosophy, and for those two years I had the privilege of being part of a small group of clever and curious minds. There were seven of us in the group, and we were mentored and encouraged by our Oxford-educated lecturer, a denizen of a famous Australian academic family, to explore where our minds wanted to go.

This was not an undisciplined experience, as we also studied Greek philosophy, which dealt with important and weighty matters relating to the purpose of life and existence. We learned Aristotelian and symbolic logic and learned to apply those principles by having as a textbook a volume called *Straight and Crooked Thinking* by Robert Thouless. In those two years I learned a lot about how to make an argument and how to defend it. It was exciting and fun to be allowed and enabled to go on adventures on the mental plane egged on by our tutor, who looked meek and mild and something like a defrocked nun but was, in fact, a great subverter of establishment conservatism and an encourager of youthful inquiry. I believed that this experience greatly aided me in bringing some form and structure to my otherwise creative and intuitive mental life. Some order was gradually growing out of the fermenting chaos.

All the while I continued my reading career and had steadily journeyed through most of the classics of English, French, German, Greek, and Roman writing. In one term holiday period, for example, I read all of Dickens. In other holiday periods I set myself the task of reading my way through all of the important Western philosophers, and I spent many torturous hours in the reading room of the Public Library of NSW and Fisher Library at the University of Sydney struggling through endless pages of turgid and lugubrious prose. I found it hard to believe that these were the writings of the greatest minds of Western thought. Compared to the luminous writings of the Greeks, the likes of Kant, Descartes, Spinoza, Hobbes, and others seemed to my youthful critical intelligence like very pale shadows.

Eastern philosophical and religious insights seemed to make more sense, and I spent some time reading, practicing, and teaching hatha and raja yoga. These experiences in Eastern mysticism sharpened my ability to gain some control of my mental processes, to quieten my mind and focus its power. This ability was to become an important skill when I began to study magic in an organized way. Around this time I made incursions into the major divisions of Christianity by attending as many different brands of church services as I could find. It was an attempt to assess whether or not I had been too precipitous as a rebellious child in dismissing Christianity as a pathway to enlightenment, but I must say I did not change my mind over much from my early years as a Sunday school resister.

I spent almost two years at the National Art School studying painting, sculpture, design, and composition. I was good enough to get a scholarship but realized that I would have to dedicate a lot of time and energy to earn a name as an artist. I wasn't prepared to do it. Being trained to "see" as an artist was a definite advantage to a magician or a psychic, though, because an artist sees things that are subtle and unnoticed by most people. An artist's view is often deeper and truer and can create shifts in perception and meaning. It is an invaluable skill to perceive like an artist and is more like my natural way. In some powerful but limited ways an artist is a more socially acceptable and respectable shaman.

I had thought the path to the truth might be discovered through art, and when I decided that this was not the case I thought the universities might be the place to look for it. I tried philosophy, psychology, linguistics, politics, and history, but I couldn't find it there either. It seemed to me that not only did the universities have no answers, they did not even know what questions to ask. It was as if I knew there was a pathway to truth, yet it remained hidden and I was on a mission to find it. I definitely fitted the archetype of the Seeker after truth, and I now know that the path to truth is everywhere, but the starting point of the journey is within oneself. The seminal questions *Who am I?* and *What am I doing here?* need answers.

As well as investigating some of what the outer spiritual practices of the East and West had to offer, I also explored the natural world. With a few like-minded friends I would regularly truant from school to go to the beach or for long bike rides and explorations around the seascapes, inlets, and coves around coastal southern Sydney, where there was endless sky, sea, sand dunes, shaded gullies, caves, and large flat rocks engraved and colored with mysterious Aboriginal carvings. Dreaming outdoors in light and water seemed a far more spiritually nourishing and joyful experience than being trapped in the gray world of algebra and trigonometry.

We would also regularly go on long bush walks and climbs in the national parks and coastal wilderness areas. I noticed that even though these walks were sometimes long endurance events I felt rejuvenated from the time I spent in the bush. As an adult I see even more clearly the benefit and necessity of spending time in the natural world. I find that as I enter the forest my energy is suddenly raised and my mind relaxes. I stop thinking and am just present and grounded in my body. Nature has been my friend since early childhood, and I see shamanic patterns in that time that were a template of what was to follow.

Hank Wesselman says that the Kahunas, the Hawaiian shamans, teach that the *ku*, the unconscious mind, loves to be in nature. The unconscious is the link with the natural world. It understands connectivity. I think that what happens for me is that the noisy intellectualizing part of the mind shuts down and I am more my real self as the unconscious comes into prominence. This ability to switch from conscious to unconscious awareness is an important skill of the shaman-healer, and it is something that the subjects of the Grail Family inquiry describe as "clicking over" and say helps them access the Elphame.

Medicine Grizzlybear (Robert G.) Lake, a Native American shaman, says that all shaman-healers must regularly replenish their energy by retiring into the wilderness. He describes the fluctuations in the shaman's energy and the healer's necessary connection to the powers of the earth:

> Sometimes the healing connection is very strong…it is influenced by a number of variables including peak days and our low periods. This is another reason why a Native healer must constantly…get recharged in the wilderness and mountains to strengthen the healing connection. (1993, 114)

I think that this escape into the natural world was something I learned to appreciate because of the time I spent as a child with my grandfather in his garden and from the times my grandparents would take the family to stay at their holiday house on the New South Wales central coast near Pearl Beach. It was a wild environment.

The house was set in deep bushland where wildflowers and many different types of ferns proliferated. Banksia men, the venerable guardian spirits of the Australian bush, watched from their perches in the Banksia trees—their grizzled gray faces with bushy stubble and eyes as old as time seemed rather scary and coldly judgmental to imaginative, naughty, and disobedient children. The air had that particularly pungent perfume of the Australian bush with its identifying signature of the Boronia shrub.

Huge native conifers lined both sides of the rutted dirt road, secretive, darkly powerful, and mysterious. Each morning there would be a new festooning of spider's webs from one side of the road to the other, anchored in the high branches of the pine trees. The webs sparkled with morning dew and hung like ropes of diamonds, heavy with the weight of it. I used to wonder about the size of the spiders that could spin such webs overnight, but I never actually saw one.

We children would wander off for hours at a time unsupervised by adults, exploring everywhere and picking bunches of wildflowers: perfumed Boronia, egg and bacon plant, flannel flowers, Christmas bush, Christmas bells, gray spider flowers, Waratahs, and sweet, shy little cerulean blue bush orchids. The old house always had that same pungent fragrance exuded by bunches of wildflowers in battered jugs and pots coloring unexpected nooks and crannies. I have never been afraid of the bush. It has always felt benevolent to me. The trees and native plants seemed to have an individual conscious presence and intention although as a young person I could not really guess at what it was. But I thought nature was definitely alive and aware.

We children splashed about in the sea shrieking like wild things and playing with the local dolphins, which were very tame and let us pat them. I think they enjoyed the games we played with them. My sister and I had names for them and practiced calling them telepathically and were surprised that they often came to the shore breakers when called in the "silent language."

Around this time also my sister and brother and I also developed a kind of sun worshipping religious practice whereby we would put down our beach towels, sit on our heels, and bow low, with our foreheads touching the earth, and say, "Hail to our great father, the sun!" We also lived very close to the ocean and spent a lot of time swimming and surfing, frequently unsupervised by any adults. I had no fear of the natural world and would swim out far beyond the breakers in deep water and float there, never thinking of sharks or the dangers of other sea creatures or of the possibility of drowning. In fact, I think I could say that I was fearless. I was at home in the ocean.

Close to our home we had discovered a secret place, a hidey-hole cubby house concealed in a huge clump of blackberry bushes. It was a small haven where adults never ventured and where we could play and dream. A small stream ran through it singing and we would spend hours making fairy barquentines and dressing tiny dolls in flower costumes and floating them down the flows and eddies of the mellifluous creek. These activities provided a kind of access to another world, a window into the world of the imagination where the designing and creating of fairy balls and feasts and other exciting events and adventures seemed like the most natural thing. We never worried about snakes and they never worried us. Fear of the natural world seems to be something contagious that is passed on to children from adults. That fear of things that creep and crawl does not usually seem to arise spontaneously in the minds of children. Our minds were open, curious, and full of delight in the beauty of the small worlds we created, and any passing snakes would probably have been absorbed as merely part of the dramatis personae of our play.

In many ways I had a wild and enchanted childhood—at least this is what my memories tell me—and the drive to discover the inner meaning of outer events was always strong and present. But the pathway to wisdom was elusive, and as a young seeker of the truth I experienced many moments of anguished frustration. The path was not evident to me in any of the Western social institutions of knowledge or religion I had encountered. I became despairing of ever finding it, imagining with apprehension the dullness of a life lived on the surface of consensus reality.

But the path opened up to me in an unexpected way that seemed completely unrelated to all my frenzied curiosity. All the searching had not revealed it, and maybe it never does, but I was persistent. I believe that persistence is a necessary quality in a seeker after truth. Persistence, commitment, and strength gained from facing the vicissitudes of life and struggling with the painful experiences it brings establishes the inner strength one needs to tread the shaman's path. Learning from ordeals brings one to the point of sufficient strength and development for the path to find the seeker. That is the paradox of the path and the real secret of initiation. Ultimately the path finds you!

The Opening of the Way and the Phenomenon of Ontological Shock

When the path found me, I discovered that I had a surprising array of psycho-spiritual abilities that emerged fully formed. It shocked me, frightened me, and caused to me doubt my sanity. I suffered ontological shock because these experiences rocked, for me, a world picture constructed on the foundation of the dominant scientific-materialist worldview. The other world had come crashing through, and although I had always had a strong interest in the spiritual and had read and speculated about the possibility of the existence of other dimensions, it was more from an intellectual position, safely remote from the actual experience. The experience itself brings with it an emotional reaction that is a mixture of fear, confusion, self-doubt, elation, and a sense of liberation. Thinking about and longing for the encounter with the hidden truth is not the same as the actual encounter. No preparation or open-minded anticipation can provide a facsimile of the real thing because even a seeker after truth is conditioned by the ontology of the familiar world even if its validity is questioned or rejected.

Traditional people from shaman cultures, for example the Australian Aborigines, call lucid dreaming experiences "strong dreams" or "big dreams" and describe visionary experiences as "using the strong eye." They place a high value upon the various kinds of psychic experiences and regard them as normal; they are considered to be conscious and intelligible contacts with the world of spirit. By contrast, I have struggled to integrate the experiences and absorb their inherent wisdom. My skeptical, rational observer self clashes with a part of my psyche that has a greater spiritual understanding and an unshakable confidence in the reality of the experiences. This recurring and conflicted experience is a battle between the intellect and the intuition. The intellect is doggedly fixed in material reality, inflexible and skeptical, while the intuition is more mentally adventurous, open, and accepting of different possibilities. Experiences of strong dreams, visions, and other psychic experiences powerfully challenge the rational worldview, shaking out vestiges of intellectual complacency and inducing a condition of psychic imbalance that I call ontological shock in reference to Professor John Mack.

Mack, a traditionally educated Harvard psychiatrist, treated many patients who had experienced unusual and frightening events that did not fit within the accepted boundaries of consensual reality. The difficult psychological and emotional adjustment he was forced to make when he concluded these people were telling the truth, that they were experiencing these events as real and that they could not be brushed aside as delusions, he described as "ontological shock." He was forced to expand his view of reality to encompass the possibility that this new world was a very different place to the old one he had accepted without question.

Yet however uncomfortable the mental and emotional adjustments Mack was forced to make, he was experiencing the strange events vicariously. It is much more devastating to the person who is inside the experience when familiar, solid ground seems to shift beneath the feet and the known world becomes far more fluid and plastic and far less certain. As the Elphame crashes through into ordinary consciousness, there are sensations of racing waves of fear and rapidly juxtaposed feelings of confusion, disbelief, and unreality as the mind swings between the physical world and the other world, attempting to reestablish equilibrium. Often there come feelings of incipient insanity and fears of being out of control. Physically there come sensations of coldness and numbness and a perception that time has stopped: a kind of breathless suspended animation and paralysis on all levels. The self has identified with a particular worldview and the intrusion of something very different into that panoramic inscape seems like an attack on the core of one's being. This shocking self-shattering is something like the experience of schizophrenia—but the center holds.

Then comes a sense of isolation and a fear that others will not understand and that one will be regarded as either insane or fraudulent. These feelings of cultural estrangement are something expressed by Hank Wesselman, an anthropologist and evolutionary biologist who became an initiate of Hawaiian Kahuna shamanism. In the book *Spiritwalker* he describes dramatic experiences of altered states of consciousness and of unexpected incursions from the Elphame (1996, 280). He discusses the polarity of feeling that accompanies such extreme events—of the exhilaration and excitement of going into an entirely new direction on the one hand and fear of alienation and rejection by his peers on the other. He expected that if he were to follow in this new direction that it would virtually destroy his academic career. It seems to me that it is a great shame that the sincere pursuit of truth in our culture can take on such an unwelcome political dimension.

Starhawk, who is an initiated high priestess, says that the sense of alienation is usual in those who have had experiences that exist outside the boundaries of the cultural narrative: "In modern Western culture, artists, poets, and visionaries, let alone witches, mystics, and shamans, are often somewhat alienated from their culture" (1999, 32). In traditional shaman cultures, in contrast, to be initiated as a shaman by being "chosen by spirit" is generally considered to be an honor.

How People Deal with Ontological Shock

The ontological shock I experienced raised fundamental questions of identity for me. I did not know who I really was anymore. I was quite slow to reconstruct the fragmented pieces of the picture into a coherent whole and slow to see its real meaning. Although I did have a kind of intellectual understanding of what it all meant, it was only through the completion of my research and the crafting of my doctoral dissertation that I was finally able to draw all the disparate pieces of the chronicle together and understand what it all meant in an emotional and embodied way.

The challenge to integration and adjustment first presented itself when I decided that although I was sane, my experience of the world did not agree with the accepted descriptions of reality. There are strong social and medical pressures in Western-style thinking that regard those who have psychic experiences to be either fraudulent or psychotic. When powerful ontological challenges occur there seem to be three options: to absolutely deny the experience, to have some doubts about one's sanity but at the same time determine to explore and possibly integrate the phenomenon, or to agree with psychiatric opinion that you are most likely psychotic. I chose the second way. I took a heuristic approach: I would experiment and explore it. I was going on this journey, but I was asking questions.

However, after interviewing some of the participants in my research, I discovered there is also a fourth way. When some people have an inexplicable or inassimilable experience, they simply compartmentalize it until they find a way to emotionally and psychologically integrate it. The process may take many years or it may not happen at all, in which case the experience remains quarantined in its isolation ward, from which it cannot break free to contaminate the rest of the psyche. The consciousness consequently remains free from the potential infection of ontological challenges from the unknown and indescribable. It is a type of deliberate forgetting, but it is something different than complete denial because it remains open to the possibility of change. I could relate to this approach and realized this was what I had done originally and that it was only later that I had decided to suspend disbelief, to take a pragmatic approach and to see what happened.

My later formal study and practice in magic and Witchcraft gave me an intellectual and theoretical framework of understanding that illuminated much of what had been formerly mysterious. My early experiences of the Elphame also seemed to set a pattern for further and lifelong encounters. Some of these events, particularly relating to matters of intuitive healing, visions, and lucid dreaming, are still occurring today, and although I am finding it easier with the passing of time and with increasing familiarity to accept their legitimacy, it is still not a completely seamless process. The ontological shock persisted until I found ways of integrating the incursions from the Elphame and recovering my psychic equilibrium, but my primary reactions were usually disbelief and self-doubt.

When the path found me it signaled the beginning of a pattern of revelatory experiences that sometimes came unbidden. At other times I experimented in a more controlled way to find what I could do and what my limitations were. My experimentation over the next several years revealed an array of psychic talents. I could see and communicate with spirits. I could heal with the energy of the hands. I could leave the physical body and return to it. I could communicate with animals and the natural world. I could influence the patterns of weather, and the other world frequently communicated with me through the medium of dreams;

visions; telepathic encounters with birds, animals, and plants; and other mystical experiences.

Because I had not worked to develop any of these skills and they simply emerged abruptly and fully formed, I had difficulty trusting my inner perceptions and myself. The self-doubt engendered then began another cycle of ontological shock. I had held the opinion that one had to work long and hard at spiritual development, so it almost seemed as if I were cheating. I thought that perhaps I was egotistical, deluded, or possibly insane. Living this way remains a psychic and emotional balancing act. The shaman-healer inhabits the umbrous zone where the two realities conjoin and walks the strange pathway between the worlds.

I did not, at that time, associate what I was doing with traditional shamanism, as the insight that connected those skills with the work of the shaman did not become more fully formed until I began the research and reading for my doctoral project. It was then, when I interviewed the subjects of the Grail Family inquiry, that I finally realized how all these individual strands were woven together to create a pattern that was based on the traditional designs of shamanism yet had a particularly modern look to it. This insight was true for me and my story, and for my investigations of the Grail Family and their stories as well.

Some Personal Experiences

I now present a range of personal anecdotes illustrating some of the magical and mystical experiences that have given me cause for reflection. This is not a complete or definitive list; it is merely a range of revelatory experiences that have relevance to the discussion and provide a foundation for understanding how a shaman is made in the contemporary era.

A Mystical Experience

When I was in my early twenties I had my first dramatic mystical experience. I had been thinking about the question of Divinity and was trying to force my mind to be the instrument that would penetrate the veil or fog that seemed to act as a barrier to knowing. As a child I was frustrated by the ineffectual nature of the intellectual mind to pierce through to clarity. As a young adult, and largely through the practice of raja yoga, I had learned to focus the mind more powerfully. I used it as a beam to burst or bore through what I perceived as a dark matrix and out to the other side, which I perceived as light and freedom. These ideas were more like intuitions than anything I could identify by using the senses or the rational mind. I was turning the question of God over and over in my mind, using its focused power to burn through whatever the resistance was, and I had not yet fully explored the idea of a feminine Divinity.

Suddenly I felt something give way and I heard a voice say, loudly and clearly, "God is Light!" The room exploded into bright golden-white light and I entered an altered state of consciousness. I seemed somehow to float over to the couch. As I lay there the golden light poured down from an unseen source all over my body. It felt very calm and like a kind of spiritual sustenance. I forgot to be afraid and basked in the light as long as it lasted, which was probably fifteen or twenty minutes, although it could have been longer as time seemed frozen.

My mind existed in a state I can only describe as a kind of dynamic tension. It had a "pinned down" feeling. All mental and emotional movement had ceased. Everything was very still and at the same time very dynamic and full of life. It is a struggle to describe this state in words, but those who have had a mystical experience would recognize it: "All mystics speak the same language and come from the same country" (Achterberg 1985, 26). Several people I have questioned about their mystical experiences have described them in a very similar way, as an encounter with living and intelligent light or energy. This is the typical experience of ecstasy described in the literature on shamanism (Eliade 1989), and many people who have had near-death experiences describe something similar.

It was not a particularly frightening experience, and I recognized in it the timeless and spaceless feelings I had had in childhood as I accessed what were clearly altered states of consciousness. What was different was the clarity of the spoken communication in a voice that was not my own. Hearing voices is generally regarded as evidence of psychosis and doubts about my sanity arose in my mind, although another part of my psyche was serene and accepting of what had happened. This pattern of simultaneous and alternating acceptance and skepticism was subsequently to become for me the familiar and repeated experience of ontological shock.

Healing by the Laying-On of Hands

In the early 1980s I discovered that I had a talent for healing by the hands. My daughter, Julia, who was three at the time, had been diagnosed with a urinary reflux problem, and the urologist I consulted told me that her ureters were not long enough and that some of her urine was being recycled to the kidneys, which could easily become infected. The presenting problem was that she was unable to empty her bladder in one attempt; an amount of urine would pass through the urethra some time after she had originally urinated, and she would become incontinent. He wanted to do a medical procedure consisting of passing a tube through her urethra and dyeing the kidneys to see what damage had been done. As she did not seem to be in any pain, I felt resistance to allowing such an invasive procedure to be performed on such a young child. I procrastinated for a couple of days, trying to work out what to do. On the third day the urologist rang me. He was angry and abusive, shouting that he wouldn't be responsible if I delayed any longer, that my daughter's life was at risk and that she would get kidney disease and die a painful death.

I am not quite sure how what follows happened, but I had an intuition that I should try to heal her myself. I set her down on the lounge room floor and placed my hands on her lower abdomen, concentrating on sending healing energy through my hands and into her body. I spent about half an hour on the front of her body and then turned her over and treated the kidneys from the back, placing one hand over each kidney. After about half an hour in that position I felt I had done enough. After this treatment the symptoms ceased, and a few days later when I took her back to see the specialist he was shocked when he could find nothing wrong with her. When I told him that I had done some healing on her myself, he was skeptical, even cynical, but he could not actually explain how, in the space of a few days, the ureters had grown to normal size and there was no further cause for concern.

Although all the symptoms had disappeared, I was not sure whether this seeming miracle had actually happened or not, and I went through some inner conflict about it. It did not have the intensity of ontological shock, but the skeptical part of myself was active and suspicious of the part that had so confidently undertaken the healing with a strangely powerful degree of knowledge and competence. The urinary problem did not recur.

Some little time later our family cat, a sensitive and beautiful blue Burmese female about two years old, began bleeding from the mouth. We took her to the local veterinary hospital for diagnosis and treatment. The veterinary surgeon tested her and concluded that she might have had a bleeding stomach ulcer. She was prescribed treatment and kept in hospital for several days, and when we brought her home we believed that she was on the way to recovery and that the correct diagnosis had been made. A few days later, however, she began to hemorrhage again. The veterinary surgeon referred us to the University of Sydney Clinic, where she was kept for several days, and we had faith that the experts at the university would find the answer to the mysterious bleeding. Several days later, when she was discharged, the clinicians told us they could find nothing wrong with her and were at a loss to explain what was happening.

After reading through my diary notes of the time, I found that the professor in charge of clinical veterinary practice thought she might have had a bleeding tooth, although this did not seem a very feasible diagnosis to me. She was losing too much blood, I thought, but hoping for the best, we took her home. The next morning we found she had been bleeding heavily during the night. She looked very quiet and ill and I thought that if we did not do something quickly, she would probably not live beyond that day. I decided to try the same healing procedure that had cured my daughter. I laid my hands upon the cat's body. I didn't think about what I was doing but entered a slightly altered state of consciousness where I concentrated on inner guidance to tell me where to place my hands. It was a quiet and concentrated state. Occasionally I would feel a light tingling and a slightly cool energy in my hands. I was desperate to save her and therefore did not get into intellectualizing about how it was impossible. I followed my intuition, which guided my methodology. The intellectualizing self-doubt came later. I gave about a half-hour treatment. An hour later the cat was up and walking around. She was eating a little by early afternoon, and by the evening she was playing, alert, and back to her former healthy self. The bleeding completely stopped and never recurred.

Once I discovered this ability to heal through the laying-on of hands, I had many experiences of curing both chronic and acute conditions. In sorting through some of my old documents, I discovered a research paper I had written in 1987 during my studies in naturopathic and homeopathic medicine. The subject was to have been a discussion of a particular method of alternative healing. I had written about some of my experiences of healing with the hands. The document contained several testimonials written by patients who had experienced healing for both chronic and acute conditions, and descriptions of what the experience had been like for them. What follows is a verbatim account of one of those accounts. Paula, a chef and restaurateur, was experiencing high levels of constant and incapacitating pain. Orthodox medical drug treatment and alternative medicine treatments of massage, chiropractic, and acupuncture provided no relief. I gave her one treatment.

She describes her experience:

> I suffered a bush walking accident eighteen months ago, which resulted in a prolapsed disc around T11-T12. I used hot and cold treatment and suffered acute pain and discomfort for ten days. When I breathed my back would spasm. I was incapacitated and had to be helped up out of a chair and bed. After ten days the swelling and tenderness reduced and a back manipulation seemed successful. I continued osteopathic treatment but my relief was short term. I had twinges of intense back pain constantly.
>
> My work required me to stand on my feet all day, which exacerbated the pain. Yoga gave me some little relief. I have not felt that any of these therapies has been a perfect or a long-term solution. I went to see Jane…to see what she could do. I was slightly skeptical about her healing but had an open mind. I lay on the floor and Jane proceeded to lay her hands on my back over the injured area. The sensation I felt was not exceptionally hot and not exceptionally cold. Warmth was felt externally from Jane's hands, but penetration felt dry and cool. We stayed like that for about forty minutes, chatting normally.
>
> After the treatment I noticed a slight initial improvement. It took me completely by surprise that a day later I noticed my pain had

entirely disappeared. I have also noticed a general improvement in my whole back condition, in that the whole area feels much stronger.

In this document I had also made some observations about my experience of healing with the hands. First, I said that I never felt tired after giving healing treatments; in fact, I felt energized. The next point I made is that I do not actually feel a lot of sensation in my hands during a treatment, although sometimes there is a slight tingling or heat and often a kind of coolness and sometimes a buzzing sensation. Over time, I had opportunities to work in this way with many other patients, both human and animal, and experienced a considerable degree of success with both chronic and acute conditions. I began to think that I might have a talent for healing with the hands.

In surveying the literature at the time, trying to get a rational understanding of how this kind of healing worked, I came across something called "magnetic healing," whereby the electromagnetic energy of one's own body is said to be used to augment the energy of the patient to affect a healing. In yoga this energy is called prana and in Taoist teaching, chi; in homeopathic medicine it is called the vital energy or life force. The danger of using one's own vital energy to heal is that it may become depleted and lead to exhaustion or disease for the healer. I never experienced this. It was obvious that I was working on a different level or with different energy.

Kenneth Meadows, an Englishman who was trained by Michael Harner at the Foundation for Shamanic Studies and also, I am informed, trained with Silver Bear and Wolf Eagle from the Medicine Society, Harley Swift Deer from Deer Tribe Metis Society, and Wallace Black Elk of the Lakota Tribe, confirms this idea:

> A shamanist does not use his own personal power to effect harmonization. Energy from his own energy-system would be speedily depleted, and in certain cases he might fall prey to the very condition he is endeavoring to alleviate. Instead he goes to a source of inexhaustible energy on a spiritual level to provide the necessary power, and is not afraid to touch it and be touched by it. (1998, 166)

The Reiki method of healing, which originated in Japan, is something like this hands-on method. Reiki practitioners say that they access the universal cosmic energy and that they do not use their own personal magnetic energy to heal. Reiki has become almost respectable in Western society and some medical workers, including doctors, nurses, and veterinarians, use it. Rosemary Hood, one of the animal communicators I interviewed, trains veterinary students in alternative medicine methods that include Reiki, and most of the other subjects of the Grail Family practice Reiki.

Talking to Spirits: Psychotherapy for the Dead

At the same time as my healing skill was unfolding, I found that with a little concentration I could also see and talk to spirits. Sometimes no concentration was needed—they just spontaneously appeared on the screen of vision.

After the burial of my father-in-law, he appeared to me in spirit form and seemed very agitated, saying he wanted to tell me something important. He said he knew I could see and hear him. He told me that he had hidden a diamond ring in a secret drawer in his old desk and that he wanted his son to have it. He wanted us to make sure it did not get sold with the desk when we disposed of his effects. We found the ring and subsequently had it valued. It turned out to be zircon and only worth about $50 at the time, so we were surprised that he thought it was a diamond and had concealed it for many years from his wife. She had died of cancer a month before his own death.

We discovered the answer to this mystery on finding some old letters among his personal papers. Apparently he had been involved with another woman some years before he married my partner's stepmother. He had brought the "diamond" engagement ring to a pub with the intention of asking her to marry him, but she died prematurely in a car accident. He kept the ring for sentimental reasons, being unable either to part with it or to give it to his wife. It was a secret he had taken to the grave, but he remembered it postmortem and wanted his son to have the jewel that had been important to him. When he first appeared to me I was unsure and wondered if I had an overactive imagination and had unconsciously concocted the story, but when the letters were found and they corroborated what he had told me, I realized that it was possible to have visual and auditory communication with the dead. There seemed to be a set of subtle senses that duplicated the physical senses. Somehow it did not seem a frightening idea because it was clear to me that his personality remained the same and his mind and emotions seemed familiar. It was only his physical body that was not present. I think that it was then I realized that the physical body is not the real person, although most people strongly identify with it.

Another interesting case involving communicating with spirits unfolded as follows. Martina, a close friend and colleague who also worked as a naturopath, rang me in the early hours of the morning. She was in a lot of pain, immobilized, and convinced she was having a cardiac infarction. I suggested phoning an ambulance, but she was very adamant that she wanted me to attend and not an ambulance. I was worried that I might not be able to discern what was happening and that she would die while I was dithering about. In other words, I wasn't confident about the outcome, but as she was a close friend I decided to go to her aid as quickly as I could. I jumped into the car and quickly drove to her house. She had sounded so horribly distressed.

I let myself into her flat and headed for the bedroom. She was sitting up in bed looking pale and drawn when I arrived. As soon as I entered the room I noticed a figure crouching in the corner farthest from the bed. It was a slight female figure rocking backward and forward. She had short, soft dark hair and appeared to be in her mid to late thirties. She was wearing a short blue sleeveless nightgown and was moaning, "I'm sorry...I'm really sorry...please forgive me. I didn't mean to hurt her."

I was a bit startled when I saw this vision, especially when my friend told me that she couldn't see or hear it at all. When I described the figure to my friend she became extremely distraught and told me that it sounded very much like a description of her mother. She asked me to get a photograph album out of the wardrobe and after turning over a few pages came upon a photograph that she asked me to look at. It was a photograph of her mother taken not long before she died. When I saw the photograph I recognized it as a picture of the person I could see crouching in the corner, in pain and afraid.

When my friend Martina was sixteen, her mother had committed suicide. This was fifteen years previously. She had experienced major clinical depression and had been treated with "deep sleep therapy" at the infamous Chelmsford Hospital in Sydney. The "therapy" involved sedating the patient, usually with narcotics, for several weeks at a time, ostensibly to give the brain time to "rewire itself." Multiple electric shock treatments were also used while the patients were asleep. Many former patients of the hospital had also suicided after this type of treatment. Martina's mother had been a very talented musician who was prone to bouts of deep depression during which she couldn't play or even function normally.

When I questioned the mother telepathically she told me that she "woke up" and found herself very disoriented; not knowing what she should do, she decided to find her eldest daughter. She considered Martina to be "very sensible" and thought that she would know how to help her, but became despairing when she couldn't attract Martina's attention. Martina could not see her or hear her, so she tried to get her attention by "squeezing her heart."

I asked what she wanted to do because she couldn't stay where she was, and I told her she couldn't hurt her daughter anymore. Her name was Cecily. She said that she would like to see her husband and that he would know what to do. They had been very close in life and he had died of a cardiac infarction just six months after she had committed suicide. He had been a well-known Australian composer, so I had an idea that I thought might work.

Martina was feeling quite a lot better, so I asked her if she had manuscripts of any of her father's music. She did. Martina herself was a talented pianist. We set up a little alter with a candle and some sandalwood incense burning. I smudged all of us with the incense, including the discarnate mother. Martina thanked her mother for being a wonderful friend and mother in life and said that she bore her no resentment for her suicide and that she understood how it had happened as a result of the inappropriate therapy she had experienced. Then Martina played some of her father's atmospheric music and after she had finished a long piece we both appealed to him by name and telepathically to come for his distressed wife. We were in a slightly altered state of consciousness, probably an alpha brain wave pattern. After a period, probably about half an hour, the atmosphere in the room cleared and became very peaceful, and when I opened my eyes I saw that Cecily had gone.

Martina felt that she had made peace with her mother, and the intense symptoms she suffered that night dispersed and never returned. I have no doubts that if left unchecked these kinds of spirit attachments could lead to chronic ill health or even death.

I have been able to communicate with many earthbound spirits, both human and animal, and to help them sort through emotional entanglements they experience as unfinished business with friends, family, and others in the physical world. The end of life is not the eternal sleep and peace many people want believe it to be because the "dead" are frequently troubled and at times seem to need psychotherapy as much as the living.

Animal Telepathy: Communicating in the Silent Language

Through a gradual process of experimentation and observation I discovered that it was possible to have clear and intelligent two-way telepathic conversations with both domestic and wild animals. What follows are some examples of my growing awareness.

I first discovered that animals could understand language spoken telepathically while still living in the city. I did some original experimentation with Bluebell, the cat who had contracted the mysterious hemorrhagic disease. One evening I was sitting quietly in the lounge room as Bluebell was whirling and dancing around the room in pursuit of a moth. As cats are usually implacable hunters, she was concentrating hard on what she was doing. I decided to see if I could get her attention by calling her name telepathically. She stopped immediately and looked straight at me. Then I also said telepathically *come and jump up onto my lap and I'll give you a big pat.* As soon as I had mentally framed the words, she scrambled across the room and jumped up onto my lap.

I was surprised that it had worked so quickly and thought that it might have simply been coincidence. So after I patted her, she jumped down off my lap to go in further pursuit of the moth. Again I called her name in my mind and once again exactly the same sequence of events occurred. She stopped dead and looked straight at me, then as I had invited her again to jump on my lap for a pat and a cuddle she repeated the behavior. I thought then that it was probably not a coincidence and that at some level animals could telepathically understand quite sophisticated communication.

I then tried training my cats by talking to them about not hunting birds. When they were kittens I took them into the garden one by one to look at the birds and to explain to them that the birds were our friends and we did not hurt them because they helped our garden. I told them that if they tried to hurt the birds, then I would be very angry and would give them a big smack. I reinforced this conditioning by doing it several times with each kitten, and if ever I saw them in the garden I would always call their name and repeat: "We don't hurt the birds. They are our friends and they help our garden." I talked to them at about the level of language one would use to a three- or four-year-old child. I've changed my opinion about this now because observations I have made more recently indicate that animals can understand concepts and language in a much more complex and sophisticated way.

At the time my family was living on an acre of land on the outskirts of a coastal town, where we were fortunate to have many native birds both living and visiting. During the four years we lived there, none of the three cats, to my knowledge, ever attempted to catch a bird.

An old lemon tree in the garden in which three families of blue wrens had built their nests was also a favorite place for the cats to laze beneath the branches. They could easily have caught any of the wrens or their fledglings, but I never saw any of the cats take the slightest interest in the comings and goings of the birds. I believe that cats can be trained in this way, especially when they are young. In older cats I suspect the hunting instinct may have become too strong to be modified in this manner, but perhaps not. Conventional wisdom describes cats as being untrainable because their instinctive hunting behavior is too entrenched, but I have trained many cats in this way. An entrenched and disrespectful human assumption about the true nature of animals prevents us from seeing them differently. They are not simply slaves to instinct but intelligent entities capable of transformative growth.

Apollo, a male Abyssinian cat I had at the time, brought a snake home as a gift. Amid all the screaming, scampering, and scrambling onto the table (by my daughter and myself), he dropped the snake down behind one of the lounge chairs where my partner retrieved it and took it to safety. Amid cries of "bad cat!" I thought I heard a soft voice say sulkily, *You said we couldn't catch the birds. I thought snakes were okay,* but I ignored it, telling myself I must have imagined it. At that stage I was not aware that animals had voices, not simply vocalizations, and could converse telepathically.

Some weeks later Apollo disappeared and we feared for his safety. One night about three days after his disappearance I walked into my study and saw him sitting in his usual spot on top of my filing cabinet. I was crying because I felt his loss very keenly, and when I looked at him he said, *Don't cry, Jane. I'm okay, and guess what? There are no fleas here!* He then disappeared from sight and I realized that what I had seen was his energy body, or ghost. What made me sure this was real and not an imaginary experience was that I had been trying to find a method of keeping fleas off the cats because I did not like putting toxic insecticidal preparations on them and had been removing any fleas each day with a pair of tweezers. The daily de-fleaing program had been a major event in their consciousness. This was the first time I was certain that I had heard an animal's voice. The next day we discovered his body in the long grass by the roadside about 100 meters from the house. A car had hit him.

As people became aware that I communicated with animals, I began to treat horses, dogs, and cats, and often when other measures had failed I could find the reason for the illness or puzzling behavior and prescribe an appropriate treatment. For example, a patient had a small male dog with an intractable rash that did not respond to any treatment. She asked me if I would have a consultation with him to see if I could find the cause. I thought it was possible that the cause could be emotional, as none of the physical treatments she had tried had been effective.

When I asked him how he was feeling, he replied, *I am unhappy and sad and I miss my friend*. I asked his owner if they had another dog or another animal that had been close to Bundgey and was not present now. She told me that he had been very close to a female Rottweiler who had been killed several months before when a car had hit her. She had been following Bundgey, running across the road, when the accident happened. Bundgey had been very depressed and had refused to eat for several days. When I asked her if the rash had appeared around that time, she confirmed that it had appeared immediately after the accident. He was grieving.

When she rang me a few weeks later she sounded excited, saying, "You'll never guess what happened!" She said that she had visited the pound thinking she might get another companion for Bundgey if she could find a nice dog. What she found was another female Rottweiler, and she decided to take her home. This dog had a friendly and placid temperament and became firm friends with Bundgey. The day after bringing the Rottweiler home, Bundgey's intractable rash completely disappeared.

Communication with the Wild World

Some few years ago I was travelling with a friend down the west coast of Tasmania. It is a place of extreme beauty and is sparsely populated. We had been camping, but on the fourth afternoon it began to rain heavily so we looked for some accommodation and came upon a wilderness resort. We stayed there for a couple of days till the rain eased. The accommodation section was originally part of the workers' quarters for a hydroelectric project, and it was built on the shores of a man-made lake. Although it was summer, the weather was chilly as well as wet. We arrived in the afternoon and were lucky enough to obtain the last remaining room. It was euphemistically entitled a "garden suite" and was basically a smallish room with two single beds and furniture that was meant to look hand-hewn, picturesque, and rustic. What earned the epithet garden suite, however, was that the large, curtained, interior glass doors could be opened out onto some patchy grass inhabited by a couple of desultory tree ferns.

We had closed the curtains that night to help keep the room warm. At about six o'clock the next morning I was sorting out the clothes to wear that day. My friend was still purring away gently, fast asleep. Suddenly there came a dramatic and distinct rapping sound on the glass doors. I ignored it, not yet conscious enough to work out that it was meant to get my attention. A couple of seconds later the same sequence of taps was repeated. I ignored it again. The third time I realized that the tapping meant something so I opened the curtains to see what was happening. There was a small, dark greenish-black colored bird with a lighter chestnut color on the throat and chest. As I had flung back the curtains it was about to launch itself at the glass again, determined to get some attention, but it saw me and aborted its plan. Instead it landed at the base of the window and looked at me intently. What passed through my mind was that it was a tame bird and had come to demand some food. When I had lived in the country, on the Far North Coast of NSW, we had a family of kookaburras who would tap on the glass of the back door of the house late every afternoon asking for something to eat.

The little bird then began a song while continuing to look at me with a fixed gaze. It was a warbling, trilling, rolling, multi-tonal song that lasted for about five or six seconds. It was obvious to me that it had meaning but I was too surprised by the greeting itself to slow down enough to attempt to decipher it. I must have looked pretty dumb because the bird looked at me again to see if I understood, and when it concluded that I hadn't worked it out, it gave an exasperated look heavenward, sighed resignedly, and then deliberately repeated the same sequence of birdsong communication. This time I got it and understood the message. It said, *My mistress bids you welcome, Lady!* The small messenger made ready to fly off. "Not so fast," I said. "Who is your mistress?" Another series of chirps and trills but different: *My Lady of Wild Creatures* came the reply loud and clear, and he disappeared over the trees and from sight.

I had done a sketch of the bird and when I returned home to the mainland I looked it up in *The Reader's Digest Complete Book of Australian Birds*. It did and didn't really surprise me that it was called a welcome swallow. Also, the reason that the little bird called me "Lady" is that this is a title used by a Wiccan high priestess. In some Wiccan groups she is known as "the Lady."

It was a shock to me, but at the same time I felt honored. I had felt very safe in the Tasmanian wilderness. There was a benign presence there that permeates the island and I felt it most particularly on the West Coast, which struck me as odd considering the violent past of such places as Macquarie Harbor and Port Arthur. In the past these places had been brutal penal colonies. As I turned these thoughts over in my mind an image presented itself to my inner vision. It was of a huge figure—a young Aboriginal woman with a beautiful and gentle face, with softly waving hair and a steady gaze. She was dressed in a possum fur cloak, which she held gathered around her, and she was holding a wooden staff. She exuded a quality of serenity. On her shoulder perched a bird, a raven with glossy green-black feathers. The raven, like the owl, is a bird commonly associated with the shaman.

Communicating with the Plant People

Many indigenous shamans claim to be able to communicate with animals, and some claim communication with the plant people and the rock people (Lake 1993), but although I had extensive experience of communication with animals and birds, I was skeptical about the possibility of intelligible two-way communication with plants and rocks. Theoretically I thought it was possible, but to have actual experience of it can be unsettling and induce a response of mild ontological shock.

Several years ago I had to attend a residential school at a regional university in New South Wales, so before I left home for a week's absence I asked my partner to water the indoor plants. When I returned home and was passing by my office door I heard a high-pitched little voice cry out *Help! Help! Help me!* There was no one else at home at the time, so I felt a little perplexed. I looked around to see if I could find where the voice was coming from because I was sure it wasn't coming from inside my own head. It definitely seemed to be separate from me.

I had a beautiful bromeliad in a pot beside the entrance door to my office, and the little voice seemed to be coming from there. I stopped and said to the plant, "What's wrong? Did something happen?" The little piping voice answered, *He forgot to water me! Can I have some water please?* I gave the plant some water straightaway, and when I later asked my partner whether or not he had forgotten to water it, he confirmed that it indeed was the case. I began then to understand that plants have consciousness and are able to communicate telepathically. I am strongly clairaudient. It made sense.

The following anecdote took my breath away at the time. It illustrates the intelligence and spiritual wisdom of plants. My good friend and I were out for a drive to admire the trees changing into autumn colors in the Blue Mountains west of Sydney. We had lived for a long time in the subtropics where we had not experienced distinct seasons. He just happened to say, "I wonder why some of the trees do that—change into such amazing colors and others don't. There must be a reason."

I thought about it but could not determine a plausible reason, so I switched over into intuitive mode. Over the years I had developed the skill of switching between ordinary consciousness and into an altered state more or less at will. I asked the question. The answer came back immediately from a large Japanese maple nearby: *It is the role of all plants to illustrate the law of cycles, but it is the particular role of certain of the deciduous trees to illustrate the principle that there is beauty in death.* I was amazed to hear this and experienced the shudder of ontological shock, but I did hear it and it made sense in terms of what I had learned through my studies in magic about life and death, the cyclic nature of the Goddess, and the symbolic nature of the physical world.

I was gradually expanding my awareness of the complexity of human and nonhuman relationships, realizing that animals, plants, and even rocks not only appeared to be rational and communicative but also seemed to have work to do and some kind of life mission to fulfill. Often that mission was about teaching and healing humans. The Grail Family participants I later interviewed confirmed this, to my surprise. Perhaps this is not so surprising, as John Broomfield writes that it is only in the last several generations that humanity has lost the ability to communicate with the natural world (1997, 97). Before this, most people came from shaman cultures that supported the belief in interspecies communication and regarded it as normal. They were in more equal relationships with other life forms, including spirits.

Weather Working

On the subject of weather working, the following examples may give some insight. During the mid-nineteen eighties my family was living on a six-acre farmlet not far from Byron Bay on the east coast of NSW, where we had established an orchard and an organic vegetable and herb garden. The house had beautifully landscaped tropical gardens and ferneries around it. These lush areas of green, however, were beginning to suffer because there had been weeks of drought, and the ground was beginning to show signs of extreme thirst. Large cracks were opening up in the fertile volcanic red soil, and many of the plants were becoming limp and brown where they had become burnt by the unfiltered sunlight. The days were cloudless and the sun merciless. I decided that I would try to make it rain because the garden was suffering so much.

I told my partner what I intended doing that particular morning as he was heading up the hill to visit our neighbor Horst for coffee and a chat. When he returned home he told me his view of what had happened. When he arrived Horst had asked him where I was, and he had replied: "She's doing a rainmaking ceremony because she's sick of the garden dying from lack of rain." They were sitting out on the outdoor patio that overlooked our property. Horst laughed and said, "Yeah, sure," and took another puff on his joint, but the laughter died on his lips as he watched open-mouthed as the following event unfolded.

The sky was cloudless and blue and the sun was shining fiercely. Then suddenly one small gray cloud could be seen travelling across the sky in the general direction of our mutual properties. It was travelling quite fast although there did not seem to be much wind around. The cloud then was observed to stop directly over our six-acre property and it began to rain solidly for about thirty minutes. I could see it was raining, of course, from where I was on the verandah of my house, but what I could not see from my position was that it was raining only on our property! From their vantage point on top of the hill, both men could see clearly what was happening. All the surrounding land was untouched by the rain, and all the surrounding sky was blue. I had asked for rain for the garden, and that was what I got. When the little cloud had deposited its water content exactly over our land, it then moved off and over the ridge to the north and out of view. I noticed that Horst treated me with a lot more deference after this experience and often seemed a little nervous in my presence.

Another interesting event occurred when I was running the library in a large suburban high school. Because I was employed as a teacher as well as a librarian, part of my duties was to take sport every Tuesday afternoon. Because I find most team sport mind-numbingly boring, it was something I did not really look forward to. The day in question turned out to be extremely hot, and the thought of standing out in the blazing sun watching a group of adolescents trying to throw a ball through a hoop did not exactly excite my enthusiasm.

For some reason libraries seem to attract those who are different—the odd, the talented, the thinkers, the creative, the flotsam and jetsam of the social assemblage—and school libraries are no exception. They are like sanctuaries for the outcast, the unathletic, the disaffected, the social rejects. Most of the kids who hung around the library and acted as helpers fitted this model, and most of them had not much enthusiasm for the afternoon's activity either (there were about eight of them present). I suggested to them that at the morning's recess break we all gather in the library and concentrate on making it rain so we could have respite from sport that afternoon. I had meant it as a bit of a joke or diversion, but they all turned up at the time we agreed; accordingly, we all sat down in my office and concentrated very hard on visualizing it raining.

When we'd finished, one of the girls who was in the girl guides said that they had learned a rain dance at their last meeting and asked if she could teach it to the rest of the group. She though it might help with the rainmaking. I said, "Sure, that sounds like a great idea," but I didn't seriously believe that any of this activity would actually make it rain, and my involvement was more about alleviating the boredom. It was just a bit of fun for all of us, but I guess I have on a deeper level always believed that anything is possible and have been willing to experiment. The library was closed to borrowers at that time of day, so the group performed their rainmaking dance without the interference of onlookers, skeptics, or disbelievers.

It was a particularly fine day, cloudless, and the forecast was that it would continue that way for several days to come. However, an hour after our rainmaking efforts, a huge and violent thunderstorm arrived. The rain poured down, the wind was so strong that it blew open the heavy doors at the entrance to the library, and gusts of wind and rain blasted in. It was like a bucket brigade was standing in the foyer throwing large tubs full of water through the door. The playing fields adjacent to the school became drenched and flooded so badly (much to the rainmakers' delight) that sport had to be cancelled for the afternoon. I was quite shocked at what appeared to be the response to our ritual for rain, and there were quite a few students who experienced firsthand the possibility that the world was quite different to the way science had represented it—there were dimensions to "reality" not known or understood by the consensus makers.

The Turning Point:
A Qualitative Shift

Out-of-Body Experiences

Even after I had determined that there was no physiological
cause, and that I was no more insane than most of my fellow
men—the fears persisted. (Monroe 1975, 39)

A FURTHER SERIES OF strange events occurred that revolutionized my
way of looking at the world and transformed my understanding of the
meaning of life and death. The shock of having to integrate into my
understanding of reality situations for which, at the time, I could find no
reasonable explanation gave rise to strong self-doubts but an equally
strong determination to discover their meaning.

It is difficult, even now, for me to write about this. I wonder what the
reader will think, and yet one part of me does not really care. In some
ways I have gone beyond being concerned with what the world thinks
about me and know that a sensitive reader is able to hear the ring of truth
in a work, that quality that differentiates it from a hoax or a fantasy. Yet
still there is a sensation of tightness in my chest that I identify as fear, and

as I inwardly explore the feeling I realize that I am about to commit to paper what feels like dangerous knowledge about my life that I may not have completely integrated.

Writing this down means giving a concrete reality to experiences which, when looked at from the perspective of mundane existence, seem improbable, to say the least. I have lived for a long time with this uneasy knowledge, and even though I have a framework of understanding into which these experiences can comfortably fit, living in a society that accepts only what is empirically proven and more or less physically observable gives a feeling of vulnerability and disquiet. I am clearly re-experiencing the vestiges of ontological shock in relation to these matters, and yet the story unfolds and it seems important to tell it.

On a fine, cold day in June I decided to have an afternoon catnap. Since early childhood I had developed the ability to drift not into sleep but into a dreaming state, an alpha or theta brainwave state, which enabled me to free my mind and rejuvenate my energy. Typically I would drift away for twenty to thirty minutes, after which I would arise feeling deeply refreshed and able to cope with the myriad duties, obligations, and fascinations with which I kept myself and my curious mind entertained and busy.

As I lay on my bed and began setting my mind into a drifting pattern, I was suddenly jolted into full consciousness by what I perceived to be a beam or a ray coming out of the north and playing over my body. I did not see it with my physical eyes; it was more like a perception of energy by a different kind of knowing. I tried to move but found that I was paralyzed. I could feel a strong vibration in my body, but I could not see with my physical eyes any movement on the surface of my skin. The vibration had spread over my whole body, from my toes to the top of my head. It felt particularly strong around my jaw and head, and there was a loud roaring or buzzing in my brain. It was like having a painless electric shock.

I became afraid that I was having some kind of seizure and might die. I was immobilized and could not call for help. I wondered if I had suddenly become epileptic, but I was fully conscious. I was unable to make any rational sense of the experience at the time, but subsequent reading in the field of shamanism has indicated that epilepsy-type symptoms have frequently been observed during rituals the shaman employs to alter consciousness. Subsequent reading in the field indicated that other Western "insider" researchers (those who have had their own direct experiences of the Elphame) have had identical or similar experiences (Harner 1990, Heywood 1966, Monroe 1975, Moss 1996, Narby 1998, Wesselman 1996). However, at the time I could find nothing in the conventional medical, scientific, or psychological literature to explain it.

After several minutes the vibrations stopped as abruptly as they had begun and I was able to get up off the bed to see if I was physically intact. I seemed to be quite normal. My head felt clear and my body was intact. After several days of normalcy I dismissed the experience as an aberration—abnormal brainwave activity perhaps brought about by stress. I knew that stress could affect the physical body in strange ways. I put it out of my mind.

Several days later, however, it recurred. After the second "attack," things returned to normal for a few days and then again, just when I thought I was safe from them, the strange vibrations struck for the third time. Even though I did not seem to suffer any ill effects from these experiences, I was worried that there was something wrong with my brain or medulla. I made an appointment to see a local GP and told him my story. He did some neurological tests and gave me a complete physical examination. His verdict was, "I've never seen a healthier person. There's nothing wrong with you." This should have been reassuring, but it was the reverse.

The vibration attacks continued every few days, and I finally pressured my GP into referring me to a neurologist. This doctor did some extensive tests and yet could discover no abnormalities in my central nervous system. It was frightening and mystifying; even the discovery of something as drastic as a tumor might have brought some relief, as it would have at least have provided a rational explanation for the seizure-like symptoms.

I was beginning to feel depressed, wondering if I was experiencing the onset of schizophrenia. Several weeks later, as the vibrations continued to manifest, I told my brother what had been happening. He listened with interest and told me that recently he had been reading a book that seemed to tell a very similar story. He offered to lend it to me.

This autobiographical work was entitled *Journeys Out of the Body* and was written by an American businessman and author named Robert Monroe. As I read his story I began to feel surprise and relief. His story was almost identical to mine, even down to the ray of strange energy coming out of the north, the fear of brain disease, and the trips to a neurologist, but what he had discovered about the vibrations was intriguing. He discovered that when the vibrations occurred, it was possible to float or to step out of one's physical body by simply willing it or imagining it. The book told of how he had discovered the meaning of the strange vibrations and how they could be used to astral travel. I had heard talk of the phenomenon of astral travel but it had never made much sense to me, as the descriptions sounded very confused and garbled, possibly even mythological, and certainly not something that happened to a normal human being. Nevertheless, when the vibrations recurred I determined to see if I could fly or float out of my body. I was becoming desperate enough to consider the possibility, although it was a deliciously scary proposition.

The next time the vibrations occurred I stayed as calm as possible and tried willing myself to float upward and out of my body, which was lying prone on the bed. I felt an upward movement and gently floated to the ceiling, my nose pressing against the ceiling. Waves of fear swept through me. I calmed myself a little, then willed myself down to earth again and found myself standing on the polished timber floorboards of the bedroom. I could feel them solid under my feet. I looked at the bed and saw my physical form lying there as if it were dead. I could not notice my body breathing. I panicked. As soon as I felt fear and thought of my body, I immediately snapped back into it as if I were attached to a piece of elastic.

Curiously, in my panic I had been jolted back into my body, but I did not feel I was properly aligned with it. I needed to get out again and lower myself back into my body more gently and purposefully so that it felt as if I was lying properly straight. This new phenomenon of leaving the physical body and returning to it precipitated an attack of profound ontological shock. It is a terrifying experience to be separated from the physical body and precipitated into a different level of being. Nothing else—none of the other weird experiences—could match it for the paralyzing level of fear and self-doubt it evoked. This experience and others like it brought me close to the edge of the abyss, and many times I feared that I had gone too far this time and was probably going insane.

The high level of fear and ontological shock, nevertheless, was not enough to deter me from further exploration. I decided to observe, to discover more or less through trial and error, "to feel the fear but do it anyway." In subsequent months I was able to practice leaving my physical body in my subtle energy body and travel to many places in the physical and the nonphysical worlds. In the Elphame I discovered that the great forests that are disappearing from the physical world because of human greed and exploitation, and the animals we have driven to extinction because of over-hunting and exploitation, have an existence there and remain in living form.

In the physical world I was invisible to ordinary sight and appeared only as a slight shimmer or movement caught out of the corner of the eye, but in the nonphysical worlds I appeared in my normal shape and density, and the inhabitants and objects of the nonphysical worlds appeared to be normally solid to my perception. By willing myself to float or fly I could quickly arrive at a destination. I told a friend that I would fly over to visit her when she was asleep and see if I could wake her up. Upon entering her room I called her name and tried to shake her awake but couldn't rouse her, as she seemed in a very deep sleep and my hand simply passed through her physical body. The next morning I rang her to ask if she had been aware that I had visited her. I described her room and the pajamas she was wearing. She said she had had a vivid dream about me.

I found that in the physical world I could easily walk through walls, which was intriguing because I remembered that when my sister and I were young we would practice standing up against our bedroom wall and willing ourselves to pass through it. What I learned from these out-of-body experiences was transformative. First, the physical body is not the real self, and it actually has no life of its own apart from the energy body. Without the subtle energy body, the physical body exists as if in a deep coma, barely breathing and with no apparent perception or motion. Second, I learned that there is no death. At what we perceive physically as death, the physical body returns to the elements from which it came, but the energy body continues to exist with mind, emotions, sensations, knowledge, and perceptions intact. The energy body cannot be perceived with the physical eyes, but those who are in their energy bodies can perceive the physical world perfectly well and with all their senses operational. Occasionally, those who are sensitive or clairvoyant can see beyond the physical world and into the more subtle worlds.

For example, when my partner's father died all the family and friends were gathered around the graveside weeping. While the pastor was droning on about heaven and resurrection on Judgment Day, I was stuffing my handkerchief into my mouth and digging my fingernails into my palms to stop laughing because I could clearly see my father-in-law standing beside the pastor, trying to shake his arm and telling him, *It's not like that at all, Neville! I am here right beside you,* and becoming frustrated because he could not be heard and the pastor was unconscious of his presence. It was a bizarre situation, and I quickly saw the sense in the old adage that you don't speak ill of the dead—because they can hear perfectly well all that is said, and if they do not like it, as the Chinese and the Native Americans believe, they could easily remain in the physical world to create misery, sometimes intentionally and sometimes unintentionally.

In his book *The Art of Dreaming*, Carlos Castaneda, an American anthropologist who conducted insider research into Mexican Indian shamanism and claimed to have been initiated into the tradition, asks his spiritual teacher and initiator, the Yaqi sorcerer/shaman Don Juan Matus, "What exactly is the energy body?" And Don Juan replies:

> It's the counterpart of the physical body. A ghost-like configuration made of pure energy...the energy body has only appearance but no mass. Since it's pure energy, it can perform acts that are beyond the possibilities of the physical body...such as transporting itself in one instant to the ends of the universe...or it can perceive as we ordinarily perceive the world. (1993, 31)

This succinct description exactly accords with my own experience. I also learned that, contrary to orthodox opinion, the mind is not in the brain. Out of my body I could think very well and experience the full range of emotions, thoughts, and feelings. The brain appears to me now to be more a storage tool and organizing principle for all the information pertinent to physical existence. It has great difficulty interpreting information from the other levels of existence; for example, what is perceived by the energy body. A strong dream may better illustrate what I mean.

One night I woke up to find that I was out of my body and floating near the ceiling again. I was shocked to wake in this way and reacted with fear. I observed that I was telepathically communicating with my partner, telling him I was frightened and unable to get back into my body. He was talking back to me telepathically, telling me to relax and to think about floating down into my body, saying, *I'm here; you're going to be okay.* Gradually I relaxed and landed back in my body. He was deeply asleep, so I shook him awake and told him what had happened. He said, "That's funny! I was having a dream in which I was an engineer on a building site and I was instructing a crane operator who was lowering a very fragile body, like an Egyptian mummy, onto the trays of two trucks parked very closely side by side. For some reason I could not quite understand, the trays were very soft and spongy. We were being very careful because it was a delicate operation and we didn't want to damage the body." This was particularly significant because at the time we were sleeping on two single soft Dunlopillo beds pushed together.

We thought that what had probably happened was that we were communicating telepathically and directly, energy body to energy body, but this information could not be communicated directly to the brain cortex. During rapid eye movement (REM) sleep the cortex is not active, and dreaming is largely an emotional event. The "old brain" interpreted the actual event by constructing a congruent set of images to explain what was happening. This experience made me wonder just how many of the experiences we call "just dreams" were, in fact, real experiences, albeit out of the body.

Robert Moss, who has done extensive research into shamanism and dream states, supports this view and says that we will never understand the nature of the mind by measuring brain waves:

> The mind is not in the brain, dreams are not in the brain…The brain is
> an elegant transcriber which boils down information coming from
> sources far beyond it…The most interesting frontiers of science are
> moving far beyond the science that is confined to the measurement of
> external reality. (Cameron 1998)

As a result of these extraordinary experiences, I experimented to see
what else I could do. If I sound somewhat blasé now, as I write this
account, I was actually quite fearful, self-doubting, and experienced a deal
of inner torment as I tried to understand what it all meant. It was as if I
had a view of myself as being a particular kind of person and now I had
to completely re-evaluate that view.

Another deeper and more mysterious self who could do all sorts of
strange and weird things lay just below the surface. Somehow I had to
find a way of integrating this new self into a revised and more complete
picture of my identity. It was as if I thought I was driving a Volkswagen,
only to find it had suddenly morphed into a Porsche. This was not an
easy change to accommodate. Like all myths of transformation and
transmutation, archetypal stories are easier to mentally appreciate and
emotionally absorb from a theoretical distance. When they are up close
and personal and actually happening in worldly life, they generate fear
and confusion, at least for a time, and they certainly generate ontological
shock.

It was interesting for me to read what other people who have had
these kinds of psychologically destabilizing, intense, unexpected, and
repeated experiences say about them. Robert Monroe describes his own
powerful experience of ontological shock that brought him to the edge
of madness and the trauma of psychotherapy treatment that could not
appreciate or comprehend his reality. He says that the main purpose of
publishing his book was to get as wide an audience as possible in the hope
that

> some other human being…may be saved from the agony and terror of
> trial and error in an area where there have been no concrete answers;
> that he may have the comfort in the knowledge that others have had
> the same experiences; that he will recognize in himself the phenome-

non and thus avoid the trauma of psychotherapy, or at the worst mental breakdown and commitment to a mental institution. (1975, 25)

Hank Wesselman says:

> I had heard other people's tales of such things as shamanic journeying and they caused me to wince with embarrassment. Now here I was, a trained scientist experiencing the awesome jolt of the real thing myself. My carefully constructed scientific worldview had begun to come apart…I wondered more than once if I was going crazy. I read into medical diagnosis, wondering if I had epilepsy or some other convulsive disorder. However, aside from these isolated spontaneous experiences, my central nervous system seemed to function normally. I had no symptoms of organic brain disease, tumors, traumas, infections, or hypoglycemia. (1996, 18)

Robert Moss, also previously an academic, had spent a childhood confined to bed throughout a series of serious illnesses. He experienced an intense inner life of strong dreams and visions. He writes that in his adult life also he was almost overwhelmed by incursions from the Elphame. As his experiences became more frequent and more intense, Moss began, like many other adults who have had these kinds of experiences, to lose the calm and confidence of childhood and to experience the confusion and fear of ontological shock. At times he also feared he would go insane because of the intensity of his inner experiences:

> In dream-like states I battled with sorcerers, and malevolent ghosts, and my own shadow self. In waking life I was now deeply divided, profoundly disaffected from previous ambitions and definitions of success. I read everything I could find that might give me a handle on what was happening…from Stan Grof's work on "spiritual emergency" to Robert Monroe's *Journeys Out of the Body*. In Joan Halifax's *Shamanic Voices* and in Mircea Eliade's classic, *Shamanism*, I found accounts of shamanic initiation that seemed amazingly familiar. They reassured me that if I was going crazy, I was going in interesting company. (1996, 15–16)

Kay Cordell Whitaker, an artist and academic who was initiated into South American shamanism, writes as an insider about the extreme terror and disorientation she experienced during her training, which involved induced out-of-body experiences. Her personal world map had to be redrafted, as the old one no longer served its purpose:

> For one who meets his death and lives again, the world changes. They
> have felt the very nature of Death, and they know it is not annihilation
> but movement...How else can one become a shaman but by a rapid
> and extreme movement of such force that it breaks one away from all
> that went before? (1991, 33)

Generally, and like Wesselman, my psychic skills appeared first, and
reading, study, and training followed, although this was not always the
case and further surprising developments appeared at later stages when I
had already begun magical training.

Magical Companions

When I met James, my second husband, we fell into each other's
arms, grateful to find another person interested in studying the Elphame
in a serious way. Both of us had separately experienced many inexplicable
phenomena and discovered that the truth of these experiences did not
reveal itself easily. It seemed to be part of the experience that one must
work hard to discover its meaning. Also neither of us had been able to
find a theoretical perspective in the psychological or philosophical literature that offered anything illuminating or concrete to help us. He has
been my friend and companion in some very strange situations, witnessing much of my unfolding shaman development, and has been a solid
backstop and sounding board.

We were both quite naive and probably arrogant at the beginning of
our studies. We had bought some books on the Western magical tradition and were busily reading through them, feeling quite smug that we
had found "the way." I read a rather intimidating fat volume called *The
Gems of the Equinox*, which was a compilation of articles written by the
notorious Aleister Crowley and formed the basis of his eclectic system of
"magick." As for Crowley himself, those who knew him reveal him to be
a complex person. On the one hand, he was extremely intelligent, well
read, kind and compassionate; on the other, he set out to shock the complacent from their spiritual sleep. At times he may have gone too far and
through that process gave his enemies ammunition to use against him,
and I am sure that a lot of the more scandalous stories about him were
hallucinations, exaggerations, and lies.

To me he is a heroic figure from another age, and I am not sure how relevant his methods and techniques are to the modern world. I don't like the involvement he had in sex magick because I see it as open to abuse and I believe there are other ways to gain spiritual knowledge and effect. It is interesting to see that in the modern world so many gurus and other spiritual teachers fall from grace and into disrepute largely through power, sex, and money abuses.

Crowley's influence had reached into the Wiccan coven in which we had become involved. Here, as elsewhere, we encountered deep problems with perceptions of standards of conduct. I had a strong sense of the importance of ethical standards of behavior in magical groups because I believed that they were essentially spiritual in their focus. This perspective was, however, strenuously contradicted by many of the people in the groups in which I was involved. They cited the Thelemite Creed, developed by Crowley and based on *The Book of the Law*, a work Crowley claimed was communicated to him by a nonphysical entity named Aiwass. This creed, in part, declares: "Do what thou wilt shall be the whole of the law." This is similar to the Wiccan Rede: "An it harm none, do what thou wilt."

The origins of the Wiccan Rede are mysterious. The English witch and high priestess Doreen Valiente is thought possibly to have been the author of the rede, and certainly very similar words do appear at the end of her poem "The Witches' Creed." But the stanza before that strongly suggests the influence of Crowley's Thelemite Creed. Some forty-five years earlier than *The Book of the Law*, philosopher John Stuart Mill wrote an influential pamphlet entitled *On Liberty*, in which he extensively explored the theme of personal liberty and its limits. Mill's thought was influential and also problematic. Perhaps the Wiccan Rede is a distillation of the secular values espoused by Mill. The question of the origin of the rede is not, therefore, definitively answerable.

It is easy to read Mill quickly and gloss over the more subtle nuances of his argument. It can seem like permission for personal license. The same risk applies with both the Thelemite and Wiccan creeds. How do we know that we understand the law, that our will is not distorted by unconscious and neurotic impulses, and when our acts genuinely harm none? In my experience magical groups are frequently riven by power plays and sexual politics that are excused as the robust cut and thrust of individuals learning to exercise their true wills. But that can be a veil for unethical, predatory, and abusive conduct as well. While there is certainly some truth to the robust cut and thrust defense, not all people who come to a magical group are suited to work in such an environment.

I became intensely aware of, for me, a conflict between spiritual development and magical development, the latter with a focus on knowledge and method. The extent to which development should embrace deeper psychological insight, leading to growing self-awareness, became a concern for me when the groups I was initially involved with actually seemed to reject the notion that any of the magical work should have any direct impact on emotional and psychological development, other than entirely within the context of the exercises and lessons provided. The focus on information and skills development did not allow for or encourage personal growth or psychological insights. It seemed to me in magical groups that often even senior members of the groups lacked psychological maturity and insight.

The Book of the Law says that "every man and woman is a star." I take this to mean that we are all luminous beings with our own trajectories or life plans and purposes and that if we conform to divine will and do not accrue karma by crashing into other people's "trajectories," and if we act from impersonal love, then we can do what we will. The problem is that we can never really know if even acting from our best intentions if we are causing harm to something or someone. To me it all means that we need to be very consciously careful about what we do magically. Because everything is connected to everything else, an action can create a remote effect that we do not intend or want (the butterfly effect—chaos and complexity theory).

The upshot is that these creeds that appear deceptively simple are, in reality, extremely complex—more like themes for deep meditation and reflection rather than a glib and easy motto to justify self-interest. Perhaps the fact that we cannot ever know for certain the consequences of our actions demands of us a profoundly reflective faith that we have done our best to assess the merits of all our actions. Even so, history is littered with instances of people in power choosing poorly and to catastrophic effect. How and how often do we listen deeply to our conscience before acting? I believe that magical and spiritual development must go hand in hand and that, in our imperfect stage of psychological maturity as humans, if we do not pay attention as to whether or not our actions adversely affect the common good, we run a serious risk of harming others.

I originally thought it would not take me long to master Crowley's work; however, at that stage I did not realize that magic was not a game to be mastered or a body of knowledge to be acquired. I was to discover gradually and painfully that it was a technology to be used on the long and arduous journey of spiritual awakening. I would ultimately realize that magic could speed up that journey considerably, but that it would never be a substitute for life. Life and how one lived it was the other half of the equation. Life itself was an essentially spiritual event, and living with grace, fulfilling responsibility, expanding awareness, and contributing something to the world through work were as important as treading the shaman's path of ordeal and initiation. Life itself is dynamic and evolutionary in the spiritual sense.

This is a Goddess view of life that supports the idea that because spirit permeates everything, nothing can be regarded as unspiritual. From this perspective wrong attitudes, bad experiences, and evil actions are regarded as opportunities for learning and spiritual growth however long it takes, although there may be earthly consequences as well as the finely grinding wheels of karma. (This is the realm of the Dark Goddess, the Crone, whose role will be further investigated later in this work.)

Both Wicca and High Magic are initiatory pathways that may lead to the development of psychic skill and spiritual growth. This is the theory and, as we were to discover, sadly not always the practice, as hypocrisy flourishes in the occult as in most other departments of human life and there may be too much emphasis in modern magic on the acquiring of personal power and too little on spiritual development. Dealing with power can lead to overdevelopment of the ego and stimulate the lower chakras. This conundrum is the cause of the many power struggles common in magical groups, where the focus can easily shift from personal spiritual development to self-aggrandizement. Many magicians have problems trying to find the balance between their personal and spiritual lives, and being on a spiritual path does not automatically confer spiritual wisdom. This conflict is ultimately resolved by the initiatory encounter with the shadow self, known in magic as the "dweller on the threshold," which I will later describe in some detail.

However, as the great German magician and Hermetic scholar Franz Bardon writes (in quaint English), magic is essentially a path of practical and unselfish spiritual development. He says:

> This type of science is only destined to the most sublime purposes... the magician is bound to ennoble his character in the course of his development to the highest degree to avoid an interruption, or even worse—a falling off from his rise. The ennoblement of the soul is going hand in hand with the rise of the development. He who aspires after occult power for futile motives will be led away from his path sooner or later; occult faculties being only by-products, a sort of compass of development and meant for the noble purpose of helping our fellow man. (1962, 268)

Starhawk also emphasizes that the spiritual purpose of power gained through initiation is not to be used for egotistical personal gain. Powers raised must be used responsibly, she says. If this principle is not adhered to, then—like the ring of Sauron in Tolkien's Lord of the Rings trilogy— it (power misused) will eventually destroy its possessor.

As my psychic skills gradually emerged, I began to study in a more formal way, first by reading and personal experimentation and later by joining several magical groups working with different methods of approaching and exploring the hidden reality. James and I gradually gained an understanding of the fundamental laws and practices of Ceremonial Magic, and we learned the safeguarding skills such as how to set up a protective environment in which to work and how to work with the elements (earth, fire, water, air). We also learned the techniques of magical invocation and evocation, as well as how to work with the different orders of subtle beings, such as the elemental, angelic, and archangelic orders, and how to get them to work cooperatively with us and other protocols of traditional magical ritual. There is a body of Qabalistic knowledge from which we received systematic teaching that structures and informs Ceremonial Magic.

As I recollect and reflect on this part of my life, another mountain peak takes shape and emerges from the mist of memory and I see flashing images of us as we were then, excited yet serious, draped in sheets and towels because at the time we had no magical robes, performing banishing rituals and invocations of the archangels of the elements, burning candles and incense and learning how to set up the altar with the consecrated ceremonial chalice and sword, and how to create the inner temple that is the sanctuary of the soul or higher self. The first encounters with power are exhilarating. One can feel in the bodily sense the intensity of the energy generated and at first it is surprising, even alarming.

At this point, however, I retained some skepticism, some doubt that the Elphame was real or that it had an existence apart from the human imagination, but I consciously adopted the "as if" philosophical position. I would act "as if" I accepted that these things were possible and see what happened. I found that to be open to all possibilities seemed to invite further manifestation of the magical, and everything became possible.

The Opening of the Doorway in the Mind

After my first ritual encounter of the power of ceremony, I had strong messages in my head and feelings in my hand that I should sit down and write something, but fear prevented my doing it. This was something new and quite frightening. The ceremony had opened what seemed to me to be a doorway in my mind, and I was not sure who had walked through it. After the ceremony I was walking through the dining room of my house when suddenly there was a long and loud cracking sound (Jung also describes a similar experience) and I felt myself being lifted off my feet and somehow transported through the air. I once again entered a kind of ecstatic state, which lasted for some time, and I have asked my partner to give his version of those events from his magical diary records.

We tended to keep magical diaries something like the Wiccan Book of Shadows, which contained records of all the ritual work we performed and anything else of interest. James's recollection of this incident is as follows:

Jane had gone to the bathroom, and Bronwyn (a Wiccan friend) and myself remained in the lounge chatting. The door connecting the lounge and dining room was closed. After a few minutes, I heard a very loud and very clear cracking sound. My immediate thought was that Jane had fallen against the dining room table (English oak) and that it had broken. There was nothing else I could imagine causing such a loud noise. I rushed out to the dining room. I recall seeing Jane in a dazed state near the French doors leading off the dining room to the bedroom. I helped her to sit on the bed and asked her about the noise. I was relieved, yet surprised, to see she was okay, despite being clearly affected by the experience. She told me that she had been "coming out of the bathroom and had been blasted across the room." As we sat on the bed, her behavior changed and she began to act as if she were in a kind of trance. She asked me to get her a pen and paper. I watched as her right hand made scrawling letters.

As I sat on the bed beside Jane, I felt as if I was in an intense radiation field and saw a bluish light surrounding and covering the bed. It was in this light that I felt the radiation. The sense of being held in a field of radiation was very intense. I felt slightly pressed down physically and sufficiently disoriented consciously to need to focus on what was going on—to stop drifting off and entering a similar state to Jane's. I formed the impression that the source of radiation was above us, but I had no idea what it was or who was responsible for it. I can't say how long the event lasted. Bronwyn remained in the lounge room and she thought about 20 minutes had elapsed.

• • • •

WESSELMAN WRITES ABOUT THE doorway in the mind and describes the experience in a similar way. He explains the importance of developing skills in seeing and communicating with spirits, and how, over time and with practice, it can become possible to call them up and see them at will. The key initial skill is, however, to control the "doorway" between the physical and the subtle world. When this skill is mastered, a new realm of accomplishment and discovery will open up.

A short time after these unsettling events, and through a contact with a well-known author, researcher, and commentator on esoteric and spiritual matters, we joined a magical order. It was run by a person who had trained in the higher degrees of Masonry and who had established a temple in Sydney. He was teaching the system of magical training known as the Golden Dawn after a famous esoteric order that was active in the latter years of the nineteenth century and the early years of the twentieth and had trained many high-profile initiates in its temples in the UK and France (these magicians included the poet W. B. Yeats and the actress Florence Farr). He explained how novice magicians might be tested by the Elphame to find out how steadfast and serious they are in relation to their magical and spiritual training. What follows gives credence to that claim.

Psychic Attack

I include this vignette because it dramatically illustrates some of the dangers of contact with the Elphame and the concept of magical ordeal. As a safeguard, it is important to have some training before attempting to enter the subtle world and work with its energies.

In this early magical period I experienced what is known as a psychic attack. It was a truly terrifying experience. This episode describes a spiritual ordeal, but the candidate for initiation can also be tested in their mundane life. All ordeals have the purpose of helping the candidate to develop psychological strength, resilience, and courage.

For three nights one cold Sydney winter I did not dare sleep. I sat in front of the fire in the grip of an inexplicable terror, almost panic, shaking, trying to stay awake, attempting to ward off the most overpowering and dread-filled feelings of malevolence threatening annihilation. It felt as if an evil energy was being beamed at me, but from where I could not fathom. I thought that perhaps I had drawn attention to myself by taking the first initiation in White Magic, and those retrograde energies that work toward human spiritual devolution now identified me as one of the enemy. Perhaps, I thought, I had come to the attention of the demonic forces or cosmic evil. The imperator of the order had said to me previously that taking the first initiation is like running up a flag in the cosmos that can be seen from the perspective of the subtle reality to be symbolically saying, "I'm pretty good. Come and try me out!"—and they do. I did not pay too much attention to this advice at the time, but I vividly remembered it during the psychic attack.

I had never felt so alone or vulnerable and was just managing to fight back the tide of darkness that sought to overwhelm me. I thought it must be something like the feeling of going insane in the time before a person really slips over the edge and succumbs. I felt powerlessness in the face of an overwhelming force that sought to engulf my consciousness. I thought it must be worse than being completely insane and therefore no longer self-aware: that struggle to retain a sense of psychological integrity, and the fear that it all may be lost.

My first inclination was to angrily fight back, but I did not have the skill. My intuition told me there must be a way out of this deplorable situation and eventually, on the third night, in desperation, after mentally asking for help in finding it, the knowledge I needed suddenly came to me. The quiet voice in my head said, *Raise yourself above it and polarize on a higher level*. It then became clear what I must do in order to survive the ordeal, but I was not sure of how I knew it or even exactly how to do it. It is difficult to find the appropriate language to describe it. My response was purely intuitive and instinctive. I was too afraid to engage in self-doubt or any rational interrogation of the experience but reacted on an instinctive level. The desire for self-preservation overrode all questions and self-doubt.

As the disturbing energy reached me, I transformed it in my heart center and sent it back as impersonal love. That is as closely as I can describe it. Suddenly the attack ceased and the ordeal ended. I had found the key. There is no denying the experience strengthened me, but it also taught me humility and caution in approaching the nonphysical reality. It was dangerous as well as fascinating. There is a Wiccan axiom that where there's fear, there's power—and as Neitzsche succinctly expresses it, "what doesn't kill you makes you stronger." These ideas are real.

Lynn Andrews, a student of shaman traditions, writes about the dangers and ordeals of the shaman's path. She also touches on the theme of the wounded healer (an important archetype of shamanism reflected in the Greek god of healing, Asklepios, and the centaur Chiron). C. G. Jung also explored this archetype. In order to be a healer, it is necessary to understand suffering by first personally experiencing it; this makes sense to me. Andrews says:

> As a shaman, you dwell in the almost fatal crack between light and darkness where the beings of mystery swim in unknown rivers of energy. It is a world of life and death and great danger...but if you live through the initiations, you have become the ultimate alchemist. Your own soul has burned through the agonizing fires of transformation and you become the Goddess on Earth. You can heal the mind and heart of your suffering brothers and sisters because you have also suffered. You have been born to heal and teach. You help to reinstate the sacred balance. (1987, 238)

In the remote past, in the Pagan and Gnostic mystery tradition, female psychic sensitives were used to make the contact with the spiritual teaching source and to transmit or interpret the teachings that were received telepathically. In the ancient Greek tradition, before the Indo-European/Olympian gods ascended to power, these sensitives were the pythonesses, or priestesses of the Goddess, who gave out prophecy they received in altered states of consciousness. With the rise and subsequent political influence of the Olympian gods and goddesses, it seems that the shrine was masculinized and rededicated to Apollo and his priesthood. The Pithia, or pythonesses, were then securely under masculine control.

Today, we would probably use the term "medium" to describe those people who are a link between the spiritual and physical worlds. Direct voice mediumship occurs when the medium's body and vocal equipment are taken over by a nonphysical entity and the body is vacated for a time by the normally indwelling personality. The medium may or may not remember what has been transacted. I was to find out that I was in the line of succession of these women shamans, but there was a difference.

Contact with a Master of the Wisdom

I found that during my first experience of Ceremonial Magic I was being contacted by a Master of the Wisdom, a discarnate teaching adept called the Master A. This kind of contact is what the subjects of the Grail Family inquiry mean when they talk about "working under guidance" or "working with spiritual guides." I also found that rather than being a direct voice medium, I was a mediator. A mediator is more like a translator: a telepath who receives messages as a kind of electromagnetic energy impulse and is able to translate the impulses into concrete language. Carmen Blacker, who studied the disappearing shamanic tradition in Japan, observed that when shamans telepathically communicated with the unseen reality, they received those communications in their native language, which supports the whole idea of translation.

A mediator has more control over the process of communication than a medium. Although mediation is part of the oracular shamanic tradition, I believe it is a modern and safer expression of it. As I have always had a talent for telepathy, being a mediator seemed to be a natural extension of that ability. In this same way, I am also able to translate the thoughts and emotions of animals, plants, and stones into language and to hear their voices. In the tradition of Western magical orders, contact with an inner plane adept meant that I was theoretically equipped to develop and run my own magical order with the adept's guidance and spiritual support.

At the time I was developing this contact I was a member of the Australian branch of a magical order based in Europe. The paradox of possessing this mediation skill meant that I was initiated at the same or a higher level than my teachers. This turned out to be an intolerable political situation, and I was not fully aware of the implications or the possible consequences. The order's Australian leader was actively seeking somebody with just my telepathic skills so that he could establish an independent branch of the order. However, he was not the kind of person to whom I was prepared to submit my skill, and he was not prepared to tolerate the presence of a desired skill he could not control. It meant that eventually my partner and I were ejected from the order, something that I perceived as an act of extreme betrayal.

I found it difficult to accept this telepathic contact with an inner plane Master of the Wisdom. At times I embraced it; at others I tried to avoid it, experiencing the swinging poles of ontological shock. I also found that when I needed help and guidance from those who presumably would know about such matters, I have never been able to find it but have had to struggle to work it out for myself, often a painful and difficult task. I had been aware for a long time, however, that I had a high level of intuitive guidance in my life, and in moments of lucidity this awareness made it easier to accept. Eventually I developed some trust in the contact, but it was an uneasy alliance and I was never really certain about my ability to work at this high level. However, the Master A gave guidance for the magical work in which my partner and I were engaged, but he was not inclined to be a fountainhead of information. He stressed the importance of experiential learning. Spiritual guidance does not usually work by imparting information but by guiding experience. He said to me, *I am not here to tell you everything you want to know, but rather to help you learn.*

He also said, *You build walls for yourself so that you can climb over them and feel that you have achieved something.* This statement challenged my view of myself, and on reflection I saw its truth. I found it hard to accept that most spiritual things were easy for me, and I often created difficulty through my skepticism, self-doubt, and intellectualizing. He told me that I had studied and developed these skills in previous lifetimes and I was simply remembering what I already knew. He also said that the sudden appearance of the shaman abilities and the out-of-body experiences were a wake-up call for me to start using them again and to feel that it was acceptable to do so. Nobody else could explain this precocious development to me and what he said made complete sense, yet I remained skeptical.

What he said about remembering prior knowledge now seems true, because it offers a rational explanation and it also fits Joseph Campbell's description of the archetypal and initiatory Hero's Journey. I have accepted the concept of reincarnation since childhood for the same reason: it made a lot more sense than any of the alternatives. I also think that the world itself is meaningful and that there is invisible intelligence and elegant design behind the manifestations of the apparently visible chaos. It is just that with our usually limited human consciousness we do not always see it or we see what we want, need, or expect to see, and worse, often what we are taught or told to see.

In the early stages of my work I found that I could not consistently and seamlessly relate or combine the different kinds of information coming from both the physical world and the Elphame simultaneously and in the process create a complete picture. At times I could do this more easily than at others, but the process was not always reliable; sometimes it worked, at others it didn't, so I experienced a swinging back and forth between the two realities. Clear and certain access to the Elphame is not always possible. Clarity comes and goes, not because the Elphame is a gossamer, illusory, or ephemeral world or a shifting reality but successful contact depends on the ability of the practitioner to alter consciousness and perception seamlessly. This is not always a reliable or repeatable process. Physical and emotional states may not allow a smooth transition into an altered state of consciousness or the consciousness of the practitioner may be actively distracted and not in a passive enough mental state to allow the entry of the Elphame onto the screen of personal awareness. It is the human element that is uncertain, and sometimes we perceive as the Bible describes it: "through a glass darkly."

Although I learned a lot from the years I spent studying, practicing, and working with several different magical orders, there was something about High Magic that I found unsatisfying. The High Magical corpus came from the largely masculine and hierarchical Egyptian, Hebrew, and Greek esoteric traditions that emphasized human dominance over the natural world and unseen worlds, the supremacy of intellectual knowledge, and the acquisition of personal power. There always seemed to me to be something very unspiritual about the way the High Magical corpus was interpreted in the modern world. It did not appear to value emotional knowledge or heart learning or promote psychological development. I was looking for something that addressed this lack, and it was then that I encountered the Old Goddess standing on my path. This meeting was to have a profound influence on my thinking, my theorizing, and ultimately my praxis. She was pointing to another Western spiritual path that was going in different direction.

Initiation into Wicca

James and I were invited to join a Wiccan coven. Interestingly, the high priest of this group was a professor at a local university who claimed to have been also initiated into a form of Native American shamanism, indicating the ease with which the indigenous tradition melded with Witchcraft. We were curious about the Wiccan pathway and both took initiation at the second degree and worked with this group for eighteen months as senior teachers, eventually setting up our own working group for study, teaching, and practical ritual work. One of the important aims of all magical groups is to become a "contacted" order or coven. That is, they seek to have contact with a teaching source from an inner plane. This contact then gives legitimacy for the order to start its own particular type of spiritual working group, whether it is a High Magical or Craft group. Our inner plane contact was the Master A. This contact gave us the legitimacy to start our own group working along a Druidic-influenced line of development.

Unlike High Magic and like most indigenous ritual, Wiccan ritual is conducted on the principle of the circle and the four directions, and leadership is viewed differently. The high priestess, because she is the link with the Goddess, is regarded with respect as the first among equals. This is a very different idea to the hierarchy of High Magical leadership, which is a lot more rigid and authoritarian. In my experience High Magic is most often conducted on the principle of the square or the cross, which creates a dynamic tension. The archetype of the circle has a very different and more fluid impact on the consciousness of the group, and fluidity is the foundational nature of the physical world.

In shaman cultures the circle is the form used for ceremonial purposes because circumambulation, dancing, or chanting in a circle raises the life force, a power that can be accumulated and used for healing or other magical operations. All shaman and traditional cultures, including Wicca, have their own particular versions of the circle dance.

At my first contact with Wicca, the body of theory and practice immediately resonated with me because it is a poetic and feminine system of magic, closely connected with the earth. The idea of the Goddess and all of the associated concepts had a direct and powerful impact on my consciousness that felt right. There was an unarguable coherence and consistency inherent in the model that resonated not only spiritually but encompassed a reality that extended into the mundane world and into the heart of science itself. I believe that the model expresses in a poetic and symbolic way a unified field theory, or theory of everything (Laszlo 2004). This is something for which science has been searching, at least since Einstein and Planck.

Although High Magic did have a theory of everything in the model of the Qabalistic tree of life, it was a much more intellectual and compartmentalized model. I saw that the Goddess model worked on all levels, from the spiritual to the mundane, yet described no such compartmentalism as I perceived in the Qabalah or dualism such as what underlies Christianity. There was, in reality, no sacred and profane differentiation, at least not in the mind of Divinity. Such a differentiation or not was in the mind and intention of the practitioner. The ideas of unity, connectivity, and relationship relative to the Goddess model seemed elegant, and the beauty and consistency of the model appealed to both my mind and imagination.

There is also a devotional and religious aspect to Wicca that attunes the members of the group to the seasonal cycles of the Goddess through the medium of the rituals of the equinoxes and the solstices and the monthly lunar ceremonies. This strong earth orientation was something that High Magic seemed to lack. As I began practicing in a system of magic that combined an emotional and devotional aspect with a corpus of intellectual knowledge, I began to feel greater satisfaction in my spiritual work. Wicca seemed a better fit for me, and I experienced less doubt than I had done in my association with High Magic. The philosophical foundation of the Goddess model also had the capacity to address many of the problems and difficulties of the modern world. The Gaia hypothesis and deep ecology, for example, had clearly tapped into the energy of the archetype, and it seemed it could provide motive power for the needed paradigm shift—a way of looking at the world that was completely different and healthier.

Attunement to the cycles of the Earth Goddess creates an intimate and connected relationship with the natural world, especially as the rituals are usually performed in the open air at remote sites away from the eyes of the profane. I began to feel a close connection with the natural cycles of the Goddess. A deep connection with nature is the catalyst that enables the practitioner to intuit the deity that is present in all life, a kind of deep sensitivity to the Goddess energy as it courses through all aspects of the world of forms, nourishing and sustaining everything. It was familiar, too, in that it was the same feeling that I had experienced in early childhood: peace, safety, and connection to a benevolent spirit in nature. I experienced this energy as sparkling, joyful, and loving, although those adjectives seem too weak to communicate real insight and emphasize the limitations of English as a mystical language. Its essential nature is impersonal love. The Goddess is in love with her creation, and she is in all her creation; as Starhawk describes it, the Goddess

> is found only through love: love of trees, of stones, of sky and clouds, of scented blossoms and thundering waves; of all that runs and flies and swims and crawls on her face—each of us our own star, her child, her lover, her beloved, her self. (1999, 29)

Those who serve the Goddess are bound by her ethic to love and compassion, to respect all living things and to honor the life force.

I began to hear the voices of first the animal and then the plant life streams, and to have a series of strong dreams that explained symbolically my personal relationship with the Goddess. Having an understanding of the model of the Goddess and its corollary, the Shaman, helped me to accept these communications as valid. Gaining some understanding of the triune Goddess archetype also helped me to reframe some of my more negative life experiences as necessary adjuncts to spiritual learning and taught me some level of detachment and also some freedom from self-pity. Sometimes the importance of spiritual learning can be eclipsed by the emotional pain involved and may seem like divine persecution rather a pathway to wisdom, but that is a misunderstanding of the process of illumination and of the role of the Dark Goddess.

Living in a culture that has been dominated by the Christian concept of a judging and vengeful creator god who lives in heaven, apart from nature and humanity, it was liberating for me to come to terms with the profundity of the Goddess and her more tolerant ways. Life itself is a sacred ritual if we see it in a certain manner. It depends on our intention. Every element of life has its own purpose and destiny; that is learning. These ideas, as they complemented my experiences of the Elphame, translated easily into mundane reality. They began to permeate my ontological and epistemological position and to influence my work in the world.

Wiccan teaching is that although Divinity is fundamentally unchanging, everything in the observable cosmos, being subject to time, is in continuous flux. Time is measured by the recurring cycles of the stars, the sun, and the moon, which revolve in fixed and permanent orbits. Time, therefore, is not a linear process but is cyclic or spiraling. The seasonal cycles are symbolic of this change. In the world of form this change is visible. Things are born, live, and pass away, and new life begins another new cycle of birth, growth, and death. In humanity the individual life cycle expresses itself in terms of reincarnation, the process of physical and spiritual rebirth by which one achieves self-awareness, self-mastery, and the ability and willingness to live in accordance with spiritual law. This is a process of spiritual refinement gained through earthly experience. An embodied understanding of this process, I believe, made me a more compassionate, empathic, and effective healer, and yet having been touched by the Dark Goddess myself, perhaps paradoxically, a less sympathetic one.

Wicca is an intuitive path to spiritual insight that emphasizes the poetic and the creative. Wiccan rituals have a simple and natural beauty, and the sacred circle will often be decorated with flowers and flaming candles, and will also often be performed outdoors in a forest or grove. The rituals will often include music, singing and chanting, and dancing. Food and wine are usually shared after the ritual, and a libation and offerings are made to the Goddess. This sharing and socialization is considered an important part of the ritual—so important, in fact, that the sharing of the food and wine will sometimes take place within the sacred space and is regarded as a sacred thing in itself. It would be my guess that the Christian Eucharist derives from a race memory of a previous form of this ancient Pagan ceremony.

I found that being connected at this level with the sacred is an experience that is overwhelmingly sensuous and beautiful, and that the view of reality from that perspective is so different to the conventional Western view—much more like the worldview of indigenous people. The Australian Aboriginal people describe feeling like they are part of the land itself and that when the land is wounded they feel the pain as well, so profound is their connection. From the position of being psychically and emotionally embedded in the heart of nature, as a part of the intricate design of the natural world, I sometimes felt freed and at others alienated from my culture, which denies the sanctity of nature and elevates the human to the status of Divinity. I felt as though I had found the Grail, not in an absolute sense, but rather I had glimpsed it and knew of its existence, and because I understood a little of its power for transformation, I wanted to discover its application in the "real" world of flesh and blood.

Throughout my life I had, through an intuitive process of inquiry and lived experience, built a framework of understanding that was based on the following concepts:

- The investigation of oneself and the inner world was the gateway to a coherent understanding of outer reality. In other words, the personal microcosm reflects the cosmic macrocosm. The physical world is therefore symbolic of an inner nonphysical reality. This idea was to be confirmed by my later studies in magic.

- Death is an important mystery that holds the key to the meaning of life. The cyclic nature of the Goddess model, combined with my own lived experience, confirmed for me the validity of the cyclic process of transition between the physical and subtle worlds.

- Being connected to nature in some way is vital to physical, emotional, and mental health. The observable physical world rests upon a foundation that is intelligent, conscious, rational, and communicative. This is essentially an animistic worldview. As humans we are part of the integrated design and capable of communication with other life streams. The world talks to us if we know how to listen to it.

- Humanity is part of a vast tapestry of interlinking and interrelating designs, and not an isolated pattern that is separate from or superior to the rest of the cosmos. Things that we perceive as separate are actually energetically connected and related in a complex yet unified reality.

- The world is an enchanted, mysterious, and magical place that will reveal its many secret powers and energies to those who have the persistence and determination to unlock them. The secret world must be approached in a respectful and honoring attitude or there will be unwanted karmic consequences that will be applied in subsequent incarnations.

As an adult I studied and taught arcane science, but I saw it as something separate to mundane life. I now see that separation as a false division, and in the work in which I am now engaged I try to integrate and honor the two worlds in my practice as a teacher and a healer, inhabiting both realities and working from the place between.

3

The Great Goddess
and Her World

With Wisdom I have rightly put the universe in order. I, the
fiery life of Divine essence, am aflame beyond the beauty of
the meadows. I gleam in the waters, and I burn in the sun,
moon and stars. With every breeze, as with invisible life that
contains everything. I awaken everything to life. The air lives by
turning green and being in the blood. The waters flow as if
they were alive...and thus I remain hidden in every kind of
reality as a fiery power...I breathe life into everything so that
nothing is mortal in respect to its species. For I am life.
(Hildegard of Bingen)

THE GENDER OF THE Divine has been historically a dynamic phenomenon and subject to change in order to serve political, philosophical, as
well as social and religious ends. This fluidity is part of the evolution of
human cultures, as peoples mix and merge through migration and invasion. Newer deities that replace the old gods and goddesses are established either through a process of violent enforcement by the conquer-
ors or are willingly taken up through the process of proselytization.

Ideas about the Divine have evolved in line with cultural, intellectual, and philosophical changes, but not always for the better. The rise to dominance of monotheism, for example, precipitated conflict with polytheistic traditions and polarized conceptions of deity as masculine. This coincided largely with the rise of the herder cultures as described in the old testament of the Bible and as suggested by modern research (Mason, 1993).

My interest in reviving and "reinventing" the Goddess in our time is more than a response to my personal experiences. It also responds to a far wider human longing for a conception of the Divine that fits more closely to our own growing insights and intuitions about the nature of reality. The Goddess is a better model for our reawakening awareness of greater interconnectedness of lives and systems, and for articulating our growing ethical and moral awareness of the implications of our conduct; it is also more rational, in my view.

There is no absolute or consistent rule about whether the Divine should be viewed as God or Goddess, male or female. What is thought to be male in one tradition is female in another. In some cases, such as the Egyptian (Theban) Ogdoad, there were equal representations of male and female deities (four pairs of primary creative agencies). So what's the point now in thinking about the Divine in gendered terms? Why does it matter?

It matters in practical terms because we humans think in gendered terms. In the West, from the latter part of the nineteenth century there has been a steady impetus to drive gender equality—the demand for greater freedom for women to be self-determining. It is a struggle not yet fully resolved. Women are physiologically and psychologically different from men. As embodied beings we think differently, feel differently, value differently. So whether the Divine is seen as masculine or feminine has important implications for what is valued socially and how "the world" in general is to be understood.

There is some contention about the historical rise of masculine energy, and whether the dominance of men transformed the conception of the Divine from primarily feminine to masculine. This is not an area where there can be proof positive. For me, however, the logic is compelling. After at least four millennia of male domination the tide is turning, and so it is vitally important that we rediscover the nature of the feminine divine.

Christianity brought the Abrahamic tradition into Europe, displacing a native tradition we now struggle to understand and appreciate, but evidence suggests that it most likely was feminocentric and magical. Christianity asserted the dominance of Jaweh or Jehovah, a masculinist and singular god apparently intolerant of rivals or equals. This is the model of the herd animal in which a single male dominates. The herd or horned god is present in the ancient European traditions as well, but not as singular or dominant agency. The feminine divine balances it. The shift to monotheism in the Abrahamic tradition is little remarked upon except that it is often thought of historically and theologically as an advance in religious thinking. However, it sprang from a polytheistic foundation in which male and female divinities constituted a complex philosophical, ontological, and epistemological order. The deity of Genesis is plural, one of a number. Then, quite suddenly and confusingly in the same account, there is only one God.

As Christianity evolved it cemented the position of a single male deity and in doing so set masculinist thought as the center of the faith. The feminine was not eliminated but relegated to a subservient status under the control of the masculine. That relegation at the level of religion permeated our culture and became "divinely" ordained as an expression of sacred will. This is true of all the religions of the book—Christianity, Islam, and Judaism.

I do not intend my work to be political, but it is beyond doubt that our world is adversely subjected to an excess of masculine energy, and a corrective must come. That corrective has been steadily emerging over the past two centuries, but it has a long way to go as yet. In this sense it is difficult to separate the political from the magical.

My conception of the Goddess as a primary gendered expression of the Divine is an attempt to create an intellectual as well as an intuitive pathway through which long-suppressed attributes of the sacred reality can flow into consciousness as a source of guidance and inspiration to those who know there is a need to bring restoration of balance and harmony to the human worldview. I think that on the level of the race memory or the collective unconscious, there exists a deep recognition of the reality of the Goddess that drives what seems to be an ever increasing desire in the Western world to rediscover the living world of spirit and magic that surpasses the dreary intellectual world created by the scientific materialistic thought police who seek to denigrate and destroy that expanding public awareness.

In the Western magical tradition the universe is considered to be a two-tiered system that interlinks physical and nonphysical reality, as they coexist as a vast sea of consciousness energy. This great matrix of potential and kinetic creative energy is known and honored as the Great Goddess. The myriad differentiated forms existing within the divine, infinite ocean of energy are diverse manifestations of the one consciousness, individuated and vibrating or pulsating at particular wavelengths, giving the physical appearance of stability, individuality, and separation but whose essential and deeper character is constant change and dynamic fluidic adjustment. In the spirit or energy world, these individuated forms reveal their true nature as energetic and interconnected and not as separated things. Relationship is therefore a foundational cosmic principle.

Observed from the perspective of the strong eye (the inner vision), the whole appears as a vast web of interconnected and interrelated living energy linking everything. Events that influence one aspect of the web of energy therefore influence the whole, and so the web is in a continual state of flux and adjustment.

Rosalind Heywood, who was a psychic sensitive, writer, researcher, and colleague of Niels Bohr, describes a personal mystical encounter with the anthropomorphic form of the Goddess dressed in blues, mauves, and purples and also describes the difficulty she had in finding the words to relate her experience. Her visionary experience gives an understanding of the shifting nature of the interconnecting web of energy. From the shamanic place between the two worlds that she observed, Heywood wrote that

> everything seemed to be in a sphere...and where objects were not only perceived from the outside but in their "becomingness"...one appeared to experience relationships...that interrelatedness was symbolized by a delicate spidery web, like the filaments on a cactus which

linked everything to everything, from atom to nebula...Nothing was static. The entire universe was in constant fluid movement...then... there appeared a supreme figure, motionless, eternally at peace...the ultimate still point at which all movement ceased. [These were] the two great opposites, stillness and movement, on which the life of the Universe depends. (1966, 233)

In this vision all dualities seemed to be resolved, and such opposites as near and far and up and down did not exist. The Great Goddess seems to resolve all dualities. Everything is united in the one.

Heywood's mystical experience of a Divinity that was simultaneously transcendent and immanent continued as she mentally framed a question while at the same time observing what was happening. She telepathically asked inwardly whether what she was observing was a mechanistic process or something that had consciousness and purpose, and whether that purpose, if it existed, had something to do with love. The reply that came gave her an insight into the paradoxical nature of impersonal love, which she struggles to articulate. In my experience impersonal love is not "cold," as she suggests on page 236 of *The Infinite Hive*. It is more like compassion and quite different to personal love that is expressed as emotional love and attachment, or sexual "love." To clarify these divisions, I would suggest that impersonal love exists at the level of the heart, emotional love at the level of the solar plexus, and sexual love at the level of the reproductive organs.

The love of the Goddess by its nature is impersonal but not cold. Heywood says that she had a vision of the Great Mother Goddess who shifted her alignment to more match that of Divinity to give some understanding of both the nature of the creative impulse and of the "impersonal" love that drove it. Heywood described the way she experienced divine impersonal love as personal and reassuring (1966, 236), which made me think that we would all experience divine love as warm and personal even if there was nothing sentimental about it.

The high priestess of the Wiccan group, because she consciously carries the energy of the Goddess, is also sometimes called the Queen of Elphame. Sometimes contact with the Goddess can be a very personal experience. For example, through a series of rituals I conducted as the ceremonial high priestess, I saw an anthropomorphic image of the Goddess appear as a woman dressed in robes of pale blue and mauve. She first appeared in the distance standing and watching and gradually drew closer to the sacred circle as the cycle of rituals proceeded. Finally she was standing just outside the sacred circle, apparently closely observing what was happening. This visionary experience was not as dramatic as that described by Heywood, but the imagery is close and the vision assured me that the Goddess takes an interest in ceremonies conducted in her name.

From a magical perspective all forms contain consciousness and all consciousness evolves through form in an individual way. (In fact, through my process of inquiry, I am coming to believe even more strongly that consciousness is the Goddess.) Everything manifesting in material form is filled with life force.

Marija Gimbutas, an archaeologist and researcher into the beliefs and symbolism of the ancient Goddess-worshipping communities, describes the way she understands that subtle energy, or the life force, permeates everything in the physical world. It is very close to Hildegard's description:

> Everything born from the earth is brimming with life force. Flower, tree, stone, hill, human, and animal alike are born from the earth and all possess her strength. Sacred groves, meadows, rivers, leafy trees, and gnarled contorted trees growing together from several stumps are particularly charged with life. The Earth Mother creates a cover for the earth that is lush, blossoming, and enchanted. (1989, 159)

But the externalization of the life force into the physical world is impermanent and cyclic, both in an individual sense as well as the whole of the physical world. In the individual sense at the moment of each death, it withdraws into the Elphame and the physical form disintegrates into its elemental constituents of earth, fire, water, and air. These are the building blocks of form and will be reconstituted into further and newer physical materializations that will be revivified by the life force. Thus the cycle of death and rebirth proceeds. The withdrawal of life energy into the Elphame can be interrupted, as several of the research subjects will describe in greater detail, and individual entities can remain stuck between the worlds, unable to move forward by either moving into the subtle world to reorganize and prepare for a further incarnation or by somehow creating another physical body from the materials available. The attempts by those who have died but are too afraid to move completely into the subtle reality can create bizarre attempts to construct another physical body and to remain in the earth sphere.

The Elphame

The Elphame is the foundational subtle reality. The etymology of the term is not completely clear, although it most likely comes from the Old Norse and can be found in that form in the *Eddur*, or Icelandic sagas. The thirteenth-century Norse poet and mythographer Snorri Sturluson describes Alfheim as a magical realm and the home of the Alfar, or the Light Elves. The term later transformed into Elphame and appears in that form in several Scots and English ballads in reference to the otherworld or the Faerie realm. These ballads include the seventeenth-century "Ballad of Thomas the Rhymer" (Quiller-Couch, 1919), a poem about a thirteenth-century Scottish prophetic and visionary figure known as True Thomas, who claimed to have visited the magical world and encountered the mythological Queen of Elphame.

Elphame literally means "Elf-home," or the Faerie realm, and it is a term traditionally and now widely used by Celtic-influenced Craft groups when referring to the subtle reality. In the Celtic pantheon the Queen of Elphame was the goddess of death and rebirth, which also makes "Elphame" a probable reference to reincarnation. In her role as goddess of death and rebirth she symbolizes the nature of reality and existence as cyclic or spiraling: all things die in order that they may be reborn on a higher turn of the cosmic spiral. This then suggests not only that humanity is reborn in the sense of reincarnation, but also that the whole of physical existence operates on this cyclic mode of coming in and going out of physical manifestation over vast periods of time. It is a kind of cosmic exhalation and inhalation.

On the microcosmic or human level the Hermetic axiom "as above, so below" suggests that periodically individual human lives also go through cycles of manifestation into the physical world and reciprocal withdrawal into the nonphysical world. I believe that ideas about reincarnation within Witchcraft come from its ancient Druidic roots, but also through more recent contact with Eastern influences, which have been absorbed through the influential work of magicians like Aleister Crowley, Gerald Gardner, and Dion Fortune, who successfully blended elements of Eastern and Western magical theory and practice to create an eclectic modern magical corpus (Crowley 1973, Farrar and Farrar 1989). Most modern groups involved with Druidry, including the Order of Bards, Ovates and Druids, agree that the ancient Druids taught the twin concepts of reincarnation and karma. Modern Druidic groups also believe in and teach these two mutually supporting ideas.

Master A has said that in the distant past only the initiates were given the full story of reincarnation and cycles of karma, and that the ordinary people were told a story that was something like the belief in nirvana, where after death the soul travels to a beautiful, peaceful place in the world of spirit to rest and recuperate after experiencing the difficulties and vicissitudes of physical life. They were not told what happens after this repose in paradise. It was thought that if they understood that further physical lives were to be lived, they would become depressed and discouraged. To the initiated, every new life was a fresh opportunity to grow spiritually; to the ordinary person, it would be seen as a further earthly burden, or so they thought. As the ancient Egyptians believed, "Milk for babes and meat for men."

I had previously believed that once an entity had reached the status of being human that he or she could not regress to a "lower" life stream. However, my little toy poodle Mimi told me when she was three months old that she had once been a person but she had done a lot of naughty things, and now because of that she had to learn to be the "perfect dog" before she could once again enter the human life stream. It made me think that transmigration from one life stream to another through the process of reincarnation is a distinct possibility. It also reinforced the idea that animals are often in a teaching role to we dumb humans.

I see the evolution of form as a means for the expression of consciousness and not as an end in itself, as evolutionary biology would have us believe. This is essentially an animistic and evolutionary view of reality in

that all living forms are considered to be centers of energy and consciousness, and from this point of view are symbols of a deeper spiritual reality.

The Qabalistic name for the Elphame is Yesod, translated into English
as "the foundation." It is the plane of dreams, imagination, intuition, and
emotion. It is the level of reality where magical effects are created before
being manifested into the physical world. Compared to the physical
world, it is composed of fine and fluid "matter," and according to the
Qabalah the element sacred to the Elphame is water, reflecting its flowing
and incorporeal nature. At many sites throughout Europe valuable offerings to the divine world—swords, shields, carriages, and other precious
metal objects—have been found in bodies of water, carefully placed there
in a ritual manner (Fagan 1996, 379; Konstamm 2003, 62–63; Scribner
2004, 67–69).

Professor Brian Bates, who has researched the religious and magical
beliefs and practices of the ancient Celtic and Anglo-Saxon societies of
the Wyrd, writes that

> water is sacred to the Goddess; without water there is no life, so heal-
> ing wells, pools, springs, streams, lakes, and the seas are her natural
> symbolic habitat. (2002, 136)

According to Bates, images of body parts have also been retrieved
from ancient wells, springs, pools, and rivers in many parts of Europe,
indicating that ancient people sought healing from the sacred waters.
The similarities with the Virgin Mary are obvious, particularly in her
aspect as Our Lady of Lourdes and other healing sites associated with
water. In Europe there are many hundreds of rivers, springs, and water-
ways named for divinities. Bates says that

> every spring, every woodland brook, every river in glen or valley, the
> roaring cataract, and the lake were haunted by divine beings, mainly
> thought of as beautiful females and associated with the Earth
> Mother...Our ancestors saw reflected in their waterways...metaphori-
> cal images of their psyches; essences of their souls, even the very
> grounding of existence, the flowing of life in which they were a mere
> droplet in an ocean of meaning. Water washed, purified and con-
> nected them with profound forces of life. Waters were sacred. (2002,
> 90)

But the images are also cross-cultural. For example, the Rainbow Serpent of Australian Aboriginal mythology, a feminine deity, lives in a watery environment. Clearly the symbolism is consistent with the common elements and motifs associated with the Goddess of distant cultures: the serpent and water and a rainbow "bridge" that joins the two worlds, reiterating the universality of important features of Goddess imagery and meaning.

For many ancient cultures water was the primary cosmic element out of which the manifest world had sprung. The earliest Greek philosopher, Thales, believed that water was the originating element of nature. In the Egyptian tradition the world arose from a great primal sea, Nu or Nun, as I understand it. The evidence of this ancient belief remains in Christianity, in chapter one of the book of Genesis: "Darkness was over the surface of the deep, and the spirit of God was hovering over the face of the waters" (New King James Version). Here the masculine energy (God) is counterposed to the feminine (the waters of the deep).

The Queen of Elphame is the Great Goddess, the conscious and organizing intelligence behind the world of forms. Her fluid and watery energy sustains the world of form. The Goddess is the Elphame.

The Cosmic Goddess and Her Lower Analogue, the Earth Goddess

As Heywood described her vision of the fine filaments connecting everything in existence, it becomes clear why the Hopi refer to the Great Goddess as the cosmic Spider Woman. She is the creator of the energetic web of life, or rather of created forms, but also the interconnecting web of life itself is made from her own substance. The Goddess is, therefore, perhaps surprisingly close to her creation, both the Weaver and the Web—not a remote deity living in rarefied and celestial separation from the created world, transcending earthly life, but an intrinsic, inseparable part of everything that is, including the human psyche. She is a Divinity that is both transcendent and immanent. It is because of the intimate connection of the Goddess and her creation that it is difficult to write about the Goddess as separate from humanity. She exists in us physically, emotionally, mentally, and spiritually; we are her creatures, and as we live in her, so she lives in us, even though in most people the spark of Divinity that signifies her presence remains an unconscious potential.

She is sometimes known as the Goddess of Death and Disease, who is often equated in Witchcraft and in the Western magical tradition with Hecate, the Greek goddess of magic and the dark side of the moon. She rules over the hidden wisdom, death, destruction, plague, battle, the otherworld, rebirth, and contact with the foundational reality. In this aspect she is very much a part of the tradition of the Crone or Dark Goddess that includes Sekhmet, Persephone, Kali, Sophia, and other wisdom goddesses. The Crone is a positive aspect of the Goddess that I associate with the hidden wisdom or the occult, although in the vulgar mind she is associated with everything that is negative: the ugly old witch with the pointy nose, dressed in black, who wreaks disease, death, and disaster upon humanity.

We don't like karma and don't see it as a necessity because we don't understand the process of reincarnation. We see the Goddess who oversees karma and reincarnation as "dark" and destructive. We do not see her as a beautiful necessity and welcome her as the bringer of wisdom—as the archetypal Grandmother of humanity. The Crone archetypes represent for women wisdom, power, and holiness, and also karma or responsibility. She is fully conscious and differentiated from the unconscious forces of instinct and reproduction.

As human consciousness has evolved over eons, our understanding of Divinity has evolved in tandem. Humanity has traditionally described its deities in accordance with its developing understanding of itself and the world, appropriately clothing the images of its lesser gods and goddesses in cultural forms that are limited by human comprehension of the Divine. The magical archetypes (which exist outside the human mind and are different to those hypothesized by Jung) therefore become more meaningful as our consciousness expands, and we struggle with a limited understanding and a limited vocabulary to describe our experience of the ineffable. We are not creating it. We invent and reinvent our conceptions of Divinity. The Great Goddess of modern Wicca is the same deity worshipped by the people of the European Upper Paleolithic (Gimbutas 1989), but different, as we interpret her in the scientific and ecological language of our time.

She remains the one deity, although she is sometimes seen in triune form (see page 80), but Divinity has many traditional aspects and lesser forms. Witch high priest and priestess Stuart and Janet Farrar say that

> such advances as herd raising, agriculture, and the development of human society inspired mankind's god-form concepts. Time-measuring, wisdom, vegetation, war and craftsman gods and goddesses evolved in step with human evolution. Which does not, we must emphasize, mean that these deities were man-made or unreal, they were and are channels [aspects] and tuning signals to cosmic reality. In the end we are all tuning to the same source. (1989, 3)

It is Caitlín Matthews' contention (1991, 3) that the Old Goddess did not completely fade away during the period of Christian hegemony and that she has never really been completely abandoned because even in the most masculinist and patriarchal of the Judeo-Christian religions there remain strong forensic evidence and traces of her presence. She has been fragmented and dismembered, but she is nothing if not persistent and flexible: a shapeshifter who transmutes herself into new cultural forms.

Marina Warner, a feminist writer and researcher into the cult of the Virgin Mary, also takes this view and contends that the figure of the Virgin Mary is modeled on Isis, the all-powerful, magic-working Mother Goddess of the Egyptians. The ancient image of the Goddess as life giver and Earth Mother gradually became fused with the image of the Virgin Mary mainly due to upward pressure from congregations who were upset by the lack of a feminine aspect of the Divine in the church's teachings.

Warner maintains that the Catholic Queen of Heaven, the Mother of God, like her predecessor the Great Goddess, is still connected with all life-giving waters and miraculously healing and restorative springs and waters (like Lourdes, for example), with trees and blossoms, with fruits and harvests, with animals, and with women, health, and fertility. She is the life force in all but name. The Virgin Mary was officially named Theotokos (mother of God) by the third ecumenical council of the Roman church in Ephesus in 431 CE—ironic because Ephesus was the great cult center of the Great Goddess Artemis/Diana. The Great Virgin Goddess, Herself Alone, was believed to have begun the process of creation by an act of parthenogenesis, with no masculine involvement. "Herself Alone" is a term I use to describe the one creator Goddess of the worlds. Marija Gimbutas describes the Earth Goddess's healing powers through the medium of water:

> Being an owner of wells, springs, and healing waters, she was a miraculous bestower of health. (Gimbutas in Muses and Campbell 1991, 47)

Like so much of the Bible, the story of Genesis seems to have been borrowed from an older Pagan Goddess tradition, and although the editors and writers of the Bible sought to eradicate them, traces of the Old Religion inadvertently and at times surprisingly appear in biblical writings. In the Bible the Goddess appears as the Virgin Mary, the mother of God; as Sophia, Goddess of Wisdom; and possibly in the figure of Eve, the Mother of All. The apple is a Goddess symbol, after all. The writers and editors of the Judeo-Christian Bible seem to have unconsciously retained the basic triune nature of the archetype, and the Old Goddess has therefore exerted her influence on Western culture, albeit at the level of the unconscious.

Mary Condren, a writer and researcher into the Goddess tradition, says her investigations suggest that its Judaic interpreters distorted the story of Genesis and that Eve and the serpent were one and the same entity symbolizing rebirth. She says that

> there is weighty evidence that the figure of Eve is based on much older stories in Near Eastern mythology and that the original Eve did appear in the form of a serpent. The name Eve, Hawwah, means mother of all the living, but Hawwah also means serpent in many Semitic languages.
>
> The image of the serpent is found frequently on the artifacts of the Ancient Near East, Sumerian and Akkadian etc. The serpent was the symbol of immortality (reincarnation)[;] as the serpent sloughs off its skin, so the human sloughs off the physical body at the end of life... (1989, 7)

Sloughing the skin for the serpent is a cyclic process that occurs when necessary, and in the same manner the "sloughing" of the human body at death is also cyclic, with necessity determined by fate and karma.

The original serpent, it appears, was not the malevolent and diabolical creature the Judeo-Christian tradition would have us believe, and it seems that a political spin that served the purposes of the patriarchy was placed on the original Babylonian and Sumerian creation myths from which the biblical story was derived. The serpent was the premier symbol of the Goddess, and it seems everything feminine was hated, reviled, and disempowered, but the inner reality is something quite different.

Throughout time the serpent symbol has represented both positive and adverse agencies, sometimes being transformed from one to the other. For example, the biblical serpent guardian of the tree of life was recast as the diabolical tempter of Eve in the Christian tradition, thus transforming Eve from an oracular role as a knowledge giver to being a weak creature incapable of clear and moral thought—a negative archetype transferred in the misogynistic masculinist tradition to all women.

Caitlín Matthews stresses the importance of the Goddess in mysticism and maintains that the major mystics of all Christian faiths have perceived Sophia, the Crone or Wisdom aspect of the Great Goddess, as the connecting bridge between physical life and the world of the eternal. In the initiatory Pagan tradition we meet the Goddess in her role as the wayshower and initiator into the mysteries. She is the Goddess of shamanism and of magic, whom every seeker of the truth must encounter. She opens the way or illuminates the path if she so chooses, but the price the seeker must pay is the overcoming of fear and ego. Matthews touches on the subject of magical initiation and its potential for changing ontological perspectives and giving psychological benefit, but she also takes up the theme of how those beneficial experiences are dismissed and invalidated by the dominant cultural discourse:

> The way of Sophia is the way of personal experience. It takes us into ways we may call magical reality—those creative realms to which ordinary mortals are called. However, the poetic, the magical, the creative inscapes of vision are often denied us by our culture. Anyone who has ever been into the world of vision knows that its power can enhance our lives. (1991, 17)

Personal contact with the Goddess often brings about a more thoughtful and refined spirituality, a shifting of values and life purpose, an opening of the heart, and a heightened compassion for every existent being. These profound personal changes lead to a deepened understanding of humanity's place in the universal schema and reconciliation between the earth and human responsibility.

The Goddess, being the single source of all created life, controls the mysteries of life, death, and renewal or regeneration. This is not a static or single creation. It is ruled by the laws of cycles, or rather of spirals, which are symbols of the evolution of consciousness and the fundamental template of the dynamic tension of living forms, from the cell to the galaxy. The inner reality of the constant motion of the spiral form creates the illusion of stability in the physical world, as Heywood's vision indicates. Gimbutas says: "The spiral or the serpent force is the Goddess's energy" (in C. Matthews 1991, 122).

In the introduction to *The Language of the Goddess*, Gimbutas discusses the meaning of the dynamism of the glyphs and symbols she believes are associated with the Goddess-worshipping cultures of ancient Europe. She says:

> In art this is manifested by the signs of dynamic motion: whirling and twisting spirals, winding and coiling snakes, circles, crescents, horns, sprouting seeds and shoots. The snake was a symbol of life energy and regeneration, a most benevolent and not an evil creature. (1989, xix)

Other ancient symbols and images of the Goddess, associated with her worship, are a white bird or bird-woman or water-bird, the frog, the spider, a white dove or white crane, the owl, the chalice or cauldron, the lily, and the rose or the rose cross. These powerful symbols reappear in dreams of modern people, as my dreams will attest, and as symbols in art and in mystical visions and meditations, announcing her persistent presence in our culture, no matter how hard we may try to rationally suppress her.

To Pagan cultures she was, as well, "Mistress of Animals" and of all nature, and mountains, forests, caves, crevices, caverns, and menhirs or standing stones are sacred to her.

The Triune Archetype

All goddesses are aspects of the one Great Cosmic Goddess some-times portrayed in triple form. I believe that ancient, preliterate people took the moon in its three phases to be a clear symbol of the Goddess in her three phases that we describe today as the Maiden, the Mother, and the Crone. These three gradually merge and blend into one another according to the law of repeating cycles so that the Great Goddess can be seen as the three in one. Suspended in the darkness of the night sky, the pale and gleaming moon must have seemed like a divine glyph pregnant with meaning to ancient people. She is born, matures, and dies with per-petual regularity, as all things in the visible world follow the same repeat-ing cyclic pattern of birth or creation, maintenance for a time, and then destruction. This is the basic pattern, template, or archetype for all life in the physical world. Forms dissipate and die to be reborn and regenerated in new forms that are the containers of the eternal life force.

It is important to give an interpretation of the triune archetype of the Goddess. Firstly, because several of the research subjects' lives were touched by one or other of the various putative aspects of the Goddess archetype, and secondly, because the idea of the trinity has been deeply influential in Christianity and other world religions. It does not take a huge mental leap to see how it is possible that the tripartite image of the ancient Moon Goddess has had a conceptual influence on the Indo-Euro-pean and Judeo-Christian religions, although over the eons these trinities have been given a gender reassignment. For example, the Father, Son, and Holy Ghost of Christianity, or the Brahma (Creator), Vishnu (Pre-server), and Shiva (Destroyer) trinity of Hinduism are, I believe, mascu-linized trinities that postdate the Triune Goddess and approximate her different aspects and powers. The Christian idea of a divine trinity must have come from somewhere, and as that faith has clearly appropriated much of the Pagan tradition, I would argue that the trinity itself has been appropriated from the Pagan tradition as well. The spiritual and psycho-logical truths of the archetype are cosmic and individual, impersonal and personal: as above, so below.

Carlo Ginzberg, an Italian professor of history, says in his book *Ecsta-sies* that his research into Witchcraft strongly indicates the widespread veneration of the Triple Goddess amongst the Celtic people during the Iron Age, approximately from 1200 BCE to 1 BCE in Europe.

Expression of Divinity in triune form is common from India to Ireland in traditional and archaic cultures, with male, female and male, and female deities making up a trinity. The idea of the triple goddess in its contemporary Neopagan and Wiccan form is the product of research and intuitive or inspired interpretation. The extent to which it is a fair interpretation of history is disputed and impossible to confirm one way or another. I share the powerful feelings of those who respond with deep intuitive appeal for the Triple Goddess of Virgin, Mother, and Crone. To the Paleolithic observers and the ancient readers of the natural world, the night sky demonstrated the truth of this most powerful glyph of the Great Goddess. Not only the moon but also the sun can be viewed as a triptych, as evidenced by the Celtic awen symbol, which represents the three positions of the sun as viewed as the summer and winter solstices and the equinoxes as viewed from the earth at the same position.

I find it interesting and informative to hear the voices of the three aspects of the archetypes as they speak to us through the world of literature. The first aspect of the triune archetype, symbolized by the new moon, the Virgin Goddess/Maiden/Herself Alone is not owned by the masculine and does not need it as co-creator. She creates everything, and everything flows from her. This is the aspect of the Goddess that was powerful before human beings were fully aware of the creative relationship between sexuality and pregnancy.

Psychologically, the archetype represents to a woman the power of finding her true self and of being her own person. To a man it represents the search for the anima, the inner feminine power of the soul, his muse, and the attainment of his inspiration and creativity. She appears alluring but also self-contained, enigmatic, remote, mysterious, and unattainable. She is all-powerful, creating out of her own substance by a process of parthenogenesis. Examples of the virgin goddesses who were powerful in their own right are Diana/Artemis, Athena, Brigit, Isis, and Cybele. I have included Isis because she can be seen as Herself Alone and also as a matrona as well as a crone or wisdom goddess of medicine and magic in her role of teacher and protector. These cross-cultural forms do not exactly equate with each other, but as Herself Alone they are examples from different cultural backgrounds of the same idea—that the Great Goddess is the sole creator, maintainer, and ultimately the destroyer of the manifested worlds.

In Lucius Apuleius's *Golden Ass* (second century CE), the author invokes the Great Goddess as Isis—Herself Alone. As she appears to him, she says:

> Here I am, Lucius, roused by your prayers. I am the mother of the world of Nature, mistress of all the elements, first-born in this realm of time. I am the loftiest of deities, queen of departed spirits, foremost of heavenly dwellers, the single embodiment of all gods and goddesses. I order with my nod the luminous heights of heaven, the healthy sea breezes, the sad silences of the infernal dwellers. The whole world worships this single godhead under a variety of shapes and liturgies and titles. (Walsh translation 1994, 220)

The Muses translation of these lines from *In All Her Names* is more stately, sonorous, and powerful:

> Behold, Lucius, I am come...I, the true mother of all things, mistress of all divine powers, manifesting under one form all other gods and goddesses. At my will the celestial bodies move through the heavens, and the winds, and yea, the abysses of hell are commanded. My divinity is worshipped by many people under different names. (Muses and Campbell 1991, 49)

The second aspect is the Mother archetype, symbolized by the full moon. She is the fertilized goddess, the earth goddess of materialization, whose counterpart is the masculine principle, the solar, phallic God.

She is the fecund, preserving, sustaining, and nurturing "Mother of All Living," the aspect of the Great Goddess seen in the figure of the many-breasted Diana or the many figures of goddesses nursing infants, like the images of Isis nursing Horus. She is also to be found in the many pietà images of the Goddess holding the dying, sacrificed God, such as Inanna mourning the dying Tammuz (in one particular version of the myth), Aphrodite mourning the dying Adonis, Isis holding Horus and mourning Osiris, or the Virgin Mary cradling the dead Christ. The Queen of Earth as well as Heaven, she is eternal. She nurtures her creation by absorbing the energy of the sacrificed gods—the sons, brothers, and lovers of the Great Mother who die to be reborn and once again expend their energy in an act of sacrificial love and fecundity that allows creation its continued existence (incidentally suggesting that the masculine principle is inherently unstable and that its true role is to serve the life force).

Emotionally and psychologically, the Earth Mother, the matrona, represents the mature woman of knowledge, earthy sexuality, pregnancy, and nurturance. In the individual human psyche this archetype also represents the balancing of the masculine and feminine powers. These two powers are like the two complementary terminals of the great cosmic battery; without their interactive polarity, true creativity is not possible. The feminine principle represents intuition and inspiration, synthesis, and relatedness. It is formative, nurturing, cyclic, and related to the unconscious. The masculine principle is logical, linear, analytical, and fertilizing, emphasizing ego consciousness and individuality.

Together they give an understanding of the relationship of self to other, or, as gestalt psychology describes it, the figure and the field, the darkness and the light, the conscious and the unconscious. They are not mutually exclusive. As the Chinese symbol of the Tao indicates, the dark feminine power, or yin, contains the seed of the bright masculine power, or yang, and the bright yang contains the seed of the dark, cool yin. If this were not so, there could be no point of relationship, and each power would theoretically remain separate, sterile, and unrelated to the other.

As individuals, as we incarnate in either feminine or masculine form. We express one of the great powers consciously and physically, and the other indirectly and unconsciously. Witchcraft teaches that on the physical level of existence the masculine is active and the feminine is passive. This is expressed sexually, as the male impregnates the female. She receives the seed and nurtures the fetus in the Grail or womb in a manner that is observably passive. On the subtle spiritual level of existence, however, the polarity is reversed: the feminine is active and the masculine is passive and receptive. This is the reason why in Witchcraft groups the high priestess leads: she has, theoretically, the direct connection with the world of spirit. In the human psyche this means that it is important to be guided by our dreams, inspiration, and intuition, our heart, but to cross-reference what we think, feel, and do, using the intellectual powers of logical thinking, planning, and physical manifestation.

In the Goddess and shaman traditions, the heart leads and the head follows. In this way we know how to live, and our lives have meaning and purpose. We understand how the individual fits into the greater spiritual whole. We have empathy and compassion for all life. In patriarchal cultures this natural expression of polarity is reversed, and we can see the results of that mistake all around us.

Within these chosen lines of the famous *Charge of the Goddess* written by Doreen Valiente, which is spoken by the high priestess and high priest at the beginning of many Wiccan ceremonies, the joyful and sensuous voice of the Earth Goddess is clearly discernible:

> For mine is the ecstasy of the spirit and mine also is joy on earth; for my Law is Love unto all Beings...I am the Gracious Goddess, who gives the gift of joy unto the heart...Upon earth, I give the knowledge of the spirit eternal...Nor do I demand sacrifice for behold I am the Mother of All Living and my love is poured out upon the earth...I, who am the beauty of the green earth, and the white Moon among the stars, and the mystery of the waters and the heart's desire, call unto thy soul. Arise and come unto me. (doreenvaliente.com/Doreen-Valiente-Poetry-11.php)

The Crone, the third aspect of the triptych, is both the distiller of wisdom and the wielder of the silver sickle. She knows both the ugliness and the beauty of existence. She is the mistress of life and death, the keeper and teacher of the mysteries, and the ultimate initiator. Her embrace means death but also renewed life, and as far as magical initiation goes, it means death of the ego, and not necessarily of the physical self. In visions she may appear as an ugly, malevolent, and fearsome old hag, but when her black veil is lifted, her true nature is revealed to be that of a laughing, beauteous, and benevolent girl who is full of life. She may appear as old and feeble in body; this appearance is deceptive, as she is strong and powerful in spiritual wisdom. Always, she is a paradox and an enigma. Assume nothing!

Sophia, or the Goddess of Wisdom as she appears in the Bible and the Apocrypha, is clearly an aspect of the Crone archetype and has had an enigmatic influence on our Western psyches. I have included the following quotations relating to the Crone because I have found them especially illuminating when I have applied them to my own journey as a seeker and to the initiatory and spiritual journeys of many of the people I interviewed for this book.

Caitlín Matthews, whose particular interest is in the hidden influences of the three aspects of the Goddess, discovers her in the biblical book of Proverbs, where she speaks with the harsh voice of the Dark Goddess of karma, suffering, death, and destruction and the "reborn" or "reawakened" experience of initiation:

> Because I have called, and ye refused; I have stretched out my hand, and no man regarded;
> But ye have set at nought all my counsel, and would none of my reproof:
> I also will laugh at your calamity; I will mock when your fear cometh;
> When your fear cometh as desolation, and your destruction cometh as a whirlwind; when distress and anguish cometh upon you.
> Then shall they call upon me, but I will not answer; they shall seek me early, but they shall not find me. (New King James Version, Proverbs 1:24–1:28)

At least, they will not find her until fear and self-doubt has been overcome and a level of inner strength, independence, and psychological resilience has been achieved. Then, paradoxically, the path finds the seeker.

In the invocations to the Great Goddess written by the witch and high priestess Vivianne Crowley, the Crone as the black Isis in her third-degree initiation ritual once again instructs the seeker:

> What you seek is perilous to you;
> for you must journey to my hidden temple.
> Through danger and difficulty
> you must make your way and falter not
> and only then can I reveal myself unto you.
> Look upon me!
> Secret am I,
> and none may penetrate my mystery...

I am fierce and terrible to behold;
dark is my countenance and stern my words;
yet fear me not,
for dark and terrible,
I am yet thy Goddess.
Approach me with love
and I will reveal myself unto you. (1996, 230–231)

The darkness turns to light when the apparently harsh Goddess of Karma transforms herself into the Goddess of Light—as the moon transforms itself through its phases from darkness to light and then back to darkness again. In Proverbs, the alter ego of the dark Goddess of Karma can be seen in her phase as the Goddess of Light and Wisdom. One transforms into the other and back again once the seeker sees her more clearly:

She is more precious than rubies,
And all the things you may desire cannot compare with her.
Length of days is in her right hand,
In her left hand riches and honor.
Her are ways of pleasantness,
And all her paths are peace.
She is a tree of life to those who take hold of her,
And happy are all who retain her. (New King James Version, Proverbs 3.15–3.18)

Marion Woodman, a Jungian analyst, and co-author Elinor Dickson, a clinical psychologist, give a detailed exposition of the revival of the Dark Goddess in their book *Dancing in the Flames*, but they interpret the Crone as Herself Alone and make a case for that interpretation. They believe the Maiden can be interpreted as the unconscious form of Herself Alone, while the Crone is the fully conscious aspect. They say the Crone psychologically

is the part of a woman's psyche that is not identified with any relationship nor confined by any bond. She infuses an intrinsic sense of self-worth, of autonomy…and gives the woman strength to stand to her own creative experience. (1996, 134)

Their thesis is consistent and interesting, but traditionally the tripartite image of the Goddess has followed the dynamic phases of the moon (waxing—full—waning).

On more of a spiritual and less of a psychological note, among the biblical Apocrypha is a document called *Sirach* (the full title is *Ecclesiasticus or the Wisdom of Jesus, the Son of Sirach*), written probably around 190 BCE. The writer tells of the ordeals, tests, and initiations meted out to those who seek to walk the "Path of the Wise" and to "raise the veil" of the Goddess. Material from it was later incorporated into Christian liturgical texts such as the eighth-century *Little Office of Our Lady*, and strengthens the idea of Mary as being cognate with the feminine presence of Wisdom in the Old Testament.

In her role as initiator and spiritual instructor, "Wisdom," like her lower analogue the Soul, stands by and will not intervene as the seeker learns the painful lessons of responsibility and self-awareness because we do not come to Wisdom unless it is by experience, which is mediated by the Dark Goddess. If we respect the Dark Goddess, we will eventually come to understand Wisdom, or Sophia. She loves humanity, but like a good and loving mother she is not always indulgent. Sometimes she must be detached and strict while allowing her children to do the necessary painful learning in order that they may grow spiritually. I have looked at several translations of the *Sirach* documents and prefer the translation used by Caitlín Matthews because I believe it is more powerfully poetic than the other translations.

The *Sirach* document of Hebrew Pagan origin says Wisdom is the companion of all flesh, but her ways are harsh and laborious. She applies the tests and ordeals that lead to initiation:

> For at first she will walk with him on torturous paths, she will bring fear and cowardice upon the seeker and will torment him by her discipline until she trusts him, and she will test him with all her ordinances. She seems very harsh to the uninitiated…for Wisdom is like her name and is not manifest to many. (Matthews 1991, 108)

However, once the spiritual lessons are learned and fear is overcome, she becomes a mentor, a sponsor, a guide, a protectress, and an inspiration. The document continues, saying that although she may appear to be a slave mistress at first, once the required painful learning is completed

> her fetters will become for you a strong protection, and her collar a glorious robe. Her yoke is a golden ornament, and her bonds are a cord of blue. You will wear her like a glorious robe, and put her on like a crown of gladness. (Ibid.)

These ideas and sentiments I found to be profoundly meaningful when I applied them to my own life experience and my initiatory journey with the Old Goddess.

In reality, these three images of the triune Goddess are not so clearly differentiated, but like the gradual waxing and waning of the moon, they tend to blur, merge, and grow into each other—three aspects of the one power. It is the same severe deity who is merciful and welcoming when she says: "I love those who love me and those who seek me diligently, find me" (Proverbs 8:17).

4

The Magical Warrior: The Shaman

During a conversation with an Aboriginal elder...the old man
explained that in the trance vision one can see a web of
intersecting threads on which the scenes of the tangible world
as well as dreams and visions are hung. Inner fears...break that
glimpse of an invisible webwork, leaving only a world of
isolated things...and with that fear the vision of the spirit
world departs. (Lawlor 1991, 373)

A NEW DISCOURSE OF healing is emerging in the Western world. It is an eclectic group of therapeutic modalities that fuses Western psychotherapy, alternative medicine, and traditional shamanic magical practices. It is another way in which the Goddess is weaving her way back into a changing cultural paradigm. In fact, the range of alternative medicine therapies that are currently available is very similar to the modalities of traditional shamanism.

This is true of herbal medicine, homeopathy (healing with strange substances whose vibrational rates match the illness to be treated, which can include such strange things as x-rays, snake venom, and disease products such as syphilis), massage, crystal healing, psychotherapy dreamwork, and hypnosis, as well as healing with energy, color, and sound. Although many of these modalities are concerned with healing the physical body, others work from the Elphame with the patient's memories, dreams, and emotions. At the extreme end of the alternative medicine continuum stand a group of practitioners who do the classical healing work of the traditional shaman, such as the psychic integration work called "soul retrieval," and employ various kinds of communication techniques to engage with spirit entities and spiritual guides.

The work of Michael Harner and the Foundation for Shamanic Studies in California has popularized the concept of shamanism in the West and trained hundreds of Western-educated psychiatrists, psychologists, psychotherapists, and other health practitioners in traditional shamanic healing techniques like soul retrieval, with apparent success. Robert Moss's workshops, seminars, and writings on the importance of strong dreaming have also popularized methods of shamanic journeying and spirit communication. The research of Brian Bates into the beliefs and practices of ancient indigenous Anglo-Saxon and Celtic shamanism has revived a popular interest in those powerful Western spiritual traditions.

The ecopsychology movement, as well, is adopting and adapting the techniques of the indigenous shaman and basing its theoretical corpus on the integrated Goddess model. Some ecopsychologists, especially those from an indigenous background, are returning to the theories, codes, and practices of traditional native shamanism and attempting to blend them with ecological principles and orthodox psychology training, creating in the process a type of fusion model of therapy. The work of William Baldwin and Edith Fiore, who were Western-trained clinical psychologists and psychotherapists but whose current methodology can only be described as "spirit releasement therapy" or "psychotherapy for the dead," exemplifies this shifting medical and spiritual paradigm. I do not think at this time the work of these practitioners could be described as a "trend" because orthodoxy remains politically powerful, but perhaps it could be described as the thin end of the wedge or the fulcrum upon which a new paradigm is slowly being levered into position.

Other practitioners from indigenous origins are turning away from Western psychological medicine entirely and exploring the old ceremonies and healing methodologies of their ancient native heritage. However, the revival of interest in the magical healing methods of the ancient traditions is not a regression to a superstitious and unenlightened past, as the positivist critique would have us believe, but an alchemical distillation of the spiritual wisdom of the ancient Pagan shaman tradition mixed with modern scientific insights that appear to validate the spiritual and mythopoetic insights of more "primitive" (low-technology) cultures (Braden 2007, Broomfield 1997, Capra 2000, Chopra 1996, Laszlo 2004).

Positivism emphasizes that only empirical data and the scientific method are valid forms of investigation and that metaphysics, intuition, emotion, and theism are basically superstition and quackery. In spite of this predictable opposition, however, shamanism is being reinvented in a rational new version for our time and codified so that its basic philosophical principles and techniques can be studied and understood by interested persons. This does not mean that these students can actually become shamans in the practical sense, but this study gives an important understanding of how shamans work and how shamanic knowledge is gained through contact with the Elphame. In recent times, therefore, and through better understanding, the word "shaman" has lost many of its former pejorative connotations and become a universal term to describe magical healing practitioners of a similar kind in any traditional culture.

The most commonly accepted previous view was that the tribal shaman suffered from a type of epilepsy or psychosis because in the Western worldview no other cause for the observable outer behavior of the shaman practitioner was supportable. (Traditional shamans often exhibit the strange vibrational states while changing consciousness, which I describe in chapter 2.) The possibility that the shaman was altering awareness and entering another level of reality or having communication with other life streams was not regarded as credible. Those ideas seemed preposterous to Western observers because they did not conform to the Western materialist discourse, and indigenous people who claimed to do such things were considered to be either quaintly deluded or deliberately deceitful. Traditional shamans who attempted to explain the function and purpose of these skills to Western anthropologists were regarded as tricksters, charlatans, or "old rogues."

Jeremy Narby, an anthropologist who studied South American indigenous shamanism, writes about this clash of cultures in some detail and demonstrates clearly how adherence to the rationalist ontological framework severely restricts the ability for a more expanded and empathic understanding. What uninitiated Western observers see of the work of the shaman is simply that the shaman has entered a "trance-like" state, but the observers are unaware of what is transpiring in the Elphame because they do not have the experience or the equipment that would allow them to evaluate the inner work of the shaman. This is where the scientific method breaks down and a researcher needs to rely on a qualitative research approach that honors the fact that the person having the experience is best able to describe it. To attempt to either deny the existence of the spirit world or to try to cram the greater reality into the lesser—that is, to explain the spiritual world in terms of the physical—creates greater confusion and dishonors the one who has actually had the experience (Narby 1998).

As Mircea Eliade (1989) accurately observed, there is an abundance of evidence to show that shamanic experience is startlingly similar enough across time and diverse cultures to indicate that there is a consistent body of honest reporting that can be taken at face value without too much Western-style reconfiguring, reinterpretation, or appropriation. A. P. Elkin (1944), who studied Australian Aboriginal shamanism, writes with a deeper, more sensitive, and respectful understanding of the subject because as well as being a trained observer, he also had a background in Masonry and therefore has a different and more magical inner picture of how the world works.

However, in light of what is being discovered contemporaneously about the training and work of the shaman, a new respect is emerging that is altering the negative and culturally biased perceptions of the past. There now exists a more sophisticated understanding that the shaman could best be understood as a kind of spiritual warrior whose knowledge and skill are usually gained through difficult and frequently dangerous experience of other levels of existence that are currently only dimly glimpsed as possible by the leading edge of Western science.

The terms "mage/magus" or "adept" are closer as a suitable descriptor, for the shaman has a knowledge and experience of the hidden spiritual reality. The word "magician" as I use it means the same thing. These practitioners are characterized by a common role, shared methodologies, and a variety of techniques that enable them to alter consciousness and work from a different level of reality. Across different cultures the role has some variations and shamans obviously have different and special talents, but they have enough in common to suggest that there is something universal, something that transcends culture, in the way in which a shaman works and understands reality.

I suggest the shaman-magician is the true priest or priestess mediating between the spiritual world and the physical world, creating a bridge or conduit of consciousness between the two. Through the means of a magical wisdom technology of altering consciousness, the shaman is a voyager into these foundational worlds, attempting to find answers to problems of healing that do not respond to more conventional methods and that may have nonphysical origins. Sometimes the shaman does not simply alter consciousness but is able to leave the physical body entirely and travel in a body of subtle energy into the deep reaches of the Elphame to find solutions to the medical and psychological problems of their suffering patients. In the other reality shamans are able to converse with spiritual beings such as tutelary animal spirits and gain knowledge, power, and insight through this communion. This contact with the subtle world by the altering of consciousness is the serious, real, and essential work of the shaman.

The Shaman's Universe

Eliade describes the shaman's universe as consisting of three levels. Middle Earth is where humanity lives sandwiched between an upper and a lower world. This is the traditional model on which most contemporary training and teaching about shaman practice is usually predicated. In contrast, the magical model is basically a binary model of physical and nonphysical reality, although the nonphysical component, the Elphame, is divided into many different levels or zones that merge into each other. Difference in vibrational rates is what differentiates one level from another. In the Western magical tradition, the "underworld" of Eliade's model is the lowest level of the Elphame and is closest to the slowest and heaviest vibration of the physical world.

Magically, this "place" is known as the "Tunnels of Set"—from the Egyptian. This lower level of the Elphame is where unreconstructed alcoholics, dope fiends, criminals of various kinds, serial killers, torturers and fanatics of various stripes continue their lurid and disgusting practices by conjuring up violent fantasies from their own subconscious minds and continuing to live out these destructive nightmares until they finally become bored with them and attempt to move through them and into a healthier spiritual environment.

Suicides are also found close to this level, shrouded in a deep gray fog that is symbolic of their state of mind, and there they remain until they also begin to feel bored by their situation and decide to let in a little light so that they can see more clearly and allow their curiosity to lead them into more optimistic patterns of thinking and behaving. As the light grows in their consciousness, so they are able to move forward.

In Eliade's model the upper world is where the shaman meets with gods and other high-level spiritual and mythological entities and cultural heroes. The lower world, or underworld, is where he or she searches for lost souls or aspects of self, or works with the aid of power animals or tutelary spirits, or battles "demons." The three zones are usually linked by a central vertical axis, known as the axis mundi, which is characterized in different cultural mythologies as the world tree, the tree of life, and so on.

This central axis passes upward and downward through the holes or tunnels in the cosmic layers that lead to the upper and lower worlds, and it is through these holes that the traditional shaman is able to pass symbolically from one level of consciousness to another and back again. Wesselman (1996) gives an intriguing account of his perception of the world tree as it apparently exists in the Elphame (although I have not seen it). As Eliade notes, different cultures employ different metaphors and symbols to describe the different means of crossing into these zones of the subtle universe. They describe symbolic pillars, bridges, doors, curtains, stairs, ropes, ladders, and rainbows as the means the shaman employs to cross from one level of consciousness to another—a kind of de facto pathworking.

Some shamans, both ancient and modern, heal by the method of lay-ing-on of hands and the transference of healing energy; some work as "suck doctors" (that is, they suck or massage any damaging energy obstruction out of the patient's body); and some are learned in plant lore and use herbs and other native plants for healing purposes. They also work as telepathic sensitives and intuitives, and part of their work involves the ejection of "evil spirits." Indigenous people believe illness that has no observable cause is due to spirit interference. The Pitjant-jatara Australian Aboriginal people, for example, call these damaging spirits "mamus" and say that when a mamu takes possession of a person's body, the whole person becomes ill (PY Media 2002).

Thus the mental and emotional effects caused by a nonphysical entity may generate physical symptomatology. In these cases physical treatment alone will not be sufficient to support a cure. The attaching spirit entity will have to be persuaded to leave before the patient is able to regain their health, something that Laura's story in chapter 11 will dramatically dem-onstrate.

The shaman also does the classical soul-retrieval work of returning lost fragments of self to their clients. A fragment of the personality may split off, usually through the agency of some psychological, emotional, or physical trauma, so that the psyche becomes more restricted than it needs to. The integrity of the personality has been breached, and so the patient exhibits a two-dimensional quality ("insufficient personality") or alterna-tively becomes stuck in a cycle of neurosis, psychosis, or, in extreme cases, even coma. The shaman leaves the physical body, or projects con-sciousness, to search on the subtle planes for the missing fragments of the psyche of a sick client, or enables clients to discover the lost fragment for themselves, as the case of Luciano in chapter 9 will illustrate.

Whatever method is employed, when the fragments are retrieved from the Elphame and reintegrated into the psyches of their rightful owners, patients experience a surprising and renewed sense of whole-ness, better health, increased energy, and psychological balance. The patient therefore has more healthy and complete choices about their responses to life. Sandra Ingerman is a modern-day clinical psychologist who has adapted ancient shaman techniques of healing to modern needs and built an apparently successful psychotherapy practice around the shamanic concepts of soul retrieval and psychic reintegration.

Many traditional shamans are able to have telepathic communication with the natural world, most particularly with animal spirit helpers (sometimes known in Witchcraft as familiars, familiar spirits, or tutelary spirits), but also with the spirits of the plant and mineral worlds. They are also able to control the weather, a magical skill known in Witchcraft as weather-working, and frequently have close functioning relationships with the elemental life streams, the nature spirits, who are the guardians, keepers, and builders of the natural world.

Shamans work from the Elphame to create strategic change in the material world. In effect, therefore, they are mediating the energy of the Great Goddess. They are the walkers between the worlds, inhabiting the borderland between the daylight world of ordinary consciousness and the subtle, shadowy night world of the unconscious and the unknown. They shift between life and "death" but see no real difference between the two states, as they are simply alternating facets of the one reality. Death in the physical world is birth into the subtle world, and vice versa. It is simply a shifting state of awareness. The knowledge that consciousness is continuous and separate to brain awareness is confirmation, especially to those who have experienced separation of consciousness from the physical body, that death is an illusion.

To understand this in an embodied way dispels the power of the specter of death and annihilation that haunts the minds of many in the Western world. To metaphorically and symbolically lift the musty black veil of the fearful Crone to find she is, in reality, a beautiful young girl frees the mind of the most fundamental fear. In fact, I would argue that fear of death is one of the important driving motivators and shapers of Western culture. I would go further to say that our understanding of the death process generally is superstitious, crudely primitive, and not at all helpful to any of us who are contemplating the prospect of crossing over.

Dreaming, or astral awareness, is an altered state of consciousness relative to mundane reality and ordinary states of perception. It is a source of knowledge and meaning and provides a connection to the Elphame that gives spiritual vitality to physical existence. The shaman trusts the knowledge and insight that come through strong dreams, and shaman cultures are dreaming cultures. Powerful strong dreams, in dreaming cultures, give spiritual insight and commentary or perhaps glimpses of a separate personal existence in the subtle world, and are regarded as gifts from the world of spirit. I maintain they are frequently real experiences of the Elphame, dressed in symbols, as dreaming comes into consciousness through the emotional and intuitive areas of the brain and bypasses the cerebral cortex, or the intellectualizing part of the brain.

Magical or spiritual initiation can also come through strong dreams, and I have included several examples of my own strong dreams to support this assertion. What follows is an example of a strong dream that indicated to me that I have a separate and different spiritual life in the Elphame of which I am only sometimes conscious. This experience also suggested that dreaming is a powerful though not necessarily consistent means of moving between the two realities. In strong dreams we are often witnesses as well as participants in the symbolism of the unfolding events. The serpent dream in the preface also demonstrates this.

A Strong Dream of the Elphame

I wake up into a scene. It feels like reality and not a dream. I am aware that this is happening and I am conscious that I am an observer as well as a participant. It is a bright night, and I see a full moon that casts a silvery light over the landscape. I am walking out of a forest clearing surrounded by giant trees. The air is still and cool, and I become aware of the drifting and lingering fragrance of flowers.

I suddenly become aware that I am walking at the head of a group of people dressed in white robes and that they have wreathes of flowers and leaves in their hair. They are carrying burning torches. I am wearing a crown of flowers and a girdle around my waist made of gold and silver cord twisted together. I am barefooted and can feel the damp grass and earth on my skin. I feel the swish of the white robe around my ankles, and it is soft and light. There is an atmosphere of intensity and a kind of a joyfulness that buzzes around us. I hear soft laughter and talk. Someone is quietly playing a pipe or a flute, and someone else is lightly tapping a drum.

Somehow I know we are leaving a ritual circle where we have created a lot of energy for a purpose, although I am not exactly sure what it was as I drift and relapse into brain consciousness. I focus once again in the Elphame as someone in the group I seem to know well, although I am not sure how I know her, pushes toward me and grabs me by the sleeve. "Don't forget your owl's feather!" she whispers urgently and puts a long, soft gray-and-white feather into my hand. I smile at her and take the feather and kiss it, then stick it into the flowery crown I am wearing. The vision fades.

• • • •

THE OWL IS A symbol of the Wisdom aspect of the Goddess, as well as a symbol of the shaman or the initiate. This bird represents the shaman's mystical ability to penetrate the unknown darkness and to understand what is invisible to ordinary sight. Much of what the shaman does seems mysterious, as there seems to the outside observer to be no apparent causal and visible connection between the action and its outcome. But the experienced shaman has mastered the technology of the subtle world of energy and can move into and out of this other reality at will, working in the darkness to achieve results in the light world of ordinary consciousness. Not all shamans have reached this level of mastery and control, however, as spiritual learning is an ongoing, experiential, gradual, and lifelong process, as is the gaining of personal certainty and the diminishing of self-doubt. My personal story is testament to that, but the owl feather that is handed to me in the dream validates my status as a shaman, and in the dream, at least, I willingly accept it. The twisted gold and silver cord represents the balancing of the masculine and feminine energies, the solar and the lunar lights and therefore by extension a connection to the higher self or soul that is genderless.

As consciousness moves backward and forward between two levels of reality, a splitting can occur that enables the practitioner to be conscious

of the two levels of reality simultaneously. In this dream my consciousness shifted backward and forward several times between the two realities, and there were moments when I was lucidly conscious in both simultaneously. This explains how, in chapter 12's case of Josephine, for
example, I am able to communicate lucidly with her in a consultation and
at the same time be aware of her deceased brother communicating with
me in a visionary experience. There seems to be a gradual shifting of conscious awareness, from full consciousness of the physical world to full
consciousness of the Elphame on a continuum, and the process can be
arrested at some point midway between the two.

The Making of the Shaman

Some shamans inherit the role and are trained in it from early childhood. There exist, therefore, hereditary shaman families, just as there
have always been hereditary Witchcraft families who preserved the
sacred tradition and secretly transmitted it to their descendants.

In other shaman communities the candidate for initiation may be
physically and emotionally fragile but not actually insane. This fragility
or sensitivity makes it easier for detachment from the physical body to
take place. In other words, the candidate is not very strongly grounded in
the physical world in the first place. However, there seem to be greater
dangers for candidates of this kind. Their fragile psychological integration is more likely to shatter under pressure. Epileptics and schizophrenics do not make strong shamans because their experiences of the other
reality are not under their control. In the case of schizophrenics, the
sense of self has become fragmented and disintegrated, making their
encounters with the Elphame frequently confusing and dangerous. It
requires a strong ego and the ability to remain grounded in the face of
fear and trauma to become a capable shaman.

In most societies where shamanism is a feature of cultural life, the
shaman is usually required to lead a normal life, perhaps marrying and
having a family, and certainly contributing to the economic and social life
of the community. He or she is often a person of considerable worldly
accomplishment with a well-balanced personality. Among the Australian
Aboriginal shamans, for example, medicine men, native doctors, or

"clever fellas" are expected to be perfectly healthy and normal (Elkin 1944). Eliade (1989) and Harner (1990) support this view that the shaman needs to be strongly grounded in physical reality as well as have the ability to work from the subtle world.

The third way of becoming a shaman is to be chosen by the spirits, and among traditional people the greatest shamans are always made in this way, whether or not the role is hereditary. In Western society, on the contrary, being chosen by the spirits can be a disturbing experience, as I have described. To be thrust involuntarily into little known or understood realms of consciousness, to become an involuntary traveler into the unknown, can for a time destabilize the equilibrium of the personality. The experience of the other reality can be suddenly thrust upon the individual, causing the powerful reactions of ontological shock. All of the Western-educated individuals I researched who had the experience of being chosen by spirit thrust upon them felt those intense reactions.

The following strong dream of being chosen by spirit reveals the ambivalence I usually felt about close contact with the world of spirit. This is one example of a series of many initiatory dreams. At a distance I feel safe, accepting, and admiring; at close quarters I feel fear and a level of confusion, fear, and ontological shock. As the dream indicates, the idea, but not always the actuality, is attractive.

A Strong Dream of Being Chosen by Spirit

I am lying on a huge four-poster bed, but without curtains or a canopy. It is in a stone room in a castle, and the walls of the room are very high. I see a long, narrow slit window up high in the stone wall. As I look at the window a beautiful white bird flies straight through it and glides into the upper level of the room near the ceiling. It is an image of grace, power, and beauty. It is some kind of very large species, perhaps a white crane. I watch it with admiration, entranced.

There is something about the bird that creates a cognitive dissonance for me, and I have a subtle intuition that although it is clearly and visibly a white bird there is something about it that is not quite right. It feels like this visible form is a disguise of some kind. All is not as it seems. Suddenly the bird veers off its high course and flies straight at me. Its speed of descent and its purpose of landing on me surprises and frightens me. It lands on me.

I gasp, wake in fright, and sit up in bed, my heart racing. It was the unexpectedness of what happened that rattled me. Originally I was thinking that I was an outside observer, but the whole scene suddenly changed and I was right in the thick of it all.

The Hero's Journey: Shaman Initiation

In *The Hero with a Thousand Faces* Joseph Campbell describes what he calls the "Hero's Journey," a theme that he sees as present in many different guises within the world's mythology. He calls this journey the "monomyth" and postulates that the Hero's Journey is really the archetypal journey of initiation. It is a spiritual journey into the unknown subtle reality, with three clearly defined phases. Through the process of the initiatory journey, the hero moves from a naïve and unaware state to the achievement of a level of self-mastery that equips him or her to become a spiritual teacher and healer. The tripartite template of the Hero's Journey accords well with my experiences as I expand on Campbell's description and add certain magical and spiritual insights I have gained by taking the journey myself.

Campbell calls the first phase of this journey of initiation the departure. The seeker receives a call to adventure—a wake-up call. The other reality comes crashing into consciousness, and the hero must leave behind the comfort and security of consensual reality and social acceptance to set out on a lonely and dangerous journey, often without a map or compass. Sometimes supernatural aid or guidance may be given, which must be taken on trust and intuition, but essentially the hero must rely on inner resources and have sufficient enough courage to find the way.

The second part of the journey involves trials, ordeals, and other obstacles that must be overcome, and the Crone steps into the picture, bringing with her confusing and often frightening encounters with the other reality. Sometimes these are the demons of one's own fears and doubts (ontological shock); sometimes the shadow self will present itself, seeking integration and acceptance; sometimes the hero will have to win over and subdue the denizens of the subtle planes who would cause harm. These expeditions into the underworld or the worlds beyond death, therefore, have attendant dangers, but sometimes the difficulties experienced are simply the blows of fate or karma, which add up to painful obstacles in the worldly life that must be somehow negotiated. Initiation into magic speeds up karma so that instead of the worldly life becoming easier, it frequently becomes more frenetic, frustrating, and difficult.

The second part of the journey also involves a meeting with the complete feminine archetype, the Great Goddess, and an acceptance of her true nature—that is, an understanding and acceptance that the nature of the universe is cyclic and that each of the Great Mother's aspects is equally sacred: Birth, Growth and Stability, and Destruction, or, as I believe the ancients may have described her triple aspect, the Maiden, the Mother, and the Crone. The initiation of the Dark Goddess or the Crone is by grief and pain. Grief and pain therefore may be important agents of change, deeper insight, growing wisdom, and spiritual growth.

There is also an encounter with the masculine archetype that shatters the illusions of the ego-self and reveals the true nature of our relationship with the Divine. This is the process known as atonement. There comes an alignment of the personal will with divine will, which has nothing to do with convincing or proselytizing others of the correctness of one's doctrinal position but does have something to do with knowing and accepting that the events of one's life are for a spiritual purpose and living life accordingly as an aware, embodied small part of a greater spiritual truth.

The seeker becomes a worker for the common good and not for self-aggrandizement. The little individual will is given up to divine will, and the life is turned around accordingly. Those things that were once important aspects of the material world become no longer important, and things of the spirit become of much greater interest than things of the "world." There is a complete shifting of the life purpose. Among all the change and turmoil it is important that the seeker remains grounded. Indeed, I think that it is quite important that the magical initiate, like the traditional shaman, act fairly normally and be regarded as a credible person, not a crank or an object of derision who may bring the sacred tradition into disrepute, because ultimately the hero's role is to become a spiritual teacher and healer to his or her community. To have gained access to greater spiritual knowledge and wisdom implies that the initiate has also acquired a greater responsibility.

In *The Chemical Wedding of Christian Rozenkreutz*, a core mythological and symbolic text of the collection of Western magical and esoteric groups who call themselves Rosicrucians, an image of the Goddess sleeping in the dungeon of a castle is presented. Christian Rozenkreutz, the symbolic hero of this allegory, uncovers the face of the sleeping Goddess. His penalty for uncovering the mystery of the Goddess is to become the porter of the Grail Castle, whereby he assumes the role of the previous porter, who was, significantly, Atlas. However, the porter's role is not only to act as a guardian of the mystery but also to facilitate access to those who are ready for the revelatory experience themselves. There is a tutelary or initiatory function as well as a guardianship role implied here.

In asserting what she sees as one of the most profound truths of esoteric work, Caitlín Matthews says that

> whomever penetrates to the heart of the mystery thereafter becomes its guardian. It is by this means that all esotericists are the sons and daughters of the Goddess...(the Grail Family), taking conscious responsibility for Nature. (1991, 254)

She also says that the torch or light of initiation passes from hand to hand down the generations of esotericists so that the mysteries of the Goddess may be preserved, guarded, and passed on via the ancient underground stream of secret knowledge.

Just as the seeker encounters the feminine and the masculine archetypes in the external world, so there is a meeting of these energies within the psyche. There is an inevitable challenge to balance both feminine and masculine because the soul has no gender, just a perfect balance of both female and male qualities, and the hero is seeking what the medieval magical grimoires called "the knowledge and conversation of the holy guardian angel," that is, an attunement and identification with the higher self or soul.

The encounter with the Cosmic Mother teaches love, forgiveness, and compassion, and the encounter with the Cosmic Father teaches purpose, responsibility, and perseverance through work.

The third phase of the journey is the return. The hero returns to the daylight world from the void or darkness with the wisdom and knowledge that he or she has acquired to teach, heal, and initiate those who have remained behind. He or she has stepped beyond the veil and experienced the greater reality. The shaman is a spiritual teacher as well as a healer. The problem the seeker now faces is how to translate into terms that others might understand the experiences of the other reality that can inform our understanding, or as Campbell describes it:

> How to render back into light world language the speech defying pronouncements of the dark...How to translate into terms of Yes and No, revelations that shatter into meaninglessness every attempt to define the pairs of opposites? How to communicate to people who insist on the exclusive evidence of their senses, the message of the all-generating void? (1993, 218)

There is a definite quality of loneliness inherent in the shaman's way, because the shaman has moved out of the comfort of consensual reality to embrace a broader cosmic and spiritual view, and the hero who has returned is destined to become an initiator to others, presenting the small part of the greater truth he or she has discovered by personal revelatory experience to a wider community. It is the revelatory experience that endows the teachings with legitimacy, and the teacher's life becomes the text.

What follows is a recent strong dream that places me in the return phase of the Hero's Journey, although still not feeling all that confident. Again, a strong dream gives an initiatory experience and illuminates what I need to know. I have experienced a small part of the truth that I am able to teach to others, but how to do it?

A Dream of the Return

I am standing on a rock looking down on a disturbing scene. Below me are many people swimming in what appears to be a vast utensil, something like a huge bowl or cauldron filled with what appears to be some kind of soup or broth. Although I cannot see the edge of the container, I know intuitively that its shape is round or, more probably, elliptical. As I observe more closely I see they cannot swim against the strong spiraling current but are being carried away in a coiled fashion and are eventually swept away and out of sight by the unrelenting force of the watery matrix, their heads bobbing up and down as they go.

Many of them are panic-stricken; others are despairing. My rational mind tries to make sense of the scene; it seems crazy. I feel powerless to help them. It would be no use to jump in and try to rescue them. I have to find another means to help them. There are thousands of them, maybe millions. Some of them are looking directly at me. Their eyes beseech me. They are filled with fear. They cry out and moan with heartfelt distress. I feel powerless in the face of the inexorable movement of the force in which they are trapped. I feel sadness and compassion for them. I need to give them something that will make this experience explicable in some way. I call out to them, "Do not be afraid! There is nothing to fear. You don't understand the process, which is why you are afraid. It is a natural process, and it is something that happens for your best interest. Go with the process and accept it, for if you fight it, it will be more painful." (I think to myself with a certain irony *I know what I'm talking about.*)

As I say the words, I begin to understand that I am speaking the truth. It is the process of the Goddess—everything is being returned to the cauldron to be reshaped and refashioned. In the short term it is great pain; in the long term it is great freedom. I have this powerful realization in the dream and know that I am having it and also that I am dreaming.

I see that some of them are listening to me and hearing the truth of the words I speak. These ones stop their panic and struggle; they keep their eyes fixed on mine, drawing strength. They become quiet. The majority continue to struggle and fight their fate blindly and full of fear.

I feel a pain in my heart and want to do more, but one part of me is philosophical. "You can only do what you can do," she says. "They will all learn one way or the other."

I sigh, turn away, and gradually return to ordinary consciousness. I am still and thoughtful and aware of heavy, sad pain in my heart. I gradually accept it because I know a greater consciousness than mine understands the rightness of it all.

The Shadow: The Dweller on the Threshold

In magical initiation an important part of the second stage of the Hero's Journey is an archetypal battle between the individual ego and the entity known as the dweller on the threshold. In Jungian terms this entity is known as the shadow, a powerful composite of energies rejected by ordinary consciousness that dwells in the vaults of the mind. To the seeker this figure represents a barrier to spiritual growth and must be overcome if further spiritual progress is to be made.

During my magical training I had a series of three frightening and powerful strong dreams that indicated the encounter with the shadow was imminent, and also a final integrating dream that I regarded as an initiatory ordeal. After this series of dreams I recognized changes in myself, particularly that I was less opinionated, self-righteous, and judging of others, and more self-aware and compassionate. Also, my shaman powers seemed to become more consistently accurate and available.

A magician or shaman has power over external evil forces only because he or she has conquered evil in him- or herself. This ability to control one's shadow side comes from knowing and accepting the evil in oneself as part of one's own being, not from denying, suppressing, or projecting the knowledge. In psycho-spiritual terms the shaman has control over the once suppressed, unconscious, and unrealized dark side of the personality, or lower being. The shadow has then been integrated back into the personality, where it is under the control of the higher self.

As well as the repressed and unacknowledged contents of one's psyche, the dweller is also the personal ego-self, which is powerfully self-important. If spiritual progress is to be made, then all self-importance and ego must be surrendered in the process known as atonement. This is the realignment of the personal will with the will of the Divine. This is not an easy thing to do because it is often difficult to know when ego is involved, as sometimes it has a subtle presence. It is also easy to be self-deluded. Generally, any fixed ideas, fanatical concepts, and rigid dogmas are to be shunned, and an open-minded, fluid, intuitive, and authentic attitude is to be encouraged.

Egotism is an impediment to spiritual knowledge, growth, and understanding. Fanaticism and self-righteousness frequently lead to vengeful, spiteful, and violent action that perpetuate the grinding of the mill of karma—that is, until we finally "get it" and realize that the only thing that will stop the relentless turning of the wheel is forgiveness. Forgiveness is not just an intellectual construct; it is an ideal that must be lived and felt in the emotions and the body so that it is grounded in physical reality. This is a high level of working and not something that can easily be put into practice. It is something that dawns gradually as those who are deeply involved in the perpetuation of the cycle of hate and violence begin to realize that all their efforts are destructive and ultimately impotent.

I have had many patients who have said to me that their reason for seeking out therapy is that they want to "put a stop to all the shit"—to end the conflict and sorrow in their own lives and relationships—and to not pass it on to future generations as an emotional karmic load. To do this is an act of love, humility, and responsibility, and a realization that what we do has a profound ripple effect on other lives because we are those lives. Just as our individual karma flows into the stream of family, group, and national karma, and finally that of humanity itself, so we are participants in shared karma, with all that entails.

The background to revenge is fear. The background to forgiveness is love at the heart level. Fear separates, but love reunites so that everything is understood as self. Karma is not a bad thing but is simply an objective way (Ma'at) of restoring the sacred balance and providing justice. What we find difficult to understand is that karma can have been created in the distant past but is only working itself out today; we don't necessarily see the links. This is a complex subject and will require reflection to discover its deeper meaning.

Joseph Epes Brown was an anthropologist and a professor of comparative religion who made a special study of the religion of the indigenous peoples of North America, particularly the Lakota Sioux. He lived with Black Elk for an extended period of time. He said that the indigenous peoples believe that human beings include within themselves all aspects of divinity. A human being is therefore a potentially complete entity who bears the universe in miniature within. They also believe that through attainment of the power of expanding consciousness, a human has the potential to live in ongoing awareness of this reality. As Black Elk has said:

> Peace…comes within the souls of men when they realize their relationship, their oneness with the universe and all its powers and when they realize that at the center of the universe dwells Wakan Tanka (The Great Spirit) and that this center is really everywhere. It is within each of us. (Black Elk in Epes Brown 2007, 34)

The Lakota Sioux believe that the creator god Wakan Tanka is a masculine entity and not feminine, but the powers that they attribute to him are much the same as those attributed to the Goddess. They also believe that the knowledge that we are all one cannot be realized unless the aspirant has been able to attain "perfect humility." According to Epes Brown, they say that human beings must

> humble themselves before the entire creation, before the smallest ant, realizing their own nothingness. Only in being nothing may an individual become everything, and only then realize their essential kinship with all forms of Life. (Ibid.)

Without this humility and the sense of unity and relatedness, we see the dark struggles that are most terribly manifested in religious wars but include all forms of exploitative and oppressive conflict. This is the struggle with shadow, externalized and projected upon others—writ larger than the individual—as a group or even cultural drama with karmic overtones. On a personal level, the work to attain that level of awareness must be internalized and then become the inner struggle for enlightenment—a process that we will all go through eventually.

Symbolically there ensues a great psychological and spiritual battle between the personal ego and the impersonal soul or higher self. The ego or the mythological dragon must be slain if the personality is to be aligned with the will of the soul (the maiden in the tower) and so discover the true life path or spiritual learning mission. The dweller puts up a good fight but in the long term cannot win out against the soul's superior understanding. However, this higher form of psychological integration may not always take place within one lifetime but extend over several.

When the shadow is unconscious or not integrated, it may constellate into an autonomous complex, creating havoc. It may result, for example, in compulsive criminal behavior, dissociative disorders of various types, or in the familiar tale of a guru, spiritual teacher, or holy man falling from grace and being condemned for various offences usually involving sex, money, or personal power abuses. This encounter with the dark self is an important part of magical training and also of psychological integration. According to the psychotherapist Alice Miller (1998), it is formed of violent impulses and unacceptable emotions such as murderous impulses, rage, hate, and anger, which are repressed as a result of pedagogical methods of parenting. Her analysis of the childhood experiences of Adolph Hitler and the subsequent outcomes of his violent upbringing is masterful.

By going within the psyche, the aspirant also becomes more acutely aware of the many mental and emotional blockages that create obstacles to further development on the spiritual path. These blockages should be cleared as far as possible before embarking on the shaman's magical journey because they can create unnecessary impediments. As an example of this type of emotional blockage, I can give an example from my own life.

As a young child I was a prolific writer, and from the time I could read (around three to four years old) I took a lot of pleasure in writing poetry, short stories, and plays. My writing was effortless and flowed joyfully and unimpeded. The impulse to write seemed to have been preprogrammed into my DNA; it felt so natural. I don't have any hard copies or concrete examples left of that sunburst of creativity that was my childhood literary life, so as an adult I can't really attest to either its brilliance or its mediocrity. All I can say with certainty is that family members, friends, and teachers who read my works or heard my readings of them thought that they were intriguing, entertaining, and engaging.

I felt supported and encouraged by the appreciative feedback I received from the small circle of the "literati" who surrounded me. I told everyone who asked me what I wanted to be when I grew up that I wanted to be a writer. Writing, to me, was a lot of fun as well as serious work. Eventually, in some way that was not really clear to me, I began to realize that those who were so approving of me and my work might not be very objective in their judgment. Questions began to form. Perhaps they encouraged me because they loved me and not necessarily because they thought my work was really good in its own way. I began to think I might need a more objective assessment.

My fourth grade teacher had valued me and encouraged my writing, but my fifth grade teacher and I had a mutual animosity. Most of the class disliked him, and he probably wasn't a good teacher because he couldn't communicate or connect with the children. He was also a communist. I had no real idea what a communist was but thought it must be something like a vampire because the very word "communist" seemed to incite hostility and anger within the local community. Somehow, even though he was generally perceived as a malign presence, I imagined that he would have enough integrity to give me some honest and objective feedback about my work.

I was around ten years old, and I had written quite a long play for someone my age. It was around twenty-five foolscap pages. It had only three characters who were child adventurers: Jack, Andy, and Mollie. I was excited. I thought it was really good. I gave him my manuscript to have a look at, and I was hoping he could give me some objective guidance about how I might refine it and polish it up to make it more professional. Some months passed with no word from him, and I became impatient to see what he had thought of it. Finally I asked him whether he had read it or not. He didn't say anything in reply but went to his desk and opened the drawer to retrieve the document. He handed it to me in silence. As I took it I noticed lots of red lines striking out many words.

It shocked me to see that for the entire twenty-five pages of the play he had simply crossed out every mention of the name "Mollie" and had rewritten it as "Molly." There was no further comment from him either verbally or in written form. He simply handed the manuscript back to me with the "corrections" and that was the end of the matter as far as he was concerned. I was dismissed.

The effect on me was intense and devastating. As soon as I saw what he had done, I interpreted it personally: "I'm no good!" I heard the words in my head as I told myself this powerful negative message. Like all children, I blamed myself and not the abuser. It hit me hard with an accompanying emotional force, like a really hard and winding punch in the solar plexus, that I was no good as a writer.

The intensely negative idea "I'm no good," along with its attendant catastrophic emotional impact, was fatal to myself as a writer. My unconscious accepted the idea at a deep level as a truth, and I immediately stopped writing. The creative writer in me died. It took many years of deliberate, painful self-analysis and many attempts at resuscitation to remember the incident, to understand the devastating effect that it had had upon my psyche, and to release myself emotionally and completely from its bondage. Eventually, I had to go through the process of soul retrieval to find and reintegrate the little girl who was a keen and talented writer into my psyche. She had been sitting in that classroom in a sad and traumatized state wondering why I had abandoned her.

These are the kinds of mental and emotional obstacles that many people experience, and if they remain unconscious they can exert a malign and toxic presence in the psyche that truncates further spiritual refinement and progress. It is important to hunt down these thought-forms and emotional blocks and to eliminate them. These problems can reveal their presence back into consciousness through regression hypnosis, through muscle testing, or even through cognitive behavioral therapy. These types of therapies and others can recognize negative and undermining thought patterns and change them into more logical, healthier patterns. Going within and searching out these self-limiting thoughts and emotions can pay big dividends for the person who has the necessary courage to face themselves and their irrational fears.

In the Earthsea books by Ursula Le Guin, the magician Ged is constantly in flight from a subtle secret enemy. Finally, in the third book, *The*

Farthest Shore, he summons the courage to finally face this hidden and malignant adversary. To his shock and surprise, he immediately recognizes the one who has pursued him all these years and who has generated such fear. It is himself!

Those elements within the personality that contain vestiges of pride and egotism, and those elements of an essentially negative, violent, and unconscious nature, resist the higher self. If the lower personality self is not brought under the control of the higher self, then power becomes an end in itself and the magician may be overtaken by those elements of the unconscious that irresistibly seek outward expression. This is the path of black magic described by Bardon (1962), in which power is sought out of egotism and self-interest. Therefore, understanding how relationships with one's parents and teachers affect the positive development of the psyche and the acceptance, validation, and reintegration of the lost or unconscious aspects of self are valuable psychological exercises. They help to achieve the spiritual and psychic integration that is so necessary for the shaman/magician to proceed successfully along the path to mastery. Again, both the material world and the subtle world have value and importance in this spiritual journey.

What follows is a series of four shadow dreams. The first three dreams, which relate to going into the unconscious and entering another world, indicated, with growing intensity and fear, that the archetypal meeting with the shadow self was imminent. The fourth dream is the initiatory strong dream.

In the first dream I walk into an empty room. It is built of stone blocks like a room in a castle and is filled with golden light. I stand in the center of the room and wonder what I am doing there. I ask where my partner is, as we were training together. A voice answers, "He's not here, but he may come along later." The dream ends with me feeling slightly puzzled.

In Qabalistic teaching the empty room is the symbol of the hidden sephiroth Daath on the tree of life glyph. Daath represents the way across the abyss—in essence a profound change of psychological state.

In order to cross the abyss safely, ego and selfishness must be left behind and fear must be conquered or the higher states of consciousness may not be attained without harm. Many magicians have become physically or mentally ill when they have tried to cross this symbolic barrier not sufficiently prepared.

> In the second dream I go into the same room. On the far wall there is now a set of steps leading down. I walk across the room, take hold of the handrail, and begin to descend the steps. I feel waves of fear at what I may find in the basement. There is a sense of threat: something is imminent and I may not like it. The dream ends.
>
> In the third dream I am standing in the basement and there is a high wall dividing the space. As I look at the wall a pair of hands appears to grab the top of the wall and someone begins to climb over it. I am afraid of what may appear. A distinctly low criminal type appears, who looks like the image of the stereotypical "Burglar Bill." He leers at me and winks. He dashes up the stairs and out into the world. I feel aghast at what I see because I know it is something dark and it is closely connected with me, and I have let him escape into the world. I feel guilty and anguished and wonder what will happen now.

Strong Dream of Integrating the Shadow

> In the fourth and final strong dream I walk down the same steps, once again feeling very afraid, and pass through a door that has appeared in the dividing wall. I step out into another world, which seems to be a kind of large park or zoological garden with lots of strange animals in cages. There are pathways and trees and it all looks quite well ordered and maintained. People are wandering through the park, stopping now and again to peer at the creatures that seem safely contained in their cages. I don't know why I feel such anxiety, fear, and trepidation. I am shaking a little, my

breath seems rather shallow and tight, and I am sweating in anticipation that something bad is going to happen.

I suddenly feel a force pushing me in the back, which compels me to walk over to one of the cages, and as I look into it I see that it contains two hideously ugly animals, looking something like orangutans but with red demonic eyes, signaling evil intentions, and entirely without the charming innocence of the real animals. One has shaggy black coarse hair and is the male, while the female has the same textured hair but red. The alchemical symbolism is evident. Both of them look dangerous and malevolent.

The force compels me to open the gate to the cage and walk in. Immediately the black one jumps onto me and hugs me tightly, with its body against my chest. It becomes glued or fixed to me and I know that I can never get it off. It is terrifying and I scream, but I quickly realize that panic is futile and will serve no purpose other than to confuse the situation further. I try to take control of my fear and begin to calm down and try to think more clearly. I can't run away or pull the creature off me, as it seems to be permanently glued to me. I experience a flash of hopelessness and a sinking feeling of inevitability. I have to think more laterally. "I'll ask it what it wants from me."

I look at the creature and ask, "What do you want?" He does not reply but gazes at me with a kind of fixed malevolence, and I know I have to work it out by myself and that it is a life-and-death test I cannot fail. Finally he replies telepathically but I hear his voice, with a hissing, rasping, threatening tone in it: *Acceptance.* I add the "or else" myself.

I suddenly have the realization that this hideous creature is part of me, and I intuitively know that to take an attitude of loving acceptance is the solution to the dilemma. I hug him and say, "I do accept you, and I love you." As I speak the words I do feel love and compassion for my denied and ugly self, and as I feel it flowing toward him, he relaxes his grip on me, and I am free. I am still carrying him but it doesn't feel like such a horrible and frightening burden. He and I walk off together along one of the paths in classical Hollywood style, off into the sunset. Somehow, in spite of all the fear, we have worked it out.

· · · ·

I THINK THAT THIS symbolic integration of the shadow has enabled me to have greater self-awareness and compassion and a to overcome fear and reactivity, although perhaps not completely. cilitated an ability to work successfully with patients and clients w ave had powerful psychotic episodes or have committed serious crimes. What appeared to be darkness has once again turned to light.

5

The Nature
of Ritual

To many, these ceremonies are no more than formal
celebrations, but to those who have some insight and
commitment to spiritual development, the unfolding rites are
full of significance and have a power to raise the Soul above the
patterned movements, words and music. (Halevi 1974, 191)

SOME FORM OF RITUAL practice is normally the means by which the
shaman gains access to the Elphame. The ceremony of gaining entry
may range from elaborate preparations involving ritual drug-taking,
drumming, chanting, or dancing, which jolts the consciousness into the
subtle world, to a far less dramatic approach that merely subdues the
constant chatter of the mind and emotions and allows the subtle intuitive world to arise in consciousness. One method is active while the
other is passive, but whichever method the practitioner chooses, ritual is
an aid to changing consciousness. I personally employ the latter method,
as do the practitioners I interviewed.

The will, the focused intention of the practitioner, is the motive force
that drives a ceremony and creates the doorway into the Elphame. The
symbolic ritual accouterments such as candles, incense, stones, garb,

words of power, and ritual gestures reinforce the shaman's intention and speak to the unconscious or intuitive mind, but the capacity for ritual to shift consciousness from mundane reality into the Elphame seems to be true whether or not the ritual has a social, psychological, or magical purpose.

From that perspective, all focused and intentional rituals are magical acts. At various levels of intensity ritual can fulfill personal, social, religious, magical, and spiritual functions by operating in sacred time and space. As the Western cultural narrative is changing to accommodate a more magical perspective that values the power and sanctity of the natural world, so is ritual becoming a more socially important and culturally cohesive activity.

In modern Australia the changing rituals around death and sacrifice are interesting to observe. These range, for example, from the spontaneous appearance of roadside shrines to accident victims that are proliferating all over the countryside, to the solemn ceremonies that are attracting growing numbers of participants to commemorate disasters and atrocities. The increasing numbers of young people turning up to Anzac Day ceremonies (Glendinnen 2006) or pilgrimages to Gallipoli and the Kokoda trail, and the memorial rituals established to commemorate the Port Arthur massacre and the Bali bombings are good examples of this trend. It is as though masses of ordinary people are seeking to make meaning of life through a ritualized practice that is knocking on the doors of the mystery that is death. They reflect a growing secular spirituality that is flourishing outside the traditional control of the Christian churches. Ella, one of the research participants, who conducts Druidic- style, Native American-influenced marriage, funerary, and naming rites, notes in her practice a parallel and general social shift away from a Christian approach to these milestone events to a far more Pagan orientation that honors a sacred connection with the natural world and the heart connection of the ritual participants. As she describes it, the participants are working from the soul or heart center, and the ritual intention creates sacred space and invites the Goddess's presence.

Ceremonies of this kind are usually conducted outdoors in the natural world, and there is usually a strong sense of emotional and spiritual connectedness among the participants. Ritual has the power to make connections at the heart level, the center of feminine power, and also the capacity to connect the participants with the underlying spirit of the natural world—the Earth Goddess.

In the cases of the research subjects Meredith, Anna, and Josephine, I had adapted and modified some of the principles of magical ritual practice to suit their psychotherapeutic needs. Using magical laws of correspondences influenced by the Qabalah, I helped them set up an altar and choose candles of certain colors, specific incenses, stones, and images, and helped them design and write rituals that would allow them to heal psychologically and spiritually.

I helped Meredith design a ritual using the correct magical accouterments and invoking the aid of the goddess Isis in her role as the Great Mother, which addressed the emotional turmoil she had experienced after having a pregnancy terminated. Anna also used an adapted magical ritual to deal with the consequences of extreme sexual and physical abuse that was undermining her health. Josephine and her family had consulted me because they had experienced a family tragedy from which they could not heal. I helped them design suitable ceremonies that enabled them to complete their healing journey and re-establish functional family relationships.

Their healing process had stalled and was restarted by a ritual process (Reeves and Boersma 1989, 90). By using an adapted magical ritual, these three women felt a connection to sacred time and space that helped them restore and transform their lives in different and powerful ways.

Many orthodox counselors and psychologists use some form of ritual as part of their therapeutic practice, and although there are pronounced differences between those kinds of rituals and magical rituals, there are some surprising similarities. Evan Imber-Black and Janine Roberts (1992; Imber-Black, Roberts, and Whitting 1988), who have pioneered the development of ritual practices as therapeutic tools in relationship and family therapy, are aware that ritual space and time are somehow different to ordinary space and time. Although their therapeutic interventions are focused to address problems of mundane and social reality, they are mindful that all intentional ritual is somehow a conduit for the sacred, and they understand its transformative power.

Roberts discusses Meyerhof's highlighting of what he considers to be one of the paradoxes of ritual:

> Ritual defines reality yet happens in a sacred time and space that is outside of the usual reality...Therapy works with the same contradiction, in that it is seen as a process to rework day-to-day interactions yet happens in a special time and space that is outside the usual boundaries of daily interaction. (Imber-Black, Roberts, and Whitting 1988, 7)

It is tempting to accord Meyerhof's "special time" with Eliade's "Original Time" (1989) and to extrapolate to the Elphame—to speculate that Meyerhof, Imber-Black, and Roberts are saying that they consider ritual to be a means of entering the Elphame and of communicating from that reality. It seems a reasonable inference to make. Eliade's concept of Original Time is the unitary point at which humanity was connected to, and in communication with, all other aspects of creation and all other life forms. It is the time before the separation into the physical world occurred. Eliade's Original Time seems very like the Aboriginal Dreamtime and similar to the concept of the Elphame. These researchers could be interpreted as exploring the proposition that ritual, therefore, is the means of purposefully reconnecting to that unified field of living consciousness, which I say is the Goddess.

In the Native American worldview apparently all beings have their own rituals that are life-sustaining and vital to the survival of the species. Medicine Grizzly Bear (Robert G.) Lake, a Native American shaman, writes:

> Human beings of all races, both past and present, have always had rituals of some kind. Rituals are natural. All living things in nature—animals, birds, fish, reptiles, bugs...have their own ritual and ceremony. Without it they could not survive. (1993, 99)

In traditional Aboriginal culture, ritual permeated every aspect of tribal life and was important in establishing and maintaining a sense of identity and a permanent and ongoing relationship with both the natural world and the spiritual world that was seen as crucial to survival. The performance of the correct ritual was also seen as the means of renewing the life force and the regenerative vitality of the natural world (Cowan 1992). The role of humanity in the performance of the sacred ceremony was a vital contribution to a kind of covenant in which humanity, the world of spirit, and nature were allied and interactive.

Witchcraft takes a similar view, believing that the performance of the seasonal and lunar rituals attunes the practitioner to the cycles of the Great Goddess and helps to maintain the harmonious balance of the mineral, plant, animal, human, spirit, and divine worlds, as this balance is not automatic. As Starhawk says, "It must be constantly renewed and this is the true function of Craft rituals" (1999, 26).

Ritual, then, is a means of respectfully acknowledging the life force, the living web of interconnecting relationships, and of taking more conscious responsibility for what we do. An important and universal rule for the building of a sacred ceremony is to treat all creation with respect, equity, and gratitude; everything else is cultural or personal. Since the old rituals of reconnection and regeneration have fallen away and been forgotten over the generations, it is not surprising that the natural world is suffering and dying on many fronts and many species are becoming extinct.

To live in a state of being connected to and immersed in the regenerative web of life can give insights that go beyond words to direct and grounded experience: a connection to the heart of things and an opportunity to rebuild oneself from the essence of the life source. A ritual is something that everyone is capable of performing, and shifting consciousness into sacred space-time means immersion in the vast sea of consciousness energy that is the Elphame. This means of regeneration is something that traditional people have understood and something that mythology teaches, but it is something that is not generally appreciated or consciously practiced in Western cultures. Many Western people, however, intuitively recognize that by merging oneself in the natural world and spending some time in the wilderness it is possible to return to the human world refreshed and renewed in some mysterious way.

The Grail legends and the Arthurian myths give symbolic keys to the importance of this understanding of the ritual processes of regeneration or renewal. When humanity is connected to its life source, the Grail or the Goddess, it may re-create, remake, and re-energize itself, and a new life cycle begins. Conversely, to be disconnected from the life source leads to feelings of disgust, despair, apathy, lifelessness, meaninglessness, and desolation.

Pathworking

Pathworkings—visualized symbolic ritual journeys in the mind— form part of the ritual practice of the magical tradition. In essence they are a series of controlled thought forms that are based on symbolic disciplines or traditions such as the Qabalah (employing the tree of life glyph). These journeys are designed to develop the power of the creative imagination and increase skill in working in the Elphame's subtle matter. The symbolism that is used constitutes a kind of map or pathway through the landscapes of the Elphame and creates a certain safety for the practitioner because these pathways and landscapes have been well used and protected over the centuries.

Some pathworkings, because of the magical potency of their symbolism, create psychological and spiritual effects of a distinct kind and involve contacting powerful archetypal intelligences and interacting within their reality. There are distinct similarities between shamanic journeying and magical pathworking, as both styles offer entry into the Elphame using symbolism that changes consciousness.

Other pathworkings can be structured using, for example, mythological or cultural images, and this type of symbolism can also have a powerful effect upon the psyche, influencing both the conscious and the unconscious mind. They do not have a specific magical or spiritual intention but work in a psychological manner to establish better emotional and mental balance. These rituals can be used in the shamanic practice of soul retrieval when split-off aspects of the personality can be returned and reintegrated into the psyche, as the case of Luciano in chapter 9 demonstrates. Dolores Ashcroft-Nowicki, a magical adept and world expert in pathworking, claims that a pathworking that is correctly constructed and uses the right symbolism works through the levels of the personality and brings

...unconscious energy into conscious form, opening up a person's life as well as awareness. A pathworking will confront us with choices in a non-rational way that can lead to greater understanding. (1987, 14)

These kinds of rituals can be successfully adapted to working with psychotherapy patients, and when designing pathworkings for such patients I often use images and symbols from the Arthurian legends, the Grail legends, and Greek mythology. Sometimes the line between the psychological and the spiritual can become blurred, especially when symbolism becomes archetypal and the images work on the many levels of the personality, as Ashcroft-Nowicki affirms.

The modified, nonmagical use of the pathworking technique in the treatment of serious physical illness is well documented in the work of Simonton (1980, 1992) and Jeanne Achterberg (1985). Achterberg and her co-authors (1994) and Gerald Epstein (1989), an American psychiatrist who uses the patients' powers of the imagination in treatment, have had a notable measure of success. However, these therapists, in the company of many others who use techniques of visualization skillfully for relaxation or healing purposes, are, I believe, not generally aware of the deeper magical origins of the techniques and are usually not conversant with the deeper and more powerful spiritual or archetypal levels of working. Since the technique known as guided visualization or guided meditation has become better known and used outside the magical tradition, it has tended to become, in less skilled hands than these, merely a "gentle walk in the meadows of the mind" (Ashcroft-Nowicki 1987, 148). As a technique to encourage relaxation it does have value, but it lacks the magical and healing potency of a properly constructed and healing pathworking.

Although most pure teachings on Western Pagan pathworking has been lost, the modern methodology has retained a strong Celtic-Druidic influence through the use of landscape and the symbology of the natural world. I certainly use these natural features in many of the healing pathworkings I have devised. These types of symbols also recur in the dreams of Western people.

In the tradition of Druidry there were three main spiritual pathways to enlightenment: those of the Poet, the Druid, and the Seer, although these sometimes appeared to overlap. The Poets were primarily the weavers of spells, and through the process of symbolic journeys in the imagination they initiated their audiences into the other world (Matthews 1991). Master A has also said that in the Druidic tradition pathworking was taught as part of general magical training and that the path was often sung—that is, the poetry was often recited as song and as an aide memoire. Melody, repetition, rhyme, rhythm, and sometimes musical instruments as an accompaniment to song were thought to increase the power and intensity of journeys into the Elphame and also help the initiates to remember these mental and emotional experiences, as this was largely a word-of-mouth tradition and memory was therefore a very important adjunct to knowledge and teaching.

Joscelyn Godwin, a researcher into Western esotericism and a professor of music at Colgate University in New York, says medieval Irish monks used a pathworking technique to explore the Elphame. She says:

> Usually the Other World is reached after an imaginary sea voyage to the West. It is full of adventures…as the voyager often meets unfallen spirits, dwelling in Edenic gardens where they celebrate a liturgy of song and sacred dance. Everything in that world is more crystalline, the fruits more delicious, the beasts and birds more tame and endowed with speech. (Godwin 2013, 87–88)

The psychiatrist Carl Jung (1964) and his acolyte Marie-Louise von Franz (1972) did pioneering work in the field of myths, fairy tales, and symbols in the modern era, and the work of Joseph Campbell (1993) has been important in showing the connection between the world's mythology and the hero's inner journey of initiation, the hero as discussed being the one seeking initiation and being invited by spirit into the greater life and a greater spiritual awareness.

However, Western magic has an ancient tradition, stretching back over many centuries, of an ordered and scientific approach to working with symbols in the deeper levels of consciousness and in the subtle planes of reality. This corpus can trace its origins at least back to ancient Egypt and to the medicine of ancient Greece, where it seems that the *therapeutoi*, the healer-priests of Asklepios, were adept in working with both the dreams of their patients and in the techniques of pathworking (Ashcroft-Nowicki 1987). She goes further to say that

> pathworkings are not new, in fact they are incredibly ancient. They were used in…Sumer. Chaldea made use of them in her fabled star magic. Others can be discerned at the heart of the old rites that come to us via the oral tradition of folklore, fairy-tales and nursery rhymes. (Ibid., 18)

The modern "discoveries" of depth psychology were already well known and understood by initiates of the esoteric and practitioners of ancient healing and magic. Asklepios, the wounded healer and the Greek god of medicine, is one of the archetypes I frequently use when constructing healing pathworkings. Isabelle and Angela in chapter 10, who are interview subjects in this book, obtained healing responses for both physical and emotional difficulties using a modified magical pathworking I devised. I called it "The Healing Waters" and made use of the archetypal symbol of Asklepios and the sacred healing waters of the Goddess.

Modern Therapy and Ritual

I concur with Meyerhof's perception that the ritualized aspects of the therapy session and the therapy room itself are important factors that enable extraordinary interactions to take place (in Imber-Black, Roberts, and Whitting 1988). Safety, confidentiality, and respect are usually preeminent in therapeutic interactions. Speaking the truth and having it accepted and honored by another is not something that many people experience outside the sanctity of the therapy room or the group circle. It seems that a discernible element of the sacred enters into therapeutic interaction, and that is as it should be because from a shamanic perspective true healing is a combination of medicine and religion, body and soul, and a meeting of the two worlds.

There is often a heightened atmosphere when that extra factor enters the equation—something like the shift in energy that happens in therapeutic groupwork when participants work from their higher selves and the ordinary world of separate objects falls away. Greater clarity and understanding manifest, and something else as well: a connected compassion that seems like love of a different quality to what we normally experience. The Goddess energy enters the gathering and a unitary state is precipitated. Some of my ex-student research participants spoke of that particular quality in group work. It is an amalgamation of tolerance, compassion, acceptance, love, and a kind of distancing or long view of what was happening. The long view is both the soul's view and the Goddess view, as the cyclic nature of the triune archetype symbolically demonstrates.

There are many ritualistic elements in the general practice of psychotherapy. For the patient, the visit to the therapist and the therapy room carry expectations of healing that are reinforced in the particular symbolism involved in the therapeutic encounter. The quiet atmosphere and the particular quality of intimacy and trust that develops between the patient and the therapist as they create a therapeutic alliance (Kottler, Sexton, and Whiston 1994), within which the truth may be spoken and accepted, encompasses some of the defined qualities of ritual. There is a feeling of focused intention and a sense of walking a pathway together, but also the repetitive and cyclic nature of the appointment: each week at a certain preordained time there is a meeting in a place and time existing outside of ordinary space and time within which extraordinary events take place. It is also common for a special ritualized opening and closing of the sessions to gradually develop.

My consulting room is deliberately set out in a ritualistic and symbolic way. I have followed some of the magical principles of the Chinese art of placement, feng shui, in the way I have arranged the furniture and objects in the room, in order to allow the life energy, prana, miwi, or chi to flow as harmoniously as possible and to create opportunity for high-quality communication (Kingston 1996, Lip 1993).

Whenever I am consulting with a client I have a crystal lamp on my desk, and as a symbolic gesture I make a point of switching it on as soon as they take a seat. As well as communicating with them verbally, I also talk to them in a nonverbal ritual way through the use of symbols and sensory data. The nonverbal communication facilitates connection and interaction. It can unlock the creative potential of the unconscious mind as the symbology of ritual speaks to, and enlists the compliance of, the unconscious as an agent of change.

Sometimes I will burn a soothing and calming aromatic oil such as lavender, and I will often have very soft classical music playing in the background, so soft as to be just audible. Usually the music will be Baroque music, Bach and Mozart, or sometimes Chopin, because these styles create an alpha or theta brainwave pattern and also open the heart, thereby helping the person relax and think more clearly by accessing the unconscious more effectively. Sometimes I will use very soft recordings of natural sounds such as the sounds of the sea or a creek running over rocks or sometimes bird, insect, or frog sounds combined with the sounds of wind in the trees because the unconscious mind is connected and attuned to the natural world. I always use recordings of the natural world when I am using the pathworking technique.

I have comfortable furniture in soft colors and usually offer clients a drink such as tea or mineral water when they arrive. When they graduate from therapy, in our final session together we will have a little celebratory glass of champagne, or a cup of tea and an elegant little cake if they don't drink alcohol, and discuss and debrief (more as friends and not so much as therapist and patient) our hopes, fears, and perceptions of our time together, perhaps now being able to laugh at some of the more dramatic and painful events if they have gained that sort of strength. This sharing of food and drink is a distinct part of Wiccan ritual practice and comes at the end of a ritual working. It is regarded as a sacred thing in itself and is an integral part of ritual work. It also acts to ground the participants and to refocus them into the physical body and the physical world after working in the subtle reality.

The Ceremonial Circle

In ordinary reality the movement of a group into a circle is an example of ritualized behavior that signals the creation of sacred time and sacred place in which exceptional things can happen. I have seen this natural movement happen spontaneously when working with classes of teenagers in the public education system and also with group therapy patients. Previously they had sat not in a circle but in a blob-shaped arrangement of chairs while some of the people present sat apart from the group altogether, signaling their disengagement. After several sessions and when the group really started to "work," it was fascinating to see that gradually and unconsciously the group members began to shift their chairs into a perfect circle and also unconsciously to often look to the center.

In magical work the sacred circle creates a ceremonial boundary between mundane and spiritual reality. The shape contains the power that is raised by the ritual or ceremony and prevents intrusion by the forces of chaos and dispersal. If a circle is convened regularly by the same group in the same place, a gradual increase in the energy present is discernible and a group thought-form, or "egregore," is created. The power of the egregore increases exponentially, adding energy or power to the work being done. The group, therefore, gradually becomes more unified, and the work becomes easier with passing time; there is less resistance on all levels. As well as in magic, I found this to be equally true in the group-work that I conducted with student groups and group therapy patients.

Gradually the work became more powerfully transformative until there was very little apparent resistance, and in terms of my experience of orthodox education and therapy in general, a level of involvement I could only describe as unusual became evident. Sedonia Cahill and Joshua Halpern, who have made a special study of the dynamics of the circle archetype in *The Ceremonial Circle*, relate the healing dynamics of the archetype, although they do not refer to it as the glyph of the Goddess but of Divinity.

The circle with the point at the center is the great glyph of Divinity. To sit in the circle, therefore, is to symbolically invite healing contact with the source of all life. When we make a ceremonial circle we create a form in which to align ourselves with the sacred pulse and purpose of life—to make contact with spirit and an awareness of the inimitability, sanctity, and connectedness of everything without us and within us.

Such is the power of the circle archetype. It helps to re-establish a sense of the sacred in our ordinary lives whereby mundane acts can become sacred through intention and awareness. All look toward the center, the Shekinah point: the place where Divinity as the shining Goddess (aparantos) manifests. It is the place of power and new possibilities.

Working in circular form throws the group members back on their own resources and enhances their creativity. It teaches a sense of openness, relatedness, and safety wherein participants may go through experiences that are deeply revealing and transforming of self. It is difficult to remain concealed in a circle. In this sense it speaks in a powerful symbolic way to the unconscious mind, suggesting that all are of equal value and equally worthy of respect.

To be really seen and heard by others in an authentic way, to be witnessed, is a rare and therapeutic experience for most people, and it generates a feeling of acceptance. It honors our human suffering, it supports our struggle, and it respects our courage. To be supported in the circle authenticates our life experiences and enables us to communicate from the heart center and not, as is usual, from the mask, persona, or armored personality self. It is a shape that encourages honesty, empathy, compassion, and impersonal love—all qualities of the soul—and therefore it encourages us to be present in our higher being and connected at the level of the heart center.

All of these measures are powerfully symbolic, suggesting feelings of healing and nurturance that are registered at an unconscious level. They have also grown out of my familiarity with the rituals of Wicca and High Magic, whereby the sensory accouterments of ritual enable a shift of the practitioner's consciousness into intuitive states. This shift facilitates the discovery of more creative possibilities occurring, both to the therapist and the client.

Because it has an inner and outer reality, magical ritual performance unites the inner and outer worlds, resonating on many levels of the self simultaneously. It enables the practitioner to stand consciously at the shaman point, the crossroads between the visible and invisible worlds, the known and unknown, the conscious and unconscious, the individual and collective, the part and whole. It also engages natural cyclic and repetitive actions that induce a unitary state of consciousness and uses sensory devices such as taste, sound, scent, and visual symbols to heighten and particularize the experience. It is a purposeful and potentially therapeutic and transformative type of action that may be performed by an individual or group.

Formal magical rituals are different to social rituals in that they raise large amounts of power or life energy that is certainly felt in a physical way by the participants. At times the amount of energy is so great that they may feel as if they are burning up with a fever or staggering under a burden of energy so palpable and tangible they are almost losing consciousness. This encounter with power makes it understandable why preparatory magical training is so important, because contact with these levels of energy can be overwhelming and even dangerous. To those unprepared for it, it comes as a shock to know it is real. The difference between psycho-social rituals, which have an emotional effect, and magical rituals lies in this element of power, which is spiritual power invoked from spiritual archetypes.

The ritual training that a witch or magician receives ideally includes both microcosmic and macrocosmic work. Microcosmic work is done within the self, within the individual psyche, and its purpose is to influence and effect transformational psychological growth by removing emotional blockages, gaining insight and inspiration, discovering prior life patterns that are harmful and clearing them, and making connections with the higher analogue of self, the soul.

Macrocosmic work is different because the shaman or witch is dealing with entities and forces that have an independent reality. No competent magical worker would consider that these entities are archetypes in the Jungian sense that they exist within the human collective unconscious. They exist within their own reality. These entities may be elemental—that is, creatures whose primary nature is earth, fire, water, or air. They may also be planetary spirits, or the symbolic inhabitants of the sephiroth (spheres of energy transformation) of the Qabalah, or any of the myriad unseen powers existing within the Elphame, including humans who have died but have become earthbound. The ritual releasing of earthbound or attaching spirits is something in which shamans from all cultures are involved and is one of the important themes of this book.

The Question of Performance

The work of academic outside observers like Victor Turner, while valid in its own way, has for me some significant limitations. In *The Performance of Healing*, a study of shamanism and ritual practices from an anthropology perspective, Turner and the other contributors, who come from a diverse but orthodox anthropology background, are writing as outside observers and not as insider experiencers. His thesis, and that of most of the other writers included in the anthology, is that the power and effectiveness of the shamanic "performance" is the efficacious element of ritual—that the ritual performance of the shaman influences the mind of the patient to induce a healing response. He sees ritual as a kind of placebo medicine, even a kind of mass hypnosis, but what he and other traditional researchers see, in fact, is only the outer working of the ritual performance.

This is not to say there is no place for performance, as the symbols used by the practitioner may have a powerful effect on both the conscious and subconscious minds of the ceremonial participants, who may reciprocate by joining in the singing or chanting to raise energy to help a tribal shaman go through the process of altering consciousness. The performance aspect of ritual may be an enjoyable imaginative experience for the audience and give them reassurance—the shaman's way of providing something for the audience to grasp or a necessary showmanship to give form and substance to what is otherwise a physically invisible enterprise.

However, there are also inner workings that are not obvious to the uninitiated observer, and it is these that produce the true healing response. The practitioner works in the Elphame to produce an effect in the physical world; this is the essence of all magical work. The outer workings merely serve to alter the consciousness of the practitioner and aid him or her to access the subtle levels of reality wherein lies the information that will lead to a cure in the case. In the Craft the inner workings involve contacting and working with energy, which is usually visualized in the form of light of a particular color frequency and entities either human or nonhuman such as nature spirits, animal tutelary spirits, or those archetypal intelligences known in the Western magical tradition as "god-forms."

Neville Drury, who researches and writes about the esoteric and cross-cultural aspects of religion and magic and is also himself a practitioner, agrees that from an insider perspective, the inner and outer worlds conjoin, blur, and merge in ritual. He confirms what was claimed at the beginning of this chapter about the considerable difference between the insider's experience and that of the outside observer:

> There are physical observances (that one can actually see) and symbolic mythic processes that are represented by the ceremonial sequence of events. Unlike the scientifically trained Western observer, who would no doubt miss much of the import of a ritual...the shaman does not distinguish between the real and the unreal worlds. The entire magical domain is an integrated expression of both natural and magical events. (1996, 50)

6

Sanity and Madness

Turning and turning in the widening gyre
The falcon cannot hear the falconer;
Things fall apart; the center cannot hold;
Mere anarchy is loosed upon the world.
(W. B. Yeats, *The Second Coming*)

IT IS PAST MIDNIGHT *and raining in a steady drizzle. Car tires make a perpetual hissing sound as the stream of traffic passes, spraying water from the roadway. The headlights and streetlights cast blobs of movable light; the cafés and pubs are emptying the stayers into the streets and closing up. Cabbies are cruising, looking for prey—preferably not too drunk or too out of it; fares are prone to doing strange things in cabs at this time of night in Sydney, a lot of it none too pleasant.*

There comes a scrabbling sound on the other side of the high stone wall, and a pair of disembodied hands grasp at the weathered top. An improbable figure hauls himself up to sit for a moment on the cold wet stones, darts a glance over his shoulder, then jumps for the street. He crouch-lands on the footpath and, recovering his balance, runs splashing from the darkness toward the lights and the lines of cars waiting for the traffic signals to change. He is barefooted and wearing one of those hospital gowns that tie at the neck and are open at the back. His thinning dark hair is dripping, plastered to his skull, and the gown is wet through and flaps open

133

as he runs. His ghostly buttocks shine pale as a full moon. He doesn't care. He is focused on a cab he sees sitting in the line of waiting traffic.

He wrenches open the door and flings himself inside, exuding menace. The occupants leave with alacrity by the other door. They're not going to argue with a madman who is wringing wet and half naked to boot. They leave the cabbie to his fate and weave a samba pathway, accelerated by fear, through the oncoming traffic to the relative safety of the opposite footpath. The cabbie, perhaps too afraid to argue, says laconically: "Where to, mate?" Or maybe he's just seen it all and nothing surprises him anymore. "Newtown, and as fast as you can go," says the specter. The tires skid and squeal, the engine snarls, and the driver spins the wheel as if he needed telling to step on it!

· · · ·

THIS IS THE STORY of a friend of mine, now an Australian novelist and poet, escaping from an infamous mental hospital. He'd had a few visions and some inexplicable psychic experiences not induced by psychotropic substances. He'd once seen a UFO, so he must be deluded because he had seen something that wasn't there. There were also some difficult situations he'd had to face as a sensitive kid growing up in a macho out-back town that circled as self-doubt and uncertainty around his sexuality. He'd decided that he'd better consult a psychiatrist to find out what it all meant. The intake shrink said that he was an incurable schizophrenic and that he was having a psychotic episode and would have to take medi-cation for the rest of his life. He was admitted that same day as a patient and his clothes were taken away. After several days of mutual observa-tion, he decided that the staff were crazier than he was, so he planned and executed the clichéd but classic escape: knotted bed sheets anchored to the heavy steel bed frame and lowered out an unlocked window.

In subsequent times he took a perverse pleasure in recounting the story at dinner parties to shock the complacent and perhaps to suggest that he was dangerous to know. He inwardly reveled as forks stopped halfway to mouths and diners swapped speedy, furtive glances before gathering composure and munching on, making little murmuring sym-pathetic noises between bouts of chewing and not meeting his eye. It gave him an aura of a kind of bravura chic to be known as an escapee from the lunatic asylum—the "bin" in the vernacular he liked to use.

Dropping this bombshell, although it was done with considerable sang-froid, carried barely discernible undercurrents of aggression. He mined it. It was something akin to Coyote, the trickster—just when you feel comfortable and relaxed in your assumptions, the rug gets pulled out from under you.

When your life experiences contradict accepted conventions of what is normal, you can expect that you will have to validate yourself, the alternative proposition being that you accept the common view that you are probably insane or at least disturbed, even though you don't feel that way. My friend had decided to trust himself and seek therapy and healing through writing. Last time I saw him, he had had several novels published and several volumes of poetry. I'm wondering if he still tells the story. Probably not, although I don't believe that he has joined the "sleepwalkers"—his view of reality will never be the consensus view—but I suspect that like many people he has "traded off" and keeps silent out of expediency when his view clashes with the received and accepted view of how the world works.

The remarkable experiences I have had cannot be explained by any conventionally acceptable worldview that is other than madness or delusion, and as a health practitioner and psychotherapist I often have had to incorporate these "mad and delusionary" experiences and insights into my methodology. I did look for a theoretical framework in psychology that could explain my experiences, but I couldn't find one. So, in a way, I have had to create my own. I know I'm not crazy, and I never made the same mistake of my writer friend of putting myself into the hands of the psychiatric establishment. But the search for understanding has been a difficult one because it's all very well to think you know something when you know it in theory, but experiencing something unusual and integrating it emotionally is quite a different matter.

The question of what is sane and what is mad is an important theme of this book, and the diagnostic decisions that differentiate those states can assume a political complexion when those questions define reality, legitimize only the dominant ontology, and disallow other possibilities. I suggest that significant numbers of people who are diagnosed as psychotic may be actually experiencing inadvertent and unregulated contact with the Elphame that they cannot control, conceptualize, or contextualize. If this assertion is true, then traditional psychiatric interventions will not be successful in these cases.

These people may be hearing voices or having visions, prophetic intuitions, or strong dreams and finding these events to be frightening and confusing. Sometimes they think and feel that they are on the verge of madness or are actually in the process of going mad. They have had experiences of the Elphame they have not been able to reasonably understand because the question of what is sane defines the boundary between experiences of ordinary and non-ordinary reality. On one side of that divide is the comfortable territory defined by the official cultural narrative and known as sanity, but on the other is the dangerous, dark, and ambiguous world of the insane.

Of course the rationalist tradition regards any encounters with non-ordinary reality as delusional, fantastic, or superstitious. Christianity, the other major stakeholder in maintaining the official cultural narrative, promulgates ideas about the spiritual world that are based upon doctrinaire descriptions of heaven and hell. The church has traditionally inserted itself between individuals and their spiritual life as the sole legitimate interpreter of meaning, and any experience that contradicts or questions its position as sole arbiter of what is real has been invalidated, sometimes violently. However, what most people actually say about their encounters with the Elphame bears no resemblance to these dogmas. The Christian discourse is therefore not helpful to them in their attempts at interpretation.

It requires a persistent intellectual effort to penetrate the confusing veneer of obfuscation created by centuries of Christian propaganda (their word), to investigate more deeply and discover that much of Christian dogma is simply a redecoration of some of the core beliefs, symbols, and mythologies of Paganism. For example, the story of the crucified and resurrected Christ can readily be seen as a reinterpretation of the mythology of the sacrificed and reborn gods, who are the consorts of the Great Goddess (Picknett 2005). Christianity has surreptitiously appropriated much of the initiatory Pagan tradition while at the same time reviling it. This level of dissimulation is perplexing and impenetrable to many people.

The Pagan tradition does offer a clear commentary on the value and meaning of individual spiritual experience, but to many people this tradition has been so dismissed, demonized, and devalued that it cannot generally be trusted. The words "pagan," "ritual," "witch," "priestess," and "magic" all possess acquired powerful negative connotations in the greater public mind. Before the enduring wisdom of the Pagan tradition can be revalued as a helpful ontological frame for spiritual experience, it will be necessary to penetrate the fog of superstition and propaganda perpetrated by the church. It may even be necessary to invent a new terminology because of the lingering taint. The combination of rationalism and Christianity that forms the foundation of the Western worldview creates an unhealthy and confusing climate for anyone who has had experience of the Elphame. We do not possess a coherent alternative, encompassing, and validating ontological frame. There is currently a vacuum in the spiritual life of the Western world, and it raises important questions about how we may understand and interpret individual spiritual and mystical experience.

David Tacey, who researches contemporary spirituality, discusses a "spirituality gap." He explains that orthodox psychiatrists are increasingly concerned about their inability to enter into any discussion of spirituality with their patients and that this limits their ability to devise suitable treatments. They have been trained in the rationalist tradition and have no point of entry into the conversation about spiritual ideas or experiences that patients regard as important. The medical model of mental illness prevents these doctors from creating a healing alliance with their patients, as there is

> an ever-present and persistent gap between patients who report that spirituality is an important element in their personal identity and mental health, and doctors...who have no way of entering...into this spiritual language and terminology. (Tacey 2003, 201)

There is also a discernible political resistance to the whole question of a shifting of the poles of sanity and madness. Cultural acceptance of changes in the boundary between sanity and madness requires a concomitant ontological shift, so any discussion of personal experiences of another reality is officially gagged or regarded with suspicion. Although the shaman-healer habitually works in altered states of consciousness and has many and varied experiences of non-ordinary reality, any rich data gained by those means is disregarded or trivialized. There are clearly important differences between a psychotic and a shaman, but Western medical science cannot theoretically differentiate them. This is another example of the many ways in which the orthodox rationalist paradigm is out of touch with a shifting cultural narrative.

What Tacey is describing must provoke reflection. Orthodox psychiatrists who cannot join with their patients in a common worldview must have great difficulty in understanding their patients' sincere descriptions of their experiences of the spiritual world. By reframing those experiences as panic attacks, delusions, or psychosis produced by a mental illness caused by a chemically imbalanced and malfunctioning brain, Western psychiatry must necessarily increase levels of fear, anxiety, and self-doubt for many patients. This lack of validation of their personal experience was an important issue for some of the research subjects and, as they described it, certainly increased rather than allayed their feelings of gathering insanity.

For the group of people who have had experiences of non-ordinary reality that are mainly benign but who have a conflicted understanding because the official cultural narrative contradicts what they know, a period of ontological shock is precipitated. When this period has passed, they are usually able to accept the reality of the destabilizing experiences and adjust their worldview to accommodate, if somewhat uneasily, their newer and broader perspective. Complete self-acceptance is generally something that happens over time. Others, like the modern shaman-healer research subjects, completely accept the presence of a subtle world and move seamlessly between it and physical reality.

Some brain researchers like Newberg, D'Aquili, and Rause maintain that the brain itself is the link between both worlds and that mystical experiences are completely natural events that confer psychological benefits upon the experiencer. Contact with the Elphame in the last analysis, they say, can be an indisputably positive experience, something that some others among the research subjects had also found. They say that significant research...seems to show that people who experience genuine mystical states enjoy much higher levels of psychological health than the public at large...Other studies have also shown that, in general, even mild mystical and spiritual experiences are associated with higher-than-average levels of over-all psychological health. (2000, 108)

These authors argue that the human brain is innately wired to accommodate the religious or spiritual unitary state or experience. Not only do they see the brain as naturally mystical, but they also observe that humans have an inborn genius for effortless self-transcendence: a capacity to become absorbed into a greater reality than that proffered through a focus on the individual personality self. The highest unitary states are achieved through a reduction of neural input into the orientation areas of the brain, which deal with the sense of self, and the creation of a cerebral sense of the space in which that self exists. In other words, humans are happiest and healthiest when connected within and when that connection is a kind of immersion or embedded state within a greater spiritual reality.

Of interest, too, is the idea that attainment of that unitary state is accomplished through either quiescence or arousal of the sympathetic or parasympathetic nervous systems that respond to rhythmic input, and one is immediately reminded of the womb experience of peace and security, which is both immersive and responsive to the dominant maternal heartbeat. David Abram (1997) reiterates this theme in his observations that humans are tuned to relationship within their life-world, intimately connected to the subtle language of the living world, and responsive to the short cycle rhythms of the solar and lunar cycles. Such immersion creates a perception of time that is an "eternal now" through the absence of marked differentiation of self and other. This is a common phenomenon experienced by mystics and others who break through the barriers of time and space to the experience of another level of mentality and perception.

The notional "paradise" state of a balanced interaction between left and right parts of the brain's orientation association areas could be described as a state of spiritual immersion in the world, a state in which "self" and "other" have no strong distinction. In this state the behavioral and relational reciprocity between humans and their life-world is harmonious and complete. That is, "paradise" is a quality of relationship to the world. The spiritual adept is the human manifestation of this state of perfect balance. There exists, therefore, a model of reality that legitimizes the experience of connectedness and immersion, which goes a long way to facilitating entry for more ordinary human beings into the spiritual life. The Goddess model gives permission to experience both connection to the spiritual world and immersion of consciousness within a greater reality. Mystics throughout the ages have reported that in the higher meditative states there is a sense of the dissolution of the separate, personal self and an intuitive understanding of the relatedness of all life; indeed, all life is perceived to be the self and the self is perceived to be all life.

Paul Brunton, a writer and researcher into mystical and spiritual subjects, talks about moments of illumination that may be induced by contemplating the natural world or by the inspiration of great art that reveals Divinity. He says that however and when those moments come

> time seems to stop, the sense that life is eternal infiltrates into one's mind, the physical environment loses a little of its tangibility, its reality fading off slightly into dream-like substance. An ethereal peace...surges into the heart and brings with it an intense satisfaction which the gratification of no mortal desire could ever bring...one senses rather than sees an intelligent purpose at the heart of things. (1970, 174)

As an aside, this fading away of consciousness of the physical world can also be frightening for the ordinary person who has no real understanding of the nature of the mystical experience as Brunton does. Two of the interviewees describe it as a deeply disturbing experience that seemed to confirm their fears of incipient insanity. Both April in chapter 13 and Tom in chapter 14 had similar experiences when the physical edifice of the "world" seemed to shift and crumble away. The interplay and interchange of states of light and darkness is a persisting theme in this enquiry whereby light turns to darkness and back again, suggesting that instability is an essential dynamic in the process of spiritual awakening.

Despite the perceived benefits of contact with the Elphame—an expanded consciousness, a sense of order at the heart of things, and an understanding of the truth and importance of a mystical connectedness with the spiritual world—the Western ontological narrative cannot validate any of these nodal positions of spiritual experience.

Those who have had frightening or confusing contacts with the Elphame, those whose experiences have been tutelary and mainly benign, and those who have had only positive and psychologically beneficial experiences can only be understood through that cultural frame to be suffering from delusions, psychosis, psychotic episodes, or to be downright lying.

From that orthodox perspective, experiences of non-ordinary consciousness are considered to be artifacts of a human mind in crisis or in retrogression to a more primitive state, possibly related to mental diseases of the hysterogenic or epileptiform type. The mind and the brain are perceived to be virtually synonymous, and the picture is complicated by the fact that the brain responds to both external and internal stimuli that appears to alter its chemistry, so it is possible to postulate that the brain itself generates maladaptive patterns of cognition.

The orthodox explanation is based on the hypothesis that the patient who is experiencing visions or hearing voices is suffering from a discrepancy of neurotransmitter biochemistry, though there are few convincing explanations of why such imbalances occur or any cogent explanation of exactly what constitutes the biochemical composition of a balanced brain.

Mental illness is thought to be possibly triggered by stress, but it is not clear whether stress is the cause of the condition or its outcome. Also, several people may experience the same kind of stressor or trauma, but not all of them will exhibit an "unbalanced brain." Although the medical model of illness is basically a mechanistic model, clearly the process of acquiring a "mental illness" is not a mechanical one. Some people, it is postulated, are genetically more susceptible to mental illness, while others have more resilience.

But this truism does not address the fundamental issues: Why does a brain become chemically unbalanced? What is the real and foundational cause of mental illness? What causes a formerly healthy brain to become pathological, apart from such obvious conditions as a tumor or physical trauma? From the world of materialist science there are vague and unsatisfying answers to these valid and important questions. There is also a general expectation that the etiology of mental illness will eventually be proven to be genetic, the result of a faulty gene, with perhaps even the possibility that gene therapy may be a corrective or curative procedure that could be employed at some future time.

Psychotropic drugs are generally prescribed to correct the hypothetical neurotransmitter imbalances and do give some respite and, in some cases, even control psychosis, but they do not generally bring about a cure. If the patient ceases to take the medication, it is likely that the condition will recur, so many people are told that they will have to take the drugs for the rest of their lives, despite the frequently overwhelming, debilitating, and disfiguring side effects such as tardive dyskinesia, obesity, life-threatening heart and circulatory problems, and sexual and respiratory difficulties.

Some researchers believe that psychotic illness causes changes to the physical structure of the brain (though this is not proven), which in turn causes changes in cognition, affect, and behavior. A fairly recent (2005) public information brochure published by the Australian Federal Department of Health and Ageing says that people with mental illness perceive

> their world differently from normal. What they see and hear and feel is real to them, but people around them do not share their experience. The person may think someone is interfering with their mind. The person has hallucinations—mainly hearing voices. Other less common hallucinations involve seeing, feeling, tasting or smelling things, which are not actually there.

This is disturbingly tantamount to saying that anyone who sees the world differently has a mental illness.

Among orthodox mental health professionals there is a strong tendency to pathologize, to particularize, and to label rather than to look at the patient's "gestalt" to determine whether the response to an unusual or unpredictable experience was appropriate under the circumstances. This was something directly experienced by Tom, who noted that the clinicians who attended him during and after his intense "psychotic episode" were not interested in his spiritual insights or his experiences of the other reality. During his hospitalization he learned that it was in his best interest to confine his conversation to platitudes and uncontroversial subjects if he wanted to avoid heavy doses of psychotropic medication. The cultural and medical pressure to conform to the consensus worldview can be extreme, and those who do not conform will most likely be diagnosed as insane or dangerous or both.

Drug treatments tend to sever the patient's connection between the neural pathways in the brain and the emotions, or the "heart" and the "head," so that a person may think that they should be angry or sad, for example, but are unable to express anger or grief. The medications seem designed to produce a schizoid type of docile personality with blocked affect, who is therefore more easily managed. Many patients dislike the drugs for this reason. Their emotional life is flat and colorless, and they commonly say that they "feel like a zombie." Others claim that the drugs have no beneficial effect, and that the physical and emotional side effects they produce are unbearable. Anna, Tom, April, and James all make comments to that effect.

Peter Breggin, a psychiatrist who has done extensive research into the side effects of long-term psychotropic medication, says that

> both drug therapy and the other heroic (surgery and electro-convulsive therapy) methods of psychiatry have the effect of reducing emotionality, creativity and self awareness and of rendering the patient more shallow, less able to have deep relationships, and are relatively inert. (1993, 66–67)

On the question of causality, why one person should have an unbalanced brain and another does not, orthodox medicine remains silent. It seems to be a random, selective, and irrational process. The underlying causes of mental illness remain a mystery to orthodox medicine. I contend that a large number of people who could be diagnosed as suffering from a "mental illness" could find their cure in the subtle world. They are most likely suffering from incursions from the Elphame that are detrimentally affecting their consciousness, but they do not have a "mental illness" that is amenable to drug treatment.

Some Psychological Models Most Closely Aligned with the Magical Model

Jung and Magical Psychology

Although C. G. Jung has been traditionally regarded among magicians as the most "magical" of the psychological researchers, and although there are areas of agreement between Jung's ideas and the accumulated magical corpus, there are also some significant differences.

According to magical psychology, each of us possesses a physical body that operates in the physical reality, but it is motivated by an energy body that has the power to operate in the underlying energetic reality as well as in the physical world. Each of us also possesses an emotional or dream body, sometimes known as the "astral body," that operates on the level of the Elphame, as well as a binary mental body that operates on the level of the intellect or concrete intelligence and also on the mental plane of pure reason. But this is a complex study and beyond the scope of this book.

Jung does not clearly differentiate these different aspects of self but tends to combine them under the title of the "Unconscious." However, the outcome, the sense of wholeness or integration, as Jung describes it, whereby all the elements of the psyche, both conscious and unconscious, are welded together in unity, is a similar concept to the magical view of psychic integration. Jung describes this as the goal of the "individuation" process, a journey that is guided by the Self: an archetype indistinguishable from the Imago Dei (in the Bible—man made in the image of God) and that exists outside time and space. As such it is not a part of the physical brain.

As I understand it, Jung is talking about an integrated personality self, whereas a shaman or magician on a spiritual path aspires to become a soul-infused personality. There is a considerable difference. Magical psychology would describe this process also as a spiritual journey that is guided by the "soul," but the soul is not the same thing as Divinity. The Western magical tradition acknowledges levels of reality other than the physical that are not created by the human mind. The human mind, in this view, resides within this greater spiritual reality. We live and move and have our being within a vast ocean of spiritual energy.

Viktor Frankl, the developer of Logotherapy, does not support the Jungian "Collective Unconscious" as the location of human spirituality. He said that Jung "misplaced this unconscious religiousness in man and allotted it to the region of drives and instincts" (1975, 74). For Frankl, our spiritual nature, while often unconscious, resides elsewhere in our being and is particularly available to will and choice, and finally to personal responsibility. I would position myself closer to Frankl rather than Jung on this matter because I see spirituality as part of our higher being and not part of our animal self or lower instinctual being.

The individual spiritual journey occurs over many lifetimes as the aspirant gradually gains disciplined control over the emotions and thought processes. The mind then becomes quiescent and subject to the personal will, and thereby impressionable to the energy of the higher self or soul. It can then be guided and inspired by the soul so that all the aspirant's thoughts and actions are for the highest good of all, and the aspirant is able to act compassionately but impersonally. One of the laws of Wicca instructs "And it harm none, do as thou wilt!" As I have previously suggested, this is a far more rigorous discipline than many suppose, and it is definitely not an injunction for personal license.

As the spiritual process gains momentum the aspirant becomes "soul-infused" and is able to have safer access to the higher spiritual powers. These powers or "gifts" give the practitioner the ability to perform what the uninformed call "miracles," but in reality they are the outcomes of lifetimes of spiritual cultivation. Unlike Jung, the Western magical tradition differentiates between the soul and Divinity. The soul or Self works for divine purpose but is not the Divine itself except in the way that all that exists is part of the Divine. The soul is not the equivalent of the Divine itself, although I would agree with Jung's insight that the soul, or as he described it, the Self, does mediate between the conscious and the unconscious.

I would also propose that the soul, like the shaman, mediates and moderates between the physical world and the subtle world. If the link with the soul is not strong, then contact with the subtle world is danger-ous, as soul contact gives a high degree of psychic protection. My experi-ence of psychic attack described in chapter 2 and the "Strong Dream of the Elphame" in chapter 4 give an indication of the protective guidance and oversight of the soul.

Jungian therapists typically do not acknowledge the subtle reality as an autonomous world but prefer to talk about the "collective unconscious," a deeper and more "primitive" level of the human mind that is regarded as common to all humanity and populated by the mythological motifs or primordial images Jung called "archetypes" (Jung 1972). He defined archetypes as typical forms of behavior that present themselves as images to the conscious mind.

He believed that these images were numinous and contained deep spiritual significance. In this view, archetypes themselves, as defined, do not have consciousness but are forms of energy (Storr 1983), and if contacted their enormous power can destabilize the individual consciousness and overwhelm reason, thus precipitating a psychotic or schizophrenic episode. In other words, consciousness can become overwhelmed by the power and content of the unconscious. The chain of causation seems to me to be not very obvious, and it is not really clear to me, again, why this would happen. It seems to be a random process, although Tom's experience in chapter 14 could be coherently interpreted from a Jungian perspective.

Jung was a product of his time (as well as being an original thinker), yet in spite of that, in many ways he transcended it. In some of his theorizing he comes close to a magical and spiritual point of view that resonates compatibly with a modern magical understanding. He recognized, for example, the importance of a human connection to the natural world (Sabini 2002). As a man of science, however, living in a period imbued with a positivist ethos, he believed that archetypes were the denizens of the collective unconscious. It seems clear that he believed that Western civilization, with its apparently more highly developed, analytical, intellectual, and scientific approach to questions of ontology, represented an evolutionary advance.

This cultural assumption permeates his writing, and although he does allow that the Self, or part of it, exists outside time and space, he generally confines his research to the mind and personality. But he is an enigma in many ways because although he came from a family that was deeply imbued with the mystical and the magical (McLynn 1996) and he had done considerable cross-cultural research into both alchemy and the spiritual and psychological belief systems of traditional societies, he did not ultimately go beyond the Western consensus version of reality that set the limits of acceptable investigation at the boundary of the physical world and the human mind. His own mystical encounters and conversations with the entity "Philemon" he preferred to describe as "archetypal"—that is, Philemon was a projection of the collective unconscious and therefore did not have an independent existence in another reality.

From a magical or shamanic point of view, however, Philemon could be interpreted as a tutelary spirit, as he appeared to Jung in the form of a kingfisher. At many points Jung comes close to the magical ontological position but never quite gets there, and from my perspective some of his theorizing seems strained, forced, and inelegant because in a sense he has had to reinvent the wheel in order to distance himself from what he perceived as primitive superstition.

Jung believed that there existed a kind of drive or a striving within every individual toward a state of unity or wholeness, which he called "integration." In this state divisions within the personality would be replaced by consistency and opposite traits would become equally balanced. This process of balancing included the synthesis of the conscious and the unconscious. The Self stands at the conjunction of the conscious and unconscious. He speculated that the Self and the Divine reflect each other. From a magical perspective I can agree with this up to a point because everything that exists reflects the Divine. However, beyond this point he seems to be saying, and at the same time not saying, that the human mind creates Divinity, and here I must disagree with him.

Jung termed the journey toward wholeness the "process of individuation" and postulated that through this process a person could become a completed, homogeneous, perfectly differentiated, and autonomous "self-realized personality." In some ways he seems to be struggling to articulate a concept of the soul, higher self, or adepthood, but he seems keen to avoid any Christian connotations and careful to maintain an attitude of secular spirituality that could give "primitive" and Pagan symbolism and motif a place in his schema.

He realized the importance of symbols and the spiritual significance of what he termed "archetypal dreams," which, he theorized, drew on material from the collective unconscious, and he also had an understanding of the initiatory function of big dreams. However, he postulated that all the figures that appear in dreams were aspects of the dreamer's own ego, whereas a shaman or magician would understand strong dreams as real and magical encounters with the Elphame. For all that, Jungian psychology and magical psychology have a close alignment in the field of hermeneutics as applied to interpreting and understanding the significance and hidden meanings of the symbolic material found in dreams, myths, and legends.

Jung believed that if mental health is to be established, the ego must be connected to the Self, but that if the ego is too closely connected and drawing too much power from the collective unconscious then the individual may suffer from symptoms of megalomania or bipolar psychosis. In extreme forms this kind of what he termed "psychic inflation" can easily descend into schizophrenia. His description of schizophrenia is something like multiple personality disorder, where there can be two or more egos present in an individual that reveal themselves through multiple voices and are not necessarily in communication with each other. He saw these separate voices as fragments of the patient's own psyche and not as separate entities or spirits, as a shaman might see them.

In describing a schizophrenic patient he exhibits an unconscious assumption as a man of his time that the developed and educated intellect represents the epitome of psychological development. He displays a kind of evolutionary triumphalism that still clings to positivist psychological medicine and, in my view, taints it. In the case below he enters the patient's world but cannot make an authentic healing alliance and clearly regards her testimony of experience as basically superstitious nonsense, as the following quotation illustrates. He is the expert who "knows":

> For about two years the right side of the body has been free of voices. Only the left side is still under the domination of the unconscious... Unfortunately the patient is not intelligent. Her mentality is early Medieval, and I was able to establish a fairly good rapport with her by adapting my terminology to that of the early Middle Ages...it was all devils and witchcraft. (McLynn 1996, 44)

The theory of archetypes of the collective unconscious has been criticized for being unnecessary and obfuscating, because researchers like Eliade (1959, 1989) and Campbell (1981, 1993), through their studies in mythology, culture, and comparative religion, had built a convincing body of evidence to show that all humans share similar common and essential experiences apart from their cultural dressing. Also, some critics have argued that the archetype is not a very precisely defined concept and is so broad as to be almost meaningless.

Reading Jung from a magical point of view convinces me that he is frequently (and I wonder if intentionally) imprecise when discussing spiritual matters. At times he touches on the metaphysical, the magical, and the mystical, but he avoids the ultimate encounter and does not come to grips with the Elphame. His biographer, McLynn, says that

> one cannot be half in and half out of science. The best approach for those who "go beyond" is to embrace metaphysics or mysticism wholeheartedly. (1996, 316)

However, Jung remained basically agnostic about questions of the afterlife and reincarnation, and undecided about the possibility of a second reality populated by independent spiritual entities having an existence outside of and apart from the human mind. This uncertainty could be the result of ontological shock or it could be more simply that Jung was consciously staying within the boundaries of the scientific and medical paradigm by attempting to contain the greater spiritual reality within the lesser physical reality, something that many contemporary scientific thinkers attempt with data that does not fit comfortably within the materialist discourse model.

His description of "complexes" as psychic fragments that have split off from the personality as a result of trauma resonates with shamanic and magical descriptions of soul loss. However, he attributes to complexes the kinds of influences that shamans and traditional people attribute to spirit possession or attachment. He maintains that complexes can interfere with intentions of the individual's will: they behave like independent beings. In the voices heard by the insane they even seem to take on a personal ego and character, like that of the spirits who manifest themselves through automatic writing and similar techniques (Jung in McLynn 1996, 416). From my own perspective the voices would be coming from independent beings in spirit.

His position is frequently ambiguous. Does he or does he not accept the existence of discrete spiritual entities that exist in a subtle reality? It seems that at times he wants to go there but then moves back to the safety of the human mind and the collective unconscious. Although there are considerable areas of similarity and common agreement, there are also significant and important distinctions between Jung's theories and the shamanic or magical worldview.

Transpersonal Psychology

Some psychologists and psychotherapists, in searching for answers to the perplexing problems of the psyche, have sought to move beyond the personality to attempt to come to grips with the concept of that deeply mysterious entity, the "Self." In the movement known as transpersonal psychology (Daniels 2005, Grof 2002, Grof and Grof 1992, Wilber 1979) there has been a fusing of Western psychological thought with spiritual concepts and practices of Eastern mysticism. Concepts such as reaching a deeper layer of the psyche by employing essentially magical practices like meditation and visualization are explored, and there is often an appreciation of the existence of the subtle energy body and its anatomy, borrowed from sources like yoga and Taoism.

Expression of the Self is also an important concept, and therefore painting, dance, sand play, and music are employed as vehicles of expression and for accessing the patient's unconscious mind. Some practitioners use imaginary journey techniques that are very similar to magical pathworkings. Charles Tart (1975), a pioneering researcher in the field, has described the transpersonal psychology movement as a "fourth force" in Western psychology, and he considers it to be a paradigm shift in insight and ontology. The other psychological paradigms are psychoanalysis, behaviorism, and humanistic psychology. The "fourth force" is spiritually reinvigorating psychological medicine.

Transpersonal psychology understands the function and role of the chakras and the acupuncture meridians as organs of the energy body. It takes a spiritual approach that rests on the proposition that there is more to a human being than the visible physical body and the personality. The corpus is an eclectic and innovative mixture that grew out of the rich soil of the human-potential movement. There are many influences on transpersonal psychology, with therapists combining methodologies and experimenting in a pragmatic way to try to break through the restrictions of orthodoxy. There are strong influences of Jungian theory, Fritz Perls' Gestalt Theory, and the ideas of Stanislav Grof and others who believed that as human beings we have the potential to become more than we are, and are, in fact, more than we appear to be.

The Esalen Institute and the California Institute of Integrated Studies have pioneered the serious study, research, and development of this kind of work, combining alternative medicine, Eastern mysticism, the spiritual insights of traditional people, and spiritual psychology with orthodox Western psychological insights. In some important ways I believe that this broad, varied, hybrid corpus creates a bridge between the mundane view of the human and the world that is orthodox psychology and a full magical appreciation of the human relationship to the subtle spiritual world. It is a strong and rich brew, not generally regarded as completely reputable or scientific by those who have the power to define reality and to withhold the imprimatur of respectability from psychological theories that might challenge the materialist philosophical position of the orthodox status quo.

There are many common features between transpersonal psychology and magical psychology. Both have a concept of reaching for an understanding of Self that makes a connection with the realm of the spiritual, and both legitimize practices such as ritual, meditation, and introspection as a way of making that connection. The main difference I see is that magical psychology possesses a more coherent and ordered corpus that has grown naturally and organically from its ancient European Pagan roots, and although it has eclectic elements, they are well blended and integrated. It is based upon the ancient initiatory tradition of the Western world and so has a natural affiliation for the Western-style psyche.

Transpersonal psychology may be too eclectic, and it has been criticized for its attempts to transplant distinctly Eastern methodologies and concepts into Western minds without really understanding the deeper complexity of the borrowed systems. Also, magical psychology is comfortable with the concept of the Elphame as having a real influence and existence, while transpersonal psychology struggles to articulate a clear theoretical foundation and is not necessarily accepting of the concept of a second subtle plane of existence.

Jungian and transpersonal psychology as movements have shifted away from orthodoxy and are tentatively reaching toward the magical. Some practitioners in both Jungian and transpersonal circles are reaching in that direction with more purpose and enthusiasm than others. What they have in common, I believe, is that they occupy the psychological middle ground, sometimes having a foot in both camps—the spiritual and the mundane—as I do. Both fields also have an appreciation of humanity as a species capable of growing toward a spiritual maturity, a proposition to which not a lot of thought is given in the world of orthodox psychology, as orthodoxy tends to see human intelligence and personality as something that is basically fixed and unchangeable.

Ecopsychology

Ecopsychology moves closer to a magical perspective and is more like the spiritual understanding of traditional people, since ecopsychologists maintain that in order to be spiritually and psychologically healthy it is important that humans develop and maintain closer ties to the natural world. Many ecopsychologists believe that our overdeveloped Western technology has taken us away from the psychologically healthy state of seeing ourselves as part of the natural world to a position of believing that we are somehow superior to it. Ecopsychology grew out of a marriage of orthodox psychology and modern scientific insights drawn from ecology and its conceptual offshoots.

The theoretical corpus is particularly influenced by "big picture" theories like the Gaia hypothesis (Lovelock 1979), chaos and complexity theory (Briggs and Peat 1999, Gribbin 2005), permaculture (Mollison and Holgrem 1978), and other holistic concepts, especially the deep ecology principles of Arne Naess and George Sessions (Sessions 1995) that describe the intricate design and function of the natural world and stress the importance of human relationship with nature.

These ecopsychologists and psychotherapists believe that if the planet is in a healthy state, then so is humanity. They tend to see nature as an intelligent and complex living force. Ecopsychology is moving strongly in the direction of a "Goddess" ontology and a shaman's understanding of the sacredness of nature. At the extreme edge of this movement to reconnect with the earth, deep ecology has assumed strong religious and mystical overtones.

Some ecopsychologists who are trained in orthodox psychology are also looking to the culture and rituals of traditional people to gain what they believe to be a deeper and more spiritual understanding of humanity's place in the web of life, based on the ideas of the Goddess model that everything is in direct relationship to everything else. Those ecopsychologists who come from an indigenous background have reached back into their shamanic tribal traditions and have redeveloped an understanding and appreciation of the other reality that is practically identical to a Wiccan or Goddess ontology, aside from the cultural dressing. They are stressing a respect for the intelligent whole that is the living world, and an honoring of the foundational spiritual world. They have the traditional shaman's understanding of the workings of the Elphame and knowledge of the importance of the influences it brings to bear on the visible world. They are reinventing the Goddess by combining traditional practices and developing Western psychological theory.

When ecopsychologist Chellis Glendinning reminds us that an essential part of being human is our intimate connection with the natural world and that we thrive when we are in close communion with living nature, she is connecting her training in Western psychology with the new hybrid spirituality. It is essentially a combination of the new scientifically based ecological awareness and the old practices, techniques, and traditions of Witchcraft and the indigenous shamanic traditions combined with modern psychological insights.

David Tacey, who trained in Jungian psychology and whose particular interest is the evolution of a new spirituality in the youth culture, writes:

> The view is often put to me that if one relates to the world as an extension of oneself, as a field animated with life and meaning along the lines of the Gaia hypothesis, then one would relate to the world

with profound sensitivity, care and concern. A kind of cosmic religious awareness becomes virtually synonymous with the ecological revolution. (1998, 5)

Leslie Gray, a clinical psychologist, Native American, and an initiated shaman, sees clear links between shamanism and ecopsychology:

> Fortunately, those who are forging this new field will not have to reinvent the wheel. We have only to look at the cross-cultural practices of perennial shamanism to find effective models of ecopsychology…it [shamanism] involves the use of altered states of consciousness…It's been practiced continuously by virtually all indigenous peoples up to today. (1995, 173)

Glendinning takes a critical view of what has happened in the Western cultural narrative that contributes to the sense of alienation and fragmentation common in individual mental illness. She sees our common culture as mentally and emotionally ill and that it will require a universal process of psychological and emotional healing as a corrective to the materialistic, mechanized, and technological culture we have created. She says:

> As the world has become less organic and more dependent on techno-fixes for problems created by earlier techno-fixes, humans have substituted a new worldview for one once filled with clean rushing waters, coyotes, constellations of stars, tales of ancestors and people working together in sacred purpose. But the ancestors from the Western world took on the crucial task of redefining their worldview in a state of psychic dislocation and so they ended up projecting a worldview that reflects the rage, terror, and dissociation of the traumatized state. They dreamed a world not of which humans are fully part… (1995, 53)

It is interesting to see that Glendinning says we have lost connection with our "essential humanity" as if the biological and psychic dimensions of our humanity are inherently interwoven and inseparable. This ideal of embodied being remains vitally important to us so long as we inhabit the earth and must be restored to be at the heart of civilized life, but it cannot become the whole vision of human being.

Gray has found ways of bringing both traditions together. In essence, her eclectic brand of psychotherapy is an authentic product of who she is. She uses Native American rattles and drums as tools of healing and as a method of inducing altered states of consciousness. She believes that ecopsychology can trace its roots to shamanism. Her ability to bring her two kinds of training and thinking together has prevented a deep splitting of her psyche. She believes that because these shamanic methodologies have been used over vast periods of time and that they are still used today by indigenous people, they have a proven efficacy and practical application that can enhance modern psychotherapy groupwork as well as individual ecotherapy practice. She says that in the ideals of universal shamanism, health means having balanced relationships with all conscious life.

> When someone is ill, shamanism attempts to restore power to them by putting them back in harmony with life. The idea that all things are connected, while a very ancient concept, is also a concept for the future. (1995, 174)

Gray believes that what is described as progress in psychological research, because it has moved from wholeness to fragmentation and specialization, is a devolutionary trend. She says this awareness came to her at the very beginning of her training in Euro-American psychology. She was irritated by the unconscious assumptions of cultural superiority and evolutionary advancement in the mind of the writer Henri Ellenberger, realizing that what was depicted as scientific progress and perfection was rather a backward trend. This knowledge was the impetus for her to take a vital interest in her Native American shamanism.

It is interesting to me that she describes health as the state of being in balanced relationships with all life because this is something I have contemplated since childhood, at least since my grandfather's death.

Olga Kharitidi is a Russian psychiatrist who spent some time in the Altai Mountains of Siberia, where an indigenous shaman initiated her. She experienced demonstrations of psychic healing and precognition as strong dreams and visions. In order to increase her intuitive and shamanic healing abilities, she underwent "operations" on her energy body. Originally she was most interested in mental illness and its causes and possible treatments from the perspective of shaman medicine. When discussing the origins of mental illness, however, her shaman teacher, or *kam*, said that all mental illness involves the absence of a strong ego, or central sense of self, or connection to a higher self. In English translation the terminology is a little confused, but what she basically means is that the personality self has become disconnected and dislocated from the spiritual soul or higher self, and therefore severed from its spiritual life purpose. In the words of her Siberian *kam*, she reports that

> diseases of the mind have only two causes, and they are totally opposite of each other. One way people can become crazy is if their soul, or part of their soul [self], has been lost. This usually happens because their soul has been stolen from them, but sometimes they may even decide unconsciously to give it away, perhaps in exchange for something else they want. The second way people can become crazy is if they are overwhelmed and occupied by a foreign power. (1999, 177)

My employment of shaman tools and techniques tends to confirm the view that soul loss and invasion by a foreign power are two of the major causes of mental illness. I would not, perhaps, go so far as to say they are the only causes.

Kharitidi has gone on to use these and other magical and shaman insights to create a successful fusion treatment methodology for mental illness. She has integrated Siberian native rituals into her psychiatric work, finding a way of integrating the two worlds and walking the pathway between them as a modern shaman-healer. She has found, as I have, that through this process of hybridization her practice has become enriched. She writes that through the discovery of her shaman healing power she gradually began to become more accepting of the other reality, and as a result became a better and more confident doctor through the study of the indigenous Siberian ceremonies and rituals and by applying them to her practice. Kharitidi developed the principles of Siberian shamanic method and insight, and the once-universal belief that everything is alive and full of spirits, into being perhaps her most effective psychiatric tool. She said that the effect of all this was that she learned more about the nature of serious physical illness as well as mental illness, and was able to heal patients in this more general way—and that she greatly expanded her practice by this means.

Shamanism
and Psychosis

The ideas of reincarnation and past-life memories, spirit
possession by discarnate conscious beings, and loss of souls
essence lie beyond accepted rational thinking. This is certainly
true within the mental health and the medical professions.
Yet traditional psychiatry and use of mind-controlling drugs,
psychotherapy and medical treatments are ineffectual in the
face of spiritual influences, and humans continue to be affected
by all three conditions. (Baldwin 2003, 217)

NONE OF THE CURRENT trends in psychotherapy, as far as movements
go, has overtly embraced the clear idea of working from a second level
of reality, although there are individuals who have come, like Gray, from
a Native American cultural background, and Kharitidi, a native Siberian,
who make use of their indigenous rituals to access altered states of consciousness. There are also some therapists who work in this field and
who do not come from an indigenous background, but these are few
and far between and risk being ridiculed and excommunicated by their
peers. Working in this way therefore could not be described as a "trend"
in any sense of the word at this time in history. However, all trends have

to start somewhere, and there is a noticeable groundswell of public opinion in favor of alternative kinds of healing techniques despite the entrenched views of orthodoxy in the healing professions.

Other originally conventionally trained Western psychologists are doing pioneering work in what has become known as spirit releasement therapy. They are finding that many intractable conditions, both physical and nonphysical, which are unresponsive to Western medicine are cured by these means (Baldwin 1995, Fiore 1988). Some others are successfully adapting the ancient shamanic practice of soul retrieval to a modern context (Harner 1990, Ingerman 1991). At the leading edge of psychology and psychotherapy, therefore, a radical change is taking place, spearheaded by those pioneering spirits who are willing to take an eclectic and innovative approach to healing, and one that embraces the ancient wisdom. They do not regard the concepts and techniques of shamanism as "primitive," and they respect the efficacy and healing power of working with traditional Goddess medicine principles and altered states of consciousness.

As a corollary to this process of going back to the future for inspiration, there is also a growing awareness that the typical worldview and methodologies of Western psychiatry and psychology are not suitable tools for working with people from diverse ethnic or indigenous backgrounds. These people frequently have their own clear ideas about the spiritual foundations of the physical world. For many Australian Aboriginal people, for example, the "Dreamtime" is not something that belongs to the mythical past or, as white Australians have regarded it, a quaint and primitive superstition, but a vital and powerful current reality. To attempt to proselytize, coerce, or pressure Aboriginal people into acceptance of a Western version of reality that sets the limits of existence at the boundary of the physical world, or separates the two worlds as does the Christian discourse, would be tantamount to abuse.

Yet this kind of coercion has been relentless, if unconscious, throughout the history of white settlement in Australia. Regarded in this way, it becomes clearer how much influence the culturally dominant consensus ontology has upon the practice of healing in any given culture, and how powerfully and politically it defines both sanity and madness. Thankfully, in the West there is a new and growing respect for the spiritual insights of traditional people, and some weakening of the assumptions of cultural superiority, even if there is little conscious comprehension. The consensus reality is under pressure to shift from many quarters.

The loosely organized and vaguely defined grass roots movement that is a mixture of magical, spiritual, and ecological ideas that legitimizes a Goddess ontology is becoming increasingly articulated. It is challenging the foundational premises of the dominant cultural paradigm. It is presently small but is growing in influence. It is redefining reality and significantly challenging the scientific materialist hegemony.

Some patients diagnosed as mentally ill or psychotic are simply more sensitive than most people to contact with the other reality. They are too psychically open and permeable and do not have ways of closing off that psychic sensitivity or controlling incursions from the Elphame. Contact with the Elphame, therefore, constitutes a danger to them. In a sense their experiences are shamanic, but they do not have the shaman's experience or training that would enable them to move freely between the worlds, to alter consciousness at will, or to have safe contact with spiritual entities. High sensitivity combined with the lack of a coherent theoretical model and a fragile emotional and psychological state can combine to lead to disastrous consequences.

Schizophrenia largely seems to be an unconscious and involuntary process, but the shaman changes consciousness by a controlled act of dissociation. Tom, whose case is explored in some depth later in the book, had been hospitalized after a series of "psychotic episodes" that he described as "shamanic experiences" or "spiritual emergencies," after the work of Stanislav Grof. Several other research subjects who were ex-patients of mine revealed a similar untrained and uncontrolled sensitivity, some with more ego-strength and emotional resilience than others. There were times when the Elphame burst into awareness and they had strong feelings of losing control. The ontological shock they experienced was profound, but the central sense of self held, at times only just. Ultimately they rejected the reductionist psychiatric explanation and embarked on their own magical journey of healing. These journeys came to embrace an ontology that included acceptance of the existence of the causal spiritual world.

I have two close friends whose psychic sensitivity and experience of ontological shock led them to seek orthodox psychiatric help, and both were diagnosed as paranoid schizophrenics—the only diagnosis possible within a Western psychiatric framework. They were hearing voices and seeing visions. They were both told, to their chagrin, that they would have to take antipsychotic medication for the rest of their lives. One was the man whose story is told at the head of chapter 6. He knew he was not insane. He had a strong sense of self, and so he looked for a theoretical framework that would explain his psychic experiences. Through the therapeutic process of his writing he found answers to some of the important existential questions that had plagued him. The other friend, after a conversation with an art therapist who told him that he was not a paranoid schizophrenic but that he had simply experienced some psychic experiences, discharged himself from a psychiatric hospital and never took any further antipsychotic medication. He went on to have a successful life and career.

Both of these people eventually found their way into the Western magical tradition and were able to integrate their psychic experiences and to see them as actual encounters with the subtle reality and not as "psychotic episodes." I have to wonder about the possible numbers of people who have been misdiagnosed in a similar way, victims of cultural blindness who have gradually come to believe that they are insane, spending emotionally barren lives regulated by permanent medication.

Anthony Storr, who studied the process of creativity, looks at the difference between creative artists and schizophrenics. Both categories of people live in a different world to the world of consensus reality. This is the world of the imagination, essentially the astral world or the Elphame. He says that creative writers and artists, for example,

> are apt to know a whole host of things between heaven and earth of which our philosophy has not let us dream. In their knowledge of the mind they are far in advance of us everyday people, for they draw upon sources which we have not yet opened up for science. (1991, 3)

He continues to stress the importance of contact with the other reality, saying that even secondhand contact has a useful purpose, as it forces us to confront and embrace our lost spiritual selves.

He stresses that even vicarious experience of another level of reality can aid in the process of psychic integration helping us individually to discover the meaning of our own lives.

Storr also believes that because of their partial withdrawal from the world of consensus reality, schizophrenics possess an original vision but usually cannot translate that vision into an art form. They do not have a sufficiently strong or resilient sense of self. This lack of a strong ego or organizing element in the psyche, the observer and interpreter of experience, leads to disintegration rather than integration of the psyche. Also their vision of the Elphame is usually confused, disordered, and dysfunctional.

Thus it seems that ego strength and emotional resilience are important prerequisites for those who travel into the second reality from the point of view of either artistic creativity or shamanic healing. These two personality qualities of emotional resilience and a strong sense of self-identity lessen the powerful and destabilizing impact of ontological shock that is generated when the two worlds collide. Schizophrenics are different to shamans. Storr elaborates on the malignant drama of schizophrenia, when the inner world becomes the outer reality, and all subtle distinctions of imagination and metaphor are lost and there is

> an intense preoccupation with fantasy…schizophrenics have a particular difficulty in making use of symbols which might create for them the bridges between what goes on inside and what happens outside… They have difficulty understanding metaphor and find it difficult to move outside of the literal and concrete. (1991, 177)

It seems that, according to Storr, "madness" reflects the inability to move back and forth between the worlds, to shift awareness from one to the other, and also the inability to think in symbolic ways. Although Storr would describe the schizophrenic's world of fantasy as the realm of the collective unconscious and I would describe it as the Elphame, an autonomous other reality, we would agree that involuntary access to that state by the psychically fragile would be detrimental to their psychological well-being. The Elphame can impinge on individual consciousness in an uncontrolled and chaotic way that may lead to "madness." Both skills— that of shifting awareness and that of understanding and using symbols as a bridge between the worlds—are regarded as important in the Western magical tradition.

Starhawk discusses the difference between magic and psychosis, noting that the difference lies in maintaining the ability to step back at will into ordinary consciousness (1999, 37). Her view supports the traditional definition of magic as the art of changing consciousness at will and places Wicca or Witchcraft and its practitioners within the ancient shaman tradition, such as the Australian Aboriginal or Native American, whereby the shamanic practitioner is able to move backward and forward between daylight and starlight consciousness, or from ordinary to nonordinary awareness as need be. At the same time he or she is also required to be a stable and grounded community member. The personal center holds in the face of the destabilizing and disintegrating force of ontological shock as the Elphame makes its presence felt.

Ambivalence is another way of dealing with unusual experiences that raise uncomfortable questions about the nature of reality. That is, the person learns to live with a paradox that involves two more or less mutually exclusive propositions, and no third way that might ultimately lead to a resolution of the dilemma. The world of the senses is ostensibly observable and reliable, and it seems that material reality can be trusted, yet the person has had an experience of another reality that is empirically inexplicable and unprovable. It seems the intellectual part of the brain does not live easily with paradox.

Many of the people I interviewed were in this position of having to grapple with ontological shock, using the tools of ordinary intellectual analysis to explain something that exists beyond the understanding of the intellect, as it has been educated. What they tended to do was conform outwardly to the accepted and received version of reality but privately and inwardly maintain unresolved doubts about it. They explored the wider truth only with trusted confidants, since having experienced the other reality in some way sets one apart even from intimates.

Some of them had strong doubts about their sanity and remained bogged down in this dilemma until treatment gave them another way of seeing what was happening to them that "made sense" (their words) and enabled them to integrate their experiences. They tended to shut away the experiences into a compartment in the mind where it was not forgotten or denied but simply ignored until they could bring it out into a safer, therapeutic environment to examine it and to see what it might mean.

Regarding the question of sanity and madness from a magical perspective, I am wondering that rather than a series of discrete "diseases" or mental illnesses there exists, in fact, a continuum from sanity to madness. As a hypothetical proposition, perhaps at one pole is the state known as schizophrenia, which as Storr suggests is an almost complete withdrawal into the other reality and a demonstrated sense of the disintegration of self. Perhaps schizophrenia gradually merges into the autism spectrum disorders such as Asperger's syndrome, where there remains a functioning aspect of self but narrowly defined and frequently devoid of social and emotional intelligence. The functioning self also withdraws into the other reality when the physical world becomes too difficult, demanding, or dangerous. Perhaps these people have lost their soul or a part of it, which restricts their ability to express their whole self. In the context of shamanism this would be described as "soul loss."

There appears to be a certain element of personal decision-making about this condition, even perhaps at an unconscious level. I consider that to be a possibility because I saw a patient several years ago, an intelligent, interactive, and charming young woman, who told me that until the age of fifteen she had been deeply withdrawn from the "real world" and had been diagnosed as severely autistic. She had spent most of those fifteen years hiding under the dining room table, doing repetitive rocking actions, or "stims." Finally, one day she said to herself: *Bugger this. I'm sick of this. I want to come out.* Previously I had not considered this element of personal will to be a factor in this spectrum of disorders.

She did indeed "come out." She taught herself to read and rapidly caught up with the rest of the learning she needed to acquire. At the time she consulted me she was nineteen, partway through a university course and achieving at a high level. In shamanic terms she had suffered soul loss but had rescued herself. This case made me think that the basis of autism is trauma and paralyzing fear not necessarily associated with the current life but perhaps even a carryover from previous lifetimes of persecution and violence.

Kharitidi (1999) describes a similar case: that of her patient Luba, who, with minimal and unconscious help from her doctor, miraculously extracted and rescued herself from what Kharitidi described as a very malignant and fast-acting form of schizophrenia.

Other psychotic states such as bipolar disorder seem to be attempts to find a balance or equilibrium within the psyche between the wildly swinging poles of personal power and powerlessness and self-love and self-loathing. At the heart of bipolar disorder is a hatred, a rejection and a blaming of self, so that the sense of self is still fragmented and the patient moves in and out of lucid states. In many such patients I have treated, the motive force seems to be intense guilt, but I wonder if these wildly swinging states are also related to shock or trauma in some way because of the similarity to the experience of ontological shock and its accompanying sensations of destabilization and of swinging between two poles until, and if, a new equilibrium is discovered.

Further along the hypothetical continuum of dysfunction are defense mechanisms such as denial, projection, repression, regression, and others described by Freud. These devices act to keep people stuck in neurotic states through lack of awareness of the broader reality and the deeper aspects of self. There is a willingness "not to know" and a semi-conscious determination to limit self-awareness. There is also a degree of cowardice and dishonesty in the defense mechanisms, as well as an infantile inability to take responsibility. The self is functioning but diminished. Often these diminished expressions of self, which seek to restrict reality to something limited and controllable, are the results of trauma and an overwhelming fear of losing control. There is a clear relationship here to the shamanic concept of soul loss. The schizoid types described by Storr (1991), who sever heart from head and intellect from intuition, would also fit into this picture, as well as those determined materialists who turn away from anything suggestive of a spiritual reality and cling to the evidence of their senses, however demonstrably unreliable. Their displays of denial seem to go quickly to angry outbursts that are reminiscent of childish temper tantrums.

Beyond these states are those who have a skeptical openness to other possibilities and a sense of discontent with the accepted and received expressions of the cultural narrative. They have not necessarily experienced ontological shock in a personal way but have a kind of intuitive expectation of something further, some underlying truth of the phenomenal world, or they have seen others go through experiences that throw the consensus version of reality into question. These people are intelligent and questioning and adopt a theoretical framework that says the human senses are not necessarily the final arbiters of what is real and there are many angles from which to view reality. It is possible to detect in these people a yearning for a personal spiritual dimension to their lives, but it is one that is not intellectually offensive.

From a magical perspective, further along the continuum is the state of ontological shock. Through the experience of ontological shock a person may go one way or the other, moving backward and forward between denial and acceptance until some form of psychic equilibrium is re-established. In this sense ontological shock is an invitation from the world of spirit to grow into greater awareness of self and of the greater reality: an invitation to begin the Hero's Journey. Some of those issued with the invitation remain stuck and unable to take up the challenge and to integrate the experience that originates from the subtle reality. Others take the impetus and extra energy that comes from the destabilization of the consensus worldview and commit to an investigation of the subtle world and a journey of discovery to greater self-awareness.

Those explorers who do take up the challenge of the journey or the path may be those who have experienced an epiphany of some kind, those intrepid seekers of the truth or the creative artist, like Van Gogh and other pathfinders and mediators of the Elphame. Like Van Gogh, Brett Whitely is another artist whose paintings show the effect of the energy body on form, and whose tortured inspiration shows humanity new ways of seeing.

The price these artistic pioneers paid for their sensitivity of perception was to take themselves on a dangerous journey that is close to the uncontrolled life-world of the schizophrenic. Perhaps this is why the modern world is so fascinated by their work; we unconsciously sense the inherent heroism it implies. This is the same Hero's Journey described by Campbell (1993): a journey through darkness into expanded states of awareness and an expanded sense of self. The Hero's Journey is the spiritual path, the journey of initiation in whatever cultural or historical setting. It is undertaken as a gift to self but also as an inspired learning experience for others.

At the other pole of the insanity-sanity continuum is the master shaman or the mystical adept, the enlightened or ensouled being who is able to move smoothly and seamlessly from the hidden reality to the physical reality and back again, and who understands the influences and nuances of both levels of existence. These people know that they are spiritual beings in physical form. The adept or master shaman seems to me to be the epitome of mental health because he or she has an expanded experience and expanded sense of self—an expanded knowledge of reality and the ability to work in a conscious way toward human and planetary spiritual evolution. In the adept, then, the personality self and the higher self have gradually become unified and at this stage of development all doubts within the personality self have been eradicated.

Brunton writes about the higher spiritual self, which he calls the "overself," a deeper, more essential dimension of the self we know. This is his term for what is more commonly that "mysterious and elusive thing called the soul," and which is, he says, the "most fundamental" part of human nature (1970, 175). It has a subtle influence that guides our being, and when we are aware of it most fully is when we act in the highest way possible, and we call it our conscience.

This is a magical view of the hypothetical sanity-insanity continuum, suggesting that the schizophrenic and the adept are at opposite poles of the same band of reality. In many schizophrenics, their sensitivity to the other reality renders them dysfunctional in the worldly sense, although there are notable exceptions, and some people diagnosed as suffering from schizophrenia function better on a regime of pharmaceutical medication. In the adept the ability to move between both realities, the spiritual and the physical, and to operate in both realities with expertise is something to which we can all aspire.

Kharitidi's case of schizophrenia referred to previously demonstrates that she spontaneously and completely cured this patient using a simple shamanic healing technique. Her Siberian *kam* had told Olga to heal from the heart and to make the heart her center of consciousness. She advised Olga to ask her inner healer to come out, and as Olga did this her focus of attention was dramatically shifted to the heart level. The patient, Luba, had not responded to any drug or conventional psychotherapy treatment and seemed to be slipping away into the complete darkness of the abyss. Luba did not exactly rescue herself, but with a little strange and unconscious support from Kharitidi was able marshal the energy to burst out of the deep psychosis that had enfolded her.

These cases suggested to me, first, that sometimes the decision to be well or ill is a personal choice, but that change in consciousness or realization takes whatever time it takes. It also raises questions about the overuse of psychotropic medication. Does the use of psychoactive drugs prevent or delay the possibility of healing because of the separation of mind and emotions, as Breggin (1993) has described? The personal will to heal may be dissipated by the severing of the "heart" from the "head," thus preventing the necessary emotional growth that will lead to the realization that will give an impetus to healing.

Kharitidi's case seemingly validates the views of R. D. Laing (1964, 1971) and other psychiatrists of the "anti-psychiatry movement" that if given the necessary support and time, many patients can work through their "mental illness" and come out the other side without the need for heroic interventions.

Kharitidi's struggle between her intellect and her intuition as she witnessed Luba's improbable healing seemed very familiar to me, and I recognized the symptoms of ontological shock. However, for her the shock was shortened because she already had had many concentrated experiences during her shaman training, which had made her doubt her perceptions and her sanity. Also, she was under the tutelage of an experienced shaman as a guide and teacher.

Kharitidi works in a very similar manner to the way I have developed my own practice. She works with the whole person, body, emotions, mind, and spirit, combining orthodoxy with traditional Goddess/shaman insights. Interestingly, she moved in the opposite direction to myself, from mental to physical medicine, while I moved from the physical to the emotional and mental. Both of us were trained and experienced in shamanic methods and had a strong interest in the spiritual. Both of us also use herbs and other alternative treatments such as ritual and ceremony as instruments of healing. Both of us had received a strong calling from the world of spirit that sent us on a journey of discovery, which overturned many of the notions and illusions we had held about the nature of our work and the nature of reality.

I have found, as did Kharitidi, that usually the more educated the person, the more powerful the challenge of ontological shock because it frequently revolutionizes what has been taught and absorbed on the professional level, and it puts one in conflict with the beliefs and practices of one's peers and one's culture. The willingness to combine the science of orthodox psychology with the spiritual insights of the Goddess model of reality and the practices of traditional shamanism may exact a price that all those who dare to think outside the square seem destined to pay. They risk ridicule and rejection, but most would probably agree with Wesselman (1996) that the excitement of discovering another level or reality of unlimited potential seems worth that risk.

The Goddess in the
Consulting Room

Gnothi Seauton: Man, Know Thyself
(inscription from Delphi's Temple of Apollo)

I BELIEVE THAT THE willingness to accommodate other ways of knowing and being, and to weave those ideas and practices into my therapeutic
work, has enriched it. The combination of practices accepted in the
Western cultural discourse with shamanic processes that operate from
the Elphame has produced significant healing outcomes for a group of
clients whose difficulties did not resolve by the sole use of orthodox types
of therapy or through the application of alternative medicine modalities.

I am normally conservative in my approach to healing, and when
patients present for treatment I first apply Occam's razor and look for
simple and physical causes. If the case does not resolve through that
approach, then I will consider an energy medicine modality—for example, color treatment or homoeopathy or emotionally based psychotherapeutic approaches. If those interventions in turn are not effective, then I
will consider using some form of spiritual healing. Sometimes being conservative is the most relevant approach, but keeping the possibility of a
spiritual intervention in reserve is an important adjunct resource.

The eleven interviews considered in the following chapters offer insights into the different ways the Elphame interfaces with mundane reality and exerts influences that are unsuspected. Its effects are not always benign, as many of the interviews indicate: pain, suffering, and physical and mental illness can all have their origins in that subtle world. Conversely, all the interview subjects discovered cures among the healing treasures of the Elphame, and many of them commented that it had been necessary to go there.

Working from the position of the physical world only did not usually precipitate a cure but gave a temporary amelioration of the symptoms while the deeper causes remained untouched. The research subjects reported that working from the Elphame was a different experience to any treatment they had received from orthodox medicine; April, Tom, Angela, Josephine, Isabelle, Laura, and James all made comments to that effect. They experienced lasting cures from shamanic medicine and had, in different ways, directly participated in their own recoveries.

They found this level of participation to be empowering, and they considered that the Goddess model gave a workable and plausible theoretical perspective on the causes of their suffering. All of the interview subjects experienced an expansive shift of their worldview. Their reports of their initiatory and healing journeys with the Old Goddess convinced me of the efficacy of the archetype and that its transformative power was valuable and effective on all levels of the psyche. It symbolized the genuine concept of holistic treatment and was efficacious when applied to physical/energetic, emotional, mental, and spiritual aspects of the patients who were involved with the research project.

Eight of the ten subjects of this chapter had experienced previous orthodox Western-style medical treatment. Some of those eight had experienced slight relief from pharmaceutical drugs, but no demonstrable healing had occurred, and the symptoms recurred and worsened when they stopped the medication. In some cases the medication itself made the condition worse or had no appreciable effect. Two people in this group, Meredith and Luciano, had consulted me as their primary healthcare provider.

Laura's doctor avoided consulting with her when it became clear that she could not diagnose the presenting problem. Josephine and April were told by their psychiatrists that their distressing symptoms were "panic attacks" and that "they would pass," but neither woman found this advice to be accurate. April had experienced ten years of ineffectual psychiatric treatment that had left her addicted to prescription drugs; Isabelle and Angela were given large doses of corticosteroid drugs that provided temporary relief from their symptoms but had undesirable side effects. Their unendurable physical and psychological symptoms returned unabated if they stopped their prescription medication.

These people reported that none of the doctors or psychiatrists they had consulted were able to empathically enter their reality. They were in the position of experts who "know" and were therefore unable to form a healing alliance with the patients or respect their inner experiences as valid (Read, Mosher, and Bentall 2004).

Both Tom and Anna had experienced devastating sexual abuse in childhood, but this information was not considered as linked to their condition although there is a body of research to show that traumas of this kind are implicated in the onset of psychosis in later life (Miller 1998; Read, Mosher, and Bentall 2004). They were also both medicated with antipsychotic and antidepressive drugs that they claimed made them worse, although in Tom's case the massive doses of Largactyl he was forced to take did lower the intensity of the mania symptoms he had been experiencing.

Tom said that when he was admitted to a psychiatric ward the medical staff were most interested in obtaining a psychiatric diagnosis and deciding which antipsychotic drugs to prescribe. They were not interested at all in exploring his reality or understanding his experience. He believed that there was no appreciation or acceptance that he may have been experiencing something real or that his experiences may have had their origins in another reality.

Tom and Anna's cases in chapters 14 and 15 illustrate the ways in which state-sanctioned medicine approaches such complex cases with methods that could be called callous, brutal, and dismissive of the patient's reality. There is a crude overconfidence and inappropriateness in judgments that are made about who is sane and who is mad. These black-and-white judgments suggest the presence of a strong and expedient political bias that defines consensus reality. Tom was deemed mad although he framed his diagnosed psychotic episode as a "shamanic experience" or a "spiritual emergency" and regarded it as a communication from the Elphame. The destabilizing elements of ontological shock, as I identified it in his story, tended to corroborate his view and perhaps, as he claimed, his "psychotic episode" was an initiatory journey.

Anna was deemed legally sane despite strong evidence that she had suffered recurrent catatonic episodes lasting for days or weeks at a time and for which she had been hospitalized, that she had regularly dissociated since childhood, had regularly self-harmed, had made many suicide attempts, was diagnosed with major depression, and had claimed to have no memory of the heinous crimes with which she had been convicted. She was diagnosed as sane because it was politically and socially expedient to view her as a criminal. The fact that she had suffered horrible and prolonged sexual abuse in childhood was not presented at her murder trial. Her high-profile barrister had failed to investigate deeply enough to discover the mitigating truth: that she might have been legally insane when the crimes were committed.

I believe that childhood trauma and pain in the form of prolonged sexual abuse, physical abuse, or neglect and abandonment plays a major role in patterns of drug and alcohol addiction, particularly in women but probably in men as well. For the past several years I have been working with female prisoners and parolees. Their stories of childhood abuse are horrific and are not really addressed or considered by the criminal justice system. In female clients I see a strong link between alcohol and drug abuse and crime. They tell me that the drugs and alcohol kill the pain of often shocking memories of the things that were done to them by trusted adults in childhood. Their need to buy drugs leads to criminal patterns of behavior, often shoplifting or robbery, for which, if caught, they are incarcerated.

Many of these women (I would hazard an educated guess that the number would be somewhere between 80 and 90 percent of women in jail) are there for crimes that have as their primary causation severe childhood trauma (usually sexual abuse of some kind) and poor attachment to parental figures. I am talking about women in detention in Australia, but as an educated guess I would expand this insight to women in most Western countries, and I strongly suspect in many Eastern countries as well. This kind of abuse and violation can lead to a shattering of the sense of self and feelings of incipient insanity. The center cannot hold. They are mostly treated for "mental health issues," and practically no one wants to lift the veil to see the truth of the underlying horrors. It is easier to prescribe a pill to treat the "mental health" symptoms than to look at what caused the shattering of the self in the first place.

I am suggesting that, like Anna, they have experienced soul loss and that a part or parts of themselves have become fractured and broken off because of the trauma they have suffered. Psychological reintegration is possible but only through the process of reuniting the lost aspects of self. Prescription drugs will never complete the healing that is required but will help only to manage the condition if they are lucky. Often they have told me that the drugs don't work or that they have horrible side effects. Commonly they comment that the drugs make them "feel like a zombie."

The state-defined parameters of sanity and madness are stark. There is no subtle or nuanced approach to the issue (and there may, in fact, exist a nuanced continuum from sanity to madness, as I have earlier proposed) and little evidence of an ability on the part of most orthodox mental health practitioners to think more sensitively about it or to look to the Elphame for deeper understanding or useful healing resources.

My encounters with the other reality gave me a different and expanded view of what is real and have enabled me to validate the experiences of the interview subjects and to eventually look for causation and a cure in the nonphysical world. Even to speculate about the prospect of such subtle influence opens the treatment options to more creative possibilities, and during this period of consulting with private patients I was steadily gaining the confidence to be more innovative and experimental. I also began to become more mentally and emotionally "immersed" in healing from the Elphame, and it began to feel like a normal and natural methodology.

Originally, I had reservations about working this way, but many patients were desperate for help and although one part of me wanted to refuse to treat them, I ultimately could not. I always said yes to appeals for help, even though I knew that more conventional alternative treatment like counseling, homoeopathy, or herbalism might not be successful and that I might be forced to use "strange" and "weird" methods that could make me vulnerable to criticism and possibly ostracism. However, the healer's drive was too strong, and their suffering aroused a powerful sense of compassion that I could not suppress.

All the research subjects were interested in giving me feedback about the outcomes of the work we had done. This was the first time I had any review of the sequels to their treatment. They were chosen because their cases were interesting and varied and contained enough contrasts and similarities to illustrate important themes. As the interviews unfolded, their reviews of their healing journeys and their efficacious outcomes surprised me. In all cases, it seemed that not only had their debilitating symptoms abated but also their lives were transformed in positive ways.

These interviews give a range of insights into the ways in which these people responded to such unorthodox treatment and look at their experience of working with the two-tiered shamanic model as a background to healing. I asked about the outcomes and also wanted to know how these treatments compared with orthodox medicine. I was also interested in understanding if their experiences had changed their views of reality.

A typical skill of the traditional shaman is the ability to talk to spirits, including the dead, who sometimes appear to be as much in need of psychotherapy as the living. They may remain "stuck between the worlds," causing havoc and illness in the lives of "living" people who do not recognize their painful physical and mental symptoms as attempts to attract and influence their attention.

Traditional people refer to these spiritual entities as something approximately translatable as "evil spirits." While there is no doubt that they are capable of causing harm, as these interviews will show, the spirits are often simply people who cannot move on and require a ritual or ceremony to help them release their fear and confusion and fully enter the Elphame. Their intentions are not usually consciously evil, although for the unfortunate victim the outcome of the attachment may be ill health, loss of energy, and feelings of incipient madness. Sometimes those attaching spirit entities also require some rational explanation of what has happened to them because we do not have appropriate cultural narratives to help people to go through the transition from one state to another after death. Therefore, the natural and normal process of dying is frequently experienced as terrifying and confusing.

Many of the research participants believed they were going insane, partly because they could not contextualize their experiences. In this sense they were experiencing profound ontological shock. The other reality was reaching into their lives in ways they could not understand. The cases of Anna, Laura, Josephine, and April all illustrate the painful and distressing confusion that may arise when the cultural narrative is deficient and their experiences appear to have no context.

April commented that her Maori husband and his relatives, who had their roots in traditional culture, had a context for understanding phenomena that originated from the other reality, but she did not and so was left with strong feelings of developing and overtaking psychosis. Other participants in the study were left in the position of not understanding or knowing what was happening to them. In addition, most had no spiritual background that might have given them an acceptable framework of understanding.

When the other reality was denied, these patients experienced a sense of painful fragmentation and disconnection. From a magical or shamanic perspective, several of the interviewees experienced "soul loss"—that is, an important aspect of self had been left behind somewhere, stuck in a past time and place. They experienced themselves as existing with a kind of hole in their psyche or with a two-dimensional feeling of unreality. For example, Luciano had lost his child self and rediscovered him locked in a symbolic dungeon in the Elphame. When he reintegrated this fragment of self, his doubts and fears relating to his sense of masculine identity disappeared.

Anna had lost her personal will and integrity, and with the help of a magical technique—the creation of an astral guardian or artificial elemental—was able to find those lost aspects and reintegrate them. When they were consolidated back into her psyche, she was able to live a happier, more normal, and fulfilling life. Angela, through a process of magical healing on physical and emotional levels, was able to change a lifetime pattern of dependency on inadequate and abusive men and to overcome unconscious fears of abandonment. When she was finally able to live as "herself alone" and reintegrate her lost child self, a man who was dependable, loving, and supportive magically appeared in her life. Her chronic and debilitating eczema also disappeared.

I was able to diagnose other members of this group of subjects as suffering unrecognized attacks from attaching spirit entities that they could not bring into consciousness or release, even though intuitively they recognized something of what was happening. I say that because of the language they unconsciously used in describing what was happening. Laura made the comment that "it was heart-wrenching," and April said, "It's the baby's father!" These were prophetic, strangely accurate comments that revealed their truths as these cases unfolded.

Josephine had experienced strongly intuitive urges to visit her brother's grave weeks before she came to consult me, but she only did so when I suggested it might be a good idea. The participants ignored the clues inherent in these statements and brushed aside their intuitions and feelings, and as many of them mentioned, their "minds got in the way" of their intuitive perceptions. Once they had some understanding of the subtle world and its capacity for influencing physical reality, their feelings of gathering madness dramatically abated and they were able to validate their earlier intuitive and accurate impressions.

The Goddess model is cyclic and therefore suggestive of past lives having some influence over a person's current reality. "Karma" is essentially the resolution of energy patterns established in prior incarnations that require restitution through action in the current life. From a magical perspective, it was interesting for me to see how it is possible for karma to seemingly follow a person throughout several lifetimes. This had apparently happened in the cases of April and Tom. In Tom's case his journey to healing required the recognition and honoring of the severe suffering and trauma of several past-life personalities, or "shells," that had become stuck between the worlds.

In April's case it was imperative that she recognize and honor the extreme suffering she had caused to others through her gullible and irresponsible actions in a past life. For both these subjects, their journey to healing was resolved through the observance of the appropriate rituals of recognition and acceptance that addressed these forsaken past-life responsibilities. Prior to doing this work I had not really understood how unresolved karma can follow a person from lifetime to lifetime until a resolution is achieved.

Kenneth Meadows explains how it is possible to heal some illnesses only by understanding the patient's karma and by obtaining clear mental pictures or other evidence that relates past trauma or actions to the presenting problem:

> The shaman understands that some illnesses, malfunctions or handicaps have karmic origins from a previous lifetime, and in such cases, modern science is unlikely to affect a cure. (1998, 170)

I have divided the ten interviews into three groups. The first four cases I have grouped under the title "Entering the Elphame" (chapters 9 and 10) because I had given those patients training and instruction in magical techniques that had enabled them to enter that world and take an active role in their own healing process. The skills they learned included ritual techniques (both inner and outer methods), meditation, and pathworking practices that used the creative imagination as a tool for healing, how to work with energy of different kinds, and the method of psychic reintegration known as "soul retrieval." These are the cases of Meredith, Luciano, Angela, and Isabelle.

The second set of four interviews I have grouped under the heading "Incursions from the Elphame" (chapters 11 through 13). These are the interviews of Laura, Josephine, April, and James. The initiatory journeys of these people illustrate some of the ways in which the Elphame is able to intrude into the "real" world to cause physical and mental health crises that are difficult to heal unless the practitioner is able to work from the subtle world. In working with these patients (excepting James, who was not a patient but my partner, and April, who was my coworker) I followed the modus operandi of traditional shamanism.

These, in the main, are cases of spirit attachments and the patients were suffering various levels of psychological, emotional, and physical trauma as a result. The spirits themselves were also traumatized and in need of psychological and emotional aid. This work could be described as psychotherapy for the dead as well as for the living. Both the living and the dead, suffering from ontological shock, were unable to contextualize their experiences of the Elphame. Ritual once again was the vehicle that helped resolve these distressing situations for both categories of persons. April's case is unique because it is viewed from four different perspectives.

The third set of interviews, those of Tom and Anna, I have grouped together under the title of "The Politics of Madness."

In all cases aspects of traditional Wiccan ritual practice were utilized. Ritual was important, whether it was performed in the mind and imagination as a pathworking or in the physical world using tangible symbols or both. The ritual forms used were influenced by my magical training and were adapted and simplified to suit the needs of ordinary people who were not initiates of the magical tradition. However, I observed that on some level many of the research participants exhibited a natural kind of piety and respect for the practices to which I introduced them, as if they intuited the sacredness inherent in them. Their response to ritual generally was very positive. The performance of the appropriate rituals brought healing to all the participants, both the living and the dead, and their healing journeys brought them an expanded awareness of the power of the Elphame and the ways in which it interacts with physical reality in both positive and negative ways. In this sense their experiences were initiatory.

Perhaps, also, these patients had been conditioned in some ways to respect the efficacy of ritual. For an hour or two each week the client enters a sacred space in the consulting room wherein a gradual mutual trust and respect and an intimate yet impersonal intensity is created. The room is quiet and separated from the mayhem of the ordinary world. Reclining on the couch, the patient is in an introverted mood, accessing content from the other reality in the form of dreams, intuitions, and symbols. For many people, as previously discussed, their therapist is the only person with whom they can be completely honest or be their truest and deepest, most vulnerable selves and be accepted and acceptable. This, of itself, is a powerfully healing experience because it encourages and empowers clients to live more authentic lives. It is also important that therapists are able to meet the client in authentic ways.

Gerald Corey writes about the importance of authenticity in the therapeutic relationship. In my view he succinctly describes the "wounded healer" in the modern world:

> It seems essential to me that counselors explore their own values, attitudes and beliefs in depth and that they work to increase their own awareness…Therapists must be willing to remain open to their own growth and to struggle in their lives if their clients are to believe in them and in the therapeutic process. (1996, 5–6)

This discussion of the quality of authenticity or genuineness shows me how important it is to be true to myself and my life experiences, and to find ways of integrating those insights into my work. Therapy and ontology are therefore intimately connected.

I see evidence of a deepening of my understanding as I moved into a more psychologically and emotionally immersed level of practice. I was becoming more open in confiding to my patients that I believed their problems could have had their origins in the other reality, and also more accepting of my insights and intuitions relating to the Elphame. The challenge for me was to inquire whether theories of physical and psychological healing could be enriched by the insights of the magical, two-tiered shamanic worldview that is informed by the qualities of the Goddess archetype: wholeness, inclusiveness, acceptance, and compassion.

By the end of treatment all the patients were free of pharmaceutical drugs. They were also generally free of the distressing symptoms that had troubled them, sometimes for many years. As a climax to their healing journeys, they were enabled to make transformational changes to their ordinary lives and, in most cases, after many years of painful struggle, were able to form stable and satisfying relationships and to normalize their lives socially in significant ways.

Perhaps there is a certain irony evident in that. The "illusory" spirit world of the Elphame, which according to the official Western cultural narrative does not exist, has a demonstrable and efficacious transformative power, according to the interview subjects, to make meaning and to create stability in their worldly lives.

9

Entering the Elphame
The Transforming Power of Ritual, Part 1

> I think when it's ritual, it's about you and your inner life…and
> maybe your soul or your spirit. It's really strong. I really did feel
> like it was connecting to a deeper level. (Meredith)

Meredith

Meredith's story comes at the beginning because the Elphame touched her life only lightly at this time. She and I had consulted to design a ritual that had its roots in the Western magical tradition. This was a ritual to be performed for a specific purpose. It was not designed to address all of her problems, although it did ultimately turn out to have some important repercussions and cascading effects into other areas of her life.

Although Meredith entered the Elphame and experienced its power for transformation, her involvement was not as prolonged or intense as some of the other cases that will follow. She had decided to have a pregnancy terminated and was suffering from deep guilt, depression, and self-reproach. This case describes how a modified magical ritual technique helped Meredith to change her dark, overwhelming feelings about the termination into a calmer acceptance of the outcomes of her decision.

This is presented as a case within a larger case: a snapshot of a brief therapeutic time within a greater healing journey.

I had consulted with Meredith for over two years and used nonshamanic and shamanic methods to help her through the grief and trauma she had experienced in her childhood and adolescence. I used the magical Grail Castle symbol as a ritual pathworking to help with the healing of her wounded child self (this method is described in greater detail in the next case of Luciano), but also sand-tray therapy and art therapy, as well as talking therapy interventions based on the Egan (1998) model of psychotherapy and the ideas of the psychotherapist James Bugental (1987). I also consulted with her mother and sisters, and conducted family therapy sessions for them.

Meredith's father was a violent alcoholic. He had incested three of his four daughters, including Meredith. Her mother had been the typical co-dependent partner of an alcoholic. She continually made excuses for him, hid the evidence of his drinking and violent behavior, and tried to help him to change. She buried her pain, shame, and guilt in her religion. Her Catholic faith was both her strength and her weakness, and she tried to imbue her daughters with the same unwavering acceptance of the situation by telling them that their father was "really a good man underneath." She also claimed to have been unaware of his abuse of the children.

When Meredith first presented for treatment she was deeply depressed, uncertain, and confused about her life. She was twenty-six and had not experienced a long-term, committed relationship. She wondered if she was emotionally deficient and incapable of maintaining a loving relationship. She did not become sexually active until she was twenty-three, when she began a series of brief relationships with emotionally remote men addicted to drugs or alcohol. These relationships were destructive of her sense of personal worth and self-confidence.

Meredith's involvement with these types of men is a pattern of co-dependence discussed in detail by the psychotherapist Robin Norwood. The basis of the unconscious attraction is to be found in the original unresolved child-parent relationship, which the child self compulsively seeks to rectify:

Because you were never able to change your parent into the warm, loving caretaker you longed for, you respond deeply to the familiar type of emotionally unavailable man whom you can try to change again through your love. (1986, 10)

Meredith felt a lot of uncertainty about her current relationship. The man exhibited the familiar pattern of addiction to drugs and alcohol. However, he treated her in a loving and respectful way and seemed to genuinely care for her. She cared for him too and although he was not ideal, he was kind and attentive, and she wanted to believe that it could be a growing and learning relationship.

Fifteen months into the relationship, she discovered she was pregnant. This alarmed her because she did not believe that the relationship was stable enough to support a child. She decided to have a termination but was not prepared for her severe emotional reaction. She said:

I had a really hard time with it. It was awful (tears come to her eyes). I just felt like I had not thought about it…that I'd taken a life and not even thought…maybe I just had this plan and this didn't fit in with my plan, so I'll not even consider it. I just felt like a monster really. It was horrible (her voice drops very low and trembles) and I felt really guilty about it…I never really thought I would have to make a decision like that, I think I really grieved…it just felt like such a loss (she is weeping) and it (the ritual) was to help me (whispers) say goodbye.

I turned off the tape recorder and asked her if she wanted to continue. After a fifteen-minute break she indicated that she did.

I have helped many female patients design a ritual to help them say goodbye to a child they have terminated and deal with the resulting guilt and depression. The ceremony places the intention in a psychological and spiritual context and not a secular one. Suppression or denial of feelings of guilt, grief, and vulnerability has an impact on the psyche and can result in outbursts of anger and other apparently irrational behavior. To bring those deeply buried feelings to the surface, take responsibility, and ask forgiveness of the life source helps the petitioner to live more honestly, albeit still sadly, as Meredith describes.

When I asked her how she was feeling about it currently, she said:

> It feels like I've found a place for it, and I'm normally okay with it. I really feel like I did the right thing and I'm okay with it. I don't feel the guilt. It's just still...sad.

I asked her how she experienced the ritual, and she describes mixed feelings. She is laughing and crying simultaneously.

> I did the ritual and it was like saying a prayer...that the time is not right...and my circumstances are not right...and I want you to be happy and that's not going to happen right now. When I light the candles I just want you to know. (She has moved from the past into the present tense and is reliving the experience.)

She begins to weep and again I turn off the tape for ten minutes. She composes herself and indicates that she wants to continue.

> I hadn't thought about it for a while...and I'm a bit surprised actually (gives an embarrassed laugh). I wanted her life to be a really happy one and I didn't think I could provide that right now, especially with the person I was with at the time, and I just said, "I hope that you come back to me one day when things would be better."

We had designed a ceremony that expressed what she wanted to say. She chose an Egyptian ceremony because she believed she had past-life memories of ancient Egypt and felt an affinity to its symbols and god-forms. She wanted to apologize to the Great Goddess as the source of all life and to ask her to take back the soul of the unborn child. The apology reconnected her with a sense of wholeness and spiritual integrity.

She said that her experience of normal prayer within the context of orthodox religious practice had felt disconnected and as if she was merely going through the motions. The ritual experience was different:

> When you're praying it's like you're talking to something out there that's not connected with you, but I think when it's ritual, it's about you and your inner life...and maybe your soul or your spirit. It's really strong. I really did feel like it was connecting to a deeper level.

Coherent symbolism is important in ritual and helps to focus the will and intention. Before commencing her ritual, Meredith would shower to signify pure intentions and smudge herself with sandalwood incense. Smudging is a shamanic practice using certain sacred dried plants that cleanse undesirable thought-forms and feelings from the auric field.

She would set up a small altar with a new white altar cloth, which also symbolized purity of intention. Sandalwood incense would be burned because it is magically attributed to Anubis, the cosmic psychopomp. It is he who escorts the dead to Amenti (the Elphame). She would have images of Anubis and Isis on her altar. Aus Set (Isis), the Great Mother Goddess of the Egyptians, is often depicted holding her child Horus, so she would have an appropriate image of Isis in the center of her altar. She would obtain a lotus or a water lily, a flower sacred to Isis, as an offering and have it standing in a vase of water. Thus, all the important symbols and relevant elements were represented—earth, fire, water, and air—and the working would be elementally balanced.

A large white candle would be lit to invoke the aid of the Goddess, and there was a small pink candle to represent the unborn child. White candles are used to invoke the Divine, and pink is the color of the energy of love as it is seen in the Elphame. This coherent set of symbols speaks to the unconscious mind, and when the thoughts as expressed in the text are charged with emotional energy, the ritual is potent and energized to influence both the consciousness of the practitioner and the god-form to which it is addressed.

She wrote a piece of text, apologizing for not being able to be a mother at that time, and asked Anubis to look after her unborn child and to return it to the Great Mother. She asked for forgiveness for herself and blessings for the child, and made an offering of the lotus and incense.

After performing the ritual, Meredith noticed a significant emotional shift. The feelings of intense guilt and emotional pain dissipated, and she regained some psychological equilibrium, but she did not have a sense of complete closure. She conducted the ritual three times on the anniversary of the termination:

> I kept the candles for a while and I did the ritual too when the year came round. (She is weeping.) I really feel like it did help me to accept it and it was okay. I didn't feel evil. I just felt a lot calmer about it. I calmed down a lot after it. I don't know if reassured is the right word...After the first time I did it there was quite a big shift, but it did feel like it wasn't quite over, and I think that's why I kept the candle. And it was really interesting because I had put it away, but then when I

broke up with Kieran and I was packing up the house, I found it again...and that's when I thought, "Oh...this actually needs a little bit more closure," and that's when I went down to the beach.

Meredith needed to work her way through the grieving process, and sometimes that process can become stalled. Ritual is a powerful means of restarting and completing it (Reeves and Boersma 1989–90). She was not really sure why she chose to do the ritual at the beach, but she went there to end her relationship with the father of the child. The ocean is, however, the quintessential symbol of the Great Goddess.

It's just something about the beach and the ocean...I really felt like it was letting go but then it was something that would, in terms of the soul, be like a letting go, but then it was something that could come back to me...there was something cyclic about it.

She is intuitively describing the nature of the Goddess, cyclic and fluid. She goes on to talk about the effects of the ceremonial work and compares it to the deeper kind of prayer she used to practice as a child, and again contrasts it with the going-through-the-motions orthodox type of praying.

When things were really bad I used to pray...and not just do the Our Fathers and the Hail Marys...I think that (deeper kind of prayer) made me stronger in a way that I really did connect with something else and it's the same thing (there is the suggestion that the "something else" may be Divinity). It's the same feeling...but I can't exactly say what it is, but that's what ritual helps me do. It just gave me calmness that was just somewhere inside me...not that it magically made everything okay, but it did resolve something. It helped me find a place where I could find some sort of strength. It's really strong! It feels different now. So, I feel like ritual's a means for me to work through things and to give myself strength.

Interestingly, the strength that she gained through her ritual practice helped her to go more easily through the dissolution of her relationship with her ultimately dishonest partner, and she turned to ceremony as the vehicle of completion. She had learned from the ritual she had performed for the unborn child and creatively extrapolated it to another important area of her life.

She said:

When I broke up with Kieran I did the ritual again at the beach. (She is weeping but she gathers herself.) When I went down to the beach to do that little ritual I also did another ritual to let go of Kieran as well... because I really feel like we must have had a connection in other lives or something. Meeting him was just like our neuroses going "click," but when I really started to feel like I couldn't trust him I actually became very suspicious and I was watching everything...not because I'm a jealous and suspicious person, but because I really started looking at it, and I kept this box and I called it a "dishonesty box." Whenever I would find something that would make me think "this isn't quite right," (she was becoming more observant, conscious, and discriminating—something that had been actively discouraged by her mother) I would put it in there. When it all hit the fan I made up my own ritual and I did it on the same day. I took the dishonesty box and I burned all the letters and I buried it and I said, "That's it! It's over now...and I don't have to be that person anymore. I'm doing my own thing. I have to let go. It's over!"

Through her growing self-awareness and focused intention Meredith found the spiritual strength to make her own decisions about her life. She had discovered a lost aspect of self, her personal will and feminine power, and reintegrated it into her psyche through the practice of ritual. Therefore, this is also a journey of restoration and soul retrieval. She had entered the world of the Elphame and found a powerful healing resource that offered her regeneration.

Ritual therefore had a transforming effect on her life. It did not miraculously fix all her problems, but it did give her a greater level of self-awareness and a sense of her own power and integrity. Regarding the termination, she had accepted responsibility for her actions and asked forgiveness in a respectful and appropriate manner, and, as she explained, perhaps made a connection with a deeper and wiser aspect of self she described as her soul or spirit. She also believed that she might have made a connection with a greater spirituality: "I really did feel like I wasn't just talking to myself."

When her relationship had broken down, she had taken an active role in freeing herself from the harmful pattern her mother had modeled. She had entered the Elphame and returned to the "real" world strengthened and more integrated in her feminine power. Like Angela (in chapter 10), she was also able to find her woman's strength, which she called her "girl power," and the independence to live on her own terms.

Luciano

Luciano's story illustrates the transformative power of pathworking and how it may work as a method of soul retrieval. His case also demonstrates how strong dreams are important psychic events that offer a commentary on the individual's spiritual journey and provide a deep spiritual insight. Luciano's strong dreams contained elements that suggested a contact with the Dark Goddess.

I had adapted the pathworking technique for psychotherapy clients. This adaptation involved the gradual construction in the imagination of a large and complex symbol called the Grail Castle. This flexible symbol represents the psyche both as a whole and in its various aspects. In early sessions, the client starts out on a journey to the castle on foot, using the creative imagination to travel along a road, catching glimpses of the castle in the distance. In subsequent sessions and as the symbol becomes more solid they would walk across a bridge, over a moat, through a portcullis, and into the outer courtyard.

In later sessions these images would firm in greater and clearer detail, and this basic image of the Grail Castle could be adapted for different clients. Different characters who populated the castle and its courtyards might also be created. These symbolic figures and spaces might be known or unknown to the client.

For example, the dungeons and lower precincts of the castle are symbolic of the subconscious, and the king and queen sitting in the throne room are symbolic of the anima and the animus. They may also represent the masculine and feminine divine powers that have knowledge of the true life-path mapped out for the individual. There is also a wise old man or woman: a type of Merlin character who resides in the turret room at the top of the castle and who has transformational or alchemical healing powers. A dragon may represent the shadow or the dweller on the threshold. In the innermost sanctuary is the temple, the place of the Holy Grail, the deepest and truest aspect of self, the soul. The Grail symbol also relates to the Goddess herself. In the Western magical tradition, the cup, chalice, or cauldron is the premier symbol of the Goddess. This is a very flexible symbolic image that may be used with an almost infinite variety of possibilities. Surprising and creative things can happen within it.

When Luciano first came to see me for treatment, he presented as deeply depressed and in an existential crisis. He was an Italian who had migrated to Australia in 1985. His relationship with his partner had disintegrated into continual fights, angry disagreements, and finally separation. Irrational outbursts and uncontrollable rages were affecting his relationships with friends. Life seemed chaotic, meaningless, and irrelevant; feelings of helplessness and hopelessness overwhelmed him, and he could see no possibility of reprieve from this unfathomable situation. He was considering suicide.

His sense of personal identity was crumbling, and he was afraid of what lay beyond the facade. Previously, he had been able to lose himself in playing the piano, but his current extreme self-consciousness had detrimentally affected that skill. When he tried to play, he became hypercritical of his performance, then paralyzed with unreasonable fear. He was having panic attacks. He was hypervigilant and oversensitive about what other people were thinking and saying about him, almost to the level of paranoia.

Sexually, too, he was in crisis. He was realizing that much of his sexual behavior was about obtaining approval from women and not about creating intimacy. He had become compulsive about asking women for sex, though he did not enjoy it. Being alone for any length of time generated overwhelming fear, and he was coming to understand that he was using sex compulsively to stave off feelings of loneliness and abandonment. He felt that his sexual behavior was not based on genuine desire but was an addictive displacement activity and a way of trying to solve another problem entirely, although he was not sure what it was:

> It's just the habits of thinking...of feeling loneliness with sex. Also the fear of others and this feeling of not being accepted and of not fitting in and always feeling a stranger. If somebody disagreed with me, it triggered straightaway that I'm not accepted...not valued at all.

He was living with his two children, a girl aged twelve and a boy aged eight. It was very important to him that he make a success at fathering. It will become clear why this was so. He said he came to therapy in order to understand what drove his behavior and to try to change it, or, as he put it, "To find reasons to understand what the fuck-up was—to try to understand what was wrong with me." He was particularly reactive when he perceived that anyone close to him tried to please him or humor him. This perceived lack of authenticity brought back a sense of betrayal that he could trace to childhood.

We were using psychodynamic techniques of bringing into consciousness peak memories from childhood that we analyzed for mental and emotional content. It became increasingly clear that many of his problems had their origins in that vulnerable time. He said:

> I hate being pleased...I want it to be true or nothing. With the knowledge I have today I also know I'm overreacting, largely because there is a need in me for confirmation that comes from my childhood and from the fact that I didn't feel appreciated by my mother. I overreacted because anytime something like that happened, my thought is, "Yeah...you're pretending to love me, but you don't really love me," and that's why I felt like that. I think my mother didn't really love me.

He had originally told me that he could not comprehend why he was in such a state. He had a "wonderful" partner, even though they were currently estranged, and wonderful children. His Italian family of origin was also "wonderful." He had not been materially deprived or obviously abused as a child. He came from a "good" family where many members were well-respected judges and magistrates. His sister was a psychiatrist working in a large Italian city. He alone seemed to be the failure, and he wondered if he were actually insane or on a journey to insanity.

Many people who come to therapy are in psychic and emotional pain but have no idea how they came to be in that state, and they will frequently give the therapist their version of their story. This version I call the "mythology" or the "legend." It is the patient's attempt to find a coherent story that will make some sense of the inner turmoil they are experiencing.

As our sessions proceeded, a deeper story began to emerge, and he was shocked that he had neither discerned it nor understood its meaning. His older sister, Roberta, was very intelligent academically and had occupied the role of family genius. Most family dinner table conversations related to Roberta's intellectual achievements and her hothouse education. The relationship between brother and sister was strained, even hostile. He always felt overshadowed, compared, and unappreciated. When Roberta spoke everyone listened respectfully, but when he spoke it seemed nobody gave him any credence or paid him any serious attention.

As his sister was the academic high achiever, he was cast into the role of the family artist: the emotional one, the eccentric. He also became "Mama's little man," and his mother attempted to meet her emotional needs by relating to him in inappropriate ways, confiding to him very personal and negative things about her relationship with his father. His mother regularly belittled and humiliated his father in front of Luciano and his sister, and he began to hate his father for allowing himself to be treated this way.

Toward the end of high school he suffered a bout of depression, during which he attempted to gas himself. He survived, and he recalled that his parents (especially his mother) seemed more embarrassed than concerned about his well-being. Consequently, after finishing high school he was sent to another town to study liberal arts at university and completed a degree with majors in history and linguistics. He felt he was being exiled. His feelings of never being loved and valued for himself had become overwhelming to the point where he sought refuge from his sense of loneliness, fragmentation, and alienation in excessive use of drugs, sex, alcohol, and outbursts of impotent rage.

When he began therapy, he seemed to be experiencing a cycle of attrition whereby old life-patterns were dissolving. It was a painful time for him, and he was in crisis in many areas of his life concurrently. His self-concept, his relationships with others, his work—everything about him was in the process of disintegration. His dreams were full of images of destruction and resurrection. For example, in one strong dream he is walking away from a desolate and devastated city that looked "like Dresden after the Blitz," but as he is leaving, on the outskirts, he finds a broken pipe with running water and stops to drink. He feels refreshed both physically and spiritually, and is able to continue his journey to where he is not sure, but he is hopeful.

This is the realm of the Dark Goddess. From the destruction of everything arises new hope and new life. He had been able to gather strength and insight from his dreams and other inner work we had done. It seemed an optimistic dream that explained to him a profoundly spiritual mystery: the truth of the cyclic nature of existence. Perhaps out of the devastation of everything would come a sense of vitality and a new direction.

He said that after therapy he could perceive the rigid roles the family played and the lack of authenticity that they displayed in their relationships with each other. He said:

> I realized that family life had set-up games…set-up roles…and these roles can kill people. It can make people very angry because they're not set on real feelings. They're set on models that we can never be or we can never keep. When you asked me what I thought I was doing in therapy, I was getting out of that network of lies and hypocrisy that was family life. It's a dangerous and hurtful way of living. I really try hard to be myself with my son.

The structure and dynamics of his family of origin was pathological, especially from an Italian perspective, where the father was traditionally honored as the head of the household. Luciano's father was continually shamed, dishonored, and rendered impotent in the family. He did not fight back but was unfailingly respectful and obliging to his wife and her family, who had pretensions to aristocratic sensibilities. To Luciano this respectfulness appeared as weakness and servility, and he was encouraged in this perception by his mother, uncles, and maternal grandfather.

It seemed reasonably clear why his image of himself as a man had been so badly damaged, and it helped Luciano to explore the dark stories of his childhood and adolescence. There was nothing particularly magical about these explorations. I was mainly using the techniques of traditional secular counseling to help him clarify his real story. Techniques like the construction of a genogram helped us to see how the family pathology had been passed down the generations and had culminated in his current existential crisis.

However, reframing his father's perceived weakness as strength helped him to gain a different appreciation of masculinity. During the Second World War his father had walked back to Italy from Russia. This was a difficult and painful journey that had required courage, focus, and discipline. His father had been decorated as a war hero for having completed it. He was not a groveling sycophant. He had made a solemn vow to God that if he survived the ordeal he would do everything to be as spiritually perfect a person as he was able to be. Viewing his father's subsequent behavior within that frame freed Luciano's mind from a rigid pattern of thinking and conditioned him to be more open to the Elphame and to experiencing the magical work that followed.

The Grail Castle Pathworking:
A Ritual Journey of Psychic Integration

I helped Luciano to gradually construct the Grail Castle image and guided him on a journey down the stone staircase to the dungeons. I did not tell him what to expect, and in fact I did not know what he would find there, but in my experience whatever is found there has a powerful and lasting effect on the mind and emotions of the seeker. It often illuminates something of great importance concerning their individual health and spiritual well-being. It is a method of psychic integration consistent with traditional shamanic healing techniques, using a powerful mythological Goddess symbology familiar to the Western psyche.

When Luciano opened the ancient, heavy, creaking door with a rusty key and walked into a damp and darkened room, it took him a few moments to adjust his eyes to the gloom. What I perceived outwardly was that after entering the dungeon he began to sob, his body wracked by huge shudders, tears flowing down his face. His face became a tragic mask, its features contorted by such deep grief there was something archetypal or universal in it. It was not the sniffling, self-pitying, personal kind of grief. It seemed to have elements of existential grief, weltschmerz, and I thought he looked as though he were weeping for all of us.

From the point of Luciano's inner vision, he saw a small boy, barely alive, half starved and manacled to the wall. He recognized that small boy as himself. He unlocked the manacles, cradling him, trying to resuscitate him and weeping for all the senseless wrongs that had been done to him. When he recalled the experience of coming face to face with his lost child self, the interview took a powerful emotional turn that was convincing in its intensity. He was transported back into that inner reality. There is a raw emotional energy revealed in the parts of the interview text where he describes the encounter with his lost younger aspect of self and reclaims it:

> I remember identifying myself with a little person and feeling such a surge of love for him and realizing *that was me!*...and it was nice. I was not as bad as I thought I was. I loved him, and I knew he was a good boy. I felt sorry for him because he'd been betrayed by the very person that's supposed to love him...and I realized that had created in me (voice drops and becomes thoughtful, then breaks) a vacuum that could not be filled, and I had lived with it. I know that certain desires and expectations I have for life, no partner can ever fulfill them for me!

He explained that the experience and the emotions associated with it were still very strong:

> I can visualize it still! The baby in the dungeon...the little boy with the chains, chained to the wall, and I picked him up. I remember the feeling, the real feeling of looking at him and being gentle and being nice to him and nurturing and hugging him and telling him...telling him that he was a good boy...and he's done nothing wrong...and he's lovely. That's what I remember! That feeling of warmth and saying that was me...that *is* me!

The shocking impact of seeing what had become of his lost child self impressed itself on his recollection. His mixed feelings of grief, shock, and palpable joy that were finally released from the prison of the unconscious gave a profound sense of liberation. I wanted to know if that catharsis and psychic integration had produced a permanent shift in his self-perception. I asked him if his sense of masculinity had changed.

> Oh, definitely! Definitely! My relation to him helped me to manhood...yeah...yeah. (he nods adamantly) It's very different now...after that experience and after understanding that what excites me is never an obvious erotic thing...what excites me are hugs and cuddles. Affection...sweetness...tenderness...yeah. What turns me on is affection. I was trying to be the macho man, and I was not.

I asked whether he thought the change was due to the psychic integration he experienced after the encounter with the child self. "Of course. Yes, it changed very much...yes. (voice drops and becomes thoughtful) It's much better now." The grieving for, and reconnection with, his lost child self was crucial for Luciano in another important way. Magically speaking, the image of the innocent child is, in fact, an image of the soul or the true self, suggesting that Luciano had lost contact with his soul and his true life purpose.

When he realized the profundity of the loss in this visceral way, a spiritual transformation occurred that cascaded into his worldly life as well. His profoundly emotional experience of reclaiming his lost child self enabled him to experience the giving and receiving of real affection in his primary relationship and to shed the false persona he had created.

In shaman cultures, the shaman usually performs the journey of soul retrieval. In Luciano's case, the use of the adapted pathworking technique enabled him to go on his own journey of recovery and restoration.

Entering the Elphame
The Transforming Power of Ritual, Part 2

> There are incredible things in this world. We call this
> the one reality because we can touch it, but there are lots
> of things we can't see…but they're there. There are energies
> around that we can use to heal ourselves. (Isabelle)

Isabelle and Angela

The stories of Isabelle and Angela are sufficiently similar and sufficiently different to allow an interesting contrast and comparison. I am
presenting them with the group of initiatory journeys entitled "Entering
the Elphame" because I had trained these women in a pathworking ritual
I call "The Healing Waters," which I had adapted from a magical pathworking. The modified working enabled them to safely enter the
Elphame and access its healing resources. The initiatory journeys of
these two women were based on a sustained level of contact with the
Elphame that eventually reached a climax of transformational physical
and emotional healing.

I treated Isabelle over a period of several years. On first acquaintance
she had been previously treated for six months by a general practitioner
who was a partner in the cooperative medical practice in which I worked.

The treatment was for an intractable staphylococcal infection that could not be treated by antibiotics. Her doctor referred her to me because the high doses of antibiotics she had been prescribing had not been effective.

She arrived in my consulting room on crutches. Her left lower leg, foot, and toes were swollen to twice the normal size, and the skin was discolored, disintegrating, and exuding blood and pus. She was deeply depressed. I treated the infection with both internal and topical homoeopathic and herbal medicines, and it responded quickly to treatment. Within a few days the swelling had subsided considerably and the skin was visibly healing. Within two weeks, the limb looked normal. The only reminder of the virulence of the infection was a discoloration of the skin that remained as a slight permanent disfigurement.

Some months later she suffered another outbreak of the infection, this time on her face. I asked her to recall what it was like. She had been having suicidal ideation and described her fear and despair:

> It was really horrible! It was on my face so I couldn't hide it, and it was pretty disgusting…like a weeping sore. Some people thought it was a burn. It covered the bottom left quarter and it was quite huge and I still had to function, like go to town and stuff like that. It was pretty scary…and then it crusted over and I couldn't smile. It was very difficult to talk. I was very self-conscious. I felt like a leper. I was completely freaking out (laughs another mirthless laugh) and I thought I would have to live with a weeping sore on my face. That was the worst possible thing! I went on another course of antibiotics, and that resolved it until I finished the course…then it came back, so I went on another course and the same thing happened: two days later it came back, and that's when it ended up covering my whole face. It came back and spread twice as big and twice as fast.

At this point she again came to me for help, and I decided to try something different. I gave her some advice on diet to improve her immunity and asked her to do a healing visualization. I gave her some instruction in using the focused power of the creative imagination. In the interview I asked her to describe what she did and how effective it was.

> That visualization to look at my face in the mirror and actually see the sore just (she struggles for the word) shrinking until it's all gone. That's what I did…until it was gone.

I had not had any feedback at the time about the way the infection had resolved and asked her if it had gradually faded, but she corrected my misconception:

> In reality it went—(she gestures from top to bottom)—it went from the top down...down...down...down and it actually...even though I never had it on the neck...it actually went down on my neck and got here (gestures to the front of the throat)...and that's when *whoosh!* It's gone!

I wanted to know how she had dealt with the ontological shock when the infection suddenly resolved. She had fought to get her skeptical intellectual self under control and to observe the process without judging it:

> I thought it was really difficult. I had heaps of resistance—"What am I doing here? Why am I doing this? It's obvious that it's there!"—but then it became relatively easy to see myself in the mirror without the sore, and when it was coming down I was really pleased but at the same time I was in two minds because the whole thing was coming down. So at the same time I tried to stay curious and observe what was happening and tried to remove myself from the whole thing. My material mind was saying "well, you've got this sore" but I knew myself without it...and I also knew that I could one day not have it. So...

She pauses as she attempts to come to terms with healing coming from another level of reality and describes the Elphame, saying:

> There's imagination taking over...allowing it to happen and making it reality. I mean...there are incredible things in this world. We call this one reality because we can touch it, but there are lots of things we can't see...but they're there. There are energies around that we can use to heal ourselves.

I asked her if the infection had recurred, and she confirmed that it had never returned:

> The most amazing thing is that even though it went on for a long time I don't have any scarring...not even any blemish or any mark whatsoever...very different from my foot. On my foot and leg I've got this permanent kind of bruise. So that's interesting too, that it actually went away completely.

ANGELA CONSULTED ME WHEN she was involved in a volatile and ambiguous relationship with a man who seemed to be losing interest. This was a familiar pattern of relationship for her (although several prior relationships had also been violent). The more reluctant he seemed, the more desperately and relentlessly she pursued him in an attempt to get some firmer commitment. When the relationship finally disintegrated, she found herself in a deep depression with obsessive-compulsive features. The trauma and pain involved in the separation were more than she could bear, and she began to exhibit a suicidal ideation. At this intensely emotional time, her hands broke out in an intractable weeping eczema.

She said that she was experiencing a split or mismatch between her inner and outer reality when she first sought treatment with me. She describes a psychic fracturing:

> I realized I was in a bad pattern. I felt like I was living my life externally…differently to how I thought about myself internally. I just wanted to bring it all together. I saw myself as wholesome and happy (ironic laughter)—as an effective person—whereas I wasn't coping at all. I could barely look after my son physically, mentally, and emotionally because of my eczema and my emotional state. I couldn't focus on anything…self-obsessed about negative things…nothing healthy or positive, and I was very concerned about the health of my child and myself.

She went on to discuss an incident when she had pressured the ex-partner into having a couple's therapy session with me. During this session he was clear that he did not want a reconciliation. She seemed to accept the reality of the separation, but when they were leaving, she pursued him outside and became hysterical. I took her son inside with me and gave him some dinner because I did not want him to be further emotionally damaged by witnessing his mother's extreme loss of self-control. She said:

> I was really obsessed! I remember coming inside and you were sitting with my son at the dinner table…and it was normal, and I remember just thinking, "I don't know how to do that anymore!" (voice drops) And I really think that was the turning point.

For many sufferers of this obsessive/compulsive pattern of behavior, the mental confusion, the emotional pain, and the accompanying depression are of such magnitude that it could be described as a life-threatening illness. The powerlessness and hopelessness the patient feels, mixed with the compulsion to change the partner into the warm and loving person they so desire, creates such a confusing mixture of intense and paralyzing emotions that death may seem the only way of achieving resolution. It is a psychic position not far removed from actual psychosis, and patients can feel themselves slipping toward the edge of madness.

Angela had been prone to allergies since childhood. When she was twenty-one she suffered a lengthy outbreak of eczema that became so incapacitating she eventually lost all her fingernails and toenails. At that time she had been hospitalized with septicemia because the open skin lesions became infected. It was only with the use of large amounts of cortisone-based anti-inflammatory drugs and huge doses of antibiotics that she obtained any relief, but the condition recurred when she stopped using the drugs.

Angela had studied the theoretical side of Witchcraft; knowing this, I comfortably used several magical techniques in her treatment program. I used these methods in conjunction with more conventional talking therapy and other modalities such as Gestalt-style role-play and journal-keeping. She had retained her old therapy journal and referred to it from time to time as the interview progressed.

I asked her about the magical work. She said:

> There were quite a few techniques that you gave me which really did help, and one that I remember was spiraling myself in silver light, starting from the ground up. You described how to manifest this ray of light and look at myself as though I had three bodies: emotional, physical, and mental. (She struggles to remember and is muddling two different techniques. She consults her journal.) Actually, I've got "golden" here (she looks surprised); I've just had a look at the page and it's golden light, but I actually remember it as silver...(laughs) I think that was to bring my three bodies together. Ah! Actually, now I remember where the silver light came from. The silver light was actually something different that was about severing cords—attachments that I had made to this man. You got me to visualize the different cords with which I had attached myself to him.

From a magical perspective, when humans are emotionally attached to something or someone we unconsciously send out "cords" of energy that bind us to the object of desire. Often these "desire cords" are created out of obsessive greed, neediness, and clinging. They drain our energy into the object. The ritual Angela describes is designed to contain energy, stop its dissipation, and reconfigure the relationship.

She describes her transformational experience of the ritual. The practice helped her to rebuild her emotional and mental self:

> I remember you teaching me how to stand with him, bringing him into my mind, standing face to face strong and warrior-like, and looking at these cords—at where they were attached—and then having this really beautiful sword that was mine and powerful, and I was able to sever them...and you actually explained to do it not all at once because it was too traumatic, and so I used to do this every time I'd think of him. I'd sever another one, and you showed me how to mentally cauterize the severed cords using a flaming torch. I found that extremely helpful. That was something that really worked for me! I felt the severing strongly, and it made me that little bit stronger to get through the day, and then it just got better and better. So I stopped draining my energy into him. I was starting to become more contained. Once I practiced and did it regularly, it became easier. I remember the first time I did it, it felt so good—a feeling that I had done the right thing.

I asked her about the personal effects of the practice. She said that it made her stronger, more self-disciplined and self-sufficient. She had begun to move from a position of powerlessness to having some control over her life. I asked her then about the golden light, curious to see what she recalled. Magical workers manipulate energy, or light, by the use of the creative imagination.

Once again she consulted her journal:

> What I did was go into a meditative state and then I drew a ray of golden light through the top of my head all the way through my three main bodies...I think the reason you were teaching me that was to ground me.

She was right, but not completely. I was also attempting to show her how to realign her bodies because I believed that the intense emotional reactions she had experienced had caused her bodies to become misaligned, and that was why she had feelings of being shattered or fragmented. When a person is "integrated" in the magical sense, all their bodies—the mental body, the emotional body, the energy body, and the physical body—are acting as one and are in accordance with their magical will or higher life purpose.

It was likely that Angela had lost her child self back at the time in childhood when the longing for the love and attention of her parents was most intense. But was not forthcoming. Her father had been hospitalized for the first of many operations for brain tumors, and her mother's attention and energy were consumed in nursing him. His traumatic illness had begun at Angela's puberty and continued into her adult years. It constituted a period of her life that was marked by angry, delinquent, and risky behavior. It was probable, therefore, that she had experienced "soul loss." Before his lengthy illness she had been close to her father emotionally.

Again, she refers to her therapy journal to discuss some further magical work we had done. She describes a sense of psychic integration, but when she said she thought the ex-partner enjoyed his power over her, I suddenly thought that it was possible he had stolen a part of her soul, albeit probably unconsciously. Soul theft as well as soul loss is part of the shamanic narrative. She said:

> You gave me some breathing exercises to increase my energy and also to seal my aura because...I remember a few instances where I'd be fine, and things would be going along normally, and all of a sudden I'd just start obsessing about him. I couldn't work out any triggers, and I remember discussing it with you that I probably had a hole in my aura that he was either attached to or he was thinking of me...Now I am never in a situation where I feel I can't take control. It was a slow process, but by learning how to do those things (her voice drops as she grapples for the right words) I feel like I filled out my body again. I mean I'm not separate, living two different lives.

Both Isabelle and Angela had consulted me also because they were suffering intense and debilitating weeping rashes on their hands. In Isabelle's case the staphylococcus infection recurred on both her hands twelve months after she had healed her face, so I thought a more holistic approach was necessary. In Angela's case the weeping eczema recurred, also on both hands, and was causing her constant irritation and disability. From a magical viewpoint, their bodies, as symbols of their emotional reality, were dramatically demonstrating that neither of these women was "handling" their lives.

I asked them to describe the condition and how it affected their functioning. Isabelle said:

> The whole of my right hand had gone bad and it was going onto the fingers of the left hand. It looked like a weeping sore. So first I feel itchiness coming from deep inside, and if I do scratch it, lumps appear...then little by little each little one of those bubbles comes up to the surface...and then they grow and start joining, then blisters, then they burst and the weeping starts...and then it grows and starts crusting.

Angela said:

> Eczema...it's so bloody awful! It never leaves...never gets out of your head. It's always around.

I treated them both with herbal and homoeopathic medicines as adjuncts to the emotional, psychological, and spiritual therapies. In Isabelle's case I oversaw her diet, and I had a therapy session with her three or four times during a week of intensive treatment. I also gave her some visualization work to do. Some we did together and some I had her do by herself. Perhaps a third of the treatment was conventional alternative medicine, or conventional psychotherapy. Two-thirds came from the magical tradition.

The main instrument of healing was a ritual pathworking I had developed and called "The Healing Waters." Participants walk out of the mundane world and into a magical forest. They journey through the forest until they came into a clearing where there is an ancient stone altar and statue of the wounded healer. I had used the archetype of the Greek god of medicine because healing is one of the main functions of shamanic magic.

The form of the wounded healer is a human-created form but the energy it contains is divine energy. Does this mean that this being is a god or an archetype? I have to confess that I am not really sure of this division between Divinity and archetype. It is a subtle distinction, and my current thinking is that a god and an archetype is the same thing. However, I am open to changing my mind on this point. According to Ashcroft-Nowicki (1987), it is still possible to tap into the egregore of this archetype and access its energy.

However, the most powerful image of the ritual is a beautiful jade-green healing pool surrounded by rocks and vegetation. I had asked Isabelle to take this journey every day. I asked her what she remembered. She said:

> We created a sacred space. There was a waterfall and a pool, and I'd go there and I'd wash my hands in the water and ask the water to take away the infection and to bring it to Mother Earth for earthing. There was a natural altar made with some stones...there was waterfall... there was a swimming hole, and around it was a creek going down and big rocks...like a natural stone altar.

I'm having trouble remembering all the finer details, and so is she. It's been several years since we did this work, but I remember how we treated the infection using the purifying waters of the healing pool. Suddenly I remembered that she had taken the skin of her hands off like gloves and washed them in the healing waters, and simultaneously she remembered too. This was an idea I had adapted from the work of Gerald Epstein (1989) and incorporated into the Healing Waters pathworking. She said, "Oh, that's right! Like gloves! Yes, that's right! That's right! It was like gloves!"

Angela recollects and once again consults her journal:

> I remember now my visualization (which I still do to this day)...was about my hands...and it was walking into a forest with a deep emerald green pool. It's really beautiful and tranquil, and you got me to dip my hands into this magic pool, take off my hand like a glove, and with my magical thread and needle sew the hand back together. I had a little satchel and it had a tiny pair of gold scissors, a tiny scrubbing brush, gold thread, and golden needles.

The gold thread was symbolic of the golden light of the energy body, or etheric body.

She also made an offering to the healing powers of the Elphame. Making an offering or a libation is an ancient gesture of honoring and acknowledgment: a ritualized gesture that shows respect and gives thanks to the Goddess, in this case as mistress of the healing waters. She said:

> You got me to do that three times a day because they were really bad…and then dip my hands back into the water once I'd sewn them, and then do the other hand, and then give the emerald pond a gift. I always had really nice gifts to give to the pond. One time I gave it an enormous pearl.

She said this is said in a softly serious manner, which precipitated laughter. It was a way of dealing with the tension between the two realities: the sudden realization of ontological shock inherent in the statement. It had seemed like a very real experience.

Isabelle also talked about the ancient stone altar and the making of offerings. Like Angela she remembers the ritual washing and mending of her hands:

> It was stone and I had to put some things on it like a flower, some incense, or a stone. I think it was about the god of medicine or healing…and then the ritual of washing the hands, taking the sick skin away, off, and scrubbing…then I'd have to fix what was torn, like sew it and cut off all the bits, and I had a needle and thread and some scissors. I'd be very, very careful to be very thorough about it.

I am interested in how real she felt her experience to be. I am exploring their experience of the inner senses and how alike they are to the physical senses. I asked about the sensations they experienced. Isabelle said:

> When you asked me that question the first thing I thought about was the coolness of the water. I could really sense it. It wasn't just like a surface thing. The water was…well, not the water itself, the energy—the energy of the water—was going right into my hands, right down to the bone. That's how it felt…yeah…and in a way it was radiating throughout my whole body, and I usually used to feel a lot lighter, a lot more positive afterward.

I asked her again about the color of the healing water because I had found that most people find it easy to visualize water. Traditionally it has been associated with purification and regarded as sacred. It seems the mind naturally wants to go to water. I had used the jade-green color because it is the color of the heart chakra, the color of the Feminine Intelligence.

She described her experience of the healing and purifying power of water:

> It was jade green...just really beautiful (her voice drops and she becomes reflective as she recollects) and quite cool...but that's the funny thing: it was cooling without being cold. Being in the water felt like being cooled from the inside out and totally clean...every pore, every part of the body inside and outside as well (her voice drops)... very...very deep (voice drops lower as she slips into reverie) There was the pool and the waterfall and this green, green water, and there were a few objects as well to put on the altar, and then washing my hands.

As she reflected on the pathworking, she suddenly had the insight that she had been active in her healing. She had used a magical technique and had been empowered by it. She had symbolically and actually repaired her hands by working on her energy body:

> That's right! Yeah, that's right! That was it! That was a ritual...and I am active in my healing and (thoughtful, voice drops) by being active in my healing, I allow it and help it along. So, yeah...I think it was very important for me to do that—to have that visualization, to know that I could take myself in a safe place and I could create beauty around me and...(her voice drops once more as she reflects) that I was active in my healing, and that healing is a process. There was an urgent need of healing then and there because of my hands, but I also knew it was an overall thing as well.

She seemed to have made a connection between the parts and the whole, that the hands needed healing immediately because she had been so incapacitated by the infection, but the therapy component was also important because it treated the whole person. She relates the time she spent swimming in the sacred pool as a time for "whole" healing also, and recalls a crucial and emotionally healing meeting with her deceased father.

> So, I think there was a complete thing. There were times when I had to completely jump in the pool and then I dived under to that cave where my father was, and I talked with him…and it was really nice! I think there was a hug—a big cuddle—and it was quite pleasant.

Her father had died several years before and there had been some long-term acrimony between them. She had previously referred to him as an "emotional cripple." When she returned from the cave and the conversation with her father, she seemed to me to be much happier and more relaxed. She had been swimming in the waters of the unconscious, using a magical technique to enter the Elphame and heal both her emotional self and her physical self. I remembered she said her father had asked her to forgive him for not having been a very good father, and that it had been a very moving experience for her.

When I asked Angela what the feeling was of being in that place, she said that she seemed more connected to the natural environment, that she had shapeshifted into an animal form, and then went on to describe something of her emotional and mental response to working from the Elphame. She also described a different perspective of her personal emotional ordeals more in terms of the Dark Goddess. She had learned to honor her suffering and to understand how it had taught her many things. It had matured her in womanly wisdom.

She does not mention the Dark Goddess directly, but there was an intuitive comprehension of her presence in that her individual woman's suffering had meaning and power. The Crone was there, standing in the shadows:

> When I went there I went more like a delicate deer or some sort of magical, mystical animal creature, and that's how I felt…but obviously I wasn't that because I was still dipping my hands in the pool. I never remember being disturbed or frightened there. It never felt bad or evil or any of that rubbish that parts of society go on with…I felt being female…that it was okay what I'd been going through, and that the Goddess was in me.

Isabelle discussed the confusion of ontological shock, but when she directly experienced the healing efficacy of the Elphame, she was able to accept that magic is not imaginary. She also describes the sacred quality of the encounter and the sense of peace and safety she experienced:

> I was a bit tentative about the whole process, but I could feel the good it was doing. I could see it did make sense. It was symbolizing what we were doing, what I wanted to do: heal, fix, start afresh...so I don't care if it's just imagination. What I know is, this is what happened! And it happened on whatever level, whatever realm, but this is what was happening and it was very beneficial. I think...I believe...my hands got better in one week (she whistles softly in surprise as she realizes)... Yeah, I think they got completely better.

Like Angela, she had felt safe in the Elphame. She intuited its magical and sacred nature and knew that it was not an experience to be treated lightly or regarded as entertainment:

> It wasn't scary or anything...and it felt really good. It felt like I could stay there (laughs) in that cave and not worry about going back to the surface or anything else. I felt really at home. It was very nice and comfortable and safe...at the same time recognizing that those moments were very special and not to be abused. There was a very strong sense of the sacred. I just felt so strongly part of the space, and the space was part of me. That's it! That's what I'm saying. It felt like a space in a bubble that was full of wonders in a way that magic can happen. This is the place where magic does happen!

I asked Angela about the healing of her hands and whether she thought it was complete. I expected her to say yes to this question because her hands appeared to show no trace of the former trauma, but instead she said that she thought the healing might not be complete:

> I would have to say that I can still see almost scar tissue, like there's a little bit of thickening where the eczema was, but I can still do everything with them and it doesn't flare up, and I don't ever get the lumps and bumps...and if I do get a tiny tingle I know exactly how to get onto it and I deal with it. So I would probably have to say that it still isn't one hundred percent...but that's okay to me because it still means I've got to be vigilant. I had used cortisone so I really had to go back to the beginning (she is talking about the homoeopathic medicine concept, which holds that the use of many modern drugs blocks a case energetically, and the blockage has to be undone before a true

healing can take place). I remember it being really full-on for a few weeks and I think for a month or two really intense and painful and sore, and then it started to resolve from there...so I'd say about four months...and considering I'd had it at various times for two years at a time, it really wasn't a long period of time.

I asked her that if she were under stress, did she think that it might recur, and strangely her previous reply seemed contradictory: "I don't think so...I have been under extreme stress, and it hasn't ever." She told me she had given up smoking, something she had unsuccessfully attempted many times before. She had moved house from Byron Bay to Townsville and started a university course. Her father had died, and she was having problems with her son and his father.

These were all major stressors. "All this full-on stuff was happening and it didn't flare up like I was expecting it to." She had not noticed the contradiction in what she had said. Perhaps I detected the shadow of ontological shock in these statements. Her intellect told her that this healing could not possibly have happened in the way that it did, but the evidence was that it had. I asked her how she had explained what had happened, but she said she had not needed to explain it; she had reached out and embraced it.

She also talked about having lost a part of herself—in effect, soul loss—and of needing to enter the Elphame in order to find healing. She said:

> I think I was hungry for it. I was so disjointed and I really felt empty. I think I was hungry for meaning...I think that was where I needed to go for healing. Perhaps there was some trauma or something in a past life...or I left part of my spiritual self somewhere.

As well as experiencing physical and emotional healing, she thought that the Goddess theoretical framework gave her a depth of spiritual insight and structure that had previously been lacking in her life. A healing had taken place for her on a spiritual level as well. She believed that in order for physical healing to have taken place, she had needed to work from the other reality. Even now she simply has to imagine the healing waters of the Elphame to get an immediate healing response. As her healing culminated, she met a kind and responsible man who was to become her life partner. As for her hands, she said:

> I just really have to think of that pond and I feel it settle down...and I haven't had any problems since. It's the magical work. It's brought a whole lot of positive stuff...peace and strength. I could control my life.

In working with me and the Goddess on her own healing, she discovered the useful, practical, and personal dimension of the feminine power of Divinity. I believe that, like Meredith, she has learned how to be her own woman—herself alone.

11

Incursions from the Elphame

Part 1

I wasn't thinking of another reality...I didn't expect you to talk
about my mother—the fact that it was my mother who had
attached herself to my heart chakra and was tapping into my
energy, and it was dangerous for me. (Laura)

THERE ARE SIMILARITIES IN the cases of Laura, Josephine, and April,
the subjects of the next three chapters. All three women experienced
incursions from the Elphame that caused intense emotional, psychological, and physical distress. Their problems were caused by restless spirits
who had become "stuck between the worlds." When they performed
the appropriate rituals those spirits were able to release their hold upon
the physical world and complete the process of transition. Jeanne
Achterberg, who has done considerable research into the processes of
death, dying, and the postmortem survival of consciousness, writes:

> The dying person literally moves into the space between two different
> worlds...We have heard many death conversations from dying people

in critical care units and hospital wards, and the dialogue most often has been about crossing over to another realm. (1994, 307)

In treating Laura and Josephine, I went straight to shamanic healing techniques because I had received flashes of vision and intuitive impressions that spontaneously revealed the spiritual origins of their difficulties. I allowed that communication from the Elphame to guide my methodology. In Josephine's case, however, I also used many of the conventional techniques of counseling to help her process a confusing mixture of suppressed emotions that related to her brother's suicide and to work through the stalled grieving process.

Laura

Laura's case illustrates the fact that contact with the Elphame can be dangerous and her type of experience may be life-threatening. It also illustrates the principle that if the problem arises in the Elphame, then the healer must be capable of working from that reality to obtain a cure. This is shamanic medicine, and it is effective in treating spirit entities who are causing illness by attaching to living humans. It is what the Siberian shaman who tutored Kharitidi (1999) described as "invasion by a foreign power."

In late December 2009 I had driven to Sydney to visit Laura, who was a friend and colleague. I was surprised to hear that she was in excruciating pain and had recently been hospitalized. She told me that the pain had been constant for several months and that it gradually had been getting worse. Recently, it been so severe she had been losing consciousness.

She said:

I started experiencing symptoms that felt like a heart attack. It was a dreadful burning pain that would come on really suddenly and then rip like a vice around the heart so that I couldn't breathe. So if I were at work I would just have to lower to the floor or just crouch. I couldn't lay flat because it was just too painful...and these episodes would last possibly twenty minutes and then start to ease off. Then the episodes started to become more frequent, more lengthy, and more severe. I remember having it on Christmas Day. It must have started about ten o'clock in the morning and I just had to retreat to a room in agony until about three o'clock in the afternoon. My blood pressure would go up and I'd be bright red and I'd be sweating and vomiting because of the intensity of the pain. I was terrified of them!

The hospital doctors could find nothing wrong with her, even though when she was admitted she had sharp, spasmodic, and agonizing pains around the heart. At first they thought it was a possible cardiac infarction. When the electrocardiograph revealed no pathology, her doctor seemed at a loss as to what to do and virtually abandoned Laura as a patient.

She said:

> She didn't contact me because I think she was confused. She had run an ECG and the evidence was there of erratic heart movement...but nothing wrong with the heart so she couldn't explain it.

Laura is an alternative medicine practitioner and therefore had also been self-prescribing many different herbal tinctures and homoeopathic drugs, but nothing was helping.

She said:

> That level of pain was really affecting my health. It was very stressful. My energies were being reduced. I couldn't sustain that indefinitely... something would have cracked.

She was depressed and despairing that both orthodox medical treatment and alternative medicine appeared to have no remedy. She asked me what I thought she should do. While she had been talking to me I had been forming intuitive impressions about what I thought was happening, but I did not want to frighten her by suggesting something was happening in the Elphame when the answer to the problem might turn out to be straightforwardly physical.

She had a history of cholecystitis, but when I asked her about that pain she reported that although the gall bladder pain had been very severe, the current pain was much worse. She was highly anxious and feared that she was going insane because her general practitioner had suggested that the cause might be psychosomatic. Although there appeared to be no physical cause, she couldn't quite believe that she was unconsciously creating something of this magnitude.

When the battery of tests was completed and they indicated that there was no pathology, I knew I had to tell her what I had seen with my inner vision. I had become aware of a situation in the other reality that was the probable cause of the pain Laura was experiencing. These insights were really more like intuitions than visions. I just "knew" that she had an entity attached to her energy body, and I believed that it was her mother.

I asked about her reaction to hearing this. She said she was initially shocked and surprised:

> I wasn't thinking of another reality…I didn't expect you to talk about my mother. I remember you talking about the fact that it was my mother who had attached herself to my heart chakra and…was tapping into my energy, and it was dangerous for me. I had imagined my mother had gone to rest…that she'd been released. So it surprised me to think that after all this time she wasn't rested and she felt she had to attach herself to me. She needed to get my attention in some way. But having got used to the idea, it didn't surprise me. I'm used to the idea of spirits being around. It just surprised me it was my mother.

I knew that her mother had died some time previously and asked her about the circumstances. It was a disturbing story. Her mother had been admitted to a nursing home after suffering a series of minor strokes that had left her brain damaged. She had become violent and aggressive and the family couldn't manage her. In the nursing home she was also frequently violent and had to be constantly restrained, tranquilized, and isolated from the other patients. Before she died she had been in a great pain and was heavily sedated with morphine.

She did not recognize Laura or her other children before her death. They had given her a standard funeral about a week after that event and had also privately performed a more personal ceremony for her. They had scattered her ashes at sea, something she had always wanted. On the basis of having performed these two funerary rites, Laura had believed that her mother was finally at rest. She also disclosed that her mother had been very afraid of dying.

I thought the following scenario was probable: she had been so heavily sedated with morphine when she died that she was confused about what had happened. Her fear and confusion had prevented her from moving into the Elphame and subsequently she found herself lost between the worlds in her energy body and had attached herself to Laura. She became what is sometimes referred to as "earthbound." Even though it had been a year since her death, it was only recently that the effects of the morphine had worn off, and she had become fully conscious and was now even more afraid and confused. Morphine appears to adversely affect the energy body.

It seemed probable that the pain Laura was experiencing was caused by her mother trying to get her attention and help in order to know what she had to do. Previously Laura had described the pain in her heart as "like a hand squeezing it." In the interview transcript she used the word "heart-wrenching" to describe the pain. I thought that was exactly what was happening. Her mother was causing an energetic blockage to the heart.

Laura said:

> I was amazed that there could be such a physical intensity…and it interested me that she had attached to the heart. I suppose I didn't think if an entity is going to attach to you, it's specifically going to hurt.

I told Laura that in my experience those sorts of attachments can cause a lot of damage and even produce cancer, heart attacks, and all sorts of things. Laura said, "Yeah…I believe it now!"

She agreed that the scenario made sense and told me that about a year previously she had awoken in the early hours of the morning feeling a weight upon her chest that made it difficult to breathe. It had felt as if someone had been lying on top of her and was trying to get up. She now thinks it could have been the time when her mother regained consciousness—that is, her mother became aware that something was not right and set about trying to get the attention she needed to remedy the situation.

The inner vision I had of Laura's mother seemed bizarre to me at the time. She exhibited a kind of behavioral dissonance. She was standing in a childish posture with a finger in her mouth, and even though she was an older woman there was a distinctly childlike quality about her.

Laura said:

> When you described her as being like a child, being a pouty, naughty
> child, it was just like "that's Mum!" She would resort to that. She was
> just like a little child. In fact, everyone used to laugh, and her mother
> used to recite the rhyme about "there was a little girl who had a little
> curl..."—you know, the one about in the middle of her forehead?
> "When she was good she was very, very good, and when she was bad
> she was horrid!" She was a nightmare! I thought, "That's exactly like
> my mother!" She would pout and stamp her foot.

I commented that I thought her mother must have been aware of the
amount of pain she was causing Laura and that I thought it was vindictive, but she said:

> I was thinking, "That's typical of my mother!" She was so self-centered
> that she wouldn't care what pain she caused anyone else. That's how
> she lived her life and so I was thinking, "Oh, that'd be right!" It would
> not be deliberate, it was just that she needed to get someone's attention
> and she would create any amount of pain...and it wouldn't matter.

I had telepathically asked her mother what help she needed, and she
said she wouldn't be so afraid if her father, Herb, could be there to help
her, and that she wanted a proper funeral ceremony. She thought the
family must have forgotten to give her a ceremony so she was feeling
hurt and angry. Laura told me that her mother had always been close to
Herb and that she had never recovered from his death:

> He was the most important person in her life. When Herb died she
> had been out of the country. It must have been a great shock for her...
> and so when she came back she was quite unstable, and she did start
> to go into a slide.

Laura went on to talk of an incident about the time her mother went
into the nursing home, describing a visitation from her grandfather, who
had communicated his concern telepathically. It had been another sudden
intrusion from the Elphame.

She said it made sense that her mother would ask for her father to
come for her:

> I can recall, about five years before Mum died, that Herb actually
> came to me one night. I was lying in bed and I felt him near, and I put

the light on, expecting to see him. I got the message that he was concerned about Mum. They were close. So when she wanted Herb, I could see why...because in spite of everything, he would always stand by her. I remember you saying that she was fearful about letting go and facing people. It was her guilt because she had hurt so many people, and I think she was frightened. She'd caused so much grief to so many people. She'd damaged so many people, including my father (who had died sometime before), who always loved her unconditionally, that she was terrified of facing them...

I invoked Herb to come to help her, and Laura and her sisters planned another funerary rite. Basically, they blessed her and thanked her for having been their mother and said that they mourned her death. I taught them the same magical technique I had taught Angela. They visualized a flaming sword to cut the cords that bound her to them. Fire, which is symbolic of spirit, cuts through the subtle energetic cords and enables emotional separation.

When I asked her if there were benefits from the performance of these rituals, she said:

> Apart from the benefit of no pain (which was like a miracle), it was really interesting to be made aware that my mother was not at rest... the fact that she had been drugged...she had still been asleep. She hadn't even been conscious of the fact that she had died. She couldn't even remember the funeral...nothing. I found it very useful to know that because it made sense to do another ritual. I thought that I had let go of her when we'd done the ceremonies initially after her death and then realized that it had meant nothing to her. I then felt (after doing the rituals) that I could fully let go and she would truly be at peace, and I felt that she could go off and be healed and looked after. I think it made her feel that she was acknowledged, so that made me feel relieved.

Six years have now elapsed since this work was done, and Laura has had no pain nor any recurring symptoms since I diagnosed the problem as originating in the Elphame and the appropriate rituals were performed. Respectful acknowledgment of her mother's life and her suffering brought about a healing for Laura and raised her level of consciousness about what may happen postmortem when people are unconscious at the time of transition. The experience has made her appreciative of the healing power of ritual working from the Elphame and expanded her framework of thinking. She said, "The pain stopped. I never had the pain again. That was six years ago…So it's shifted my thinking."

I asked her whether she considered this to be a valid way of working. She said:

> I found the whole experience fascinating. It was the most appropriate method in this case. There was no other way of dealing with it. One needs to shift consciousness in order to deal with a problem such as this…What was needed was a therapist who could actually engage in communication with a being that does not exist in our dimension.

I also asked for her impression of the efficacy of ritual, and she answered with a depth of understanding and insight about ritual's nature and power, saying:

> I feel that ritual is very important because it can actually shift energies. It can alter dramatically even physical events. In her case it freed her… allowed her to move on. She felt she couldn't make the shift until she'd been recognized in this dimension. It was very important to her.

12

Incursions from
the Elphame

Part 2

I think things are true on many different levels. Having an
experience with someone who is dead now but still alive in the
spirit form has changed me. As we went along it just all kept
feeling right, but it was a feeling more than a rational sort of
thing in my heart. You just have that feeling: "This is true!" or
"This has some meaning and some value." (Josephine)

Josephine

Josephine was a young woman who lived with her partner, Heath, in
Perth, Western Australia. Their relationship had become fixed in a pattern of angry fights and recriminations. Heath perceived her to be the
instigator of the disharmony and had paid for her to fly home to the far
north coast of New South Wales for several weeks to see her family and
find a therapist. At our first consultation I saw a tall, willowy young
woman with an air of passionate intensity. She did nothing to emphasize
her femininity, however, as her hair was cropped very short and she wore
boyish gray shorts, a buttoned-up shirt, and no makeup. The anomaly

between her clearly feminine beauty and the odd boyishness of her presentation created a cognitive dissonance.

She described herself as "having a short fuse," particularly in situations she considered unjust, and said when she was angry it felt as though she were "sitting on top of a volcano." Her disproportionate anger frightened and shocked her. She explained how the disagreements she had with her partner over quite insignificant things could escalate into fiery shouting matches during which she lost control and "ranted and raved." This happened when she thought she was being "unfairly treated" by him or "not looked after properly." Those phrases became significant as I began to put the pieces of this case together.

I asked her to close her eyes, relax, and drift back to the first time she could recollect feeling the volcanic rage. I induced a light hypnotic state, and as she lay back in the chair I noticed something strange: her appearance began subtly to change. She began to look even more like a young boy, and I thought at first I was hallucinating but the impression remained and intensified. A background came into focus, and I saw the boy standing in an overgrown field. His eyes held a sorrowful, wistful look and gazed straight at me. The vision overlaid my consulting room, and I was conscious in two different levels of reality simultaneously. This experience changed the way I viewed the case.

She returned to ordinary consciousness and reported she had gone back to the time of her brother's death, approximately ten years earlier, and began to weep in huge sobs that wracked her body. When she became more composed I asked her about his death, and she related a tragic story.

She was the eldest of four children and had a brother twelve months younger, with whom she was very close, and two much younger sisters. When he approached puberty her brother, Zac, had become troubled and had been caught several times stealing. This behavior climaxed when his primary school rang to say that because he had been caught stealing again, he would be suspended. His mother was distraught and contacted a telephone counseling service to get some help and guidance as to how to deal with Zac's problem. On the advice of the crisis counselor, she severely castigated Zac when he arrived home, telling him how angry and upset she was that he was so untrustworthy and how he was bringing shame to the family. Zac listened, stony faced, and when she had finished the denunciation, he walked silently away. Josephine and her mother assumed he had gone to his bedroom to sulk. The younger sisters were playing in the lounge room.

Their father was at work. Zac walked into his parent's bedroom, took his father's gun out of the wardrobe, loaded a bullet into the chamber, put the gun in his mouth, and pulled the trigger. At the sound of the gun discharging, his mother rushed to the room to find his body slumped in the wardrobe. The walls, bed, and floor were covered in spattered blood. He was eleven years old. The impact on the family and the larger community was profound.

Three or four days after his death, but before the funeral, Josephine said that she was next door talking to a neighbor and heard her name being called. She said:

> I thought it was my Mum calling me. So I went over to my house and I heard someone calling, "Josie! Josie!" I asked my mother, "What do you want?" She thought I'd been calling her. She'd heard someone calling, "Mummy! Mummy!" So…we both heard our names being called.

The voice sounded as though it was coming from a distance, but it was very clear. She said that neither she nor her mother had called out, and they wondered if Zac was somehow trying to communicate with them. It happened several times: "It didn't make a lot of logical sense… but I did know that someone had been calling out to me."

She struggled to find a rational explanation. The cultural narrative did not allow for a clear communication from the other reality. Madness lay in that direction, as did ontological shock, so she remained ambivalent about who had called her name, but it was possible it was Zac. Her younger sisters had no doubts about Zac's presence or the fact that they could communicate with him. Young children are better connected with the Elphame than most adults, and the well-known phenomenon of imaginary friends is one of the typical ways young children are easily able to accept it.

Josephine said:

They talked about him like he was there…and sometimes would say, "He was calling me and he was up here and I was talking to him!" But I don't know if he was a spiritual presence or if it was their childish imagination.

The family had lived on a multiple occupancy community that had its own burial ground, and arrangements were made to have Zac's funeral there. The burial was simple; everyone was in deep shock, barely going through the motions. The grave was unmarked and in time became over-grown. The family never visited it. The parents hardly ever mentioned his name, especially the father, who distracted himself with work. There were no overt taboos about mentioning him but a tacit agreement was operating. His death was a painful and irresolvable conundrum. They discarded all his belongings. It was almost as though he had never existed.

Josephine, meanwhile, had become an angry and rebellious girl, both at school and at home, without really understanding why. She had no way of processing her complex emotions and had to take off the pressure by frequent angry and displaced outbursts, but as we worked she was able to access her feelings. She was angry with herself because she "should have known how things were for him" because they were close and she "should have been able to comfort him." She "could have prevented his death."

There were important things she needed to say to him but they remained unsaid. She was angry with him for leaving her, for both she and Zac had felt misunderstood by their parents and had formed an alliance of mutual support within the family. She was also guilty about feeling such anger toward her brother. She also felt anger toward her parents for not realizing she was a child when these shocking events had occurred and had needed their strength and protection, but she had been treated like an adult. She had to take responsibility for her mother and the younger children, and she had coped with the police interviews on her own.

She had been forcibly initiated into the adult world. She blamed her mother for the harsh things she had said to Zac that had precipitated the suicide. She felt she had been robbed of her childhood and could not reclaim it. She became seriously ill and nearly died after Zac's suicide, and she was hospitalized for several months. I wondered, though, how much of the seething emotion was hers and how much might have been Zac's. Her mother told me, "We almost lost her as well. She was so ill."

When I suggested that she drive out to Zac's grave and spend some time there, she responded positively. We speculated that if she talked to him and said what she really wanted, he might hear. In the following session she said that it had been very beneficial to go to the burial site. She had talked to her brother and felt a strong sense of his presence, but she was shocked at the overgrown, unkempt appearance of the site and the difficulty she had in finding the grave.

We discussed how Zac might feel about his grave being neglected and what might possibly be done about it. It was then I told her about my vision of Zac during our first consultation. Josephine imagined that he would feel unloved and abandoned by the family because his grave was treated disrespectfully. We speculated that he might be stuck between the worlds, unable to move on into the Elphame without their forgiveness. This was not something she could easily accept, however, and it was a struggle for her to imagine this as a possibility.

During the next few sessions we discussed how to rectify the situation. She wanted to mow the gravesite, plant a tree, and install an inscribed headstone honoring Zac. She was startled when I suggested that she try to involve her family in the project, believing they would not cooperate. However, when I suggested to her that she ask them to come to her next therapy session to explore the idea, she agreed, and they came. Josephine described their compliance as "a miracle."

They decided the father would mow the site and the other members of the family would weed the area and pile stones on Zac's grave to prevent it becoming overgrown again. They would obtain a headstone with the inscription ZAC, BELOVED SON AND BROTHER. FORGIVEN, NOT FORGOTTEN! They would plant a tree in remembrance. The family would then conduct a ceremony to say goodbye, each in their own way. Then they would light a candle and, holding hands in a circle around the grave, they would ask his grandfather to come for him, as Zac been close to him.

The members of the family moved closer to each other and some necessary grieving and healing occurred. When I received a card from

Josephine the following Christmas, she indicated her relationship was going well and her frightening volcanic anger had subsided. She felt much more normal. Although she was not at the stage where she could completely forgive her parents, she felt as though she was moving toward forgiveness.

It became clear that Josephine used three discernible selves to deal with the foundational theory behind her therapy and that at times these three selves were in conflict with each other and struggling to be dominant. This conflicted mental pattern demonstrates the thought processes of ontological shock.

The first self was her strong rational mind, which was highly skeptical and dismissive of the idea that there could be any communication with the Elphame. This self coped by denying and repressing any ideas and feelings to the contrary and by continually casting any such suggestions into doubt. "Dead is dead! This is a load of crap!" said this self. This self is no-nonsense and practical. It does not waste time processing emotions or contemplating possibilities. It is focused in the here and now, with the realities of physical survival. It is the skeptical intellectual self.

The second self is open-minded and ambivalent. It did not make definitive and conclusive statements about the nature of reality but left the door open to possibilities:

> I didn't expect it...I didn't see how it quite related to the case either, but it was very strong...It struck me that you were being genuine, and so it gave me something to think about.

This self is also pragmatic:

> I thought, well, I'll view this as another optional tool and go with it and see where it goes...and if nothing comes of it, or if I feel that I haven't been helped by it, well, it's just another experience, and if it does, well, then, I stand to benefit from it, so I might as well have an open mind.

She was using the magical "as if" technique, allowing herself to suspend disbelief and to act as if it were true.

The third self is intuitive and spiritual. This self became stronger as the case unfolded, but she struggled at times as her skeptical voice intruded, and she experienced the psychological tremors of ontological shock. But gradually she began to use her intuition more confidently and to trust its insights. This self turns naturally to prayer, meditation, ritual, and the spiritual. It has an inherent grasp of the sacred and the mystical. This is the voice of the intuitive self.

Josephine said:

> I think things are true on many different levels. Having an experience with someone who is dead now but still alive in the spirit form has changed me. As we went along it just all kept feeling right, but it was a feeling more than a rational sort of thing in my heart. You just have that feeling…"This is true!" or "This has some meaning and some value." Intuition, that's the word! Things sort of kept seeming to click, a bit like putting a puzzle together, and I thought it might not be what my mind wants, but it's feeling right. Then I'll keep trying it out, and as we go along it's starting to make some sense to me and I'm starting to get more interested in this idea. My intuition was saying, "Yes, this is right!" and what you were saying was ringing true to me and saying that this was really important. I did feel that was what Zac wanted, and that felt right in me. It seemed to come together that way…and it made sense and felt right!

In the process of doing this interview with Josephine I discovered there was vital information she had not imparted in therapy. The fact that she had withheld such information made me reflect on the fragility of the therapy process. Without the vision of the boy standing in the field of weeds, I would have been groping for clues. The vision was the key because it provided a link with the suicide and with Josephine's own symptomatology, as well as the powerful promptings she had to go to the gravesite and "do something." The vision drew all the pertinent elements together.

She finally revealed she had previously been experiencing intense panic attacks, and although when she first consulted me she briefly mentioned them, she now gave important details. She found it strange that her doctor had said the attacks were caused by stress because they first occurred when she was feeling happy, relaxed, and excited about a new job. She had similar painful heart symptoms to Laura, but also overwhelming suicidal ideation.

She said the first time she experienced an attack:

I wasn't stressed about anything, and that's why I thought I was having a heart attack…and then after that attack I was just very, very upset and completely suicidal. All I could think of was suicide and where Zac was buried, and all this stuff was going around in my head. I thought that if I went to see Zac's grave and talked to him maybe I'd feel better. So I was interested in what you said, and I wanted to go to the grave to see if I got any sort of presence…feeling that he was around there. I felt this calling to go there all the time, and I'd been dreaming about it, so what you said tied in with things I'd been experiencing that I hadn't told you about.

She described the powerful emotional pull to visit the grave:

I felt that it couldn't be put off any longer. I felt this compulsion that was against what I personally wanted to do. It was becoming very strong and combined with the panic attacks, I thought, "I'll go there and I don't know what is going to happen." I didn't have a plan or anything but I knew I had to go.

At this point she gave in to her strong intuition and allowed herself to be guided by it: "I felt like I was being pushed…having a wind behind the car or something…like it was something I should be doing!" At the grave she discerned a strong mixture of powerful emotions and was finally able to differentiate her own feelings from Zac's. She felt

really strong feelings of unhappiness…and it seemed to be from outside me. I thought it was something external to myself…that I had my own sadness and my own feelings of anger and guilt…but this was separate. I felt like it was almost too much to bear.

She decided to take remedial action but, as things turned out, the ritual for Zac was not performed in the way we had discussed during the family consultations.

I wanted something that would blend in because it's such a natural setting. So I went to a quarry and got a giant rock. I needed my dad to help me with it because I wouldn't be able to pick it up. I needed his car and his manpower to help me, and I thought, "Well, I'm going to write my own stuff on it!" I thought, "What would Zac like?" and I meditated on it for a few days, and I came up with the idea that it would be nice to have a natural rock, a really big rock with *Zac* written on it. We cut back all the lantana and my mum and sisters and me pulled out all the weeds, and then we rolled it into place...and we all stood there, and I said, "We all love you and miss you, Zac. I'm so sorry it took so long to get this here."

The simplicity of the ritual seemed appropriate to the needs of an eleven-year-old boy, and it had a quality of spontaneity that identified it as something that came from the heart. I asked her about therapeutic outcomes. She had confided to me during the therapy sessions some three years before that the depressions and rages she experienced were cyclic, but she revealed more information now:

From when Zac died up until I came to see you, about every six months I'd just get overwhelmingly upset and I'd cry and cry and cry...crying for Zac, not for other things in my life. You know when you cry so much that you just can't stop? Then it would go away...and just sort of quietly build up again. I wasn't aware of it. I didn't think it up, but it would just be around. After going to see you and going to the grave, and doing all that, I've never had it happen again.

On the matter of the relationship difficulties and her uncontrollable rages, she said:

I still had arguments with Heath, but I felt a lot more objective. They'd be more about what the problem was rather than whatever it was inside me as well as the problem. It was more like the anger wasn't there any more...and whatever issues came up, it was just that, we dealt with. There wasn't a big explosion in me waiting to boil over.

I asked about the panic attacks. She said, "I've never had them again. No. No...I've never had another one ever." She went on to talk about her experience of the ritual and its sequel:

I remember making a promise to Zac (at the grave). I got this feeling it was important that he felt he wasn't forgotten, and so I said that I'd light a candle and have a rose in a vase on his birthday, and I'd do that every year. I haven't done it because the amazing thing was that each time his birthday came round after that, I didn't even realize it was his birthday. I realized two days later or more.

I am left wondering why she thought that was a good thing. It puzzles me that her tone sounds optimistic, even amused. A question mark hangs in the air—"because I hadn't even thought about him." (She means in the morbid and obsessive way of the past. She has been able grieve and to let him go.)

Josephine said:

> Occasionally I thought about him in a nice way…but I'd forgotten all about it and the day passed without me having even realized it… because that proved to me that some healing had happened and something really had been achieved. I know that I remember him and care about him, but it just feels settled in me. It feels resolved…

She said that on his birthday several years ago she was at a restaurant, and when she went outside she felt his presence and thought she heard his footsteps behind her. She had a strong intuition to do the ritual for him. She said:

> I thought someone was behind me and I turned around but no one was there…and I actually felt quite happy. I felt that Zac was with me and I said, "Oh, hello, Zac!"…and when I got home I did the ritual, and that was the only other time I felt his presence.

13

Incursions from the Elphame

Part 3

Everything around me—my reality—starts to shimmer.
The walls of the room feel like they're coming toward me.
If someone is in the room with me, I feel like they're
screaming at me so loud that I can't really
understand what they're saying. (April)

April

This case was one of the first times that I worked as a shaman-healer. It is unique in several ways. First, there is a methodological difference to the previous cases presented in that I entered the Elphame as a medium rather than a mediator and allowed an attaching spirit to speak through me.

This is something I do not normally do, as there are obvious dangers to the practitioner. Second, although this is another case of an incursion from the Elphame, the set of circumstances or karmic events that motivated this attaching entity had occurred in the distant past and not in April's present lifetime. Third, my partner James took the active role in talking with the entity, and I took the passive-receptive role. What are presented here are the perceptual perspectives of four people: myself as the medium, James as the investigator, April as the patient, and the entity, Richard, who spoke through me.

A general practitioner had referred April to me because she had been unsuccessfully treating her for what she believed were stress-induced panic attacks for six months. April had previously been treated, also unsuccessfully, with antidepressant and antipsychotic medication for ten years by a psychiatrist.

Like Josephine, April confided to me that the panic attacks occurred when she was relaxed, never when she was stressed. She had become addicted to the prescription drugs, although they did not ameliorate the symptoms that were causing her high levels of fear and anxiety.

Her main symptoms were as follows. She experienced being attacked by shouting voices filled with rage, disturbing visual imagery (seeing figures and scenes projected on the wall when she elevated her vision above the horizontal plane), overwhelming and terrifying feelings of incipient madness, powerful suicidal ideation, and the physical world moving, shimmering, and dissolving, the solid appearance of physical reality seemingly breaking down into an energetic state, then finding herself entering the Elphame without any conscious control. She was being psychically attacked from the Elphame but also involuntarily slipping into that fluid reality.

She gave a description of the quality of her experience in her interview. She speaks in the present tense although the symptoms have since abated:

> Everything around me—my reality—starts to shimmer. The walls of the room feel like they're coming toward me. If someone is in the room with me, I feel like they're screaming at me...so loud that I can't really understand what they're saying. It stops me hearing properly... and as that happens I have to run to the toilet because my bowels just give way and then I get the "I'm going to commit suicide" feeling. If I'm in the car and I get one, the suicide idea always takes on and I'm going to crash. "I could run into that car and I'd be dead and I wouldn't have to deal with panic attacks again!"...and then I just feel very hot... my heart races as it wears off. I found when I'd start to get one I'd take

the pills because if I don't…I never come properly out of them. I get to the hot, agitated stage and stay there…I might stay like that for ten or fifteen minutes and it comes again…so it's like a continuous cycle.

I asked her if she remembered the first time she had an attack, and she described a frightening feeling of incipient madness:

I was in the car with Brendan (her husband) and I said to him, "I feel really weird and I'm really scared something's happening to me." He took me home and we went to bed. It was nighttime and he just held onto me and said prayers because I was very distressed, because I thought I was going mad…crying "I'm going mad! I'm going mad. I'm going to go mad!" It's like your senses go haywire. You know your eyes can't see properly. You can't hear properly. The walls can't possibly be moving, you think…but they are!

She describes a significant but confusing sensation of being aware of two separate personalities in her body:

You feel like you're two people. You feel like you can stand and look at yourself, but you can't get out of yourself. It's like you're split. It's horrible!

When she was referred to me it was because none of the orthodox medical strategies were working and she was waking in terror every night with a full attack in progress. The darkness made the experience even more terrifying. She said, "It was awful…I'm losing my mind. It's really going to get me this time. I am really going to go crazy this time!" Her descriptions made me suspect that she had been invaded by what Kharitidi (1999) calls a "foreign power."

She reported that at our first meeting I told her that people in spirit form surrounded her, and she had made diary notes to that effect. I was cautious about explaining my thinking about this to April because to most people this is a very frightening idea, but she was married to a Maori and because of this cultural link and the easy acceptance in traditional Maori culture of the existence of the other reality, she was more accepting than I expected.

I detected relief and surprise in her tone that I was able to think about the problem in terms of the other reality. However, she does reveal a certain ambivalence: she is both "scared" and "not scared." This quality of ambivalence is an integral component of ontological shock. She confirmed that such ideas were well accepted by her Maori relatives:

> I was used to it...sitting at the table having a cup of coffee and someone says, "Oh, Jack's here!"—and Jack's been dead for ten years (laughter) and nobody bats an eyelid. "Oh, how are you going, Jack?" (more laughter) So it wasn't that. It was more like a reality to me...that I kind of lived in but was scared of.

She also recorded in her diary that at the consultation I asked her to talk to the spirits and ask them to leave, and that I had warned her that further strange events might transpire. Subsequently, when she returned home she found her front door open although she distinctly remembered locking it when she had left.

She also experienced some strongly symbolic visual imagery:

> As I looked out my front balcony on the first floor, I could see a number of figures fighting. I knew that it was over my future...whether to stay or whether to go. I can still see them...off the ground outside... and some were black and some were white. The figures looked like two groups of monks wearing hooded robes. One group was wearing black and the other, white. Their faces were concealed, so I believe that they symbolized the impersonality of karmic forces. Despite that, the figures were animated and seemed very personally real. They were screaming at each other: I knew I was looking at whether I was going to go insane or not...that's what they were fighting over.

She believed the symbolism of the black and white had probably come from her Catholic upbringing:

> White was good and black was evil. The devil's black and the angels are white. I was so afraid that the black figures were going to win and take my sanity right there and then...and it was like I was watching something about me but I couldn't say anything. I couldn't do anything, but it was about my future.

She said she felt helpless and powerless as she watched and waited to see what the outcome would be, unable to influence what seemed to be an archetypal battle between good and evil for the prize of her soul and her sanity. I asked her what else was happening about that time, and she described another strangely prophetic incident.

I can remember ringing you up one night because of this noise in my pantry, and that was when I was first saying, "It's the baby's father!" (a long pause) When I was fifteen I had a baby, and she lived for ten minutes...and a couple of years later her father was killed in a car crash but he had always wanted me to have another baby. He was badgering me...and I just had this thought in my mind when this started to happen...I was thinking it was Nelson, the baby's father.

Although we did not realize it at the time, the attaching spirit did indeed turn out to be the baby's father, just not the particular father and particular baby she had supposed. When I began working with April I had some understanding of these matters, but I did not realize that invasion by a foreign power can recur over many lifetimes until some kind of resolution or restitution is achieved.

I agreed to work from the Elphame for April to see whether I could find the cause of her psychic instability. When I relaxed, shifted consciousness, and entered the Elphame, I immediately became aware of an extremely angry and aggressive voice. It had a harsh, grating, ugly quality. It sounded demonic. More alarmingly, it was saying, "Kill the witch! Kill the witch!" As far as I knew, *I* was the witch, and this sounded like a death threat. I struggled for calm and gradually realized that the voice was not threatening me, it was talking about something else entirely, and it desperately wanted to be heard.

April asked me what I remembered of the first session. I had started out asking telepathically who was there and asked for an identifying name. The entity gave the name Richard. Knowing the name of an entity creates a connection that can be used as leverage.

I said:

I remember first of all just sitting really quietly and tuning into what was going on, just clearing my mind and trying to focus on what was happening, letting whatever came up...and the first thing I heard was this horrible voice saying, "Kill the witch!" (laughter)

April responded:

And you went "shiiit!" (more laughter) I can recall you speaking as Richard and saying to James, "I've got more power than you," and I can recall James's answer to that was "Because you've had to tell me that, you don't, and I know you don't."

We had not previously discussed this experience in any detail. She said:

> It's interesting to hear your side now because at the time I was just so...(long pause; voice breaks and tears well up behind her eyes)... yeah. (long sigh)

She was too disturbed to be making cool and objective observations of what was transpiring. She was desperate for a solution.

I asked her for her impression, and she replied: "Please God, make it stop! Make it be the end!" I wanted to know if she had experienced ontological shock as a result of our work, but it seemed she had not. (The incursion itself was experienced in that way.) She was intuitively completely accepting but understood the danger of openly confiding to other people.

Like Laura, she said that she had never feared the truth of it, but added, "Yet if you told someone about it, they'd think you're mad. But to me it was the most sane thing I've ever done."

James questioned Richard. He was angrily obsessive and gradually unfolded an incredible and lurid story. He had made it his mission to force the person known as April to atone for a heinous act she had committed in the distant past. The intuitive visual impressions I received about the place and time indicated ancient Pagan Britain.

In that time, April had been his wife and had been involved in a group practicing a form of black magic that involved human sacrifice. Consequently, she had taken their youngest child, a baby, to be offered as a blood sacrifice. After the ritual murder she became deeply depressed and had drowned herself, leaving Richard to raise their other children on his own. He had became consumed by these events to the point of attaching to her in spirit form, life after life, to make her pay for the terrible thing she had done.

I asked James: "What was your experience of being there and what happened?" He had worked in normal consciousness. He said:

You started off quite still, and then there were progressive movements of the head and hands and then you started speaking as Richard, who was expressing a huge amount of anger and grief, and my response was to attempt to identify who he was and what his relationship to April was—that he was, in fact, the entity we wanted to contact. I took a very cautious attitude, and having established that he was the person, he expressed very strong negative feelings toward April. He wanted revenge and believed April should be punished.

He said he had wanted to develop a dialogue to enable Richard to move through his anger and confusion, so James conducted a highly focused interchange that would deflect Richard's emphasis on April's guilt and redirect it to his own feelings of frustration and futility:

> I was aware that the space the entity was in was not the same as physical space and there were perceptions available to him that weren't available to me. My job wasn't to help him resolve all of his dilemmas but to get him to the point where he was prepared to not pursue his attachment. Once I was aware he had a sense of entrapment about being where he was, I was able to focus and to heighten the dilemma in his own mind, and there was a sense of grief there as well. I was able to bring those things together. He did feel futile, but also he couldn't stop what he was doing. It was an obsession. He had surrounded himself with a kind of fog, and he had trapped himself. I proceeded to examine that sense of entrapment and uncertainty. I was focused on argumentative trickery…moving him to the point of turning the discussion on his dilemma, on his feelings, and on his grief rather than paying attention to April.

Even though the recounted events happened long ago in "earth time," they were current in Richard's consciousness, as he existed in "original time." He/I began to sob as the story gradually emerged. I could distinctly feel remorse and a sense of betrayal. It made me speculate that the human experience of time has less to do with linear perception and more with emotional intensity. I was conscious in the two realities simultaneously. My skeptical observer was asking: "Am I making this up? Could I be such a convincing actress?" I was feeling the swinging poles of certainty/uncertainty redolent of ontological shock.

I asked April if she realized I was a bit uncertain about the whole process. She replied that she had complete faith in me and it had never crossed her mind that I was even slightly uncertain.

James reminded me that this was the first time we had worked for a patient in this way, which could explain my doubts. Previously we had worked on our own or with members of a magical group, and under the guidance of a spiritual teacher. James, like April, did not experience ontological shock. He had sufficient experience and expertise to judge the phenomenon as genuine.

He said:

> Your capacity to be in contact with discarnate entities was something we'd been working with for some time, but this was the first time we'd actually attempted it in a therapeutic context. I'd had experience of talking to discarnate entities who'd spoken through you before, so I felt comfortable with doing that. From the time that your ability to do this had become apparent, I'd taken a great amount of effort to read extensively on the subject of mediumship and mediation…and that had meant that as an observer I was able to apply tests, to observe, to take a very disciplined approach.

I asked April about the quality of the entity's voice. It had scared me, and I wondered how she had responded. She said:

> It was a deeper voice…it was different…husky, deeper. I wouldn't call it scary. I was like, "Wow, it is really him!" I can remember him saying that he had followed me through lifetimes to take my sanity because I had sacrificed a child.

I said, "He also said that you'd drowned yourself. You'd gone insane." April said (after a long, thoughtful pause), "Do you know I can't swim?" I responded, surprised, "Really? That's the first time I've heard that…" I heard the inaudible "click" as another piece of the jigsaw fitted into place, and I realize that I am still putting the pieces of this case together. The click seems to signify that my understanding has gone to another level, and I know I am on the right path. I think it is an alignment of the intuition and the intellect—the aha moment.

She continued,

I can't even wash my face in the shower! As an adult I've had two people try to teach me to swim, and the minute I go under water, I can't... I don't know how to stand up.

As I had spoken as Richard, I had sensed him become calmer and eventually consider his own spiritual progress. He finally understood that by obsessively attempting to exact revenge upon April, he was keeping himself stuck in an unhealthy dynamic and injuring himself spiritually.

April said:

I can remember James asking him what I could do in this lifetime to make up for whatever I'd done...and there were two requests he put on me.

After giving the matter some thought, he decided he wanted a ceremonial and heartfelt apology. He also asked that she always protect children. The symptoms disappeared. What can I say? It seemed so improbable, so melodramatic, but it worked when nothing else had. Conventional medical treatment had failed, as had physical alternative medicine interventions.

James said:

He wanted to be certain that she was sincere and was able to have a sense of grief for what she'd done. I asked her what she remembered of Richard's requests.

She said:

That I apologize and that I would promise to always protect children. I have really put that into my life and tried to do it very hard...I'm doing already what has been asked of me so I don't have to carry this anymore. It wasn't the me who sits here that did that. It was me at a different stage.

She had been working for a time as a volunteer in child protection, preparing children who had been physically and sexually assaulted to give evidence and supporting them in court. As a consequence of her heartfelt apology and reassurance, Richard was able to move into the Elphame.

She said:

You got him to go to another place. I know he had to go. He had gotten from me what he came for...and he went.

James said:

> Richard was able to say to me that he became aware of a very power-
> ful presence...someone who'd come to help him to take him to the
> next stage. (James had asked the Master A to help Richard.)

Finally, I inquired about the outcome of this working for April's
health. She reported that she might have a very mild cluster of symptoms
every few years. She was not taking any drugs, and the suicidal ideation
had disappeared. All thoughts and feelings of going insane had also van-
ished completely. She said that the visual and auditory symptoms and
their intensity and frequency had diminished "immensely."

When I asked her to compare the intensity of the symptoms she
experiences now with the symptoms she experienced previously, she said
she feels she has control over what happens:

> I might think the walls are a bit shimmery and wrinkly and so I'd
> think, "I'm not buying into this!" and get up...do something. If you
> were talking, you may be just a little louder, but not like you're
> screaming at me up close. Once I got up and started to do things, then
> I might need to go to the toilet, but I wouldn't have to run. They are
> unbelievably diminished. I don't even think about it and to have even
> that happen is so rare...very, very rare.

The mild body response she experiences now is, she thinks, a kind of
stress habit and not a reaction to entity attachment. "This is what my
body will do at times because it was used to doing it." She believed that
she was 95 percent cured.

I asked her about ontological shock and whether she thought her
worldview had shifted because of her experience. She said that it had
changed her view of reality in important ways. It made her more reflective and aware, for example, that incidents from past lives could have an
important influence on the current life. She had also become more tolerant of people with mental illnesses, perceiving that their difficulties may
involve incursions from the Elphame, even over many lifetimes. She said
that she frequently wanted to approach them and say:

> Is it just this lifetime of torment or is it lifetimes of torment that has
> made you like this? You don't know what they're carrying. I never do
> it, but I feel like saying to them, "Why aren't you looking to the other

side because you may find answers there that will ease your mind—
that will make sense as to why you are what you are today?"And I
never do it because I think people will think, "Oh, she's just a crack-
pot!" (laughter) I realize now people's disturbed minds may come
from other lifetimes…I think if there was more of this sort of thing,
more people would get peace of mind.

She added:

It seemed so right! It made sense! At last somebody really does know!
It was so sane to me…so real. I can't stress enough how "real" all the
weird stuff was (laughter)…and how weird all the "real" stuff was.
(more laughter)

She reflects on the restorative and healing power of ritual:

I believe that I, to the best of my knowledge, am making up for what I
did. I hope to God I learned something out of it all. Because it's amazing how rituals make so much sense—the peace that it brings immediately.

She excitedly recalled an incident I had forgotten, a time when she
had rung me in a very disturbed state and asked me to come to her house.
I arrived carrying my magical sword and conducted a banishing ritual,
working in the Elphame to remove negative influences from the premises
so she could get some rest. She said, "When you came with the sword to
the house, the peace I immediately felt was so deep and so real. It is real!"

She also talked about her conflict and confusion when her personal
experience clashed with the medical model of reality. She had existed for
eleven years in a state of ontological shock and said:

I was so desperate for an answer because all the time I used to think,
"There's got to be a reason for this!" You just know that there's a reason and nobody can give it to you. A psychiatrist talks to you and
you're thinking, "Oh, you've got no idea!" But you go through the
motions because society tells you you've got a mental problem. The
psychiatrist says you have to take these drugs and you think, "Well,
he's a doctor. He knows *da da da* so I have to take these drugs," but it
keeps gnawing away at you: "There's something not right here!" He's
telling why you're like that and you're thinking, "No! There's more!
There's something more! There's got to be a reason why this happens," and then when you two came along, *that* was my reality.

Now I work solely as a telepathic and intuitive mediator and not as a medium, as it does not feel appropriate to allow someone to express their negative emotions through my physical body. The mediator is not so closely attuned to the entity but is a more like an objective translator. What I perceive happening during the telepathic process is that my mind acts as a receiver of the thought waves or impulses, and then transfers them to my brain. My brain then translates them into the English language.

The mediator or telepath has control over the process so that the dangers of spirit possession are reduced. This may also help explain how telepathic communications are perceived in the native language of the mediator, something that Carmen Blacker (1975) had noted. I asked James how he made coherent and logical sense of this case.

He replied:

> I'm not unfamiliar with strange phenomena. I've had experiences, which satisfy me that there are things that happen that are outside consensual reality. For example, I've been outside of my body consciously...so whereas before that was an enticing idea on which to speculate, having experienced that, even though it was only once and briefly, it was clear to me it was no longer a case of mere speculation.

He reminded me that he had also been a psychically sensitive child and that in his late teens had admitted himself into a psychiatric hospital in Melbourne. He had no ontological frame to interpret incursions from the Elphame, and after being diagnosed as paranoid schizophrenic he was told he would have to take antipsychotic medication for the rest of his life. Fortunately, an art therapist told him that, like many others, he had simply had some psychic experiences. "Consensual reality," she added, "has no explanation for these phenomena except madness." He immediately discharged himself.

He saw a link between what we had done and the traditional practice of driving out devils or evil spirits, and said:

> Here was a condition that was not amenable to conventional therapeutic modalities, and it was resolved by an activity that had been respected in other cultures...the driving out of devils or various forms of purification...or cleansing or banishing.

He also saw the therapeutic value of what we had done and adopted an evidentiary perspective:

> I experienced participation in a therapeutic methodology that delivered results...and one can engage in endless debates as to whether the description of what happened is objectively real or whether what we've simply done is come up with a discourse style that enables us to articulate a process. I know that conventional medicine will deny the methodology, but I don't think on any good grounds. They might certainly deny the explanation, but then again any form of discourse has the purpose of providing the capacity to talk about an experience... the trick is not to interpret one discourse in terms of another but to allow the validity of the discourse and the methodologies associated with it and assess them on whether or not they "deliver the goods"... in which case one could say that the classical, rational, medical model or discourse sometimes delivers the goods and sometimes doesn't, and you can't negate its validity on the basis of its failure any more than you can confirm its validity on the basis of its success, and I think the same with what we were able to do. We can't absolutely validate the methodology because we were successful.

However, that was not my purpose. My purpose was to allow a number of people to talk about their experiences and to facilitate discussion by providing a theoretical and experiential framework. The shamanic approach to medicine has a long, honorable tradition and a holistic gestalt approach to healing.

James continued:

> If a person has a spiritual problem, they can't necessarily go to a doctor who will prescribe a spiritual solution, whereas in your case you have a whole range of things you can apply, whether it's herbalism, flower remedies, homoeopathy, ritual practices, and ultimately the work that resolved April's problem. It seems to me that is much closer to the multidimensional and multifaceted approach of the shaman. A shaman may send someone off to do a ritual to redress the balance. An imbalance has arisen in the world as a consequence of something that they've done, and my sense is that is a far more sophisticated notion of human well-being. It's something that accesses the physical and the emotional, the psychic and the spiritual, and it looks at the whole person in the world in which they are living...looks at their behavior, their attitudes, in terms of the scope and sophistication of

it…I think it is superior to the conventional medical approach that is very narrow, very reductionist—ultimately a very limiting approach. We've progressed on the material level, but we've regressed on the psychic and spiritual.

It is always easy for James and me to get into analytical discussions, and to become overly mentally focused, so I tried to get him to discuss the experience in a more emotional way. He said:

It was very intense…challenging. It demanded a huge amount of focus and a case of very much thinking on my feet because I felt I had to maintain control of the dialogue, listen very carefully and keep him focused, allow him enough opportunity to say what was necessary but not let him become too focused on venting his wrath. I found it very important to listen in huge detail.

As he spoke I discerned strong parallels between working in this way and psychotherapy practice. I had a realization: It's almost like doing psychotherapy. It *is* psychotherapy! Psychotherapy for the dead!

We had worked as a team, each of us contributing our own particular skill, but I realized the important oversight role James had played. I also realized that a strongly rational part of my own awareness was overseeing things as well and commenting on what was transpiring, not in a negative way but in the sense of splitting consciousness and of being simultaneously aware in two levels of reality. One part was accepting and intuitive, while the other was very much rooted in the physical world and offering skeptical opinions. I had told Josephine that "both things were good," that is, skepticism and intuition, and I reflected that I was coming to the realization that cross-referencing between the two realities may give a more complete and accurate picture than the simple acceptance of one or the other. There was a third way.

I had decided to interview both April and James as well as writing about my own experience, and to present this work as a four-cornered case, looking at points of concurrence and disparity, and inquiring into the one series of strange events from four differing perspectives. Viewing this case from four differing perspectives, I believe, has added a richness of insight and detail to what had transpired. It also gave me confidence in the accuracy of the work we did because of the subsequent positive changes in the quality of April's health and life.

14

The Politics of Madness

Part 1

The system is not there to support you. The system is designed
for people who are out of control. Unless there was no other
way and you actually needed to be medicated to get out of the
state you're in, you wouldn't go near them. (Tom)

Tom

Tom realized that circumspection was necessary when he was hospitalized for an intense "psychotic episode." He, however, framed the incident differently as a "shamanic" or "transpersonal experience." In his
view, the Elphame had unexpectedly crashed through into normal waking consciousness, but he found it was too risky to reveal anything about
his inner reality to his "mental health" workers at the double risk of being
labeled schizophrenic and of being continuously heavily medicated.

It became politically expedient to remain silent about the reality of his
inner experience. He said:

They were trained to look for pathology, so anything that's not within consensus reality is a symptom of pathology. They weren't interested in my process. They had no concept of process. The system is not there to support you. The system is designed for people who are out of control. Unless there was no other way and you actually needed to be medicated to get out of the state you're in, you wouldn't go near them. It's not for any non-consensus reality experiences or how to deal with them...they're only trained to see things in terms of pathology rather than the events having meaning and being part of a process.

Tom's story shows, in stark contrast, the difference between practices arising out of the medical model of mental illness and the Goddess model of working that honors the insider's intuitions and empathically works within their reality. In the Goddess-oriented model of treatment the therapist is not the expert who "knows" but a companion and guide on a healing journey into the Elphame. Tom gave a vivid description of his humiliating and disempowering experience of conventional psychiatric treatment.

He had crashed his car into a telegraph pole in response to hearing voices and consequently had been sectioned and incarcerated. He angrily remembers what happened:

> The cops jumped on me and some guy who looked like a refugee from the fucking Gestapo Medical Team gave me this fucking great big needle, then strapped me in a straitjacket and took me to Coffs Harbor Psychiatric Hospital, where I was given large doses of Largactyl and Valium and placed in an observation room. The antipsychotic medication reduced the energy of the state I was in. I spent four days in that room, and I was so heavily medicated that I can't remember what happened, and then I was put in the lock-up ward...The whole emphasis was on medicating me. There was absolutely zero interest shown in what was actually going on...(pause) They were mainly concerned with coming up with a diagnosis that I was bipolar because then they told me that I have to take lithium...and even then they didn't explain the process to me.

When Tom first approached me for treatment, about two months after he had been released from hospital, he confirmed that he had been diagnosed as schizophrenic and bipolar but added that he rejected the psychiatric diagnosis. He valued his "psychotic" experiences as part of an important process that could possibly lead to a deeper understanding of reality. After hearing his story, I believed he had experienced a frightening incursion from the Elphame that had affected his life on every level.

He believed the experience was fundamentally positive but that it had been mismanaged medically, mainly because of the political limitations of the cultural narrative. He was not aware of my interest or training in shamanic healing and said:

> Many people can experience a transpersonal experience, but because they don't know how to deal with it, or ground it, or go in and out of it, they lose it. It's not doing them any good. (long pause) Drugs actually interfere with the process. Within a shamanic context it could be called an "initiatory experience" or a "spiritual emergency" or like "unconscious material erupting" or the collective elements manifesting through an individual and working stuff out.

As a sequel to the psychotic episode and subsequent psychiatric treatment, he was living in isolation as a fringe dweller on what he described as the "nut pension" in a shack on the outskirts of town, separated from friends, family, and community, and still suffering the effects of the spiritual emergency that had overwhelmed him.

He had experienced an acrimonious divorce that had divested him of much of his material affluence, as well as any contact with his children. He claimed he suffered from poor memory, no imagination, and no emotion. He existed in a cyclic and recurring state of psychic and emotional numbness and several self-graded levels of depression with attendant symptom patterns. The third and deepest state he described as "being a cabbage."

His levels of depression he named as one, two, and three, with three being the most mentally and emotionally distressing and debilitating, as well as having a physical symptom pattern like chronic fatigue syndrome. As he had found the antipsychotic medication detrimental in its effects, he wanted to explore the possibilities of psychotherapeutic treatment with me.

We worked together for over three years, during which time we experimented with many different methodologies both conventional and shamanic in order to find a cure, but as Tom believed that he had no creative imagination and was highly fearful of any ritual practice, the possibilities for successful shamanic treatment gradually became more limited. It was, however, by a process of attrition combined with my willingness to innovate that a successful method was finally developed.

In the process we created a healing alliance, or what he termed "a dyad." Sufficient trust and empathy had developed between us to enable the process of intuitive healing to unfold. He said, "It's like a process happens which is outside of your conscious mind." His deep fear of ritual originated in his belief that he had in past lifetimes suffered brutal ritual abuse. This aversion meant that I had to be extremely adaptive and to give up any struggle to impose on him whatever preconceived ideas I had about the nature and progress of therapy.

Whether or not we always agreed with what we were doing intellectually seemed to be irrelevant, but we allowed ourselves to develop sufficient relaxation and trust to be guided on a magical journey from the edge of madness. This was an intuitive and pragmatic process that was not always comfortable. There were elements of ontological shock for me in this process because it meant being willing to be guided by faith and intuition and more or less abandoning the intellect and its preconceived ideas about how therapy should unfold and entering the dark realm of unknown potential—the unknowable void. It was another application of the Hero's Journey narrative, and I vacillated between doubt, as my skeptical intellectualizing self got in the way, and acceptance, as I learned to let the intuitive process unfold and remain comfortable with it.

I wanted to know how different it was for him working with me compared to his experience of conventional psychiatric medicine. He stressed the importance of facilitating the process of unfolding and the advantages of working with the intuition. This is a more passive, feminine approach to the healing journey than the heroic methods of psychiatry.

He said:

> One difference is the recognition that there is actually an internal reality and there's a process that is the individual's own process…and that things occur within a wider framework, which recognizes things other than the normal consensus sensate view of reality. There's the recog-

nition of a healing process rather than a mechanical-type process where certain chemicals aren't being produced. (thoughtful pause) The map of the human psyche is very limited in psychiatry.

I asked him what it was like for him to have worked in an intuitive, guided way, and with a person who could accept his process and his experiences, and he said:

It was heartening to find somebody who actually is open to what is going on…that doesn't see it in terms of pathology. It is very heartening if you have a unique experience to have it accepted. I don't think you can really change or move unless you accept where you are. So it's totally different from psychiatry.

I asked him whether having his experiences validated had been important to his healing, and he confirmed that it was:

It's like obtaining meaning in the subtleties of things that happened. Any assistance with that is really helpful. It's a bit like going to a foreign country and not knowing the language…Even though you can walk around and experience things, you're at a loss to communicate.

I then understood that he saw my role as that of a guide and companion in an unknown world, or another reality. It was important that I could go on that journey with him.

The method I used that proved to be most successful was ultimately quite simple. I induced a deep relaxation during which he seemed to be able to access certain incidents and contact personality fragments we believed had split off in past lives. We achieved this access by working with feelings and intuitions and by altering consciousness to work from the other reality. When we allowed the personality fragments to speak and process their emotions, Tom began to experience some relief from his symptoms. At other times we allowed the various affected physical organs, or the symptoms themselves, to speak.

Accepting Tom's experiences as real was very important to his process of healing, as was my ability to work as if all was possible—that is, to accept that the body and the symptoms can have communicative consciousness, and that the symptoms are symbols that can speak to the imagination and intuition. We assumed a particular symptom had intelligence and consciousness and was trying to communicate something by its presence. By this process of decoding, we allowed the symptoms to tell their story and were gradually able to peel away layers of maladaptive beliefs, ideas, and behaviors.

As the debilitating mental, emotional, and physical symptoms dissipated, the process of recovery became exponential. Tom said:

> I think that deep relaxation takes me to a place I wouldn't normally be able to access. It loosens things up. (thoughtful pause) The thing that makes a big difference is dialoguing with the symptoms or the aspects that are displaying the symptoms and the process of releasing them or integrating them. Most of them seem to be from prior lives. It was basically a process of past-life regression. We went back to a time when the symptoms actually happened. This work seems to produce a great deal of change. Those symptoms disappear totally afterward.

I asked him to give a concrete example. He said:

> Hmmm...I had severe pains around the heart, and it was strong enough for me to actually go and have a medical examination. They'd usually be there in the morning when I woke up and at other times, and also I felt very lethargic and sort of drugged, and what came out was I'd been given a strong narcotic and, while still alive, my heart had been cut out. There was this narcotic feeling which felt like it was left over in the energy body. (long pause) It was almost like the soul or whatever was still stuck there and lost. We allowed the heart to talk for itself. I can't remember whether it was an integration or sending it to the afterlife, but it was after that the symptoms disappeared—the energy picked up and the feelings totally disappeared.

By "integration" he meant the physical heart damage from the prior incarnation had translated as damage in his current energy body's heart chakra. Integration meant repairing the old heart energetically and integrating or merging it with the current heart. "Sending it to the afterlife" meant persuading the past personality fragment to release its hold on Tom's body, emotions, and mind and to take itself to the Elphame. This was a kind of a reverse shamanic soul retrieval process, although from a prior lifetime.

Robert Lake, a Native American shaman-healer, says that if he asked a patient who complained of stomach pain what it was like and if the patient responds, "I feel like my stomach is twisted up and full of snakes!" the shaman would respond, "We'll talk to the snakes and find out why they're tormenting you" (Lake 1993, 142). This is similar to the way in which I approached Tom's healing: by talking to the symptoms as symbols of a deeper reality. By "not allowing your mind to get in the way" it is possible to work in a more holistic way in which inner and outer, past and present, conscious and unconscious are all interlinked and mutually influential.

I asked him for another example, which he gave but also expanded on what he had said before:

> A feeling of having my skull or scalp removed and my brain exposed... those symptoms seem to have totally gone since we did that process. The mind-blowing part is that this actually works! The quietness of it compared to other methods—it's sort of homoeopathic. I expected a much stronger experience. The experiences seemed to be almost made up or constructed, but they seemed to have the desired result. It's almost like you have to invent a story to fit the feeling, but once the regression's done it always seems to work, even though it feels like the mind's saying, "Bullshit, you're just making it up!" You've got to stand back from your reactions—part of them are skeptical.

He is talking about his reaction of ontological shock and how he copes with it by "getting his rational mind out of the way."

He found the method quietly reassuring. There was no noisy or uncontrolled abreaction or catharsis, yet it had proven effective. He found working from the Elphame to be a gentle process. This is something on which Laura and April had also remarked.

Tom was an accountant and had a strongly rational, skeptical intellect, but at the same time he had an interest in spiritual and mystical matters. He had trained for many years in aikido, a Japanese martial art which emphasizes patience, self-control, and self-discipline as a route to spiritual growth. However, he had stormed into the Elphame, hungering for the experience but unprepared for the level of energy he encountered. The ability to handle high levels of psychic energy is the mark of the magical initiate.

He explains the apocalyptic visionary experience that marked the onset of the "psychotic episode":

> I had been practicing aikido and meditating quite a bit...I was down at Belongil (Byron Bay, on the far north coast of New South Wales) practicing tai chi and chi gong, and I had this really intense experience. Up in the sky (the sky wasn't there anymore) was this coal-black face rumbling forward...and then this sort of god, this huge sort of human figure looked out, and it was like, "You've got to fix up all the mistakes you've made!"

I inquired whether he thought he was somehow responsible, and he replied:

> No, no! Not me—him! He fucked up when the parameters were set up in the beginning. (long pause) I'd been practicing this meditation of making things that were infinitely large, small, and pulling them in...and spontaneously it felt like the top of my head opened up and I felt like I pulled it in through my crown chakra...this giant spirit. It was like those rock paintings from Western Australia. (I asked if he meant Wandjina.) Wandjina...right! It was like a giant one of them... and I thought, "Oh, fuck! What's going to happen?" I thought some sort of major transformation...and I thought, "Oh, maybe this is some sort of archetypal mythical memory or something." I'd never had those types of experiences or imagined things...my imagination is very poor.

I asked what it was like having that altered consciousness. He said:

> It wasn't what I'd expected. I was punting on what the guide books say when you have this sort of transformational experience. It was supposed to take you into a world beyond the normal grotty pain of human existence to some sort of blissful, high energetic state...and it would dissolve all your pain. But it was a terrifying experience!

The "psychotic episode" had lasted for around ten days, and there were several things about Tom's detailed descriptions that supported my contention that what Western medicine describes as "psychosis" are actually uncontrolled and culturally inexplicable incursions from the Elphame. I believe there is a nexus between powerful experiences of the subtle reality and so-called psychosis.

In support of that view, he described a cognitive dissonance existing between what he was observing and his inner dialogue. The inner dialogue was describing an alternative reality—a world of meaning—so the things he was observing in the outer reality became symbolic:

> I had this knowing, like the mental trip would be going on and all of a sudden, it's like you've tuned into the wrong station. You'd see just normal people, but the dialogue in your head was telling you something else. I couldn't figure out what the fuck was going on! It was like someone projecting mental energy and whatever they're thinking just goes all into your mind, so you'd go to the golf club and there's this geezer couple sitting there morosely drinking scotch and water…and they're supposed to be the devils and the angels that have come back together…and there were other interestingly bizarre episodes where I felt I was playing golf with this really muscular blue sort of creature who would jump into people's bodies.

He describes an intuitive perception:

> I could sort of sense it…but you know reality comes and goes. (He describes the experience of heightened awareness that is called paranoid schizophrenia.) Your mind with its limited experience tries to make sense of it, so it will say, "Oh, the CIA's there!" or something, or some clandestine information or "There's these fucking pricks in the bushes!" It was real and unreal…you know what I mean?

His description of CIA operatives hiding in the bushes, which would normally be diagnosed as paranoid delusions, he framed as the mind's attempts to offer a rational interpretation of what was happening in the other reality. In other words, it was the intellect's way of dealing with the ontological shock of the other reality impinging on ordinary reality—of normalizing experiences and explaining away the unusual when it had no frame of reference.

He seemed to be saying that madness is created by the intellect when it is overwhelmed by information that it cannot process and that comes from the other reality. I would say that if this happens and the sense of self is very weak or undermined in some way, the mental structure can collapse and what is called schizophrenia results. When the sense of self is strong, then it is ontological shock that is experienced and not psychosis.

I was also intrigued that he described an experience that seemed very similar to the traditional shamanic skill of shapeshifting—that is, the ability to change into an animal form. Perhaps an alternative explanation for the following could be that he inadvertently released an animal spirit helper that he had contained within his energy body. The practice of keeping animal "familiars" is something common to shamans from many cultures. In Australian Aboriginal culture, according to Elkin (1944), who had interviewed some of the remaining "clever fellers," initiates often retained snakes and stones and other objects within their energy bodies to be used in magical rituals in a controlled way.

In Tom's case this was an uncontrolled experience. Tom's contention that his psychosis was a shamanic experience may have been accurate:

> I am walking along that beach at the back of Belongil, and suddenly there was this fucking giant eagle coming out of my head...that was really freaky. I could actually see out of the eyes of this eagle, and then it transmuted into this pterodactyl-type creature and there was this huge vortex coming out of me with first of all the eagle and then this more primitive-type creature in this vortex, with me at the bottom.

I was interested as he talked of being conscious in two realities simultaneously, especially as he describes the other reality as the "world of meaning." This experience sounds very much as April had described it. The physical world seems to shimmer, flicker, and disintegrate, and the person becomes aware of another underlying reality. Tom said:

> It was like I was coexisting in a separate reality along with the normal consensus reality. I could function and carry on a conversation but the other reality was becoming stronger and stronger. It was like our normal world and another world were lined up. They had conjoined. Like a cycle where you know they move at different speeds and at this time they were actually coexisting...and it seemed like the other world had much more meaning than ordinary everyday life. Things became more and more bizarre...like I was standing on the earth and the world would dissolve.

He struggled for an analogy. The solid form of physical reality seemed to shimmer and break down, as if the veil between the worlds was being torn apart or dissolving:

You know in the old days when the film in the projector wasn't very good? Flickering, and you could see there was nothing physical behind it, but…I could feel the solidity of the ground. This world is sort of parallel to the other one in some ways, but in others it's totally different…it's sort of like a subtle version, and all the events had gone on and the cycle has brought them back together again. It was just so overwhelming, I just couldn't cope anymore with the bizarreness and the world collapsing…going flickering and black around me.

I asked him how he would describe the changes he perceives in himself as a result of having done this work. He described a gradual and exponential transformation:

Initially the unreal sorts of feelings and experiences were very strong and dominating. Everything was suppressed and acutely depressed… just absolutely no feeling, staggering through chronic fatigue–type symptoms. Over time they've gradually lessened. The bottom two levels of depression have disappeared, so the states of being totally (he makes a crashing sound) when there's absolutely no feeling…the muscles ache…the joints ache…every movement, every thing, every thought you have, requires intense effort…those are nonexistent now, and the energy levels have increased as well. Sometimes there's actually feeling and emotion!

He went on to say that he belonged to a manic depression support group and he had observed that except for himself, all the members seemed to be getting worse. He attributed this to the fact that he refused to subscribe to the medical model. He did not agree that he had an illness or a disability that must be chemically managed. He valued the psychotherapy we were doing and found it to be efficacious.

He then described a recurring strong dream that was part of his symptom picture and had persisted for ten years. It was a dream about a test for which he had not studied and had strong fears of failing. It invariably preceded a lengthy episode of level three major depression. He laughed as he said:

The depression lasted two or three weeks, if not more, when I first started therapy…and then by the end it would last for a day or an hour. (a breathless pause—he's almost bursting) But what I haven't told you was the other night I had a dream where I'd already passed the test, and I didn't have to sit for it. (pause) I'm still waiting for the results! (explodes into laughter)

His voice thickened with emotional intensity as he continued, "I thought that was a monumental dream in the scheme of things...it's a dramatic turnabout, isn't it?" It was, and it was this strong dream that signaled the end of his therapy and of our healing journey together.

15

The Politics
of Madness

Part 2

I felt like I was losing my mind. I was determined
I was going to give it my best shot. If it was going
to work, I had to give it my all. (Anna)

Anna

WARNING: This case contains material that may be distressing to some
readers, as it contains explicit descriptions of sexual and physical abuse. I
have left the transcript as Anna told it and have not sanitized it because it
reveals the depth of the severe trauma that she suffered in childhood and
therefore gives the reader some greater understanding of how and why
such heinous crimes came to be committed. It also shows that magical
techniques of healing have efficacy when applied to very serious cases
that have a strong psychological and psychiatric focus.

. . . .

THIS IS A COMPLEX story, not only because of the inherent intricacies of
Anna's journey from the edge of madness, but because of the variety of

roles I needed to assume as her therapist in order to accompany her. Sometimes I was her therapist working with the various techniques of conventional therapy, and other times I worked with the magical techniques of a traditional shaman.

Ultimately I took on the role of a social justice advocate, negotiating on her behalf with several government agencies that treated her with a callousness that bordered on the vindictive. I worked with Anna for more than two and a half years, and probably came to have greater knowledge of the finer details of her case and its antecedents than most of the many professionals who had consulted with her over the years.

She was thirty-seven and on parole when she first consulted me, and when she told me the reason for her imprisonment I was shocked and wondered whether I could suspend judgment sufficiently to be a suitable therapist for her. At age seventeen Anna had been sentenced to life imprisonment for the suffocation murders of three infants left in her care as a babysitter. She was also sentenced for the attempted murder of two other young children. She had served sixteen years in prison and was released on parole under truth-in-sentencing legislation, largely because she had been a model prisoner.

At the beginning of our second consultation I told her that I had spent several days reflecting on what she had told me, wondering if I could cope with her case, especially as it appeared that, based on what she had told me, other therapists either had mishandled it or had avoided coming to terms with it. I had strong reservations but I had thought about it carefully and was prepared to accept her as a patient. When I later interviewed her as a research participant, she revealed that when I told her I had reservations about taking her case she had been surprised because I had shared something of myself with her.

She had not experienced an authentic therapeutic relationship or alliance in any of the considerable and extended therapy she had received since her arrest. It was then, she said, she felt she could work with me, that there was hope and that this was a turning point in her life. There could be honesty between us. With the other therapists she felt a gulf between themselves and herself, as though they "were on a pedestal looking down on me." With me, she said she felt more equal and that I valued her as a human being despite what the world thought of her. This was not quite the way I had thought about it, but I was willing to suspend judgment and see how things unfolded, and I had been honest about my uncertainty.

The quality of authenticity is a vital part of the therapeutic relationship. Gerald Corey, a researcher into the efficacy of psychotherapy, believes that the quality of authenticity that exists between patient and therapist is indispensable to successful treatment:

> The therapists' techniques are far less important than the quality of the therapeutic relationship that they develop. Indeed, therapists are not in business to change clients, to give them quick advice, or to solve problems for them. Instead, therapists heal through a process of genuine dialogue with their clients. (1996, 5)

I believe this insight is important, as it is the quality of the relationship that provides the fertile ground for acceptance and healing, but both parties to the healing alliance need to be brave enough to work with the truth. As I worked with Anna a pattern of insight gradually began to emerge. This pattern traced a series of tragic and traumatic life events that converged to make a murderer of an apparently kind, intelligent, and sensitive person.

She was the unwanted child of a teenage pregnancy, and from infancy her mother had emotionally and physically abused her. Her father was an alcoholic by his early twenties and was also addicted to gambling. Her mother coped with the stress by becoming "strict." This meant frequent beatings and other colder disciplines for Anna and her siblings. As the eldest child she had no memory of ever having been kissed, cuddled, or nursed by her mother and was frequently told that she had ruined her mother's life. Her father abandoned the family when she was five.

Anna's parents divorced, and her mother remarried. The stepfather was quiet and uncommunicative, remote, and detached from any emotional involvement with the children. The home was always clinically clean and there was always enough food, but it was a cold and loveless climate in which to grow, and Anna was always aware of an aching need for love and acceptance. At age eight her maternal uncle had began to show an unprecedented interest in her, ostensibly giving her the attention and affection she craved by giving her presents and treats and telling her that she was "special."

In reality, he was grooming her for a future of sexual abuse that began when he showed her pornographic magazines. The abuse escalated to mutual masturbation and oral sex that was repeated a couple of times a week. Sexual intercourse began about age eleven. To keep this illicit activity secret he manipulated her into powerlessness, self-loathing, and confusion. He continually reinforced the suggestion that she was the one responsible for the abuse. At about age twelve, in a sex education lesson in her first year of high school, she finally realized how reproduction occurred. She tried to tell her uncle that she didn't want to do it any more. He raped her violently, telling her it was too late to say no, that no one would believe her, and that "it's not going to stop until I say so!"

This was the first of a series of violent, terrifying, and humiliating anal rapes. Her sense of betrayal and hurt was profound, and she began to view herself as a scapegoat, sacrificing herself to her uncle's cruelty to save the other children in the family. She feared that if she denied or thwarted him, he might abuse his own young daughters. The scapegoat role in childhood was a foretaste of the way in which society would condemn her in the future.

She vividly described the violence and humiliation of the rape:

> That had to be the worst pain I've ever felt. I wanted to scream. He held my head into the pillow. I guess he knew it was going to hurt like hell…and it did. When he finished I tried to roll over…lost control of my bowel. There was blood everywhere…I thought, "This time he's killed me! I'm going to die from this!" This was the same uncle who had treated me so nice…He was totally cold and saying all the stuff Mum had always said…I was "never going to amount to anything." "No one would ever want me."

She reported that she frequently thought of suicide during those years but did not know how to achieve it.

From the early days of the sexual assaults she had dissociated from the trauma in the way that many child victims do. The experience of being sexually assaulted by a trusted adult is such a confusing and disturbing occurrence that the child's psyche cannot integrate it. Part of the consciousness fragments. She said, "It was easier for me to go along with it and imagine while it was happening that I was not there." In this way Anna lost an important part of her psyche, personal power, and autonomy.

It was while she was in this fragile and disturbed state that the murders took place, although she has always claimed that she has no memory of them. Her history of abuse and her dissociative episodes suggested she was telling the truth when she made this claim. None of her history of sexual and physical abuse or psychosis was investigated at her trial. If it had, the verdict might well have been different.

When she first approached me for treatment she was suffering extreme mental stress and emotional pain and living like a fringe dweller, isolated from community support. A psychiatrist had prescribed her antidepressant and antipsychotic medication, which she claimed had no beneficial effect and made her "feel like a zombie." She also had a mental health caseworker who exuded hostility when I attempted to discuss her case with him and exhibited no trace of compassion. She had been raped several years before our meeting, but because she was an ex-offender and had been convicted of heinous offences, the police refused to believe her and did not investigate the crime or charge the rapist. As a result of the rape she became pregnant and delivered a baby girl to whom she became a devoted mother.

Due to a series of misperceptions, the Department of Community Services removed the child from her care not long before I took up the case. This was another devastating blow, and I believe that she was psychotic in the early months of treatment. In my estimation the police, the Department of Health, the Department of Community Services, the Criminal Justice System, Corrective Services, and Probation and Parole treated her as less than human. A representative of the Department of Community Services said to me that "it was better that her human rights were violated than another child be put at risk." It was easier for these bureaucracies to see her as evil and to make a scapegoat of her than it was to look a little deeper to find that the truth was more complex and less politically and emotionally satisfying.

As an adult she had made many suicide attempts and regularly self-harmed. At our first consultation it was obvious she had been slashing herself recently as her arms and legs bore masses of scar tissue. Early in treatment I tried to teach her a relaxation practice, but she dissociated and it proved very difficult to get her back. Each time I tried a therapeutic intervention that involved some kind of inner focus, she would dissociate and lapse into a catatonic state, and although I wanted to use hypnosis these experiences indicated I would have to proceed slowly and cautiously. Ultimately I was able to use hypnosis successfully, but that was after two years of experimentation with other therapeutic approaches. She wanted to see if under hypnosis she could regain any memory of the crimes.

After my experience of the first dissociative episode, I managed to get her back to conscious awareness, and being cautious I drove her home and made sure she got safely inside. I noticed that she had a beautiful poster of a tiger. At her next appointment I remarked on it, and she told me that her Chinese astrological sign was the tiger. This gave me an idea as to a possible safe place to make a creative start in her treatment.

I decided to use the tiger archetype or totem to help her develop the strength and courage she was going to need to deal not only with her life, but also with her therapy. Because she seemed to relate positively to the tiger symbol, I was hoping that a real spirit animal guide might decide to help her. If that strategy did not work, then she could build what in magic is known as an "artificial elemental." This is a deliberately formed mental image that is gradually built up and reinforced by repeated visualizations. Once the form is built, it is then charged with emotional energy. It becomes "alive" and can operate in the Elphame or in physical reality. Many magical workers build them to protect their homes or ceremonial places from unwanted incursions from the Elphame. They function as psychic guardians.

The other reason that influenced my decision to work in this way was that Anna herself would be in charge of the process and would therefore, perhaps, feel more empowered. I hoped it might lessen the chances of further dissociative episodes.

I asked her to set up an altar with a white candle and some incense. I also asked her to put the picture of the tiger on the altar and buy a tiger's-eye stone and keep it on the altar. We designed a simple ritual for her to do each morning. She was to wash her face and hands as a symbolic act of purification before starting and then to sit facing her altar and concentrate on relaxing her body. When she was sufficiently relaxed, she was to focus on her breath for a few minutes and then ask the totem or the archetype of the tiger to help her develop the strength, courage, and grace to cope with the ordeals she was to face.

She was then to imagine that she was breathing in and being filled up with those qualities from the tiger in the picture in whichever way felt most natural. When she went out she was to take the tiger's-eye stone wrapped in a yellow cloth. This would act as a protective talisman; if she felt her courage slipping, she could hold the wrapped stone and feel its energy flowing into her. When she returned home she was to put the stone and the cloth back on her altar until she needed them again. Anna became committed to the ritual and began to feel positive results. She said that she did feel stronger and more confident, at least in daylight hours and in the "real" world. The dream world was a different matter.

As we began to explore the childhood incest in some detail, she began to experience flashbacks. This is a common pattern of post-traumatic stress disorder sufferers. She had flashbacks from time to time in the past, but these latest ones took the form of vivid dreams with full sensory detail. The dreams were so real that she felt they were actual events, which indicated to me that strong dreams were not always benign events. Her sleep patterns had become very disturbed, and she was distressed that her uncle seemed still able to violate her although twenty years had passed since she had seen him. I thought that there was a strong possibility that these visitations were incursions from the Elphame and her uncle was continuing his abuse from the Elphame by visiting her in his energy body. I decided to extend the function of the tiger totem to provide further protection.

I asked her when the dreams happened if she was a child or an adult, and she said that it varied. She described the experience of the strong dreams:

> Sometimes it's just the reliving…It's me at the different ages when I was going through it and at other times it's me now, going through it again. It's the same stuff he used to do and I'm still just as powerless as an adult when it's happening as I was when I was a child. They were so real that I'd actually feel the physical pain…like it was actually happening. The feeling that he was there was incredibly strong. I'd have to get up out of bed and I had to look for him…I checked the lounge room and the kitchen and the bathroom to reassure myself that he wasn't there.

Flashbacks associated with post-traumatic stress disorder are usually repetitions of the original trauma, as if the needle has somehow become stuck and the record of recall endlessly repeats itself.

Obviously some of the dreams were repetitions of past events, but the dreams of her adult self that were taking place in real time were unlikely to be the usual kind of flashback. I had suggested that these may have been real events but were taking place in another reality. I asked her what she had thought about that idea. She replied she had suspended disbelief, although she remained ambivalent:

> I was prepared to try anything to stop it from happening. I couldn't explain it myself. I couldn't figure out how a dream could be so strong and so real. It was horrible! When you were talking about him still being able to visit me on an astral level…I accepted that. I thought, "It's the only way it could be happening!"

I asked her to build a visualization of the tiger and to charge it with emotional energy. It was to be her night guardian and prowl through the flat keeping out any unwanted visitors. As she continued to use the image of the tiger she reported that it became more distinctly visible and real to her and that she could feel its presence. I asked her what the experience of doing the tiger rituals were like for her.

She coped with the ontological shock by remaining hopeful but still ambivalent.

> I hadn't done anything like that before. I guess I went into it thinking, "I don't know if this can work, but I'm willing to try anything!"…I had an open mind. I didn't totally think this was a load of crap, but there was a little doubt in my mind. "How can this really work? He's so strong!" I didn't know if anything could stop him. Nothing stopped

him in all those years, but it was a case of I had to try something. I felt like I was losing my mind. I was determined I was going to give it my best shot. If it was going to work, I had to give it my all.

She was desperate enough to give the artificial elemental she was creating sufficient emotional energy to animate it. I asked her how it had worked. She said it was quite a slow process and it took a few weeks to develop the tiger to the stage where he would be frightening enough. As she continued her visualization, however, he changed from being very small, two-dimensional, and immobile to becoming animated, three-dimensional, and huge. He also began to accompany her when she went out. As the tiger became more materialized, she became more confident. Interestingly, she did not program him to be violent. His job was to wake her up as the violent dreams began. She affirmed that he did this job well:

I'd feel the presence of my uncle and I'd wake up straightaway, which was something I'd never been able to do before. I never saw any vicious attack or anything like that...it was just that he managed to wake me up. He was doing his job because it was saving me and sending my uncle on his way. I felt peace and calm when he was there, but there was an energy of fear around him...anybody he came in contact with, other than me, would be afraid.

I thought that what she meant was that the tiger was so clearly a powerful force, he did not have to exude aggression. His mere presence would be enough to frighten most astral intruders. She had him stay on her bed. She said:

There were times when I'd wake up and I wasn't scared like I had been...I knew I had the dreams but I'd lay in bed with my eyes closed and just reach out and he'd be there. I could hear and feel his breath! I started off having him patrolling round and sitting guard at the door... and that worked to a degree, but my uncle was still getting through that so I had to do something that made him closer. He had to actually stay with me in order to do the job he was meant to do.

I asked whether doing this work had changed her worldview. She described some conflict between her skeptical rational mind and the reality of what she could evince was happening when working with her creative imagination.

As her work gradually became more successful, her original skepticism shifted and she became accepting of the Elphame.

> I was taking him whenever I went out of the house, so for me it was real. On days when I felt like I'd had a really bad night and I had to go out, I needed a form of protection with me that was going to safeguard me, so I'd take the tiger with me. I'd have the stones in my pocket and he would be with me...so I guess it gave me more of an open mind, whereas before the tiger I guess I may have thought, "Oh, bull!" (laughter) It's shown me how strong your mind can be. I was probably more thankful than anything else, even though it took me quite a few weeks to get to the point where it was actually working. I was just grateful that something was finally working.

When I asked her about the effects of the ritual on her health and on her life in general, she said:

> I started to feel physically and emotionally stronger...well, strong enough to go to the police, which I'd often thought about doing but had always backed out at the last minute; I'd never made an appointment to see them or anything. I've never had any power or control over what happened to me until this. I felt like, "Hey...I can get rid of him! I can be in charge!"

When she went to the police to report the childhood sexual assaults, this time she was treated with respect and the police mounted a serious investigation. She had also started a relationship and was eventually happily married. Her partner was supporting her attempts to gain regular access to her daughter, the child of the rape, and they had started legal proceedings to that effect. At the wedding I could see how different she was from the person she had been. There was a distinct shift from passivity and powerlessness to some observable evidence of autonomy and self-confidence.

Like Tom, Anna had begun the journey of recovery. She had suffered soul loss and the tiger elemental had helped her to reclaim her lost aspect of self, will, and personal power. I mentioned to her mother that I could see big changes in Anna, and she attacked me, saying, "You shrinks are just a bunch of do-gooders!" in a very nasty and aggressive tone. However, toward the end of the evening she came back to apologize to me and to say that yes, she could see in Anna really big changes for the better. She couldn't, however, get past a certain level of denial. She would not or could not accept that her younger brother was Anna's sexual abuser.

Anna went on to say that over the past couple of years she had become complacent and had stopped working with her tiger totem, and that the dreams had occasionally returned but they were like ordinary vague, shapeless dreams and had none of the terror, malignancy, and immediacy of the psychic attacks.

What is presented here is a snapshot of a particular magical aspect of Anna's longer healing history that was a mixture of conventional and magical therapy. This was a particularly significant aspect because it worked on several levels of efficacy at once. Not only did it offer her protection from devastating attacks from the Elphame, it also provided her with a means of healing and of transforming her mundane life.

Anna's case is a also a bridge between entering the Elphame and incursions from the Elphame because the ritual technique gave her a means of entering the Elphame and offered some psychic protection. However, I had also trained her in a response to the terrifying incursions from the Elphame that had disturbed her sleep for many years. Her testimony dramatically illustrates some of the limitations of orthodox psychiatric drug treatment and demonstrates the healing possibilities of shamanic medicine that works from the causative level.

At the time I interviewed her for this project, she revealed some further information that cast a different light on her case and may have, if it had been revealed at her trial, influenced a different outcome in her verdict. She said that when she was about sixteen her mother had given birth to a male child but had not shown much interest in him. Anna then took on the mothering role and felt like she was able to give and receive love from her little brother. She came to see him as her baby and took great care for his nurturing and well-being. He became a source of happiness and joy for her and a way of redeeming her personal deprived and unhappy childhood. They became devoted to each other.

All this changed when the little boy almost died from SIDS, or cot death. She said that her mother had gone out and left her in charge of the baby. She had gone to sleep and when she woke up she found he was blue in the face and had stopped breathing. She called an ambulance and the paramedics managed to revive him, but this experience left her with feelings of deep dread that something she so highly valued could be taken away so suddenly and shockingly. Several weeks later, as she prophesied and dreaded, the baby really died from cot death. She could not watch him and protect him twenty-four hours a day. She was in an agony of guilt and self-reproach.

At the time this terrible event occurred, she was making a little money from baby-sitting—she was still at school. She remembered thinking, "Why do these children who are so neglected by their parents thrive like weeds while my baby who has had such love and care was taken away from me so early?" The emotional pain she suffered was indescribable, overwhelming, and blinding. She felt her life had ended, and she couldn't make a fight of it any longer. Although the evidence of her guilt was circumstantial, this is the context, unknown and uninvestigated by the criminal justice system, in which the murders are said to have taken place.

16

The Grail Family

> Those who have supped from Ceredwin's cauldron or
> from the Grail are knitted together by ties stronger than those
> of blood kinship—they are the brothers and sisters of the
> cauldron or the Grail Family. (C. Matthews 1991, 218)

THE TITLE OF THIS chapter has been borrowed from Caitlín Matthews, who used it to describe the group of magical workers who have maintained and perpetuated the ancient shamanic tradition throughout past ages and into the modern world. What they all have in common is a tradition of working from the Elphame by the shifting of consciousness. They are healers who utilize the hidden spiritual powers of the subtle world in their work. (I use the term "healers" in the widest sense of the word. It includes not only the area of physical healing but also emotional, psychological, energetic, and spiritual healing.)

As Matthews describes it, the light of hidden knowledge has been passed down the generations from hand to hand over centuries. During dangerous periods of persecution, the torch was passed on in secrecy through the process of initiation. The flame of Goddess knowledge, therefore, has never been completely extinguished and in our time has reignited a new ground fire of interest in the ancient spiritual wisdom and in the traditions of shamanism. The Holy Grail, I believe, is the Great

Goddess herself. She is the vessel from which all of creation flows into existence.

The network of modern shaman-healers who are the interview subjects of this chapter represent the visible peak of a largely invisible Neopagan and shamanic magical subculture that is expanding and gathering an undercurrent of momentum for change. This change is of the order of a paradigm shift. Recent studies that support the idea of this proposed cultural shift are giving increasing credibility to the validity of the spiritual insights exemplified in the animistic ontology and epistemology of ancient and traditional shaman societies (Abrams 1997, Bates 2002, Berry 1990, Broomfield 1997, Lawlor 1991, Narby 1999, Perkins 2005, Tacey 2000, 2003).

In the West the newly found respect for those insights is fueling the search for a more integrated and holistic worldview that honors the sanctity of the natural world as a symbol of a greater spiritual reality. There is a growing acceptance that the discourses of traditional and archaic people are not primitive or superstitious but reveal a sophisticated and integrated vision of the world that could act as a corrective to our apparent headlong rush to environmental disaster.

In the Western world we are progressively questioning our cultural assumptions and values, and the ontological patterns that have sustained our civilization in the past are shifting and changing. Although this shifting of values is exciting and dynamic, it is not yet coherent or cohesive, and the search for a different and more spiritual worldview has not yet solidified into something completely grounded and practicable. It is patchy, tentative, and experimental.

No modern blueprint exists that can be followed to give clear guidance about how to successfully integrate these new/old insights, as this movement is not a simple reversion to the past but a synthetic, dynamic, and modern re-flowering of the ancient wisdom. However, the following interviews do give some indications of the ways in which the theoretical model can become grounded as lived experience in our time. They give a new understanding of how the Elphame influences the modern physical world and how that understanding can be successfully translated into a corrective.

Pressure to shift the cultural narrative, therefore, is coming from "below"—from many people who are beginning to acknowledge and talk about their experiences of the Elphame without experiencing the shame, fear, and embarrassment that kept them silent in the past—and the sense of the magical and spiritual is once again weaving itself back into the cultural discourse despite the best efforts of determined materialists to ward it off. It has taken root at the level of popular culture, in magazines (particularly women's magazines), literature, music, television, film, and a new generation of adolescents and young people searching for a spirituality that involves a magical and spiritual connection to the natural world.

In 1994 researchers in the United States found that a growing number of people rejected the mechanistic model of reality and that 33 percent of the interview sample reported having had a mystical experience. The research findings of the same study also concluded that 58 percent of the sample considered nature to be sacred or spiritual (Elgin and Le Drew 1997, 19–20).

In a more recent Australian study, conducted by Monash University, two thousand people answered an online survey that asked about their paranormal experiences. The study is entitled "The Nature, Incidence, and Impact of Parapsychological Phenomena." Researcher Beverly Jane said that some of the surprising outcomes of this study were that 70 percent of respondents believed an unexplained or "irrational" event changed their lives, mostly in positive ways; about 70 percent claimed to have seen, heard, or been touched by an animal or person that "was not there"; 80 percent reported having had a premonition; and 50 percent claimed to have memories of a previous life (Jane 2006).

In the book *Paranormal America*, three professors of sociology, Christopher Bader, F. Carson Mencken, and Joseph Baker, project that "the percent of the population reporting at least one paranormal belief will grow from 68 percent to 72 percent over the next thirty to forty years." These are big numbers, and although the studies examined are American I think this trend could be extended to the rest of the Western worldview and that these figures suggest a changing paradigm with a populist foundation.

Many current films and television programs, including *Medium*, *Ghost Whisperer*, and *Psychic Detectives*, seriously and respectfully deal with the subject of contact with the world of spirit. It is also notable that many current films and television programs employ the artistic device of contact with spirits who frequently appear to loved ones or who are felt to be present and influential.

Strong dreams, intuitions, visions, out-of-body experiences, and other communications from the Elphame, therefore, are something that many ordinary people experience, although usually not as a regular occurrence. They are mostly singular events. In the past, discussion of these events was culturally unacceptable, but due to the findings of studies like those above, I sense that this prohibition is slowly being lifted.

Once my patients know that I am accepting, they often confide their "weird" experiences to me, at first rather reluctantly, but they are ultimately relieved that I haven't dismissed them or tried to convince them they are having hallucinations or delusions. The Elphame touches the lives of many ordinary people. It seems clear that there is an increasing disconnect occurring between what is fermenting at the level of popular culture and how reality continues to be defined by the keepers of the ontological keys.

In the ancient Goddess tradition the shamans would have been mainly women: priestesses of the Goddess, like the pre-Indo-European pythonesses of ancient Greece. These women worked in altered states of consciousness, linking the prophetic and intuitive world of the Elphame with the mundane world of physical reality. Accordingly, this group of interview subjects is mainly composed of women healers. They practice what is sometimes called White Witchcraft, although they themselves would probably not describe it in that way. The majority would more likely describe themselves as medical intuitives or practitioners of vibrational medicine.

They are intuitives and telepaths who have consistently reliable clairvoyant, clairaudient, and clairsentient capabilities. They communicate with the spirit world and with other life streams using the interconnecting web of subtle energy. They do not use substances to alter consciousness but have developed a fast and natural means of changing consciousness and moving between the two worlds. Many of them have described the method as "clicking over" from ordinary consciousness to an intuitive mode that gives access to the spiritual world. Although they are children born of the Western scientific materialist paradigm, philosophically they have moved beyond it and redefined their place in the world, their human identity, and their relationships with other life streams.

Although I had originally planned to interview them as animal communicators, to my surprise and fascination I found they were something quite different, and I discovered that many aspects of their stories were startlingly similar to my own. In their range of psychic abilities, healing modalities, and ontological perspectives, they were very like me. Many of them were natural telepaths, some of whom had discovered their ability in childhood and considered it to be completely normal.

Others had worked to develop their latent ability as young adults, but the important framework that gave coherence and structure to their reports was an adherence to an integrated Goddess ontology. This worldview may not always have been clearly and rationally articulated as a theoretical model and often was more alluded to and unconsciously accepted than expressed as a straightforward set of guiding principles. Nevertheless, it was obvious that their personal and professional lives were imbued with the philosophical truths of the Goddess reality.

As I began the interviews they behaved as though they expected that because I was an academic researcher I would be dismissive and belittling of their work. However, through the process of the interviews we discovered a mutual empathy, affinity, and respect. Once they realized that I respected their experiences and their work and showed an understanding of what they were talking about, they were surprisingly open about the things they revealed. In fact, many of them subsequently expressed gratitude that I was doing this research and thought that it was very important to have it "out there" in the public domain.

To that effect, I have made generous use of their own words to describe what they believe are some of the seminal influences of their lives and works. I believe that their own words carry an emotional force that reveals the depth of their spiritual understanding and ontological perspective.

Simon

Simon is the partner of Bernadette. Bernadette has established a reputation as an animal communicator and works for zoos, racehorse owners, wildlife parks, and private clients to telepathically inquire into the hidden causes of disease. Simon has an academic background and comes from a family with a strongly conventional academic ethos. His father is a former professor of theoretical physics. Simon's acceptance of the Elphame came by a process of empirical observation and intellectual evaluation. He saw that Bernadette's success rate when working from the second reality to find remedies for her clients' formerly intractable illnesses was far beyond the probability of chance.

He also became fascinated by the potential for healing he perceived in the hidden powers of the mind and emotions, and he ultimately developed a degree of sensitivity that enabled him to make emotional attunements with animals:

> A teacher in a workshop I attended spoke to a room full of people and said, "I want everyone here to meditate, for the next thirty days, on contracting a really horrible debilitating disease." Everyone in the room tittered and he said, "How many are willing to do that?" And of course no one would raise their hand, and he said, "Well…if not, why not? Because you believe that you can give yourself that disease by doing that, don't you? So why isn't the converse true?" So if thought is inherently creative, it becomes a matter of how creative is thought. How powerful are our minds? And to me all of that kind of washes together. Scientists have their prejudices. They like things that can be measured, but science doesn't explain everything and never will.

He believed that the physical sensory evaluation of phenomena that is the basis of the scientific method was unreliable because it involved a kind of prejudice toward one particular perspective. He had intuitively adopted the magical "as if" position and was willing to act as though a world of experience existed beyond the physical senses. He said:

> So if we accept that there are things that we can't see, touch, feel, taste, or smell that exist, that are valid, then to me it becomes a no-brainer. Sure, then that opens up the entire possibility for the world of spirit and the world of psychic communication and all of that.

He was convinced that the possibility for extrasensory experience was innate but that not everyone had worked to develop it and some people were necessarily naturally gifted in those skills. The normal curve applied:

> To me it's like tennis. Everyone can play tennis, but not everyone is Venus Williams. I believe that everyone is born with the gift for extra-sensory phenomena, but not everyone's good at it. Bernadette's a lot better at it than I am, but that doesn't mean I can't whack the ball over the net.

As a young person he was not particularly sensitive, but as he became convinced of the existence of the second reality and accepted its validity, he gave himself permission to become more intuitive. He further described his rational process of acceptance of the "irrational":

> A lot of people have spiritual crises or epiphanies, like near-death experiences. I didn't have anything like that. To me it was a lot more subtle and less tangible. I'm comfortable with it because I don't believe we can explain everything with the five senses. I could probably convince myself that I was making it all up except that there's too much external evidence for it. There's no point in denying it. There's no gain. Whereas there is gain in being open to learning...acting "as if"... being willing to believe that these things can exist.

When I asked him how his family reacted to his interest in metaphysics, he described a closed-mindedness that is common among scientists who reject all interest in phenomena that do not fit within the assumptions of the scientific paradigm:

> I don't talk to them about it. My dad's very analytical and scientific, so he's not really open to it at all or interested either. He'd think it was quackery, but I've seen enough results, especially from Bernie's work, that are way beyond coincidence...and that validate it.

Bernadette

Bernadette and Simon live on a large property in Southern Queensland. They take in aged and abandoned domestic animals, offering them a home, food, and medical treatment while they live out their final years in an atmosphere of love and care. At the time I visited them to conduct the interviews they were caring for thirteen or so horses, twenty or so dogs, and thirty cats, as well as several llamas. They also tried to accommodate the needs of the native animals that dwelt on their acreage and to integrate what they were doing for the welfare of the domestic animals with the requirements of the wild environment. Therefore, they used no poisons, even in the house, and were involved in organic farming methods, natural medicine treatments, and shamanic methods of communication with the spirits of the native plants and animals.

They were attempting to live their ideal, trying to integrate a modern lifestyle with the needs of the natural world, living in communication and harmony with the other life streams that shared their environment. They envisioned an interactive and connected existence based on the belief that all is consciousness and has spiritual purpose. They were experimenting, as I had done, with the model of the Goddess as lived experience.

Bernadette talked about using ritual as a vehicle for showing due respect for the natural world and honoring the Goddess worldview. She said:

> I try in my own life to show that sort of respect of traditional people for the natural world, even when I'm picking grass for our budgies. I will say, "Which ones want to come? Which ones are ready? Withdraw your energy!" And I don't pick any until I've done that. It's about honoring and respecting...and doing what you can to communicate...and to show respect by doing a ceremony. We are all one...even a newt or a fly or a frog has consciousness. Everything has consciousness.

She had previously trained as a natural medicine practitioner. At the time of the interview she was working professionally with people who engaged her services as an animal communicator, medical intuitive, and naturopath. She usually worked remotely—that is, she did not need to have physical contact with the animal but used the web of subtle energy to make contact and discover what the deeper problems were. Sometimes she worked from a photograph. I was surprised to hear that when she does a telepathic consultation, she writes either with a notebook and pen or by sitting at a computer and letting the words flow into her mind and out of her hands. Both of these types of communication can be described as automatic writing. Like the traditional tribal shaman, she said she also works with quartz crystals and other stones to amplify and transmit energy. She revealed that as a child she realized all things had consciousness and she felt an acute sensitivity and a mystical attunement to the natural world:

> I knew it was a gift I had. I would hear stones. I'd be aware of stones on the ground and apologize to them if I tripped over them. I was aware of trees as living beings and aware of their pain when leaves were stripped off them and would rush to their defense. I tried to get people not to stomp on ants…I was always very sensitive to the natural world.

I asked her what sort of reaction she got from other people and whether or not she thought that things were changing. She said that in her view things were changing for the better and that "as a young person people thought I was quite weird…that I was a total flake." (laughter) But more recently she observed that a shifting attitude was emerging at the level of ordinary people and popular culture. The level of respect for the natural world had been steadily rising. People were actively seeking to re-enchant the world. She said:

> Ordinary people, and especially children, seem to be more aware of the sacredness of the natural world. Just recently when some journalists were here and I refused to use insecticide on flies, they respected me. There's something changing…especially at the level of children in our society, and it's all about the idea that magic is real and magic actually exists.

Katie

Katie has a degree in social science and completed studies in natural medicine. She began treating her own pets with natural medicines in the mid-1980s and went on to qualify as a naturopath with the aim of working solely with animals. She has also been instrumental in the development of courses in natural treatments for animals and in the formalization process of qualifications for practitioners.

Her ability to work as an animal communicator and intuitive did not emerge in a haphazard way. She was not naturally sensitive as a child but developed these skills as a young adult, approaching this new learning in an organized, logical, and determined manner. She confided that she had used various trainings, techniques, and devices to shut out the usual intrusive intellectual commentary and heighten her intuitive powers. This systematic developmental process was the way she coped with ontological shock. She took control of the process of psychic and telepathic development. The Elphame had not overwhelmed nor surprised her. She had sought out expressly spiritual experiences but believed that her already heightened interest had most likely come from past-life familiarity.

When I asked her what she thought were the benefits of working with the intuitive process in treating animals with respect and communicating with other life streams, she took an ecopsychology or deep ecology position that emphasized relationship and interconnection. She also saw the political implications:

> There are many benefits for mankind. I believe that we're changing consciousness as we open to the energies around us...I think the greater picture is to help us move on to a lot more open relationship with the world around us, the whole environment really, and also with other humans. If we could all communicate and develop these faculties and open the heart, then maybe we wouldn't have the sorts of conflicts we have now.

Donna

Donna had been diagnosed in early childhood as autistic, a diagnosis that was later revised to Asperger syndrome, a condition less limiting but still on that particular spectrum of neurological disorders. She said:

> In those days a lot of people (who were diagnosed as autistic) were considered to be mentally retarded and treated as such...and through a lack of understanding they fulfilled the medical prophecy.

She and her family, however, did not subscribe to that diagnosis. She said:

> I had a mother who said, "No, this is not right!" Because, I mean, at three years of age I'd tear into her and say, "I was lying in bed pretend-

ing I was dead...and where will the me be in a million years?" and "Mum, where was the me a million years ago?" And she'd just look at me dumbfounded. (laughter)

Clearly Donna is a high-functioning person, and although her patterns of syntax are at times unusual, her communication style and narrative power are dramatic and compelling. She described herself as a "lateral thinker," possessing "an ability to look at things from a totally different perspective." On the basis of what she later confided to me about her ability to work both with animals and humans in innovative ways, I could only agree.

Her family had owned a stud farm and shown thoroughbred horses, and from an early age she had shown a distinct aptitude for working with them, especially with nervous and difficult horses. She believes that our animal companions are constantly attuned to us in emotional ways, and that the way to communicate something to them is through visualization. She believes they pick up our thoughts and feelings through pictures and thought-forms, sometimes manifesting our illnesses even before they manifest in our own bodies, showing us by physical example the magical power of thought reinforced by emotional energy. Much of their relationship with humans is therefore symbolic. Many of the other subjects, including Joanne, Rosemary, and Katie, mentioned this symbolic relationship between humans and animals.

At the time of our interview she was driving horse-drawn carriages through city traffic as a tourism service, but she also drove matching pairs of white and black horses for weddings and funerals, respectively. They were Percheron, French draft horses, immensely strong and with an even temperament, elegant in feathered, jeweled headdresses reminiscent of Le Grand Epoch. She drives the horses in dangerous city conditions and believes they trust her implicitly to know what to do to keep them safe because of her ability to communicate telepathically and in pictures.

She said:

> We're working horses in the harshest conditions in the world. This is the only city in the world where horses run like taxis. We go anywhere in normal traffic. Sometimes we have to go down through the flames at the casino...massive flames that go off every hour. You can feel the

heat from 500 meters away and the horses will stand underneath those flames. There's a couple of hotels where you've got to go down through a basement car park...and there's flashing light. The conditions are the worst you could ever work animals in.

Caroline

Caroline had a nonconformist kind of personality and an earthy, humorous exuberance that was appealing and infectious. She had worked as a veterinary nurse for some years but had previously driven trucks she described as "big rigs" and had managed a McDonald's fast food restaurant. She had always been interested in animal behavior and had always worked with dogs and horses, but a watershed occurred for her when she read a book by Arthur Meyers entitled *Communicating with Animals*. In the back of the book was a list of people who worked in the field, and she wrote to all of them in an attempt to find someone to teach her because she had developed a strong interest in learning the skills of telepathic communication.

Several of the people recommended in the book contacted her, some suggesting that she do a Reiki course because it would help to develop her sensitivity and intuition. Through personal experience she shifted her position toward energy healing from one of antipathy to acceptance because of her first-hand observation of its power for healing:

> So I did Reiki 1 and I hated every bit of it...and then my horse, Doc, got Ross River fever and was dying, so I asked my Reiki teacher to give him an absent healing, figuring I had nothing to lose.

Her Reiki teacher, as well as Katie, used telepathic communication skills, and a local veterinary surgeon treated her horse with different kinds of alternative medicine modalities. Most significantly, perhaps, through the processes of her own telepathic communication, Caroline realized that she herself was complicit in Doc's chronic ill health:

> There was a lot of emotional stuff. Doc had been in South Australia working cattle and it wasn't unusual for him to have ten or twelve people on his back in a day. He was a quarter horse and he wasn't happy and I'd had him for two years before the Ross River fever and I'd

essentially done no riding. The care was getting horrendously expensive, and Doc wound up feeling like I wanted him to get better for what I wanted out of it, rather than him getting better for his own sake.

I asked about her emotional response to this information and whether she had discussed the cascading expense in front of Doc:

I felt really bad, and I did bitch about the money at times...people do. They talk and they don't think animals are taking it in, and of course they are.

Although she was originally skeptical about animal communication, she had attempted it with Doc, and I asked about his response. The speed of Doc's physical response that she described surprised me.

She said:

I'd read the book, but I certainly wasn't convinced. So I took him to the stable where no one else could hear and felt like a complete dickhead. (laughter) I explained I loved him and I was really upset that that was the way he perceived it...and I thought he knew I loved him, and I did want him to get better for his own sake. (long pause) In less than twenty-four hours his gum color had improved. He was starting to eat again, and he was able to stand up. He was on the road to recovery. This was before we had started any other treatment.

This dramatic healing response convinced her of the efficacy of energy medicine and animal communication. At the time I interviewed her she was working as a part-time veterinary nurse but also acted as a diagnostic consultant to several local veterinary practices near Melbourne. She also did remote or absent healing, sometimes working, like Bernadette, from a photograph and sometimes intuitively.

I was interested to discover that she also worked with humans doing psychic rescue work and acted as a guide to the dead. She was working in another of the roles of the traditional shaman, that of the psychopomp, helping earthbound spirits to release their hold on the physical world and move into the Elphame.

Susan

Susan worked as an animal naturopath in the Blue Mountains near Sydney, using homoeopathic treatments as well as the usual naturopathic modalities such as herbs, vitamins and minerals, and diet modification. In order to select the appropriate remedies she usually dowsed. That is, she used a pendulum and a witness from a client, usually a hair, feather, or fur sample, and while holding the biological sample she would hold a pendulum over a chart of remedies until it responded to the appropriate treatment. This process is sometimes called radiesthesia. In this way she bypassed the intellect and went straight to the intuition because she had found that the laborious intellectual way of selecting homoeopathic remedies—that is, by repertorising—was not nearly so accurate or effective.

She also worked as an animal communicator with her four Saluki hounds as assistants. She referred to them as the "doctor dogs." She believed they offered valuable insights into her cases. If it is true, as many of the interview subjects believed, that animals have their own lives and destinies apart from the desires and requirements of their human owners, it seems that some animals have a life mission to act as healers, both for their own kind and for the humans in their lives. Susan's Salukis fitted the profile of tutelary spirits and healing animals.

She said:

> With the Salukis I have now...the younger dogs Fehn and Mariah do the communicating. Mollie and Basha 2 don't talk much now, but they do give yes and no answers. If they yawn and make a whining sound or they blink and smile, I'll know it's a yes. If they look away, it's a no. Mollie is the healing dog now, and most of the time when I'm working she'll come and lie on the carpet near me, and when I'm dowsing she'll either confirm or deny the remedy.

She showed me the behavior on a segment from a television program about her work, and I also saw Mollie confirm, with a big yawn and a small whining sound, a remedy for my own hay fever.

Although to some people her methods may seem unconventional, they have been spectacularly successful, and over the years Susan has become well known as a healer. Many of her cases have been publicized in the press and on television, and she has made several appearances on popular nationwide television shows dealing with animals and demonstrating her methods. She credited her first Saluki hound, Basha 1, with accurately prescribing his own successful treatment for his case of distemper and for bringing to her attention other animals living in the area (inner Sydney) that required treatment for various health problems.

This was how she believed she originally learned her trade as a shaman-healer. She credited her animal patients as tutelary spirits. At this time, in her early thirties, she had developed RSI in both wrists and was unable to work. She said:

> The only thing I could do was walk…I'd just go out with the dog and I'd walk all around the streets and anybody I saw with a dog, I'd talk to them and say, "Do you know your dog has a problem?" But I had absolutely Buckley's of trying to convince the people. They just branded me the "Mad Dog Lady." I even had people make hex signs at me in the street. (laughter) It was nightmare stuff!

She continued explaining how she treated her animal clients and how she believed she had learned from them. She said:

> But most mornings I'd open up my door and there'd be five to ten dogs sitting on my doorstep. I never had trouble convincing them! I'd try to find out where they lived, and I'd go back and hassle their owners…and they just hated my guts. So in the end I just used to make up dinners for them all, and I'd put on all the herbs I thought they needed and I'd throw them over the various backyards or they would arrive at my place at the appropriate time and I'd feed them. They were my guinea pigs. They taught me everything. I learned so much from those guys.

I sense that these events still retain a deal of emotional power for her, and the interview seemed to be gathering intensity. When I asked her to talk about a particular case, she chose the case of a horse that had been selected for treatment by Basha 1.

She said:

> He found an ex-trotter that was living on an old building block. She was in the most terrible condition and I started feeding her. All the owner fed her every day was half a bucket of moldy chaff and the block was covered in rubbish. I drove past there a couple of weeks ago

and I remembered what it was like (her voice trails off and drops to a whisper as she reflects)...She was kept in an area most people wouldn't keep a rabbit. Anyway, I fed her and got her looking good...and he hated me. If he saw me he would scream abuse. If he caught me on the block again he was going to have me up for trespassing...and I'd yell back.

She said that she had tried to get the Royal Society for the Prevention of Cruelty to Animals to take up the case but legally there was nothing they could do because the owner was technically feeding the horse. She also approached the government department that owned the block in an attempt to get them to cancel his lease, to no avail:

> After I'd spoken to fifty million people, none of them were going to take any responsibility...I had to give up. (her voice drops and breaks) But in the end the horse could have gone to Harold Park Raceway and won a race. She looked so fantastic! (she becomes reflective again and sighs)

Tears are coming to her eyes, and I can feel the emotion rising as her voice becomes shaky and then finally breaks. I am also feeling swept along with the rising tide of grief.

> So when I left Sydney I had to leave her...and within six months she was back looking exactly the way she was before. (she is weeping) That happened to a lot of my animals. The animals knew I had to go. I remember the day I left...they all came around to say goodbye. (weeping) It was...terrible!

I switched off the recorder for ten minutes. I asked her whether she wanted to continue with the interview, and she said she did. She thought it was important that these stories were told and that people needed to know that animals were sensitive and intelligent beings.

Rosemary

Rosemary had been referred to me as an animal communicator, but she described herself as a practitioner of vibrational medicine. She had been trained in conventional medicine and had worked first as a physiotherapist and then as a veterinary surgeon. She practices integrated veterinary medicine in Perth, Western Australia. She had previously worked in a clinic that practiced a style of veterinary medicine that combined natural therapies with orthodox treatments. Rosemary has also trained as a Reiki practitioner and currently runs training sessions for veterinary students and practitioners in alternative veterinary medicine and in Reiki healing. She perceives a growing interest among vets in legitimizing complementary and energy medicine. They are becoming increasingly convinced of its efficacy. She also practiced remote healing.

She said:

> I started doing distance Reiki…actually for another vet. I lived a long way from where she worked, so she said, "I don't suppose you could help?" So I eventually ended up working for her doing distance work.

I asked how open her employer was to energy healing. She explained that she sensed there was a growing public acceptance in general and that her employer had dramatically shifted her position over time:

> At the time she was open but skeptical, if you know what I mean. Now, every member of the clinic has Reiki. (laughter) I remember her very clearly—and I'm sure she doesn't remember saying to me—"I can see that Reiki does something, but I'll never do it!" (laughter)

She is also trained in acupuncture, kinesiology, homoeopathic medicine, and flower and gem essences, and she also uses dowsing or radiesthesia and telepathic communication as diagnostic techniques. When I asked how she came to be involved in alternative veterinary medicine, she surprised me by saying that it was because she had become disillusioned by the conventional medical treatment of her special-needs children, and when those treatments had failed she had started looking for more effective modalities. This desperate search eventually led her to alternative and energy medicine, such as homoeopathy and Reiki, and into a radical reordering of her previously conventional spiritual understanding.

She said:

> My eldest son is disabled…severely developmentally delayed, and he had uncontrolled epilepsy and he's autistic as well. Eventually I had three children under four, and two of them had asthma and one of them had uncontrolled epilepsy. I remember sitting in a doctor's office

and I had my eldest son's antibiotics…three times a day, plus his epilepsy medication. I had intermittent Ventolin for one of my other children, and the doctor was telling me that my other son needed to be on a nebulizer three times a day. I thought, "I can't do this! I'm just a full-time nurse! There must be a better way!" So that really made me start searching, and whatever worked on me or my children, I learned.

She later translated the success she experienced in treating her children with alternative medicine into her veterinary practice. Her open-mindedness and growing intuitive powers then led her to experiment with various types of energy healing and ultimately with telepathic communication.

Joanne

Joanne worked as a veterinary nurse, medical intuitive, and animal communicator employed by a veterinary clinic that offered conventional treatments. The pioneering clinic offers orthodox treatments as well as a wide range of alternative therapies, including homoeopathic and herbal medicine, acupuncture, craniosacral balancing, flower essences, Reiki, kinesiology, and animal communication.

When I asked Joanne about her background and how she came to be involved in this work, she described a series of strong dreams and spiritual contacts with the Elphame that guided her career choice and suggested to her a way in which her love of animals and her concern for their well-being could be translated into paid work.

She said:

I was travelling through London and I started to think, "I'm really sick of doing the shit-kicker sort of barmaid jobs!" And through my dreams I started saying, "Someone please show me what I'm meant to do," and I started to have, night after night, dreams of working with animals in all sorts of situations. I can remember the strangest one: walking through a paddock and finding a walrus, and it was dying because it was so far from the ocean, and just sitting with this walrus and holding it while it died, and I thought, "Hmmm…that's a pretty strong indication!" I have always had such a deep love for animals ever since I was tiny. It took those dreams to make me think, "Why can't I turn that natural affinity and love for animals into a profession that can make me some money?" So I came back home and started my vet nurse training.

The other influence that fueled her interest in shamanic methods and alternative medicine was that Reiki, homoeopathic and herbal medicine, massage, and acupuncture had successfully treated her mother's pattern of chronic ill health. Although she previously had been skeptical, she had found these experiences of strong dreams and observations of her mother's improving health to have been initiatory, describing them as "eye-opening." Like Donna, Susan, and Bernadette, she remembered having the ability to talk to animals in childhood and regarded it as "normal" and "as something that everybody did":

> I think I have always spoken to animals. One of my earliest memories is sitting on the front path talking to my cats. I just wasn't aware that other people didn't, so I didn't think there was anything amazing about it.

Ella

Ella worked as a marriage celebrant and also conducted and designed ceremonies for funerals, the naming of children, coming of age, and other milestone life events. It became clear to me that she was a ritualist possessing a sophisticated comprehension of ritual's deeply sacred nature and magical power to open the heart.

She described the sacredness of ceremony and the spiritual bonds created in the group:

> The guests are carefully chosen. They are not just there as witnesses or observers, they are really there to participate in their hearts. There's a unity among those present. It's a deep experience for them as well. They understand that it's not just words that are being spoken. It is myself participating from my heart center as well and entering into it with the couple and inviting them all into this sacred space where we all participate with them. It gives even more unity to the bond. There's such a depth to that sort of ceremony. I'm drawing everyone together. I feel that very much. The way you speak the ceremony goes beyond their own defenses and into their own hearts. When they open their hearts to each other, then something else comes in.

I wondered if she was talking about the Goddess or the Shekinah here, but I did not want to question her too directly about this or put ideas into her head. I let her pursue her train of thought and she began to describe the power and process of magical invocation, again stressing the deeper level of connection with the sacred. She went on to discuss some of the common elements of the earth-based religions of traditional societies, indirectly comparing common elements of her own practice and describing the similar patterns of philosophical foundations. This was something many of the other interview subjects had also mentioned.

She said:

> I'm very careful…I won't conduct a ceremony for a "dress up" experience because of the power. I say to people, "You are asking the old gods to come and bless your union. If you're asking the gods of the four directions to come in here, we're not just saying empty words. Is this what you really want?" When we're invoking the four directions the words are very, very powerful and I do love the old ceremonies and the old ways. I'm talking about the beliefs of the Druids…the earth. To me they bond with many of the other traditions—the Native Americans and the Aborigines; the earth spirits; earth, fire, water, air…all of the elements. It really doesn't matter by what name you call it. It's honoring the earth energy.

She had been referred to me as an animal communicator, but I was not surprised when, like the other practitioners, she revealed that she possessed many skills and powers common to the ancient shamanic tradition. She lived and worked within the model of the Goddess reality. She communicated both telepathically and clairvoyantly with spirits both human and animal, and she was frequently briefed postmortem on what the dead required in their funerary rites.

She hears the voices of the dead and sees them with the "strong eye," and she has observed that the dead frequently attend their own funerals and make their presence felt in various ways:

> I've been making funeral arrangements when the person's picture has actually fallen over, trying to let you know he still exists. Sometimes it's so hard when I'm standing facing a hundred people, and the dead person I'm talking about is standing at my left shoulder and they're

looking down at what I'm about to read and giving me little words of advice. (laughter)

She was in the process of developing a fifteen-acre property into a sanctuary for ten sighthound rescue dogs. The sanctuary was the idea of one of her Saluki hounds, Yasmina, whom Ella believed had taken the role of a tutelary spirit. Several times throughout the interview she remarked that "animals were ensouled beings" and said:

> A Saluki really changed my life and got me into communication. Yasmina is still part of my being. She died in October, and the following July I was in California at the Kinship with All Life Conference. I'm sure she led me every step of this journey. I see her—she used to run ahead of me when we were out walking. She would run ahead on the path, and she'd turn and look at me: "Come on, Mum. Salukis are for running, not walking at your pace!" and I see her ahead of me on my spiritual path doing the same thing: "Come on! Get with the program!" (laughter)

It seemed very clear to me that although she had not specifically trained in the magical or the Wiccan tradition, she was most certainly a shaman and a priestess. She understood the invocatory power of ritual and how it can change and shift energy, which is the basis of magic and something on which Laura had remarked. She knew that ritual is a means of entering the sacred and working from the heart center of Goddess energy and power. She was unique among this group in that she was the only one who conducted magical rituals in public and, in fact, made her living from that practice. Although both Bernadette and Helen also understood and made use of ritual, they did not take it to the same level of public performance.

She saw, as those who followed a shaman's path saw, that the role of animals in our lives was that of tutelary spirits. Her worldview is animistic, and she understood that all is consciousness and all is related and connected. She had conscious contact with the Elphame and frequently, like Bernadette, Helen, and Caroline, took on the role of the psychopomp, aiding the spirits of the dead to cross over successfully into the Elphame. She does not directly name the Goddess, but she lives the Goddess and I recognize a spiritual sister. She said, "God is not in the church but in everything. The Divine is in everything—in nature, in the dawning sun." That aspect of the sun is symbolic of new life, but she also honors death, symbolized by the setting sun. She assumes the role of the psychopomp, who is the companion and guide of the departing spirit, with the compassion and respect due to all those who strive and suffer. In that sense she is a priestess of the Dark Goddess.

Helen

Helen had also been described to me as an animal communicator, but when I spoke to her she corrected that perception. She did some work in that field but mostly worked with people as a spiritual healer and medical intuitive. She accepted the validity of her experiences, knew that her perceptions of the other reality were real and useful, and like a traditional shaman was able to move seamlessly between the two realities. She was not plagued by self-doubt or feelings of incipient madness but had a serene presence of mind and acceptance that the coexistence of the two realities was something completely normal and natural.

She did not appear to suffer from ontological shock, although she admitted to having had some past mild doubts and had from time to time asked herself, "Am I making this up or is this real?" She considered these doubts to be normal but added:

> I think there's a really powerful, overwhelming feeling when you know that it's real. I think you really know when it's pure and when it's not…but it often gets mixed up because our mind is so busy. You don't have to question it. It just feels different.

When I confided my experience of ontological shock to her, she stressed that I should "get out of my head and trust my heart more":

> The most important thing is dropping into your heart all the time… that's important…and what feels right here (gestures to the heart) and getting out of your head.

She had been raised in a family where there was a strong interest in metaphysical subjects, and after leaving school at eighteen she had began studies in naturopathy, herbal medicine, massage, and nutrition. During her teens she had begun to study tarot cards as a guide to developing her intuition and had been experimenting with automatic writing.

Some years later she was introduced to energy healing by her massage therapist:

> I was having some therapy with my massage teacher and I was quite amazed when he started taking his hands off my body and I was having these strange feelings going on, and I quizzed him about that and he said, "Well, this is easy. This is just having guides work through you, which is similar to what you're doing with your automatic writing, but this is in healing mode." So he showed me how to do that, and from then on I read everything I could find about spiritual healing and started practicing it. So I work in a guided way—spirit guides work through me.

She means that discarnate teaching entities work through her and guide her healing practice. These experiences developed into a lifelong interest. Susan, Bernadette, Ella, Joanne, and Katie had also remarked they felt the presence of spiritual guides. Helen said:

> I've studied many different forms of healing. I'm also a Reiki master and I've studied Chiron healing and all sorts of energy healing. So I work sometimes hands on, sometimes hands off. I receive intuitive information and I flow with what happens, so I'm working with energetic blocks in the person's field generally.

I was interested in the clearing of entities and asked her to talk a little more about her work in that field. Like Caroline, she clears entities from houses and other spaces, including those attached to the energy field of certain people. I was interested to hear that her work in this field involved the overcoming of fear and the invocation of love, as this had been an important feature of my own initiatory experiences.

She said:

> It's easy to do if you've got no fear. You've got to get totally out of fear. I often have the spirit trying to be totally terrifying. It's real haunted house stuff a lot of the time. They send some really creepy images to try to get rid of me. All I do is the same as when I'm working with a client. I just try to bring love through and I let myself be guided.

I asked her about the purpose of the spirit trying to get rid of her by using "creepy images." I had not had experience of spirits who were reluctant to leave the physical world once they knew what had happened and how they had become stuck. She said:

> They often don't want to go, but they usually crumble after a while and I get to their fear…and I quite often see spirits standing there crying and quite remorseful and scared. I've had spirits that have been really lost and stuck…Sometimes I'm picking up on things that are not human and are just sort of fear energies that have evolved like fragments. They turn themselves into something bigger and scarier as they are fed fear, but usually underneath there's just a scared person.

There are many different types of energies and entities to be found in the Elphame. Some are benign and some are malevolent, which is why maintaining caution and having some prior knowledge of what to expect are very important attributes when approaching this level of reality. Also, ideally the aspirant should have some training in self-defense, even something as simple as spiraling white light around the energy body and quieting fear by gaining control of the emotions.

17

The Modern Shamans

Such physicians may be trained in what may be called
techno-shamanism, an exotic yet rigorously schooled
combination of ancient magical principles and future
technologies. (Radin 2010, 331)

IT WAS REMARKABLE FOR me to discover that the Grail Family worked
as multi-skilled shaman-healers inhabiting the place where the two
worlds intersect. I had previously assumed that animal communication
was what they did, and that was how they were originally referred to
me. I had also assumed this after reading the book *Conversations with Animals* by Lydia Hiby, as this kind of telepathy seemed to be a highly developed yet singular skill, but I soon realized that they all possessed a range
of skills apart from this specialized telepathic ability. They worked as
healers and therapists in their own practices, with two or three exceptions employed as diagnosticians or medical intuitives working closely
with conventionally trained veterinary surgeons and doctors.

However, all the research subjects shared an array of common skills
and talents and an interest in a broad range of alternative medicine modalities, including homoeopathy, herbalism, acupuncture, naturopathy,
Reiki or other subtle energy healing, and other techniques of vibrational

medicine. They prescribed remedies from the repertoire of conventional, physical, and alternative medical treatments, as well as intuitively diagnosing the subtle energetic origins of disease and working with light, color, and energy. They therefore worked from a place between the two worlds, successfully combining both physical and subtle energy treatments.

Reiki energy healing is something very like the natural hands-on healing ability I had discovered in myself years before. Some of the group credited Reiki with the development and refinement of their psychic sensitivity. Simon, Bernadette, Caroline, Helen, Rosemary, Katie, and Joanne had all been trained in Reiki. Many of them, including, Katie, Bernadette, Helen, Caroline, and Donna, worked with human clients as well as animals. Although they had a large repertoire of healing modalities, with their human clients they tended more to spiritual healing and spirit dispossession.

Medical intuitives work from the Elphame to diagnose and sometimes prescribe treatments for health problems that have their origins in the energy body or emotional body of the patient (Brennan 1987). They are able to see into the subtle levels of reality using the strong eye to find the origins of physical health problems, sometimes before they have manifested in the physical body and sometimes after physical manifestation. Although mostly disdained by mainstream science, this is an emergent and growing field in Western medicine. Some doctors, particularly in the United States and England (Brennan 1987, Welch 2002), take a pragmatic view and employ medical intuitives as diagnosticians. Barbara Brennan, for example, has worked in this field for many years, successfully locating, diagnosing, and treating the subtle energy causes of disease. Before taking up this type of healing work she had worked for NASA as an astrophysicist, so having a scientific background does not necessarily mean that a person has a closed mind.

All the members of this group of subjects were able to speak in "the silent language," having the ability to communicate telepathically with animals by using the gossamer web of subtle energy that links everything to everything else. Sometimes the telepathic communications they received were more like a feeling attunement or a physical or energetic rapport. They felt referred pain and sensation in various parts of their own bodies that worked as a kind of sympathetic magic enabling them to pinpoint exactly where the animal was experiencing suffering. Simon, Rosemary, Katie, Joanne, and Bernadette worked with this type of energetic and emotional attunement.

Sometimes, using the inner senses, they saw clear mental pictures or symbolic images of what had happened, but some of them also heard precise and accurate verbal communications from their animal clients and companions in clearly identifiable signature voices, in the way that I did. Simon, Bernadette, Caroline, Helen, Rosemary, Katie, Joanne, Ella, and Susan were all clairaudient, and they gave many examples of their skill in this regard. For example, Caroline told a story about staying with a friend who had two dogs, one of which was sick. She decided to stay the night to be available if the dog's condition worsened and arranged to go with him and the dog to the veterinary surgery in the morning.

She said:

> He hit the scotch and staggered to bed about three o'clock in the morning, and this other dog was there—this old cocker spaniel. I crashed out on the couch and woke up and looked at the time… turned on the kettle and walked to the bedroom door and banged on it and yelled, "Coffee's up!" And I heard loud and clear—this little cocker spaniel sitting on my feet as I was banging on the door said, "It's going to take a lot more than that to get him out of bed this time of the morning!" And she was right! I had no idea he wasn't a morning person, and you literally had to kick the door down, go in and pour the coffee on his head.

Caroline, Helen, Ella, Katie, Rosemary, and Bernadette were also clairvoyant and used the strong eye in both active and passive modes. That is, they could actively tune into the Elphame or they could render themselves into a more passive state and allow the Elphame to arise onto the screen of consciousness.

On the emotional level Simon and Bernadette believed that they had the ability to align themselves with the emotional state of the animal they were attending and could feel if anxiety, grief, or distress were present. Caroline could discern fear and feelings of abandonment and also could detect cynicism. Katie, Donna, and Helen believed that animals they treated felt anger, fear, emotional hurt, relief, grief, disappointment, frustration, and agitation at not being understood. Liz, Bernadette, and Ella thought that animals are constantly attuned to us in emotional ways and therefore pick up our thoughts and feelings, often reflecting back to us images of our own dysfunction in the physical and emotional illnesses that they exhibit. Donna, Ella, and Bernadette said they thought animals could teach us about loving without expectations; that they worry about us and care for us in ways we perceive only dimly, if at all; and that they can make our lives better in so many ways if we are open to them.

Tutelary Spirits

Ella was certain that animals are "soulful beings" and tutelary spirits, and Susan agreed that she had learned much of what she knew about healing from her Saluki hounds; they are teachers and healers in their own right, with their own pathways of spiritual development. Many of them believed that they had been personally spiritually inspired by animals and thought that animals could provide powerful spiritual guidance to humanity, particularly by embodying such abstract concepts as unconditional love, sacrifice, and forgiveness. They said that animals have the power to deepen our spiritual understanding and positively influence our life's journey. They also believed that animals, like humans, have their individual life's journey of learning.

Ella commented on the healing power of animals:

> The comfort they can bring to humans is extraordinary. I don't think any human loves us in the way that a dog loves us. There's no love like that. I truly believe that it is a dog's role to teach us about loving without expectations. My passion is for the animal world. I would do anything that I could…to make people realize that these creatures have a soul. They come back time and time again for service to humanity.

Donna holds a similar view about the relationship between the human and the animal world, and told me that through her carriage work with the horses she had developed positive relationships with many of the city's homeless people and street kids. Because of this unique connection, the Department of Human Services had employed her as a youth worker for over three years. I thought it was particularly interesting and elegant that her carriage work and her street work fitted together in an organic way, whereby the street work grew naturally out of her work with the horses. There seemed to be a kind of spiritual economy in operation.

In a way, what she was doing was similar to my work in education. She was taking an opportunity to connect with children and helping them to heal, starting from the position of her mundane work but eventually moving into a more spiritual field as her connection with them became stronger and they became more trusting. I asked how the process worked and how she had become associated with the Department of Human Services. This innovative way of working she described seemed to be another potent means of the Goddess discourse model operating in the "real" world.

She said:

> I use the animals—the animals are actually the bridge between my world and their world. I've met all these people while I've got the horses with me, and they all build a relationship with the horses. People love the heavy horses. What happened was that a lot of the kids the Department of Community Services were dealing with started mentioning my name. Most adults that start getting mentioned to the department in association with their kids are either selling them drugs or getting them to steal for them or prostituting them, and my name kept coming up, but it didn't come up in correlation to anything but "Oh, Donna bought us a coffee the other day, and she's got a new horse!" And they thought, "Hang on, who is this person?" So they finally made contact with me, and that led to a full-time working relationship.

She went on to say that the street kids she worked with were often addicts, involved in serious crimes such as theft, drug trafficking, assaults with weapons, and prostitution. They had mostly been resistant to the various attempts the department had made toward their rehabilitation. These failed attempts included the usual youth work, diversional therapy, social work, counseling, and psychiatric interventions. Nothing worked. She described her clients as follows:

> The kids that I deal with are very, very hard. I don't think they can afford to feel a positive human emotion because if they could, they wouldn't be able to cope with who they are. Because they do rob people in laneways; they do hold knives at people's throats; they do sell themselves for a hit of heroin; they do rob their parents; they do con everybody they know...and they hate people. People are just scum. They learn very quickly that if they intimidate, they get what they want. They're very cunning and manipulative. These are kids as young as twelve.

She described how, paradoxically, the street kids loved and protected the horses, and I asked her what she thought happened between the street kids and the horses that magically created a climate of such trust and hope. What was the alchemical ingredient that enabled the psychic transformation from hate to love? The horses, she believed, operated straight from the heart. There was no incongruity between their inner and outer expression. They erected no emotional barriers:

> I believe the animals in their naked emotional state have the ability to make the street kids feel a seed of kindness...just a seed of kindness. (voice drops) I believe that the animals initiate that seed of kindness, and then...that spreads and includes me as well. The horses reach them. The horses bring them to the carriage, and I stand back and I just say hello. The next week I ask them their names, and it evolves over a period of time, but it's always the horses they come for. They're always patting and touching the horses, and the street kids all say the same thing—always the same thing: "This horse loves me, doesn't he? He loves me?" And I say "Yes, he does."

She mimics the eager piping quality of a child's vocal tones: "Does he need any water? I'll go and get water for you." The horses had become a focus of positive and reciprocal loving interaction for the street kids, who had found the human world rejecting, cynical, violent, ugly, and exploitative. It was not possible for the kids to make positive relationships with others in the human world. It was too late, and too much harm had already been done, but the intense emotional relationship with the horses was therapeutic and redemptive for them. Paradoxically, it was through the steadying and loving presence of the animals that the kids were rediscovering and healing their own partially eclipsed humanity. Donna describes the fiercely protective and loving attitude of the street kids to the horses with the following anecdote.

> On New Year's Eve I went in to the city and the horses were pelted with beer cans and God knows what else, but eight street kids made a ring around the horses, a protective ring, and they were ready to murder anybody who hurt them. The human condition is still within them. They wouldn't be alive if it wasn't. Because they love the horses and if any of the operators were seen to be cruel to the horses, they'd have a lot of problems with the street kids.

Like Susan and Ella, she reflects on the role of animals as tutelary spirits to humanity, teaching patience and unconditional love. Most of us are blind to this awareness, however, and unconscious of the sacrifices they make:

> Animals are so selfless. They're here to teach us about unconditional love and how to live in the present. When a human looks at you like these animals look at you, it's total unconditional love. You see it!

Animals and
the Elphame

All creatures—from stars to humans to insects—share
in the consciousness of the primary creative force, and each,
in its own way, mirrors a form of that consciousness.
(Lawlor 1991, 17)

HELEN, BERNADETTE, JOANNE, KATIE, Caroline, and Rosemary
thought that animals worked in spirit as well as in physical reality and
are more closely connected to and accepting of the Elphame than is
humanity. They also maintained that animals did not fear death in the
way that many humans do because of their strong relationship to the
world of spirit and the knowledge that death did not mean annihilation
of consciousness. They accepted death as a release from suffering and
embraced it when it came, and the intuitives believed that humanity
could learn from the animals the true nature of death as simply a transformation from a physical to an energetic existence.

For example, Joanne said she had no difficulty with euthanasia and
that animals will often ask their owners to "let them go" because they are
in extreme pain or discomfort. Her ability to see into the Elphame had

reassured and convinced her that they experienced joy, freedom, and transformation through the cyclic process of death and rebirth:

> I've seen what happens through my third eye...I can remember par-
> ticularly a cat that we had euthanized. I saw her spirit or soul lift from
> her body. She had extreme renal failure, and her soul lifted from her
> body and she reverted back into a kitten. I saw her playing on the end
> of our examination table and then she just sort of slowly faded. They
> don't have that attachment to physicality that we do. With animals it's
> "oh, well, out with the old and on with the next one!" Although they
> share many human characteristics with us, I think that's one thing
> they can definitely teach us. I'm always astounded how easily they let
> go, and if we could let go so easily in death I think it would be great.
> They maintain such a strong connection to the spiritual plane all
> throughout their lives.

Rosemary also said that she had seen this kind of transformation many times when animals had been euthanized. When they left the physical body and she clairvoyantly tracked their progress into the Elphame, she saw that in their energy bodies they appeared to be young, playful, and full of vitality.

Caroline said:

> All animals accept death. I've met one or two that were afraid, but
> there's usually very little fear of death. Animals know they will reincar-
> nate, whereas we have this whole fear of death thing...I remember
> going to someone's funeral about two years ago and sitting there and
> thinking, "This has absolutely nothing to do with what I know death to
> be." The whole ceremony was so alienating from what it actually is,
> and it doesn't help that the church says that animals don't have souls.

When animals were able to "have a voice" they were able to process the emotions that often manifested as physical illness. The reports of the interview subjects indicated that when the process of emotional expression was facilitated, the physical symptoms of their patients often resolved spontaneously. They described the similarity of what they were doing to psychotherapy practice with humans, and I agreed that there were startling similarities. As with Caroline and her horse, Joanne gave another powerful example of how humans are implicit in the illnesses that their animals manifest. This phenomenon is illustrated by the following description. Joanne said that a couple had brought a dog to the clinic that was suffering from severe allergies and digestive problems that had not responded to conventional treatments.

She tuned into the dog from the Elphame using the strong eye:

> The first image I got was of it as a puppy. So I started to talk to the owner about its birth, and she said it was the runt of the litter. This dog had a really overshot underjaw so its bottom jaw stuck out a long way, which made it look, I thought, really cute. But she said that when she went to pick him up, she was really disappointed because of the way he looked. That was her first emotional response to this dog: it was, "Oh, God, he's so ugly!" And as soon as she said "ugly," the energetic and emotional ripple that went through this dog's system was quite astounding. It was amazing! And when I told her that she said, "Oh, it wasn't just me who said it! The breeder said it, and the kids said it." And I said yes, but that's been his first and lasting impression of himself—that he is ugly, he's unattractive; he's unattractive externally and he's also becoming unattractive internally as well. So we started doing some emotional sentences with him. You say the sentences and you measure the emotional response.

When I asked what sentences she had used, she said she had used "I am ugly" and that she had asked the mind to become conscious of the unconscious emotional content of the sentence. The surrogate says the sentence repeatedly as the two large energy channels that run alongside the spine were stimulated by another practitioner using a chiropractic adjustor. She said:

> Basically what you are doing is teaching the body not to react emotionally to that sentence anymore...to recognize it and to let it go using a very small chiropractic adjustor, a clicking thing that we use to stimulate the energy meridians.

When I asked how the owners responded to this new awareness of being complicit in the dog's ill health, she said:

> The male owner burst into tears...and the female owner said, "Oh, I feel so guilty. I say it to him as a joke, like 'you're my ugly baby' and things like that, but I always say it in a loving voice." And I said, "But it's a self-concept of his, so if he hears that word it just reinforces what he thinks of himself. It wouldn't matter what kind of voice you said it in."

She went on to say that the physical problems the dog had been experiencing began to heal quickly from that time forward, indicating the close relationship between unconscious emotional states and physical illness.

While I was finishing interviewing Bernadette, I dimly noticed that one of her dogs had walked in, sat on my feet, and began to give me a few gentle pats on the leg with his paw. He looked something like a cross between a corgi and a cattle dog. He persisted for seven or eight times while sitting at my feet, whining softly and looking directly and intently at me. It was clear that he was trying to tell me something.

Bernadette said:

> Well, he came home specially to thank you. He believes in the work that you're doing, and that's why he came in. Otherwise he wouldn't have bothered. He is Patches—he's a brilliant dog.

As soon as she translated Patches' message of thanks for me, he happily got up and went outside, and I could sense the relief he felt that he had managed to penetrate my abstracted consciousness. He had wanted to thank me. Bernadette had said that humans unconsciously and consciously created pain and suffering for animals, and Patches wanted things to change.

In the light of this new knowledge about the psychological similarity of animals to humans, it does not seem such a huge mental leap to accept that it is possible to have meaningful and intelligent telepathic contact with the animal world and other life streams. According to the American animal communicator Lydia Hiby (1998), we are in constant intuitive communication with animals and other life streams but mostly ignore the reality and deny the possibility because it is not consistent with consensus reality and the cultural discourse that places humanity at the top of the evolutionary pyramid and regards animals as objects or things to be exploited for our comfort and convenience. We do not want to think it possible that they are very like us. That would mean a radical ontological shift that would change everything.

Donna had said that in her experience many people had good intuitive powers but did not trust them. She described the fear, denial, and inertia most people experience when asked to see reality differently. She touches on the problem of habitual patterns of thinking and the threat of ontological shock. I had asked her about what stopped us being able to accept what we already suspect we know, and she said it is a combination of laziness and fear:

> If you can break your pattern of thinking and if you can step outside the square and look at what the American Indians and the Aborigines have always known, then it opens up a whole new world...but that's scary because ninety percent of society cannot look at anything other than what they know or believe because that brings into jeopardy everything, and you start mucking around with people's belief systems and suddenly they're very nervous.

A strong mystical and mutually supporting relationship between the human and animal life streams is one of the cornerstones of traditional shamanic practice. One of the first requirements of novice shamans is to acquire animal spirit guides and helpers and to build a relationship with them. These guides give invaluable assistance to shamans working in the landscapes of the Elphame, often helping them to avoid the many real and present dangers.

According to Michael Harner, in the mythic past tribal people believed that humans and animals were able to converse, and animals were portrayed in an essentially human physical form that revealed the close relationship between the two life streams. Although the mythological past of human-animal unity is lost in ordinary reality, Harner maintains it still remains accessible to the shaman in non-ordinary reality (1990, 57). That is, by entering the Elphame or by altering consciousness the practitioner has access to aid, insight, and spiritual wisdom from the animal life-stream and from animal spirit helpers and guides.

Human-animal communication has ancient and respectable antecedents, and in shamanic societies it is a sign of a developing spiritual prowess. Modern animal communicators and nontraditional shamans like Ingerman (1999) and Harner have acquired a telepathic ability that has been lost to the majority of human beings. Tribal people have retained it, especially those who have been chosen for shaman training. Harner observes:

Thus, when a man becomes a shaman among the tribes of the Western desert of South Australia, he acquires the power to speak to birds and other animals." (1990, 58–59)

He goes on to say that the Jivaro, a South American tribe with whom he did extensive fieldwork, believe that if an animal speaks to you, it is evidence that the animal is your personal totem or guardian spirit.

This is a similar concept to that of the witch's familiar that remains present, if in a parodied form, in children's fairy tales and in the Western psyche generally. Unfortunately, the demonizing of witches by the Christian church has spread a taint that includes their animal guides and companions that continues even into the modern era.

Ontological Shock

Some of the group had gone through periods of self-doubt and experienced the destabilizing tremors of ontological shock as their ability to work in the Elphame unfolded: struggling, as I had done, to trust the intuitive process. They discussed the interference they experienced from the intellectual part of the mind, gradually devising means of preventing the intellect from intruding upon the intuition and "getting in the way" of the revelatory experience. Bernadette described this process as "forcing all the noise out" so that the mind became quiet and receptive.

Some of them, like Helen, Susan, and Joanne, seemed to move seamlessly between the two realities, while others, like Caroline and Simon, managed to maintain a skeptical openness to what was happening in the Elphame, acting "as if" it were valid, unconsciously adopting a magical approach. This open and experimental attitude enabled them to think outside the box and be innovative, which they regarded as an invaluable aid to their healing work. They described this process as lateral thinking.

Caroline said:

If you'd told me five years ago I'd be doing this for a living, I would have had you institutionalized. (laughter) But the greatest skeptics are the greatest believers in the end. One vet said, "Well, I would have said it's all shit...but I've known Caroline for years and if she says there's something in it, then maybe there is!" People are a lot more open-minded than they used to be.

I asked her more directly about her level of self-doubt and acceptance. Her answer surprised me, as she stresses the importance of being a grounded person and of learning through personal experience. She had experienced the darker side of the Elphame and the way in which unprotected contact with the world of spirit can cause depletion of energy and ultimately illness:

> I probably would have trouble accepting it of I hadn't experienced it firsthand. The fact that I was really sick and it got to the stage that I was terrified of being in the house I was in...Once you've lived through it, it changes your thoughts and perceptions. I got really sick and had to find a professional ghostbuster. There were several ghosts in my house and he got rid of half of them for me, and I learned to do the rest.

Ella's struggle with ontological shock was more protracted and more like my own, and like myself, she often censored what she heard or omitted to relay any information altogether. However, she had worked through long periods of self-doubt and ontological shock to the point where she was comfortable enough to simply pass on any impressions that came to her uncensored. It took time for her to trust both herself and the intuitive process, and to be open to the possibility that communications from the Elphame were real and useful in the process of healing. She said that her father had communicated with her after his death, but she found it very difficult to accept that she was not distorting what she was hearing. She discussed her feelings of unreality when the Elphame and the physical world collided, and the disorienting experience of ontological shock. It was easy for her to dismiss intuitive contact with the other reality as a fantasy, wishful thinking, or even delusion:

> They were the words that he would say, but that's what I found difficult sometimes, to distinguish between is this real or is that just what I want to hear? It's easier when it's someone you don't know.

She was also wary about possible damage and discredit to her professional reputation and consequently was very selective to whom she revealed her telepathic and psychic abilities. She confided to me that in the conservative town in which she lived and practiced "it is all too easy to wear the fruit-loop label." She also said that at first it had been difficult for her to trust me as a researcher and agree to allow me to tape-record the interview. The reason for this degree of caution she believed came from past-life experiences of harassment and persecution. That insight also resonated with me as a possible cause of my own prolonged struggle to accept my shamanic abilities.

Quieting the Intellect

Most of these modern shaman-healers had reached a level of confident expertise and worked through a purely intuitive process. As diagnosticians they simply knew what was wrong in a flash of insight and cross-referred this knowledge later through the slower intellectual process. They went straight to the causal level, into which the intellect cannot venture, to make meaning. However, many of them spoke about first having to quiet the relentless chatter of the intellectual part of the mind so that they could access the intuition. The intellect can block access to the intuition if it is not quiescent. This is obvious during episodes involving the swinging poles of ontological shock. It also explains why in laboratory research into paranormal phenomena the results are often inconclusive or not easily repeatable. The rigidly applied scientific method is not always a good way of measuring the validity of these kinds of events.

Rosemary reported that she renders the intellect passive or quiescent so that she can access intuition. The healer gives up intellectual control, suspends disbelief, and does not allow the critical rational intelligence to interject or offer up opinions. Katie used various meditative techniques to shut off her "logical voice" and have more accurate access to her intuition. She was also conscious of spiritual guidance when she was working. Joanne has an intuitive understanding of magical techniques of focusing the mind and having a clear intention of purpose. She said:

> I think if you have presence, focus, and intent, you can probably do anything. I think that's the hardest thing to do...to really still yourself and be present.

When I asked Susan how she worked, she answered that she worked from the unconscious and that she also worked under guidance from her animal helpers and spiritual beings. She also agreed it was important "to keep myself out of the process," that is, to keep the judging and evaluating intellect out of the process. Ordinary waking consciousness is not the right tool for the job:

She said:

> I just have to be careful to keep myself out of it…I'm not actually thinking about it, so my mind's not getting in the way. I'm not intellectualizing it. When you're working with a pendulum, you're working with energy. It's the same with kinesiology.

She makes her consciousness passive to the impressions that rise from the Elphame in a way she describes as "tuning in." It is an introverted, reflective, and ritual process:

> If I come in here to my consulting room and it's just me and the dogs, I light a candle and I sit down and I just hand it all up to those little angels who are helping me, plus my four little ones down here who are helping me. Then I just ask for guidance while I work. I'm tuning in on an energy level, and it gives me a reading on that animal or person.

Helen also said that she worked in a receptive "right brain" state that allowed spirit guides to work through her. She added that her practice was currently changing to the point where she was working more simply with an unadorned intuitive process and that her healing practice had become more "free-flowing because of this." Her hands had become a powerful diagnostic tool, and she thought that by running her hands through the living energy field of a patient she could sense and remove blockages, even blockages like Tom's that have originated from past-life trauma. She mentioned removing "energy spears" and other impediments that needed to be cleared from an individual's psychic or energetic field.

She said:

> I've had to take the shackles off people's legs and all sorts of strange things. I'm a past-life regressionist as well, so all sorts of things happen when I do a session, particularly around a regression. Sometimes when I'm doing a healing I see past-life energies that need clearing. Sometimes the energy that we were stays with us to protect us and holds us back in many respects.

What she said made sense of the healing methodology I had employed in Tom's case. I had worked intuitively, but she gave me something of a theoretical background to the strategy I had used to clear what he and I had assumed to be past-life influences.

Spirit Dispossession

Helen and Caroline both do a considerable amount of work in the field of spirit dispossession. Helen gave an example of this sort of work with the following case study. She had been asked to visit a family living on a farm outside Melbourne. They had been experiencing strange and disturbing phenomena since they had recently begun to dig a new vegetable garden. They were hearing a lot of strange sounds at night, and many of the farm animals were acting as though they were spooked. The family suspected that spirits might be involved.

She said:

> And what I noticed was a whole heap of Aboriginal spirits outside. I asked the family if they'd been doing anything to the land, and they had been doing some digging where they shouldn't have, according to the Aboriginal spirits. I went out to where the digging was taking place and there was a group of Aboriginal spirits there...and one in this warrior outfit, standing in front of me with a spear, looking really scary and saying: "I don't want to talk...no more talk," and he turned around and went away. I'm thinking, "Oh my God. What do I do?" I'm this little girl and I'm surrounded by all these angry Aboriginal spirits. So I prayed, and within minutes the whole area was encircled with light. It's really common for Aboriginal spirits to be causing problems where people are doing stuff on sacred land.

The word "prayed" may be misleading. What she actually did was invoke the aid of her spirit guides. She had used many shamanic skills in this episode. In order to solve the family's problem she used clairvoyance, clairaudience, the aid of spirit guides, her knowledge of energy healing, and her animal communication skills. She worked as a traditional shaman would have worked under the circumstances. She said that the Aboriginal spirits had communicated to her the things the family needed to address in order to avoid further incursions from the Elphame:

The family had to change their plans with what they were doing on the property. They were digging in a burial ground, so that caused a lot of problems and put a lot of fear into the horses that were on the property, and the spirits had energetically speared the dog as well.

She said that one particular night the clients had heard the dog barking and heard the horses galloping around and all sorts of other strange noises. The dog had been trying to do his job of protecting the farm and the family. The next day the dog was really weak around the back, hips, and legs, and it looked as though a car had hit him.

She used the strong eye to find out exactly what was wrong:

> I got very strong images that an energetic spear had been put through his hips. This dog also needed a lot of healing around the fact that he couldn't do his job properly, which was to get rid of the intruders. The spirits had put some sort of sticky stuff around his face so he couldn't bark. He was communicating with me, showing me pictures of what had happened: the tribe doing a dance over in this area of the garden and how he had tried to go over there but they'd chased him away, and he'd tried again and then he got the spear.

She went on to say that after she had done the invocation and the family took the advice not to dig in the area, everything became quiet and returned to normal on the farm, although the dog required a few counseling sessions and some energy healing to overcome his traumatic experience.

The Grail Family subjects all shared the Goddess view of reality, seeing the world as an integrated and interconnected web of energy in a constant state of interactive, intelligent, and communicative relationship. Humanity, they believed, had its assigned role in this rich design, but it was not necessarily a role that assumed a greater spiritual importance in relation to other life streams. From this ontological perspective, they regarded all life as having its own valuable place in the complex and sacred tapestry that is the "All."

There were clues to this ontological perspective in Hiby's writing on animal communication that I had not absorbed at the time I was reading her work. She relates that as a child she talked easily with animals, but as an adult the usual skepticism set in. This gradual and growing skepticism was something that many of the research subjects also experienced, and it seems that children are generally more easily and consistently connected to the Elphame but lose their sensitivity as they grow into adulthood. I believe that this loss has something to do with the way in which we are educated and conditioned not to trust intuitive or emotional knowledge.

Even so, Hiby says:

In my heart of hearts I always knew that all living beings shared some existing form of communication...My work with animals reinforces my belief in the powerful connection that weaves together humans, animals, and the universe we share. (1998, 4–5)

Katie and Bernadette believed that telepathy was possible because the subtle energy links joining all things create a communication network. They believe that we receive impressions of light energy and give it meaning using the physical senses and other decoding mechanisms of the central nervous system. They also see that we exist within a vast matrix of consciousness energy.

Katie said:

When we come back to the unity of consciousness, we realize that we are all one and so that whatever we vibrate to, we attract similar vibrations. I see the world and consciousness as within this big bubble or balloon. It's like broadcasting a thought, a thought-form, which is a form of energy. It's just at the level of the subtle fields, not at the level of the five senses. So, we receive information as energy and translate it with the five senses, but it's energy, which is light. The whole theory of telepathy is just one form of receiving psychic energy. I just use the term "psychic" purely because it's nonphysical energy.

Joanne, like Caroline and Simon, stressed the importance of adopting the "as if" position and being open to possibilities. She also believed there are subtle energy links connecting everything in the two worlds:

It's just being open to it. More often than not the biggest obstacle is people just being open to the possibility. I think we have a connection with everything.

Ella sees the important potential for change inherent in the model of the Goddess. In her view, humanity is part of the whole and should not be dominant in the scheme of things. She is also clear about her understanding of the Elphame as a multilayered reality. She said:

> I think it can lead you to a whole new way of being...and being in the
> world, not just being the human animal that is over everything...but
> being just a part of it all, and realizing that we are just a part of it; there
> are certainly lots of other planes where I think people who've loved us
> exist, and also animals who've loved us exist, and also the greater gods
> and goddesses.

Rosemary used a culinary metaphor to describe the web of relationship that exists within the whole. We are all one, but we are not as one. She said:

> To me we're all minestrone soup. (laughter) We're all energy but we
> take on different forms, but basically, we're all the same soup. So you
> might be a potato or a pea, or some of the liquid, but we're all really
> soup.

I found her comment to be very interesting, particularly in the light of "A Dream of the Return," which I described on page 104. That strong dream vehicle had used a similar metaphor. It was clear they understood their work in remote healing and telepathy, for example, as possible because of the inner subtle energetic connections between all things in the universe.

A Shifting Worldview

They all believed that public acceptance of what they do and the way they work is increasing exponentially. Most modalities of alternative medicine have become well accepted in Western society and in some cases have entered mainstream medicine. Rosemary said that a veterinary surgeon friend of hers had remarked that ten years ago, when he first trained in acupuncture, he disliked using it because it attracted the "lunatic fringe" of society, but now it was ordinary people who asked for the treatment. He had a distinct impression that orthodox medicine was slowly changing its attitude to energy medicine. Even something as controversial as animal communication is slowly becoming more respectable. Joanne remarked that people who are on a spiritual path find no difficulty in accepting animal communication because they accept the actuality of telepathy in general.

This group of healers generally agreed that while there are many people who cannot accept what they do, there are also others who are prepared to suspend judgment, especially when their "weird" healing treatments are spectacularly successful. This is particularly so when clients have previously tried many orthodox treatments that have failed. Bernadette, Rosemary, and Helen remarked that when the healer "has integrity and stands in their own power," it makes it easier for skeptics to shift and be more open-minded. Defensiveness invites challenges, they say.

Rosemary observed that in the ten years she has been practicing vibrational medicine she has not been challenged and has only once been called "weird" by a client, and that was in the recent past. At the time I interviewed Joanne, a documentary film had been made about the energy work that was being carried out at the veterinary clinic where she worked. There had been a big public and positive response to the program:

> The amount of phone calls we received from so many people all over Australia saying, "Good on you! Well done! It's so good that stuff's finally getting out there!" It was really pleasing and also humbling that there were so many people who were supportive and into it. It's fantastic!

The Restorative Power of the Elphame

Rosemary and Ella made interesting observations about the ways in which the Elphame sustains the healer and supports their energy. This was something that I had also observed from my own experiences of energy healing with the hands and with massage. Patients had often commented to me that it must be very tiring to massage someone for an hour or more, but I never felt tired after doing hands-on healing of any kind. Instead, I always felt more energized. Rosemary described the feeling of entering the Elphame and also commented about its capacity for healing:

> You're alert but you're very relaxed...if you're tired when you go into that state, you come out of it feeling rejuvenated. It's a healing space, and I guess all your senses are affected.

She also spoke about the reality of the Elphame, in that she experienced it as being more "real" than physical reality:

> The physical world is a little more dull, whereas the other world is much sharper. To all intents and purposes, it's just as real as the physical world...and I'm well aware of where the demarcation is.

Ella has had evidence of the healing power of ritual, and she is able to call in extra reserves of energy when she needs them. She is also conscious of working with guidance from the Elphame, especially when performing funerary rites. The powerful negative emotions of the grief-stricken participants, she finds, can drain her own energy:

> I do call on lots of extra energy and power to surround me during those times because I could not do it on my own strength. If I do it on my own strength I'm a "cot case." I can't work very much because it takes so much out of me, whereas when I ask for help, I'm sustained.

She said that help also comes from the Elphame as inspiration. Sometimes when she is writing a script for a ceremony, for example, it will change itself in the process and the changes are beneficial:

> Sometimes the words are different. I will have written something, but sometimes other words will come into my mind that add to it.

The Grail Family group, then, was familiar with many of the healing practices of traditional shamanic medicine, including Witchcraft. Ella, Susan, Helen, and Bernadette, in particular, used the power of ritual invocation to good effect in their work. They were also familiar with the magical use of the creative imagination as a way of influencing material reality, especially involving the use of various colored light.

Ella described a marriage ritual she had conducted and the amount of palpable energy it had attracted:

> Sometimes it is unbelievably powerful. I was conducting a ceremony in a couple's living room—not out in nature or anything. The energy was incredibly powerful through the whole ceremony because of the intent of the two people. I was holding my service book and my hands were shaking, and when they showed me the photographs afterward there were through, out of, and around my head lightning strikes and halos of light. That was the power of the energy in the room.

Katie works with color and also teaches her clients to use it as a visualization practice in treating their animals at home. All of the healers used the inner senses to make contact with and work from the Elphame, and they all used some form of hands-on healing treatments that facilitated the flow of universal energy. They were able to use the range of the skills of a Wiccan shamanic practitioner, although as far as I understood they had not been initiated into Wicca or into the Western magical tradition.

None of them would call themselves witches because of the negative connotations of that word in the public mind. Ella also prefers not to use the word "Pagan" to describe her work. She prefers the word "Druidic" because in the public perception "Pagan" is a synonym for sorcery. She believes, however, that because many clients are asking her to perform Druidic ceremonies, there is a fundamental shifting of the Western cultural discourse back to our Pagan roots, and that is a good thing. Sadly, because of this semantic and cultural disapproval and confusion, however, I believe that an important part of our Western historical, cultural, and spiritual heritage is being lost. At the very least, the links between shamanism, Druidry, magic, and Witchcraft as spiritual practices are not clearly or instantly identifiable.

None of the group claimed to be able to leave the physical body in their energy body—to astral travel—although many of them were strong dreamers. In fact, Rosemary specifically mentioned that she did not leave the physical body and "was not one of those who walk on the astral plane." It would have been interesting to inquire into the degree of ontological shock they might have experienced if they had been precipitated out of their bodies, as it is through this experience that ontological shock arises in its most intense and frightening form. In general, they were natural psychics who had developed and refined their sensitivity and skill in vibrational healing in various ways.

The Aftermath

With my research I had discovered another branch of the perennial shamanic world tree, a modern grafting of the universal shamanic tradition. I had previously believed that the scattered seeds of the "lost shaman tradition of the West" had found fertile ground in the Western magical tradition, but most particularly in the modern form of Witchcraft or Wicca. What I ultimately discovered was something quite unexpected: this was a group of people who were not initiates of that magical tradition; nevertheless, they lived and worked within the Goddess tradition as healers and psychic sensitives. They were a modern hybrid manifestation of the ancient tradition of the universal shaman.

As Matthews described it, they were the heirs and mediators of the ancient tradition of the Great Goddess; the keepers of the flame; the servers of the Holy Grail; part of the Grail Family reborn into a modern context, treading the Path of the Wise as had the intuitives and healers of countless generations over vast epochs of time and throughout the numerous and varied cultures of humankind.

I realized that my magical understanding had been fragmented and that this piece of research had helped me to reassemble several missing pieces of my own personal magical jigsaw puzzle and reframe my own life experiences. It drew together the various and disparate threads of myself that had always circled around the central themes of magic: my psychism, my training in ceremonial magic, my research, and my ongoing battle between the intellect and the intuition.

It helped me to realize at a visceral level that I was, and always had been, a shaman in the classical sense, but I had only ever seen it dimly. It helped me to redefine myself and see more clearly the strong links between my spiritual life and my work in the world. Although I had speculated vaguely and intellectually about the possibility of a shaman identity, I had never been completely comfortable with the idea emotionally. There were times when I accepted it and other times when I was filled with doubt. I had previously thought of shamanism as something that was to some degree qualitatively different to magic and Witchcraft, and although I thought I had related the way in which I worked as a healer to shamanic medicine, I had, in retrospect, a shallow understanding.

The confusion had come about because before my research began, I had not so clearly linked Wicca with universal and traditional shamanism. The interviews with the Grail Family group helped me come to terms with my true identity and find my place in what Caitlín Matthews calls "the Sisterhood of the Cauldron" (1991).

Also, this segment of my research was to be influential on my professional life as a therapist. It gave legitimacy to my eclectic approach to therapy and changed my thinking about the whole subject of shamanism. It made me aware that in the modern Western world there existed a group of healers who worked within the ambit of traditional shamanic medicine. I entered a new world.

Previously I had combined orthodox psychological theory and conventional alternative medicine with the practical and spiritual corpus of Western magic and modern Witchcraft and had thereby devised an eclectic, hybrid methodology that contained many elements that were similar to what I understood ancient shamanic practices to be. For example, being able to talk to spirits gave a different and deeper understanding in devising and applying treatments. However, the interviews with these ten healers both deepened and broadened my interpretation and enabled me to put together further pieces of the puzzle that made the underlying pattern of similarity far more discernible.

Like many people, I had previously vaguely thought that shamanism was a type of superstitious and primitive performance or sympathetic magic, a throwback to the Upper Paleolithic, and although I knew that there were traditional practitioners following the ancient magical formulae, I had not fully realized that modern transmutations existed that could properly be called "shamanism." For example, I knew that traditional shamans had the ability to communicate with animals, but it was not until I interviewed this group that I realized what I had experienced was not an aberration—telepathic communications with animals could be as clear as normal conversations that human beings held with each other. Other people also had this ability, and it was something that was common to shamanic healers from diverse cultures, both ancient and modern. This was an eye-opening initiatory experience for me.

I found that my understanding had gradually moved from a position of being mostly outside the Goddess experience in my work in education to one of being immersed in a shared reality that included a wholehearted acceptance of the two-tiered model of reality that is the Goddess.

I discerned a certain elegance in the way it had all begun to fall into place and a certain fittingness in the way it was working out in the world. I also felt that something that had greater wisdom than I did was guiding the process of my learning.

I believe that my research raises important issues that may lead to a redefining of how we see ourselves as human beings in relation to other life forms on our planet. If there is truth in these insights and experiences, then we must question our current understanding of our relationship to the earth and, indeed, our relationship to the cosmos. It appears possible that animals are more like human beings than we, as a culture, care to admit. This possibility challenges our view of animals as commodities to be experimented upon, cruelly killed, and exploited as resources. Contrary to the Cartesian view that they are "soulless mechanisms," they do have emotions, feelings, thoughts, and self-awareness. The repercussions of this knowledge could be profound and could contribute to an ontological shift that strongly challenges our current views about the nature of reality.

My Grail Family interviewees are in the vanguard of the reemergence of women's medicine, or Goddess medicine, that emphasizes treatment of the whole person; using natural medicines such as herbs and diet; working with intuitive processes by "revisioning" the problem; and working from the Elphame using energy healing and shamanic techniques that restore the balance. It therefore engages the physical, emotional, mental, and spiritual aspects of the human psyche, restoring balance on one or many levels of being simultaneously. This methodology is very similar to traditional shamanic medicine that also uses natural physical medicines like diet, herbs, and stones, but it also works from the second reality to bring about change in the physical world and redress any emotional, psychological, or spiritual imbalances in the patient's life that might be contributing to their ill health.

This methodology is qualitatively different to Western medicine with its emphasis on drugs, surgery, and other heroic treatments, and on teaching people ways to manage their illness and disability by learning to live with it. The usual metaphors of the Western cultural narrative relating to medicine are about "fighting a battle" against or "winning the war" on disease, and nature is generally regarded as an enemy that must be overcome or defeated. There exists in orthodox medicine, as in most other departments of Western life, the positivist expectation that technology, not nature, will provide the answers we seek and need for healing, although there is evidence that this attitude is slowly changing.

Millions of people worldwide have sought out the services of alternative and energy medicine practitioners, and the numbers are growing. Public acceptance is pragmatic if not coherently theoretical. Most of the interview subjects, for example, had found that orthodox medicine did not have the answers they sought for their own and their families' health problems, and they had therefore investigated the healing possibilities of alternative medicine and mystical treatments with more success. Many of my own patients consult me as their primary healthcare provider. It seems shamanic medicine has been entering our culture, subtly and gradually altering our worldview by the back door, over a period of forty years or so.

Be that as it may, Susan sums up the ambivalence that many people in our culture feel about contact with the Elphame. On the one hand there is a growing acceptance, and on the other there is fear and rejection. In her practice she is careful and wary and does not confide her healing contact with the Elphame to everybody. The ancient taint remains strong, particularly within the context of fundamentalist Christianity:

> I don't usually tell people straight off that I dowse. I come in here (to her dispensary and away from the consulting room) because a lot of people think this is really weird, and a lot of Christian people believe it's the "work of the devil." I mean, there are some weird and wonderful things going on around (long pause as she reflects)...out there! (laughter)

The efficacy of the combination of physical and mystical treatments that have their origins in the Elphame gives credibility to this eclectic healing methodology. These practitioners combine an understanding of alternative medicine physical treatments with a willingness to use energy treatments and explore more mystical practices in order to find healing resolutions for their suffering clients. It seems to make no difference whether they are human or animal. In fact, their treatments for both animals and humans are very similar between both life streams, and this raises further important questions.

Rosemary, for example, believes that our cruel treatment of food animals has broken a sacred covenant, and she has been a vegetarian from choice since early childhood. Caroline commented that she was considering vegetarianism herself because it does not seem reasonable "to eat something that can talk back to you." Bernadette discussed the importance of respectful ceremony when taking the life of another species and how we are so careless and disrespectful about what we do. These are some spiritually valid concerns that require serious consideration.

In my view the shaman is both a healer and a teacher. With the exception of Rosemary, who is also a teacher, the Grail Family subjects work with the healing side of the archetype but not necessarily with the teaching aspect. In the latter sense they are not fully initiated heirs of the universal shamanic tradition, and although they achieve successful healing outcomes for their patients, their methods are ultimately different to my own. I make use of symbolic and actual journeys into the Elphame—that is, from time to time I separate from my physical body in order to explore that reality.

The other Westerners I have researched and who have been "chosen by spirit" also have that ability to separate from the body and to take the Hero's Journey. Shamans from traditional cultures also claim this ability. It is interesting to note that neither Wesselman (1996), Monroe (1975), Heywood (1966), Moss (1996, 2005), Whitaker (1991), nor Castaneda (1993, 1999), who were all able to leave their bodies and walk on the astral plane, were healers; they were a seemingly random selection of ordinary humans who were accorded frightening, fascinating initiatory experiences of the different levels of the Elphame. Brennan (1987) is the exception in this group, as she was a medical intuitive who could also leave the physical body to operate on the many levels of the Elphame. The members of this group are teachers in the sense that they have written about their experiences of the other world and therefore have taken on the educative function of the archetype.

Also, with the exception of Ella and possibly Helen, the Grail Family are not Qabalists and they are not ritualists. Ella and Helen are intuitive ritual practitioners and are not guided in their practice by Qabalistic knowledge. Helen and Katie are the only members of this group who suggested in their interviews that they used pathworking or visualization practices in their work. The more free-flowing, intuitive, and guided approach that they usually employ may be a higher way of working, and I am not claiming that one methodology is superior to another. Nevertheless, this is one considerable difference between their manner of working and mine. I frequently make use of my magical training and Qabalistic knowledge in the healing work that I do, although this is not an invariable practice and there are times when I too use a purely intuitive and free-flowing approach.

It seems to be a rare thing in Western cultures to find both sets of skills—the teaching and healing aspects of the Shaman archetype—united in the one person. To find both an intuitive healing talent and the ability to leave the physical body and enter the Elphame in the energy body is unusual. Ingerman (1991) has this skill, as she is both a healer and "one who walks on the Astral Plane," in the classical sense of the universal shaman. She searches for lost fragments of self in the subtle world and reintegrates them into the psyches of her patients. Kharitidi (1999, 2001) is also a skilled healer and a traveler into the Elphame, as is Brennan, but it seems that in the modern Western world in general, it is unusual to discover the full spectrum of shamanic skills in one individual.

It seems the Shaman archetype, like the Goddess archetype, has been shattered in Western culture and is presently in the process of being reinvented and restored in a new form that is pertinent to our time. The skills of our lost shaman tradition are being rediscovered and restored but at present exist mostly in an incomplete and fragmented form.

All in all, these interviews show how the theoretical perspective of the Goddess translates into lived experience, but it implies a radically different ontological and epistemological focus. Whether we make such a conceptual shift voluntarily or have it thrust upon us by force of circumstances will make for interesting observation in the coming years.

19

Drawing the Threads Together

But we must not forget that Consciousness is the
fundamental one common reality, despite all
manifestations and attributes. (White 1988, 78–79)

THIS WORK HAS BEEN an exploration of how and why I came to see the world differently and to explore the consequences of that different vision. That ontological shift was not a matter of a relaxed and intellectual choice but something into which I was precipitated, more or less involuntarily, through a series of relentless and unexpected encounters with the Elphame. The resultant ontological shock of being confronted by the apparently real from within a culture that denied the existence of any plane of reality other than the physical became the dynamic tension that led to my seeking a model of reality that could accommodate my experiences.

As a result of that investigation I discovered the presence of a tradition of thought and practice that had both ancient roots and a contemporary presence. The Western magical tradition affirmed both the real presence of the spirit world of the Elphame and the possibility of disciplined contact with it.

The Wiccan model, an aspect of that tradition, is informed by the idea of the dynamic interaction of two great archetypes: the Great Goddess, who is the symbolic, anthropomorphic image of the conscious intelligence of the visible world and whose energy animates and orders it, and the Shaman, the spiritual warrior who has gained direct and personal knowledge of the subtle world through the psychologically and spiritually refining process of ordeal and initiation.

Through the initiatory process the shaman has learned to overcome fear, develop compassion, and gain the ability to alter ordinary consciousness at will. This level of spiritual development theoretically gives the shaman the confidence to make the Hero's Journey into the darkness of the "unknowable void" and return to physical reality bringing new spiritual insights that can be grounded as lived experience. Although that is the basic template of the shaman's role, the reality is sometimes different. It is not always a smooth process of transition.

I have described in some detail my experience of reluctantly being "made" into a shaman. It was a natural consequence of that experience to want to investigate how the spiritual knowledge I had gained from my journeys into the Elphame and my training in magic and Wicca could be grounded in physical reality as lived experience. I was interested to discover what the practical benefits of that process of spiritual attunement might be.

The interviews with former patients who had experienced successful treatments originating in the other reality give a broad understanding of the range of conditions that can respond to shamanic healing methods. These conditions have their origins in the energy body, emotional body, or mental body of the patient. The interviews indicate that several of these people had spirit attachments or had lost an important aspect of their psyches, and they therefore represent the classic shaman patients who have suffered "soul loss" or who have been "invaded by a foreign power." When those lost fragments of the psyche were reintegrated, or when the attaching spirits were recognized by the appropriate rituals and thereby helped to cross over into the Elphame, the patients reported beneficial results.

Some who became competent in using their creative imaginations made guided and symbolic ritual and pathworking journeys into the Elphame. By the employment of a magical technology, they themselves were enabled to perform remarkable healings and cures of their formerly intractable conditions. They became free of the debilitating symptoms from which they had been suffering, sometimes for many years, and all of them became free of any dependence on pharmaceutical drugs. Their physical and psychological health and well-being were noticeably improved, as was their sense of personal empowerment. These benefits were lasting. Their lives in general were transformed, as they reported better social adaptation and more fulfilling personal relationships.

I detected relief and gratitude not only in the words they spoke, but also in their vocal tones and body language, and it was not simply about being free of debilitating symptoms. Their gratitude and relief were also connected to having, for the first time, a workable and comprehensible spiritual frame of reference. Many of them commented that "it made sense…something finally made sense."

Although they believed that orthodox medicine had not provided effective and lasting cures, they had suffered profound ontological shock when the Elphame had crashed through into their consciousness. Sometimes they had existed in this uncomfortable state for long periods, with no intellectually acceptable explanation of the underlying cause. Finally, they experienced treatments that were effective and reasonable when interpreted through the discourse model of the Goddess and the Shaman. They said they experienced many varied and positive benefits when shamanic-medical insights were applied to their physical, psychological, and spiritual difficulties and maladies.

On the personal level, as my research has evolved over time, my learning has been intense and also eye-opening. As I draw the threads together, I am surprised to discover that my role in the interview process is the same role I have traditionally played as a teacher, healer, and psychotherapist. I am not the expert who knows everything, but I am flexible and attuned to expect the unexpected and the unlikely. I am therefore a competent witness, supporter, guide, and companion to those who are embarking on their own spiritual and healing journeys.

From a human perspective, the Goddess is unpredictable and cannot be second-guessed. There is no guaranteed formulaic response or methodology that ensures success. I have learned that to embrace her in each of her aspects, with courage and gratitude, is better than running away in panic and fear; it causes less pain in the long term. I have personally traveled into the unknown darkness, leaving behind the safety of consensual reality, and returned to the familiar world of daylight consciousness. That journey has tested both my resilience and my psychological balance. I understand something of the Hero's Journey and something of the responsibility incumbent upon those who have undertaken it. They must take up the role of the psychopomp, the spiritual guide and initiator who facilitates in others a gradual unfolding of greater realization and awareness. I realized, as I reviewed and processed the interview transcripts, that I had facilitated deeper realizations of both past and current events for many of the subjects while the interviews were in train. This realization was, paradoxically, both surprising and predictable.

I also interviewed ten practitioners whom I initially understood to be animal communicators but ultimately revised that description to see them as contemporary shaman-healers. I found their interviews to be valuable in two ways.

First, it was therapeutic for me personally to make contact with a group of practitioners who lived and worked within a different reality and who were demonstrably sane and well adapted. Their lives were grounded as lived experience within the two-tiered Goddess model. Their backgrounds and experiences were different to mine, yet similar enough for me to see many broad connections between their stories and my own. They made it easier for me to ground my personal narrative in the meta-narrative of the Goddess and the Shaman, and besides, as Moss (1996) has remarked, if you are going to go crazy, it is better to go in good company.

They also showed me with greater clarity how to combine, seamlessly and fearlessly, my mundane and spiritual lives. They said that if the healer stands in their power it helps skeptics to shift, and that if I had "dropped into my heart" more frequently and with greater faith, perhaps

I would not have experienced ontological shock with such intensity. There was wisdom in both those statements.

Second, they helped me to understand on a larger scale how it was entirely possible to live within a Goddess cultural narrative in the contemporary world and imagine more of what that might possibly imply. They were doing it by example. It seems that it requires only a shift of perspective to see humanity as directly connected to everything that exists, and as no more or less important than other spiritually evolving life streams. This seems a simple change to make theoretically, but the emotional toll of attempting that shift in practical terms can be considerable, and for many people it is not as easy as it sounds. The ontological shock experienced can be profoundly disruptive, threatening, and distressing, and they resist it because identity is intimately connected to ontology. To change ontology can seem like an attack on self.

The Grail Family also helped me see with greater clarity that to adopt a respectful and appreciative attitude to the natural world necessarily links us to its foundational and communicative intelligence, the Great Goddess. We may then realize how closely related to other life streams we really are. Connected to the vast web of energy we call "life," we can choose to participate in it with a deeper and more compassionate understanding, knowing we are a part of it and that we are not standing alone, traumatized and alienated at the top of the evolutionary pyramid. As Ella remarked, we can learn from animals and other life streams as tutelary spirits if we are open to it. We do not have to be "the human that is above everything"; we can be "just a part of it all...just a part."

Just recently I was reading a book by Kuhn called *The Tree of Knowledge*, first published in 1947. I was surprised to read something that was very similar to the way I had described the teaching function of the natural world to early people. I thought what I had said on this matter in the introduction to this book was original, but it seems that there is nothing new under the sun. He said that the ancient sages learned from observing the natural world, and the Earth Goddess was, in effect, the first teacher of truth to ancient people:

The sky, the earth, the ocean; vegetation and animal life; the universal daily phenomena of natural forces supplied the materials able to clarify the speech of truth...every tree, bush, insect, worm, beast, every tumbling rill upon the hillside, every cloud, snowflake, mist and rainfall, was each in its way a visible delineation of cosmic principle...For these processes and creations were themselves the outward visible manifestation of the Soul of the Universe...They were Universal Spirit's ideas that were now crystallized in material form in the outer world. (Kuhn 1947, Loc 48 Kindle Edition)

In virtually every field of contemporary inquiry, complexity and interconnectedness are emerging as dominant features and considerations.

The ancient magical and mystical tradition would appear to have much to offer the contemporary world. It can offer a model of a state of mind that is able to embrace deep complexity and interconnectedness with clarity and poise, and to imagine practical means of aligning and attuning human activity to greater spiritual realities. Applying such a state of mind to the knowledge now available to us constitutes a paradigm shift with potentially profound implications for the way we educate our children, for our notions of therapy, and for our descriptions of human identity.

Elements of our culture are coming to revalue other ways of knowing and being. There is a growing public interest in shamanism and Wicca, particularly among the young who are searching for a spirituality that includes a re-sacralization of the earth. I experienced shamanism as based upon empirical knowledge and rational investigation—eventually. The shamanic model is not inherently irrational, but because of its deeply spiritual nature, a grounded understanding of its processes must be based upon personal experience, as spiritual development is not something that can be achieved vicariously.

The model does demand, however, that we honor, not discount, knowledge that comes as feeling, emotion, intuition, imagination, dreaming, and in the silent language of telepathic communication. If we are able to do this, then we are back in touch with the Great Goddess and reconnected to the web of life. The ground of our being is transformed, and we understand in a deep and visceral way that other ways of knowing and being complete our human identity.

By being curious enough and experimental enough, readers of this work will be able to put into practice some of the ideas and methodology presented here, particularly those using the powers of visualization in a focused way. On a more cautionary note, however, there are obvious dangers in untrained people attempting such arts as spirit dispossession, astral travel, pathworking, hypnosis, and even the construction of an artificial elemental. I am a trained hypnotherapist, magical worker, naturopathic physician and psychotherapist, and while I am not trying to discourage amateurs from trying some of the techniques I have described, it should be understood that while designing something that appears as innocuous as a guided visualization, there can be traps for the unwary. If you want to try something, exercise caution and recognize that you may have limitations.

As an example, a former patient of mine who was a trained musician began professionally mentoring young musicians. To help them with their performance she also began using some of the techniques I had used with her, particularly deep relaxation and visualization. As part of a visualization exercise she had devised, she had one client mentally jump off a tower and float in the air. He began to panic in the light trance state she had introduced, and she had great difficulty in bringing him out of that state. She subsequently found out that he had a great lifelong fear of heights. He was traumatized by this experience and refused to attempt any further work of this nature. To remember the Rede in its most all-encompassing insight is an important component of any magical work: "An it harm none..."

So this work is not really intended as a self-help book but rather it is to be considered as something that might help readers to think outside the box when it comes to looking at ways of healing illnesses both physical and emotional/mental and, if possible, to find a reliable practitioner to work with them. It is also designed to help those who have had experiences of the Elphame that they cannot contextualize and to normalize those experiences so that they no longer generate fear or lead them to suspect that they might be going crazy. I also want to reassure readers that magic is real and that it can affect our lives for the better; it is not all about ego, power, and status, but it is our birthright and it can be used for the betterment of humankind. It reconnects us with our spiritual roots and opens a pathway into a more spiritually aware life that so many people in the disillusioned Western world are seeking.

The researches of Elgin and Le Drew (1997), Newburg, D'Aquili, and Rause (2001), Jane (2006) and Bader, Mencken, and Baker (2010) into large population samples reveal that many ordinary people whose mundane lives are ordered by the economic and political necessities of the Western meta-narrative have experienced many extra-rational events. This research begs the question: if thousands or possibly millions of modern Western people claim to have had unmediated contact with the Elphame are not demonstrably delusional, diseased, psychotic, fantasizing, or lying about their encounters, how do we accommodate that "uncomfortable" data within the present dominant cultural discourse?

The marginalized voices have spoken and given truthful testimony of their healing journeys with the Old Goddess and the Shaman.

So mote it be!

Bibliography

Abram, David. *The Spell of the Sensuous*. New York: Vintage Books, 1997.

Achterberg, Jeanne. *Imagery in Healing: Shamanism and Modern Medicine*. Boston: New Science Library, 1985.

Achterberg, Jeanne, Barbara Dossey, and Leslie Kolkmeier. *Rituals of Healing*. New York: Bantam Books, 1994.

Alford, Alan F. *Gods of the New Millennium*. London: Hodder and Stroughton, 1997.

———. *When the Gods Came Down*. London: Hodder and Stroughton, 2000.

Andrews, Lynn V. *Crystal Woman*. New York: Warner, 1987.

Andrews, Ted. *Animal-Speak: The Spiritual & Magical Powers of Creatures Great & Small*. St. Paul, MN: Llewellyn, 2001.

———. *Enchantment of the Faerie Realm*. Woodbury, MN: Llewellyn, 2005.

Apuleius, Lucius (trans. P. G. Walsh). *The Golden Ass*. Oxford: Oxford University Press, 1995.

Ashcroft-Nowicki, Dolores. *Highways of the Mind*. Loughborough: Toth Publications, 1987.

Bader, Christopher D., F. Carson Mencken, and Joseph O. Baker. *Paranormal America*. New York: New York University Press, 2010.

Baldwin, William. *Spirit Releasement Therapy*. Terra Alta: Headline Books, 1995.

Bardon, Franz. *Initiation into Hermetics*. Wuppertal: Dieter Ruggerberg, 1962.

Bates, Brian. *The Wisdom of the Wyrd*. London: Ryder, 1996.

———. *The Real Middle Earth*. London: Pan, 2002.

Berry, Thomas. *The Dream of the Earth*. San Francisco: Sierra Club Books, 1990.

The Bible, New King James Version, 2015; https://www .biblegateway.com/passage/?search=Genesis+1

Blacker, Carmen. *The Catalpa Bow: A Study of Shamanic Practices in Japan*. London: George Allen and Unwin, 1975.

Bookchin, Murray. *The Philosophy of Social Ecology—Essays in Dialectical Naturalism*. Montreal: Black Rose Books, 1995.

Braden, Gregg. *The Divine Matrix*. Carlsbad: Hay House, 2007.

Breggin, Peter. *Toxic Psychiatry*. London: HarperCollins, 1993.

Brennan, Barbara A. *Hands of Light*. New York: Bantam Books, 1987.

Briggs, John, and F. David Peat. *Seven Life Lessons of Chaos*. Crows Nest: Allen & Unwin, 1999.

Broomfield, John. *Other Ways of Knowing*. Rochester: Inner Traditions, 1997.

Brown, Joseph E. *The Spiritual Legacy of the American Indian: Commemorative Edition*. Bloomingdale: World Wisdom Books, 2007.

Brunton, Paul. *The Quest of the Overself*. London: Rider, 1970.

———. *A Search in Secret Egypt*. York Beach: Samuel Weiser, 1984.

Bugental, James. *The Art of the Psychotherapist*. New York: W. W. Norton, 1987.

Cahill, Sedonia, and Joshua Halpern. *The Ceremonial Circle*. London: Mandala Books,1991.

Cameron, John (ed). *Changing Places—Re-imagining Australia*. Woollahra: Longueville Media, 2003.

Cameron, S. "In Your Dreams: The Dream Work of Robert Moss," *The Australian Magazine*, October 3–4, 1998.

Campbell, Joseph. *The Hero with a Thousand Faces*. London: HarperCollins, 1993.

———.*The Masks of God: Occidental Mythology*. London: Souvenir, 2000.

———. *The Masks of God: Oriental Mythology*. New York: Arkana, 1991.

———. *The Masks of God: Primitive Mythology*. London: Souvenir, 2000.

———. *The Mythic Image*. Princeton: Princeton University Press, 1981.

———. *Myths to Live By*. London: Souvenir, 2000.

Capra, Fritjof. *The Tao of Physics*. Berkeley: Shamballa Publications, 2000.

Carroll, John. *Western Dreaming*. Sydney: HarperCollins, 2001.

———. *The Wreck of Western Culture*. Melbourne: Scribe, 2004.

Castaneda, Carlos. *The Active Side of Infinity*. London: Thorson,1999.

———. *The Art of Dreaming*. New York: Aquarian/Thorson, 1993.

———. *The Teachings of Don Juan: A Yaqui Way of Knowledge*. London: Penguin, 1976.

Cavandish, Richard (ed). *Man, Myth & Magic*. New York: Marshall Cavandish, 1995.

Chopra, Deepak. *Creating Health*. New York: Houghton Mifflin, 1996.

Churton, Tobias. *The Gnostics*. London: Weidenfeld & Nicholson, 1987.

Clifton, Chas S. (ed.). *Witchcraft & Shamanism: Witchcraft Today, Book Three*. St. Paul, MN: Llewellyn Publications, 1994.

Condren, Mary. *The Serpent and the Goddess: Women, Religion and Power in Celtic Ireland*. San Francisco: Harper, 1989.

Corey, Gerald. *Theory and Practice of Counselling and Psychotherapy*. Pacific Grove: Brooks/Cole Publishing Company, 1996.

Cowan, James G. *The Aborigine Tradition*. Shaftesbury: Element, 1992.

Crotty, Michael J. *The Foundations of Social Research*. Crows Nest: Allen & Unwin, 1998.

Crowley, Aleister. *The Commentaries of AL*. London: Routledge & Kegan Paul, 1975.

———. *Magick*. London: Routledge & Kegan Paul, 1973.

Crowley, Vivianne. *Wicca*. San Francisco: Thorsons, 1996.

Curott, Phyllis. *Book of Shadows*. London: Bantam, 1999.

Daniels, Michael. *Shadow, Self, Spirit: Essays in Transpersonal Psychology*. Exeter: Imprint Academic, 2005.

de Quincey, Christian. *Radical Nature*. Montpelier: Invisible Cities Press, 2002.

Denning, Melita, and Osborne Phillips. *Psychic Self-Defense and Well-Being*. St. Paul, MN: Llewellyn, 1992.

Diamond, Jarrod. *Collapse: How Societies Choose to Fail or Survive*. Melbourne: Allen Lane, 2005.

———. *Guns, Germs and Steel*. London: Vintage, 1998.

Drury, Neville. *Shamanism*. Brisbane: Element Books, 1996.

Eckersley, Richard. *Well and Good*. Melbourne: Text, 2004.

Egan, Gerard. *The Skilled Helper*. Pacific Grove: Brooks/Cole,1998.

Elgin, Duane, and Coleen Le Drew. *Global Consciousness Change: Indicators of an Emerging Paradigm*.1997; www.awakeningearth.org.

Eliade, Mircea (ed). *The Encyclopaedia of Religion*. New York: Macmillan, 1987.

———. *The Myth of Eternal Return*. Princeton: Mythos (Princeton University Press), 1991.

———. *The Sacred and the Profane*. New York: Harcourt, Brace & World, 1959.

———. *Shamanism*. London: Arkana, 1989.

Elkin, Adolphus Peter. *Aboriginal Men of High Degree*. Sydney: Australasian Publishing Company, 1944.

Epstein, Gerald. *Healing Visualisations: Creating Health Through Imagery*. New York: Bantam, 1989.

Fagan, Brian M. (ed). *Oxford Companion to Archaeology*. New York: Oxford University Press, 1996.

Farrar, Stewart, and Janet Farrar. *The Witches' God*. Blaine: Phoenix Publishing Inc., 1989.

———. *The Witches' Way*. Blaine: Phoenix Publishing Inc.,1984.

Fiore, Edith. *The Unquiet Dead*. New York: Ballantine, 1998.

Fortune, Dion. *The Mystical Qabalah*. London: Ernest Benn Limited, 1976.

Foucault, Michel. *Madness & Civilization*. New York: Vintage Books, 1973.

———. *The Order of Things*. New York: Random House, 1970.

Fox, Matthew (ed). *Hildegard of Bingen's Book of Divine Works with Letters and Songs*. Rochester: Bear & Company, 2014.

Frankl, Viktor. *The Unconscious God*. New York: Simon and Schuster, 1975.

Freke, Timothy, and Peter Gandy. *The Hermetica*. New York: Jeremy P. Tarcher/Putnam, 1999.

———. *Jesus and the Goddess*. London: Thorsons, 2002.

Gairdner, William D. *The Book of Absolutes*. Canada McGill-Queens University Press, 2009.

Gardiner, Philip, and Gary Osborn. *The Serpent Grail*. London: Watkins, 2005.

Gardner, Laurence. *Genesis of the Grail Kings*. London: Bantam Press, 1999.

———. *Realm of the Ring Lords*. Melbourne: Penguin, 2000.

Gimbutas, Marija. *The Language of the Goddess: Unearthing the Hidden Symbols of Western Civilization*. San Francisco: Harper and Rowe, 1989.

Ginzberg, Carlo. *Ecstasies: Deciphering the Witches' Sabbath*. Chicago: Chicago University Press, 2004.

Glasser, William. *Reality Therapy*. New York: Harper & Rowe, 1965.

Glendinning, Chellis. "Technology, Trauma and the Wild," in T. Roszak, M. Goines, and A. Kanner (eds), *Ecopsychology: Restoring the Earth, Healing the Mind*. San Francisco: Sierra Club Books, 1995.

Godwin, Joscelyn. *The Golden Thread*. USA Quest Books, 2013.

Goleman, Daniel. *Emotional Intelligence*. London: Bloomsbury Publishing Company, 1996.

Graves, Robert. *The Greek Myths*. London: The Folio Society, 2001.

Gray, John. *Al Qaeda and What It Means to Be Modern*. London: Faber & Faber, 2003.

———. *Heresies Against Progress and Other Illusions*. London: Granta, 2004.

———. *Straw Dogs: Thoughts on Humans and Other Animals*. London: Granta, 2003.

Gray, Leslie. "Shamanic Counselling and Ecopsychology," in T. Roszak, M. Goines, and A. Kanner (eds), *Ecopsychology: Restoring the Earth, Healing the Mind*. San Francisco: Sierra Club Books, 1995.

Gribbin, John. *Deep Simplicity*. London: Penguin, 2005.

Grof, Stanislav. *Spiritual Emergency*. Los Angeles: J. P. Tarcher, 2002.

Grof, Stanislav, and Christina Grof. *The Stormy Search for Self*. Los Angeles: J. P. Tarcher, 1992.

Halevi, Z'ev ben Shimon. *Adam and the Kabbalistic Tree*. London: Rider, 1974.

Hancock, Graham. *Supernatural*. London: Disinformation Books, 2006.

Harner, Michael. *The Way of the Shaman*. San Francisco: Harper, 1990.

Heywood, Rosalind. *The Infinite Hive*. London: Pan Books, 1966.

Hiby, Lydia. *Conversations with Animals*. Troutdale: Newsage Press, 1998.

Hillman, James. *The Soul's Code*. Sydney: Random House, 1996.

Horgan, John. *The End of Science*. London: Little Brown & Co., 1997.

Imber-Black, Evan, and Janine Roberts. *Rituals for Our Time*. New York: HarperCollins, 1992.

Imber-Black, Evan, Janine Roberts, and Richard Whitting. *Rituals in Families and Family Therapy*. New York: W. W. Norton & Co., 1988.

Ingerman, Sandra. *Soul Retrieval: Mending the Fragmented Self*. San Francisco: Harper, 1999.

Jane, Beverly. "The Nature, Incidence and Impact of Spontaneous Paranormal Experiences," Monash University online survey, *ABC Science* online, 17 November 2006.

Jeynes, Julian. *The Origin of Consciousness in the Break-down of the Bicameral Mind*. Boston: Mariner, 2000.

Jung, Carl G. *Four Archetypes*. London: Routledge & Keegan Paul, 1972.

——— (ed.). *Man and His Symbols*. London: Aldus Books, 1964.

Kharitidi, Olga. *Entering the Circle*. San Francisco: Harper, 1999.

———. *Master of Lucid Dreaming*. Charlottesville: Hampton Roads, 2001.

Kingston, Karen. *Creating Sacred Space with Feng Shui*. UK: Hodder Headline, 1996.

Kinney, Jay, and Richard Smoley. *Hidden Wisdom*. New York: Arkana, 1999.

Knight, Christopher, and Robert Lomas. *The Hiram Key*. London: Century Books, 1996.

———. *Uriel's Machine*. London: Arrow Books, 2000.

Konstam, Angus. *Historical Atlas of the Celtic World*. London: Mercury, 2003.

Kottler, Jeffrey A., Thomas L. Sexton, and Susan C. Whiston. *The Heart of Healing*. San Francisco: Jossey-Bass, 1994.

Kuhn, Alvin Boyd. *Lost Light: An Interpretation of Ancient Scriptures*. Filiquarian Publishing, 2007.

———. *The Tree of Knowledge*. Seattle: Kindle, 1947.

Laing, Ronald David. *Self and Others*. London Penguin, 1971.

Laing, Ronald David, and Aaron Esterton. *Sanity, Madness and the Family*. London: Tavistock, 1964.

Lake, Medicine Grizzlybear (Robert G.). *Native Healer*. Wheaton: Quest Books, 1993.

Laszlo, Ervin. *Science and the Akashic Field*. Rochester: Inner Traditions, 2004.

Lawlor, Robert. *Voices of the First Day*. Rochester: Inner Traditions, 1991.

Le Guin, Ursula K. *The Farthest Shore*. New York: Simon & Shuster, 2001.

Lip, E. *Out of China*. Singapore: Addison-Wesley.

Lovelock, James. *The Gaia Hypothesis: A New Look at Life on Earth*. Oxford: Oxford University Press, 1979.

Mack, John. *Abduction*. New York: Simon & Schuster, 1995.

Macken, Deirdre. "Leunig Drawing the Line on Creativity and Other Curly Issues," Melbourne: News Extra, *The Age*, 1995.

Maslow, Abraham H. *Religions, Values, and Peak Experiences*. New York: Penguin, 1976.

Matthews, Caitlín. *Sophia: Goddess of Wisdom*. UK: Mandala, 1991.

Matthews, Caitlín, and K. B. John. *The Western Way: A Practical Guide to the Western Mystery Tradition.* London: Arkana, 1985.

Matthews, John. *Taliesin: Shamanism and the Bardic Mysteries in Britain & Ireland.* London: HarperCollins, 1991.

McLynn, Frank. *A Biography of Carl Gustav Jung.* London: Black Swan, 1996.

Meadows, Kenneth. *Shamanic Experience.* Shaftesbury: Element, 1998.

Mill, John Stuart. *On Liberty.* Kitchener: Batoche Books, 2001.

Miller, Alice. *Thou Shalt Not Be Aware.* New York: The Noonday Press, 1998.

Mollison, Bill, and David Holgrem. *Permaculture One.* Australia: Transworld Publishers, 1978.

Monroe, Robert. *Journeys Out of the Body.* London: Corgi Books, 1975.

Moss, Robert. *Conscious Dreaming.* London: Rider, 1996.

———. *The Dreamer's Book of the Dead.* Rochester: Destiny Books, 2005.

Murray, Margaret. *The Witch-Cult in Western Europe.* Oxford: Oxford University Press, 1921.

Muses, Charles, and Joseph Campbell (eds). *In All Her Names.* San Francisco: Harper, 1991.

Narby, Jeremy. *The Cosmic Serpent: DNA and the Origins of Knowledge.* Blaine: Phoenix Books, 1998.

Newberg, Andrew B., Eugene G. D'Aquili, and Vince Rause. *Why God Won't Go Away.* New York: Ballantine Books, 2001.

Norwood, Robin. *Women Who Love Too Much.* London: Arrow Books, 1986.

Pearce, Joseph Chilton. *The Biology of Transcendence.* South Paris: Park Street Press, 2002.

Perkins, John. *Confessions of an Economic Hit Man.* London: Ebury Books, 2005.

Picknett, Lynn, and Clive Prince. *The Templar Revelation*. London: Corgi, 1998.

Picknett, Lynn. *The Secret History of Lucifer*. London: Robinson, 2005.

Plumwood, Val. *Environmental Culture: The Ecological Crisis of Reason*. London: Routledge, 2002.

PY Media. *Australia By Numbers: Ngangkari, Fregon 0872*. Sydney: SBS Television, 2002.

Quiller-Couch, Arthur (ed.). *The Oxford Book of English Verse: 1250–1900*. Oxford: Clarendon, 1919.

Radin, Dean. *The Conscious Universe*. New York: HarperCollins 2010.

Read, John, Loren R. Mosher, and Richard P. Bentall (eds). *Models of Madness*. New York: Brunner-Routledge, 2004.

Reeves, Nancy C., and Frederic J. Boersma. "The Therapeutic Use of Ritual in Maladaptive Grieving." *Omega*, vol. 20, no. 4 (1989–90), 281–29.

Regardie, Israel. *The Golden Dawn*. St. Paul, MN: Llewellyn, 1971.

Roszak, Theodore, Mary E. Goines, and Allen D. Kanner (eds). *Ecopsychology*. San Francisco: Sierra Club Books, 1995.

Sabini, Meredith (ed.). *The Earth Has a Soul: The Nature Writings of C.G. Jung*. New York: North Atlantic Books, 2002.

Sagan, Samuel. *Entities: Parasites of the Energy Body*. NSW: Clairvision, 1994.

The Scottish Pantheon website, 2006: http//www.surfsouth.com/strix/scottishpantheon.html.

Sessions, George (ed.). *Deep Ecology for the Twenty-First Century: Readings on the Philosophy and Practice of the New Environmentalism*. London: Shambhala, 1995.

Sheldrake, Rupert. *The Rebirth of Nature*. London: Rider, 1990.

Shepard, Paul. *Nature and Madness*. USA: University of Georgia Press, 1998.

Simonton, O. Carl. *Getting Well Again*. New York: Bantam,1980.

————. *The Healing Journey.* New York: Bantam, 1992.

Sitchin, Zecharia. *The Stairway to Heaven.* USA: Avon,1983 .

Starhawk. *The Spiral Dance.* San Francisco: Harper, 1999.

Storr, Anthony. *The Dynamics of Creation.* London: Penguin, 1991.

————. *The Essential Jung.* London: Fontana Press, 1983.

————. *The Soul's Code.* Melbourne: Random House, 1996.

Strassman, Rick. *DMT: The Spirit Molecule.* Rochester: Park Street Press, 2001.

Symington, Neville. *A Pattern of Madness.* London: Karnac, 2002.

Tacey, David. *The Edge of the Sacred.* Sydney: HarperCollins, 1995.

————. *Renchantment.* Sydney: HarperCollins, 2000.

————. *The Spirituality Revolution.* Sydney: HarperCollins, 2003.

————. "Youth, Spirituality, and Old Religion," paper presented at Catholic Education conference, University of Melbourne, June 1998.

Tart, Charles (ed.). *Transpersonal Psychologies.* London: Routledge & Kegan Paul, 1975.

Temple, Robert. *Netherworld.* London: Arrow, 2003.

Turner, Victor (ed.). *The Performance of Healing.* New York: Rutledge, 1996.

Valiente, Doreen. *The Rebirth of Witchcraft.* London: Robert Hale, 1989.

Valiente, Doreen, and Evan Jones. *Witchcraft: A Tradition Renewed.* Blaine: Phoenix Books, 1990.

von Franz, Marie-Louise. *Creation Myths.* Boston: Shambhala, 1995.

————. *An Introduction to the Psychology of Fairy Tales.* New York: Spring Publications, 1972.

Warner, Marina. *Alone of All Her Sex.* London: Vintage, 2000.

Watson, David. *Against the Megamachine.* New York: Autonomedia, 1997.

————. *Beyond Bookchin.* New York: Autonomedia, 1996.

Welch, Robyn E. *Conversations with the Body*. London: Hodder & Stoughton, 2002.

Wesselman, Hank. *Spirit Walker*. New York: Bantam, 1996.

Whitaker, Kay Cordell. *The Reluctant Shaman*. San Francisco: Harper, 1991.

White, Stewart E. *The Unobstructed Universe*. Columbus, Ohio: Ariel Press, 1988.

Wilber, Ken. *No Boundary: Eastern and Western Approaches to Personal Growth*. Los Angeles: Center Publications, 1979.

———. *Sex, Ecology, Spirituality: The Spirit of Evolution*. Boston: Shambhala, 1995.

Wilson, Colin. *Rudolph Steiner: The Man and His Vision*. London: Aeon Books, 2005.

Woodman, Marion, and Elinor Dickson. *Dancing in the Flames*. Crows Nest: Allen & Unwin, 1996.

Wright, Ronald. *A Short History of Progress*. Melbourne: Text, 2005.

Yalom, Irvin D. *Concise Guide to Group Psychotherapy*. Washington: American Psychiatric Press, 1989.

———. *Theory and Practice of Group Psychotherapy*. New York: Basic Books, 1985.

Zukav, Gary. *The Dancing Wu Li Masters*. USA: Bantam, 1980.